BIOGRAPHY AND CRITICISM

General Editors
A. NORMAN JEFFARES
R. L. C. LORIMER

12

CONFLICT
IN THE NOVELS
OF D. H. LAWRENCE

YUDHISHTAR

CONFLICT
IN THE NOVELS
OF D. H. LAWRENCE

OLIVER & BOYD

EDINBURGH

1969

OLIVER & BOYD LTD

TWEEDDALE COURT

EDINBURGH I

Class no. 823·91
LAW

FIRST PUBLISHED 1969

PRINTED IN GREAT BRITAIN

BY T. AND A. CONSTABLE LTD.

EDINBURGH

SCOTLAND

Preface

LAWRENCE's vision of life finds expression in his novels in terms of relationships; and they can be fully appreciated only when they are seen as imaginatively conceived and artistically organised revelations of man's relationships to his circumambient universe. These relationships, as it happens, are fraught with conflicts. Depiction of human relations and the conflicts in them is the most distinctive feature of a Lawrence novel. In this study I have attempted to show that the best way to understand the meaning as well as the structure of Lawrence's novels is to approach them by recognising that his purpose in writing them was to reveal to us "the changing rainbow of our living relationships".

This book is not offered as a comprehensive study of Lawrence's novels. A great deal more needs to be written about Lawrence's work. I have, for instance, not attempted to draw a comparison between Lawrence and other novelists—English or European—though such comparisons are, of course, implicit when one speaks of Lawrence's greatness as a writer. Again, no attempt has been made to relate Lawrence's work to his social and cultural background. However, the basic pattern which the novels closely follow has been, I hope, sufficiently clearly revealed. It is this pattern of relationships and of conflicts in relationships which provides the clue to a proper understanding of all Lawrence's fiction.

How much I owe to earlier critics of Lawrence is made fairly obvious in the course of the book itself: but I should perhaps add that I found Lawrence's own letters and other writings far more helpful, in coming to an understanding of his novels, than any critical discussion of them.

This book is substantially a Ph.D. thesis submitted to the School of English, Leeds University. I am indebted to the University of Leeds for the award of a Postgraduate Research Studentship which enabled me to complete this work. Thanks are also due to the Charles Brotherton Trust, the Sir Ernest Cassel Educational Trust, and the Afro-Asian Educational Trust Ltd for grants received.

I am most deeply grateful to Dr A. C. Kettle, whose constant encouragement and guidance in the preparation of this work proved extremely helpful in a number of ways. Sincere thanks are also due to Professor A. N. Jeffares and Mr G. M. Matthews for their help and valuable suggestions.

YUDHISHTAR

ACKNOWLEDGEMENTS

For permission to quote from the works of D. H. Lawrence, acknowledgements are due to Laurence Pollinger Ltd., and the Estate of the late Mrs Frieda Lawrence, as well as to Messrs William Heinemann Ltd.

For permission to quote from *Apocalypse,* from *Assorted Articles* and *Reflections on the Death of a Porcupine* (both now contained in *Phoenix II*, edited by Warren Roberts and Harry T. Moore), from *Etruscan Places*, from *The Symbolic Meaning*, from *Twilight in Italy*, from *The Rainbow*, from *Sex, Literature and Censorship*, from *Studies in Classic American Literature*, from *Sons and Lovers*, from *Women in Love*, from *Fantasia of the Unconscious* and *Psychoanalysis and the Unconscious*, from *The Letters of D. H. Lawrence*, from *Aaron's Rod*, from *The Collected Letters of D. H. Lawrence*, and from *Kangaroo*, acknowledgements are due to The Viking Press, Inc.; for permission to quote from *The Plumed Serpent*, to Alfred A. Knopf, Inc.; for permission to quote from *The White Peacock*, to the Southern Illinois University Press.

Contents

Abbreviated Titles

Works by D. H. Lawrence

Collected Letters	=	*The Collected Letters of D. H. Lawrence*, 2 vols., ed. Harry T. Moore.
Fantasia	=	*Fantasia of the Unconscious and Psychoanalysis and the Unconscious.*
Letters	=	*The Letters of D. H. Lawrence*, ed. A. Huxley.
Miscellany	=	*A D. H. Lawrence Miscellany*, ed. Harry T. Moore.
Phoenix	=	*Phoenix: The Posthumous Papers of D. H. Lawrence*, ed. Edward D. McDonald.
Poems	=	*The Complete Poems*, 3 vols.
R.D.P.	=	*Reflections on the Death of a Porcupine and Other Essays.*
S.C.A.L.	=	*Studies in Classic American Literature.*
S.L.C.	=	*Sex, Literature and Censorship*, ed. Harry T. Moore.
S.M.	=	*The Symbolic Meaning: The Uncollected Versions of "Studies in Classic American Literature"*, ed. Armin Arnold.
W.P.	=	*The White Peacock.*

Works by Others

Daiches	=	David Daiches, *The Novel and the Modern World.*
Hough	=	Graham Hough, *The Dark Sun: A Study of D. H. Lawrence.*
Leavis	=	F. R. Leavis, *D. H. Lawrence: Novelist.*
Moynahan	=	Julian Moynahan, *The Deed of Life: The Novels and Tales of D. H. Lawrence.*
Nehls	=	Edward Nehls, *D. H. Lawrence: A Composite Biography.*
Vivas	=	Eliseo Vivas, *D. H. Lawrence: The Failure and the Triumph of Art.*
West	=	Anthony West, *D. H. Lawrence.*

I

An Approach to Lawrence

How is one to approach a writer like Lawrence?
Lawrence has always been something of a problem
to the critic. Is one to think of him as primarily an
artist, or essentially a moralist, or both? Should one discuss
him as a novelist in a tradition? If so, is that tradition to be
that of the English novel, or a larger European tradition? Or
is he, more than a writer in a certain tradition, an innovator, a
"tablet-breaker", a rebel? Or again is he both? To what
extent is Lawrence an autobiographical writer, and what effect
has this on his work as a novelist? Can one completely divorce
Lawrence the man from his work and consider his novels
purely as self-sufficient works of art? How far was Lawrence a
psychoanalytical writer? How much a symbolist? How
fruitful is a consideration of Lawrence as a nihilist likely to be?
—These are some of the questions critics of Lawrence have
found themselves faced with, and which they have, in their own
ways, tried to answer—though neither, it must be said, with
much success nor consistency.

Much critical work has by now appeared on Lawrence as a
writer, and anyone not closely familiar with Lawrence-
criticism is very likely to have a feeling that everything worth
saying has already been said. Many of the books, essays, and
articles on Lawrence are, in their limited way, certainly quite
valuable. But no critic has so far discussed at length the
distinctive qualities of Lawrence as a novelist. What most
critics have done is merely to comment on the most easily
explicable in Lawrence's writings; and when they have tried
to do more than interpret the obvious, they have generally
become either muddled or misleading. There is surely, as a
rule, more than one legitimate, and fruitful, approach to any

great writer. But whether a critic sets out to discuss a writer's work as "art" on the basis of some aesthetic theory, or seeks to bring out its significance in terms of human values, there is little justification for any literary criticism that does not help deepen our understanding or increase our enjoyment of creative literary works. A large proportion of Lawrence-criticism, owing to its failure to recognise the essential in Lawrence, does neither.

"The critic's first duty to a genius", says W. Y. Tindall in the preface to his book on Lawrence, "is to try and understand his meaning." The rest of his book, *D. H. Lawrence and Susan His Cow*, is Tindall's attempt and, in the main, his failure to understand Lawrence's "meaning". But he must be given credit for at least trying to understand his subject; and he has, since the publication of the above book in 1939, considerably modified his views on Lawrence. Many other critics, however, have not even made the attempt. Without waiting to find out what Lawrence was trying to say in his novels, they first arbitrarily decide what he must have been trying to do, and then go on to blame him for not doing it well; or they feel dissatisfied with Lawrence for not being the novelist of their conception, for not concerning himself with what they think should be the concern of all novelists. Middleton Murry, for example, declared in his *Son of Woman* that the only true life of Lawrence was to be found in his works, and then proceeded to blame the works for not telling the truth. Eliseo Vivas, a very different critic, does practically the same thing by first telling us that works like *Aaron's Rod*, *Kangaroo*, and *The Plumed Serpent* can be considered only as biographical material and not as novels, and then goes on to criticise them for not being truthful and honest as biography. And the complaints of Harry T. Moore, F. R. Leavis, Eliseo Vivas, David Daiches, W. W. Robson, and others, that Lawrence is not always objective or impersonal enough an artist, or that he occasionally violates the canon of aesthetic distance in his novels—these complaints, we shall see, are not relevant in the case of Lawrence, and are based on a static, fixed conception of what a novel is, or ought to be.

In a letter of 20 May 1929, Lawrence wrote to Murry: "We

don't know one another—if you knew *how* little we know one
another! . . . Believe me, we belong to different ways of
consciousness, you and I, . . .".[1] After Lawrence's death,
Murry acknowledged the truth of this in his *Reminiscences of
D. H. Lawrence*, admitting that he had never faced the real
Lawrence,[2] that he found it difficult to understand Lawrence's
ideas. One way in which Murry's misunderstanding of
Lawrence found expression was in his refusal to see the artist in
Lawrence. "Lawrence", said Murry, "was not, primarily, an
artist; he knew it, he declared it, his books reveal it."[3] "Art
was not his aim."[4] "He is and always has been a moralist."[5]
In his later writings, however, Murry comes much nearer an
understanding of Lawrence when he grants that Lawrence was
an artist, if one accepts the view that the supreme purpose of
art is to reveal to man what he is. He still insists that concentrating on Lawrence's literary genius, ignoring to what
purpose he employed it, is "a kind of outrage to his spirit":[6]
but his contention that a mere "artistic" appreciation of
Lawrence is inadequate in that it does not correspond to our
experience of Lawrence's writing, is surely a valid one.
Anthony West goes further than Murry in condemning an
aesthetic approach to Lawrence's work by describing such an
approach as "something of an absurdity",[7] for he believes that
Lawrence was a religious leader and life-changer first, and only
incidentally a writer. It is, says West, a mistake to treat
Lawrence as a literary man: "his novels are intended as
moralities . . .",[8] "they were not supposed to be works of art."[9]
West's is an extreme position: but there are other critics who
have stressed the larger moral import of Lawrence's work.
Stephen Spender says Lawrence "was a creative writer, not
merely in the aesthetic sense, but in the sense that his writing
was a constant search for a new life . . .".[10] Arnold Kettle has
pointed out that "it is part of Lawrence's greatness as an artist
that he had no use for art for art's sake—in the way the phrase

---

[1] *Collected Letters*, II, p. 1154.   [2] *Reminiscences*, London (1933), p. 26.
[3] *Op. cit.*, p. 167.   [4] *Son of Woman*, London (1931), p. 146.
[5] *Reminiscences*, p. 234.
[6] *Love, Freedom and Society*, London (1957), p. 56.
[7] West, p. 73.   [8] *Ibid.*   [9] *Op. cit.*, p. 104.
[10] *The Destructive Element*, London (1935), p. 182.

is generally understood. . . . He is out to help us to live."[11]
David Daiches finds Lawrence a disturbing writer in the sense
that he forces the reader to question his own life: "You cannot
simply accept his vision of life as interesting or illuminating or
aesthetically satisfying; you are compelled to apply it, to use it,
to test it, to wonder about it."[12] Kingsley Widmer also
affirms that Lawrence sought to transform existence, and that
"without taking some account of his religious quest we fail to
confront Lawrence's work".[13]

Aldous Huxley writing his introduction to *The Letters of
D. H. Lawrence* provided a corrective to views like the one
expressed by Murry that Lawrence was "beyond art", by
reiterating that "Lawrence was always and inescapably an
artist"; that he was an artist first of all; and that it was
therefore impossible to write about him except as an artist.
Richard Aldington supported Huxley in this, saying Lawrence
was above all a great literary artist. Even T. S. Eliot, in his
foreword to Father William Tiverton's *D. H. Lawrence and
Human Existence*, said in effect the same thing by underlining the
need for books about Lawrence "by critics who know him only
through his works". Most recent studies of Lawrence have, in
varying degrees, sought to assess Lawrence's achievement as an
artist.

The most frequent trick employed has been the convenient
one of dividing Lawrence into two: Lawrence the artist and
Lawrence the prophet. Lawrence the artist—so the argument
goes—wrote the aesthetically satisfying works—especially the
stories—in which the vision of the artist is fully realised,
rendered dramatically: all praise to this Lawrence. But in
other works—especially in the later novels—the intervention
of Lawrence the moralist is skilfully detected, and then, as if
to make the earlier praise sound more plausible, Lawrence is
severely condemned—for not living up to the critic's conception
of an artist-novelist. Thus H. T. Moore writes that while
The Rainbow and *Women in Love* had an integration, nearly all
Lawrence's subsequent fiction has "awkward moments,

[11] *An Introduction to the English Novel*, II, London (1962), p. 115.
[12] Daiches, p. 178.
[13] *The Art of Perversity*, Seattle (1962), p. 203.

digressions, collapses of theme and structure",[14] and doubts if books like *Aaron's Rod* should technically be called novels. F. R. Leavis, probably Lawrence's staunchest champion and most sympathetic critic, also observes in *D. H. Lawrence: Novelist* that the novels that succeed *Women in Love* are not achieved enough to be wholly impersonal works of art because "something like a direct involvement of the author . . . is evident in them . . .".[15] Dr Leavis remarks elsewhere in the same book that to appreciate Lawrence "is to revise one's criteria of intelligence and one's notion of it".[16] One only wishes Dr Leavis had realised as well that to appreciate Lawrence is also to revise one's criteria of art and one's notion of it. W. W. Robson complains that Lawrence permits himself liberties incompatible not only with Flaubertian principles of art, but with the practice of any art, and that even in novels like *Sons and Lovers* and *Women in Love* "the 'frame' of the book is broken and we are drawn into the quarrel as if it were real life, forced to take sides, to want to intervene".[17] Two recent full-length studies of Lawrence which professedly concern themselves only with his writings as art are Eliseo Vivas's *D. H. Lawrence: The Failure and the Triumph of Art* (1961) and Julian Moynahan's *The Deed of Life: The Novels and Tales of D. H. Lawrence* (1963). Vivas, who claims he would be "the first to insist" that responsible criticism must have a theoretical basis in an aesthetic,[18] says in the preface to his book: "This study is not concerned with Lawrence the man."[19] He, however, adds on the next page that he is not altogether indifferent to biographical data; and, having said that, goes on, in the first few chapters of his book, to trace Lawrence's failures of art back to "subjective factors". We are then told that Lawrence was "oppressed by a sense of social inferiority",[20] that he had a "yearning for a homosexual relationship",[21] that he was a "physical bully",[22] and—perhaps as a model of sound aesthetic judgment—the following:

[14] *The Life and Works of D. H. Lawrence*, London (1963), p. 154.
[15] Leavis, p. 147. [16] *Op. cit.*, p. 27.
[17] "D. H. Lawrence and *Women in Love*" in *The Modern Age*. Harmondsworth (1961), p. 292.
[18] Vivas, p. 283. [19] *Op. cit.*, p. vii. [20] *Op. cit.*, p. 56.
[21] *Op. cit.*, p. 57. [22] *Op. cit.*, p. 195.

[Lawrence's] own conduct and his own desiderata are the norm, they define the ideal. A deviation from *his* style of living is wrong. Either you—whoever you may be, whatever your heredity or upbringing may have been, whatever your aims and commitments—manage your sexual life the way I, David Herbert Lawrence, by the grace of God and my fiat appointed teacher of mankind, manage mine, or you are wrong, and nothing can alter that fact. Never mind the fact that I, David Herbert Lawrence, am a sick man trying desperately to shed my illness in book after book unsuccessfully. Never mind the fact that I, David Herbert Lawrence, have suspected at times that I am a bit dotty. Never mind the fact that my mother mangled my development. It still remains an incontrovertible fact that I, David Herbert Lawrence, am, by the grace of God and my own fiat, the standard. You are not like me, you say? Obviously not—and that is what makes you wrong.[23]

Mr Vivas no doubt expected this to pass for literary criticism. It only shows how difficult it is to come to terms with Lawrence on "artistic" grounds alone. Vivas's aesthetic objection against Lawrence, however, is that he disregards the principle of artistic distancing and—as for instance in *Sons and Lovers*—commits the artistic crime of "dragging the reader into the quarrel".[24] Moynahan's book is "a study of Lawrence's major works of fiction as works of art",[25] and the author, we are told, has "tried to avoid a preoccupation with . . . the moral significance of Lawrence's message and career". In practice, however, Moynahan's critical method is, luckily, not so exclusive as he, for some reason, wants to have us believe it is.

All this aesthetic criticism of Lawrence is based on a narrow, fixed conception of art. It takes for granted certain rules or principles as axiomatic. But there are not, there cannot be, any fixed, static principles of literary criticism valid for all time. Any really great writer forces us, in one way or another, to reconsider and extend our ideas about the nature and function of literary art and its forms. Applying irrelevant aesthetic principles to Lawrence's novels serves not the least purpose.

---

[23] *Op. cit.*, p. 132.   [24] *Op. cit.*, p. 193.
[25] *The Deed of Life*, London (1963), p. xiii.

Lawrence was an avowedly moral writer—moral in the widest and best sense of the term. He believed that his genius was essentially religious, and that he wrote from a deep moral sense. He was impatient of art "too much cooked in the artistic consciousness".[26] He did not, he declared, "care a button" for neat works of art. Writing to the Italian critic Carlo Linati, Lawrence said:

> But really, Signor Linati, do you think that books should be sort of toys, nicely built up of observations and sensations, all finished and complete?—I don't. . . . I can't bear art that you can walk round and admire. A book should be either a bandit or a rebel or a man in a crowd. People should either run for their lives, or come under the colours, or say *how do you do*? I hate the actor-and-the-audience business. An author should be in among the crowd, kicking their shins or cheering on to some mischief or merriment. That rather cheap seat in the gods where one sits with fellows like Anatole France and benignly looks down on the foibles, follies, and frenzies of so-called fellow-men, just annoys me. After all the world is *not* a stage— not to me: nor a theatre: nor a show-house of any sort. And art, especially novels, are not like theatres where the reader sits aloft and watches—like a god with a twenty-lira ticket—and sighs, commiserates, condones and smiles.—That's what you want a book to be: because it leaves you so safe and so superior, with your two-dollar ticket to the show. And that's what my books are not and never will be. You need not complain that I don't subject the intensity of my vision—or whatever it is—to some vast and imposing rhythm—by which you mean, isolate it on a stage, so that you can look down on it like a god who has got a ticket to the show. I never will . . . whoever reads me will be in the thick of the scrimmage, and if he doesn't like it— if he wants a safe seat in the audience—let him read somebody else.[27]

It is pointless to analyse Lawrence's novels laboriously in order to come to the conclusion that Lawrence is not the kind of writer he himself never wanted to be; or to blame him for not writing the kind of rounded-off books one could "put on the shelf" and admire, which he refused to write. As early as in

[26] *Mornings in Mexico and Etruscan Places*, p. 107.
[27] *Collected Letters*, II, pp. 826-7.

January 1909—Lawrence's first novel was published in 1911—
he wrote in a letter to Blanche Jennings that he would rather
write crude live things than beautiful dead ones. Discussing
Lawrence's novels as "a series of discrete aesthetic organisations
to be valued solely for richness of texture and internal coherence
of organisation"[28] is no more useful than trying to abstract his
ideas from his art and discussing them as if they were some kind
of philosophy or religion. Lawrence was both an artist and a
prophet at once; and his moral intention and his art are
inextricably bound up together. To bring them together, to
join them was, in fact, Lawrence's declared intention. He says
in his essay "Surgery for the Novel—Or a Bomb":

> It seems to me it was the greatest pity in the world, when
> philosophy and fiction got split. They used to be one, right
> from the days of myth. Then they went and parted, like a
> nagging married couple, with Aristotle and Thomas Aquinas
> and that beastly Kant. So the novel went sloppy, and
> philosophy went abstract dry. The two should come together
> again—in the novel.[29]

In Lawrence's novels whatever is moral is expressed in artistic
terms, and all his artistic effort is meant to be moral. If his
novels have a message, the novels themselves are that message.
E. M. Forster rightly called Lawrence a "prophetic novelist";[30]
and the only "way to deal with prophets who are also artists",
says Graham Hough, "is to respond to their art".[31] Leavis's
attempt to see a novel like *Women in Love* both as a "highly
organised work of art" and as having a "significance in terms
of basic human problems and the fate of our civilization"[32] is
undoubtedly justified.

Lawrence once said: "One has to be so terribly religious to
be an artist."[33] And even though he was not prepared to
subdue his art to any "metaphysic", he acknowledged that he
wrote because he wanted men and women to change, and have

[28] The words used by Eugene Goodheart to describe this attitude in *The
Utopian Vision of D. H. Lawrence*, Chicago (1963), p. 39.
[29] *Phoenix*, p. 520.
[30] *Aspects of the Novel*, Harmondsworth (Penguin) 1964, p. 146.
[31] Hough, p. 5.
[32] *Times Literary Supplement*, 19 Apr. 1957, p. 241.
[33] *Collected Letters*, I, p. 189.

more sense. Explaining his views on the relation of art and morality, Lawrence wrote:

> The essential function of art is moral. Not aesthetic, not decorative, not pastime and recreation. But moral. The essential function of art is moral.
> But a passionate, implicit morality, not didactic. A morality which changes the blood, rather than the mind. Changes the blood first. The mind follows later, in the wake.[34]

It is well to remember the distinction Lawrence makes here between implicit passionate morality and didactic morality, because, while he does not believe that a work of art is immoral just because the artist has any dominant idea or purpose, the immorality comes in when the artist puts his thumb in the scale to pull it down in favour of his didactic purpose—which is quite often directly opposed to his passional inspiration. Art, in a way, *is* utterly dependent on the artist's vision of life (or philosophy or "metaphysic")—even if the artist is at first not conscious of it. Every work of art "adheres to some system of morality". But, adds Lawrence, if it is really a work of art, it must contain the essential criticism of this morality to which it adheres; for while all systems of morality are of temporary value, useful to their times,

> Art must give a deeper satisfaction. . . . The degree to which the system of morality, or the metaphysic, of any work of art is submitted to criticism within the work of art makes the lasting value and satisfaction of that work.[35]

Do Lawrence's own novels give this "fair play all round" which he demands of art? I think they largely do, even though this is not at once obvious, and most of Lawrence's critics have failed to see this—probably because of certain preconceptions with which they have tended to approach him. Lawrence, of course, had his own views, his own "theory of being and knowing": but he also knew that while a novel must have the structural skeleton of some theory or metaphysic, it becomes a treatise if the novelist fails to make his metaphysic subserve the larger artistic purpose. Lawrence did not set out to write his novels in order to convince the readers of the truth of his own

[34] *S.C.A.L.*, p. 162.   [35] *Phoenix*, p. 476.

B

beliefs or ideals. In fact he believed no one has the right to
impose his ideals on another person, for that is ideal bullying,
to Lawrence the most hateful of things. Lawrence's own views,
of course, do find expression in his novels: but they are not
presented as absolute truths. To Lawrence there are no
absolute truths. He was acutely aware that his own views could
be only relatively true, true for the time being. "Away with
eternal truth", he says. Truth lives from day to day, and even
art can only tell the truth of its own times. Perfect art is a lie
because it is perfect only when abstracted from "that context by
which and in which it exists as truth".[36] Hence Lawrence's
high praise for the novel: the beauty of the novel is that in it
everything is true in its own relationship, and no further. The
novel, if it is really a work of art, contains no didactic absolutes;
and even if the artist or the novelist sets out to point a moral,
the tale as a rule points the other way. It is in this context that
Lawrence recommends trusting not the artist, but the tale.

> Oh give me the novel! Let me hear what the novel says. As
> for the novelist, he is usually a dribbling liar.[37]

What about Lawrence himself? Isn't he, too, a "dribbling
liar"? Shouldn't moral judgments in a work of art be implicit?
Why should Lawrence shout over the voice of the novel and
not let the novels speak for themselves? The answer is that
moral judgments *are* implicit in Lawrence's novels, in that they
supply the imaginative evidence for whatever judgments are
made, and that Lawrence does let the novels speak for
themselves.

Critics have frequently complained that in Lawrence's
novels characters like Birkin, Somers, Lilly, Mellors act as
mere mouthpieces for the novelist. The reader, it is said, is
not left free to decide for himself: he is forced to side with these
characters, and against others like Anton Skrebensky, Gerald
Crich, Hermione Roddice, and Clifford Chatterley,[38] for

---

[36] *Op. cit.*, p. 475.   [37] *S.L.C.*, p. 80.

[38] It has been suggested to me by Mr C. G. Martin that it would be useful to
draw a distinction between characters like Hermione Roddice who are presented
by Lawrence with impartiality and those like Clifford Chatterley and Gerald
Crich who can be said to have the author's deep sympathy even while they are
severely criticised.

whom the novelist has nothing but unjustified contempt. But these complaints, however widespread, are only imaginary. The critics first divide Lawrence's characters into two categories —the good ones and the bad ones—and then imagine that the good ones must represent Lawrence himself, whereas the bad ones probably stand for all that Lawrence wanted to condemn. This neat division, however, has no basis in fact. There are no wholly good or wholly bad, wholly right or wholly wrong characters in Lawrence's novels. No character in any of Lawrence's novels can be said to be the author's mouthpiece or to have his wholehearted approval. Similarly no characters are singled out for outright condemnation. And if we see nothing good in Gerald Crich or Rico or Clifford Chatterley, it is to be attributed not to an artistic failure on Lawrence's part, but to a critical failure in ourselves, a failure of perceptiveness and discernment in us as readers. Having decided beforehand that Lawrence created these characters only to damn them, we find in them only what we look for.

Lawrence as a rule projected aspects of himself and his ideas imaginatively into various different characters of his novels. In fact it would be hard to find out a major character in any of his novels who is not, in some way, Lawrence himself. A critic who fails to see Lawrence projecting some facet of his own self in characters like Miriam, Gerald Crich, Hermione Roddice, Aaron Sisson, Kangaroo, and Clifford Chatterley, fails to recognise Lawrence's genius as a novelist. Lawrence was an intensely self-critical writer. Characters like Birkin in *Women in Love*, who resemble Lawrence in some ways and express some of the opinions Lawrence himself expressed elsewhere outside his fiction, are not spared the criticism of the novel. Birkin is made to look ridiculous in his moments of deadly earnestness. We must laugh, Lawrence believed, "at ourselves and everything. Particularly at our sublimities. Everything has its hour of ridicule—everything".[39] Lawrence's "heroes" and "heroines" are not presented to us as models to be admired, nor is their conduct offered as a standard to be accepted by the reader. What they are and what they do is

---

[39] *S.C.A.L.*, p. 70.

true for their own context, for their own particular time, place, and circumstance.

> So, if a character in a novel wants two wives—or three—or thirty: well, that is true of that man, at that time, in that circumstance. It may be true of other men, elsewhere and elsewhen. But to infer that all men at all times want two, three, or thirty wives; or that the novelist himself is advocating furious polygamy; is just imbecility.[40]

Whatever the novelist advocates is incorporated in the total structure of the novel. Lawrence is nowhere concerned with forcing our sympathies for or against any particular character. What one resents most in a novel, he says, is "having one's sympathy *forced* by the novelist, towards some character one should never naturally sympathize with".[41] Lawrence presents impartially things as they are, or as he sees they are, in their varying relationships. Whatever a reader accepts as true or valid is left to be determined by his own sensibility, not dictated to him by the novelist. The novels present to us dramatised experience so organised as to define for us aspects of "the human condition"—in both its implications and its possibilities. They help us see ourselves and the world we live in more clearly: they tell us what we are, and could be. In doing so they also heighten our sense of values, sharpen our sensibility, and make life a richer experience. But it is no part of the novelist's business to offer solutions or cures for mankind's ills. One often hears it said that while Lawrence's diagnoses are correct, the cures he prescribes are unacceptable. F. R. Leavis says that Lawrence's analyses are always irresistible, but that he sometimes cherishes the illusion that his art also provides positive "answers" to the large issues raised. "It is then", Leavis continues, "that we make our severest criticisms."[42] These "severest criticisms" are, however, entirely misplaced, for nowhere in his novels does Lawrence offer any answers or solutions. Those who go to Lawrence's novels hoping to find there any ready-made answers are bound to be disappointed. The novels explore and reveal, and leave it—as they should—to

---

[40] *S.L.C.*, p. 73.   [41] *Phoenix*, p. 352.   [42] Leavis, p. 70.

the individual reader to solve for himself the questions and problems his personal life, or his civilisation, confronts him with. Lawrence unequivocally states that "the business of art is never to solve, but only to declare".[43] As a human being Lawrence had his own views about what life should be like, and how this could be brought about. But his own conclusions are not offered as conclusions of the novels. It is not at all necessary to agree with Lawrence's ideas in order to appreciate his greatness as a novelist. The *correctness* or otherwise of Lawrence's beliefs expressed outside the novels is not relevant to the assessment of his novels as works of art. It is ridiculous to pass moral judgments on Lawrence's social, political, or philosophical ideas and offer these as valid literary criticism of the novels. But while there is no justification for bringing in Lawrence's beliefs stated outside his fiction in order to arrive at literary judgments on their basis, these views are undoubtedly helpful in trying to clarify Lawrence's meaning. No adequate literary criticism of Lawrence can even begin without a proper understanding of Lawrence's closely connected ideas about art, morality, life, human relationships and the conflicts inherent in them.

Lawrence's dictum that the essential function of art is moral becomes clearer when we see the close correspondence between his views on art and on morality. "Art", he says, "displays . . . the living conjunction between the self and its context",[44] whereas for him the "essence of morality is the basic desire to preserve the perfect correspondence between the self and the object . . . ".[45] The business of art is "to reveal the relation between man and his circumambient universe",[46] while morality is that delicate, changing balance between man and the circumambient universe which accompanies this relatedness. Art reveals things in their different relationships.[47] The relation between things changes from day to day. Therefore art which reveals these changing relations is for ever new. But a new relationship also means a new morality, for "the only morality" is to let each "relationship form of itself",

[43] *Phoenix*, p. 461.   [44] *S.M.*, p. 117.   [45] *Fantasia*, p. 226.
[46] *Phoenix*, p. 527.   [47] *Op. cit.*, p. 524.

naturally.[48]   Indeed "nothing is true, or good, except in its own living relatedness to its circumambient universe".[49]

It is important to bear in mind the special sense in which Lawrence uses words like morality, good, evil, truth, sin, God, etc., when discussing his views on art, especially on the novel. Morality for Lawrence is not a set of rules or prescriptions. On the contrary, he characterises morality based on ideas or an ideal as "unmitigated evil". Morality, pure morality, is only "an instinctive adjustment which the soul makes in every circumstance, adjusting one thing to another livingly, delicately, sensitively".[50] Anything that damages this delicate adjustment is sinful and immoral. Our main business is to be fully, vividly alive. That which brings into us a stronger and deeper flow of life is good and moral; that which impairs this flow is evil. "There is only one sin in life, and that is the sin against life":[51]

> Evil, what is evil?
> There is only one evil, to deny life. . . .[52]

To sacrifice oneself to anything or anybody whatsoever is the vilest deed a man can do, ". . . the vilest cowardice and treachery".[53] As to saving one's soul, how and why should the soul be "saved"? One can save one's pennies, Lawrence remarks,[54] but how can one save one's soul? One can only live one's soul. The business is to live, be really alive. Real living is the only truth: "The problem of truth is: How can we most deeply *live?*"[55]

A man can, of course, do nothing with his life but live it: but every man has to learn to be himself, his real spontaneous self. It is by no means easy for anyone to come to his "spontaneous-creative fullness of being".[56] And yet all that matters is that each human being shall *be* in his own fullness, so that he can meet life sensitively and responsively in every one of its moods and aspects, without imposing on it some theory or some arbitrary goal or some mechanistic vision of his own. One cannot, however, live in sheer full spontaneity by one's instincts

---

[48] *Op. cit.*, p. 531.   [49] *Op. cit.*, p. 525.   [50] *Fantasia*, p. 76.
[51] *Phoenix*, p. 745.   [52] *Poems*, II, p. 24.   [53] *Poems*, III, p. 119.
[54] *Selected Literary Criticism*, ed. A. Beal, p. 8.
[55] *Collected Letters*, II, p. 933.   [56] *Fantasia*, p. 248.

alone; there must be a "perfect harmony between the conscious intelligence and the unconscious, preconscious prompting...."[57]

Mental consciousness is an invaluable aid in our coming to full spontaneous living: but the mind or intellect by itself is only the "glitter of the sun on the surface of the waters".[58] In a letter to Ernest Collings, in which he compared life to a flame for ever upright and flowing, and the intellect to the light that is shed on the things around, Lawrence said:

> We have got so ridiculously mindful, that we never know that we ourselves are anything—we think there are only the objects we shine upon. And there the poor flame goes on burning ignored, to produce this light. . . . A flame isn't a flame because it lights up two, or twenty objects on a table. It's a flame because it is itself. And we have forgotten ourselves. We are Hamlet without the Prince of Denmark. We cannot *be*. . . . The real way of living is to answer to one's wants. Not 'I want to light up with my intelligence as many things as possible' but 'For the living of my full flame—I want that liberty, I want that woman, I want that pound of peaches, I want to go to sleep, I want to go to a pub and have a good time, I want to look a beastly swell today, I want to kiss that girl, I want to insult that man.'[59]

Living consists in doing what the life in us really wants to do, not what the ego imagines we want to do. And to find out how the life in us wants to be lived is terribly difficult. It is in the performance of this difficult task that mind can be of great use, as an instrument. Mind or intellect can never control or direct the life mystery if only because "our volition is always subsidiary to our spontaneous arrival".[60] There should be some measure of control so that every deep desire can be fulfilled in its own fulness and proportion. But this control must never be for its own sake. Mental consciousness is not our goal or aim.

> We want *effectual* human beings, not conscious ones. The final aim is not to *know*, but to *be*. There never was a more risky motto than that: *know thyself*. You've got to know yourself as far as possible. But not just for the sake of knowing. You've

---

[57] *S.M.*, p. 229.
[58] *Apocalypse*, p. 308.
[59] *Collected Letters*, I, p. 180.
[60] *S.M.*, p. 26.

got to know yourself so that you can at last *be* yourself. 'Be Yourself' is the last motto.[61]

Knowing is, in a way, antagonistic to being. The more we know the less we are: the more we are in being the less we know. In our modern civilisation, as knowledge has increased, wonder has decreased, and men are left thoroughly bored, dead. And yet, paradoxical though it might seem, we have to know all before we can know that knowing is nothing. We have to go on knowing more and more until knowledge "suddenly shrivels and we know that forever we don't know".[62] Our aim, therefore, is to know how not-to-know; in other words: how to be spontaneous in full consciousness.

> Yet we must know, if only in order to learn not to know. The supreme lesson of human consciousness is to learn how *not* to *know*. That is how not to interfere. That is how to live dynamically. . . .[63]

Living, then, is not mere existence, not just doing certain things—"running after women, or digging a garden, or working an engine, or becoming a member of Parliament".[64] A thing isn't life just because somebody does it, and an artist ought to know this perfectly well:

> The ordinary bank clerk buying himself a new straw hat isn't "life" at all: it is just existence, quite all right, like everyday dinners: but not "life".
>   By life we mean something that gleams, that has the fourth-dimensional quality. If the bank clerk feels really piquant about his hat, if he establishes a lively relation with it, and goes out of the shop with the new straw on his head, a changed man, be-aureoled, then that is life.[65]

When an artist or a novelist writes about this transformation in the bank-clerk, he writes of "life". It must, however, be added here that in talking of life Lawrence does not have any vague, abstract, or mystifying concept in mind. Life, he maintains, is inconceivable as a general thing. It exists only in living

[61] *Fantasia*, p. 64. [62] *S.C.A.L.*, p. 123. [63] *Fantasia*, p. 72.
[64] *R.D.P.*, p. 148. [65] *Phoenix*, pp. 529-30.

creatures. In the beginning of the individual creature is the beginning of life, and life has no beginning apart from this.

> Life is not and never was anything but living creatures. That's what life is and will be, just living creatures, no matter how large you make the capital L. [66]

Every individual creature has a soul, a specific individual nature. This individual soul within the individual being is, has always been, and will always be the only clue to life and universe. "Life is individual, always was individual and always will be." [67] This life in the living individual is for Lawrence the only thing that is really important. Life with a capital L is nothing but man alive.

> For man, the vast marvel is to be alive. For man, as for flower and beast and bird, the supreme triumph is to be most vividly, most perfectly alive. Whatever the unborn and the dead may know, they cannot know the beauty, the marvel of being alive in the flesh. The dead may look after the afterwards. But the magnificent here and now of life in the flesh is ours, and ours alone, and ours only for a time. We ought to dance with rapture that we should be alive. . . . [68]

It is Lawrence's constant, persistent concern with, and exultance in, life as lived in individual beings which made one critic remark that Lawrence was "terribly, overwhelmingly in love with life", [69] and occasioned Katherine Mansfield's comment in 1922:

> He [Lawrence] is the only writer living whom I really profoundly care for. It seems to me whatever he writes, no matter how much one may "disagree", is important. And after all even what one objects to is a *sign of life* in him. He is a living man. [70]

Lawrence was a "living man", and he transmitted the life in him through his creative work by ". . . kindling the life quality where it was not". [71] It was his belief that all work done with real interest, all creative work, becomes a fountain of life for

---

[66] *Fantasia*, p. 16.   [67] *Op. cit.*, p. 147.   [68] *Apocalypse*, p. 307.
[69] André Maurois, *Poets and Prophets*, London (1936), p. 187.
[70] Nehls, II, p. 159.   [71] *Poems*, II, p. 179.

others.   In one of his letters he defined a hero as one who touches and transmits the life of the universe.[72]   This is what his own work pre-eminently does.

Life, in Lawrence's view, starts crude and unspecified, and then seeks continually and progressively to differentiate itself. It proceeds to evolve out of an undifferentiated mass ever more distinct and definite forms, as if its purpose were the production of an infinite number of perfect individuals, each individual distinct from all others.   The final aim of every living thing, creature, or being is the full achievement of itself.

The highest goal for every man thus is the goal of pure individual being.   But this goal cannot be reached simply by the rupture of all ties, for the individual is truly himself only when he is in genuine living relation to all his surroundings.   It is only through a living dynamic relation with others that we can come to our own particular and individual fullness of being: it is the correspondence between the individual entity and the external universe which is the clue to all growth and development.   Our whole life is, indeed, one long effort to establish a "polarity" with the outer universe, human and non-human. Life, according to Lawrence, is nothing but a vivid relatedness between man and the living universe that surrounds him.   For mankind it is this relation between man and his circumambient universe which constitutes life:

> If we think about it, we find that our life *consists in* this achieving of a pure relationship between ourselves and the living universe about us.   This is how I "save my soul" by accomplishing a pure relationship between me and another person, me and other people, me and a nation, me and a race of men, me and the animals, me and the trees or flowers, me and the earth, me and the skies and sun and stars, me and the moon: an infinity of pure relations, big and little, like the stars of the sky: that makes our eternity, for each one of us, me and the timber I am sawing, the lines of force I follow; me and the dough I knead for bread, me and the very motion with which I write, me and the bit of gold I have got.   This, if we knew it, is our life and our eternity: the subtle, perfected relation between me and my whole circumambient universe.[73]

---

[72] *Collected Letters*, II, p. 994.   [73] *Phoenix*, p. 528.

This view of Lawrence about life being a series of relationships between man and his circumambient universe is central to all his work. All his novels are concerned with revealing these relationships. This is the main theme of Lawrence's entire literary output—imaginative as well as discursive. Lawrence's concern in the novels with human relationships has been recognised to some extent by a number of critics, especially in recent years.[74] However, despite this verbal recognition of the importance of relationships in Lawrence's work, hardly any critical discussion of his novels has given these relationships the central place which they occupy in the novels themselves. Neither have Lawrence's views on the nature of various relationships been fully understood, nor has any attempt been made to discuss the novels as imaginative and artistically organised revelations of these relationships. It is, nevertheless, quite certain that unless full recognition is given to the place and importance these relationships have in Lawrence's fiction, all criticism of his novels will continue to be strictly limited in value. As long as critics are content with merely applying to these novels certain rules or criteria derived from a formal study of other novels, no adequate assessment of Lawrence as a novelist is likely to emerge. If the business of art is to reveal, then Lawrence's art makes this revelation in terms of human relationships; and it is the theme of relationships which is the essential clue to the meaning as well as the structure of all Lawrence's novels.

"The amazingly difficult and vital business of human relationship," Lawrence complains, "has been almost laughably underestimated in our epoch."[75] We need a theory of human relativity much more than the universe does, for we have our very being in living dynamic relations. Man must maintain himself in true relationship to his contiguous universe, as he did once. Lawrence found in the carvings, drawings, and

---

[74] See Arnold Kettle, *An Introduction to the English Novel*, II, p. 118; Mark Spilka, "Was D. H. Lawrence a Symbolist", *Accent* (1955), p. 54, and *The Love Ethic of D. H. Lawrence*, Bloomington (1959), p. 10; J. Middleton Murry, *Love, Freedom and Society*, p. 13; Mark Schorer in *A D. H. Lawrence Miscellany*, ed. H. T. Moore, p. 286; Herbert Read, "On D. H. Lawrence", *The Twentieth Century*, CLXV (1959), pp. 562-3; and Daiches, p. 181.

[75] *Fantasia*, p. 245.

paintings of old Egyptians, Assyrians, Hindoos, and Etruscans a marvellous quality of "living relationship between man and his object! be it man or woman, bird, beast, flower or rock or rain".[76] Whether it was an Assyrian sculpture of a lion, or an Egyptian hawk, or an African fetish of a pregnant woman, or an early Greek Apollo, or an Ajanta frescoe—Lawrence could discern in them all the "exquisite frail moment[s] of pure conjunction".[77]

This conjunction, however, is not always exquisite or pure: the relations might be living and changing, or they might be static and dead. Modern man, Lawrence observed, was increasingly depriving himself of vital contacts. Nearly all his relations were old, mechanical, dead. "What we want", Lawrence wrote in *Apocalypse*, "is to destroy our false, inorganic connections, especially those related to money, and to re-establish the living organic connections, with the cosmos, the sun and earth, with mankind and nation and family."[78] Of the organic relations, Lawrence's novels deal mainly with the man-woman relationship, though by no means only with this. For besides his relation to the woman he loves, man is, or should be, related to the family, to other men and society, to birds, beasts, and flowers, and beyond all these to the cosmos. All Lawrence's efforts were directed towards bringing about a living, harmonious relationship between man and the world he lives in. Man's deepest desire, Lawrence said in a letter to Catherine Carswell, is "a wish for pure, unadulterated relationship with the universe".[79] The relationship, Lawrence explains elsewhere, is threefold: the relation to the living universe; the relation of man to woman; and the relation of man to man.[80] In each of these relationships a circuit of vital flow, of dynamic vital interchange, is established. But one cannot insist on this flow, or in any way force it. The moment anybody insists, the flow is gone. The relationship has "to happen, . . . almost unconsciously. We can't *deliberately* do much with a human connexion, except smash it: and that is usually not difficult. On the positive side we can only most carefully let it take place, without interfering or forcing."[81] In fact human beings are

---

[76] *R.D.P.*, p. 140.   [77] *Ibid.*   [78] *Apocalypse*, p. 308.
[79] *Collected Letters*, I, p. 467.   [80] *S.L.C.*, p. 263.   [81] *Phoenix*, p. 191.

more or less connected, more or less in touch, until—as happens
too often today—they kill the sensitive responses in themselves
or begin unnaturally resisting their connexion with the living
cosmos and with other human beings.

No human being can develop except through a vital relation
with his surroundings. Actual living is, therefore, a question of
direct contact. As early as in January 1910 Lawrence was
saying, "What we all want, madly, is human contact."[82] An
individual can never be purely a "thing-by-himself"; he can
exist only in relation to the external universe.

But a mature individual not only lives in a perfect harmonious relation to the universe around him, he is also perfect
in himself. The ultimate attainment for man is the attainment
of his perfect, unique self. "One is one and all alone and ever
more shall be so. Exult in the fact that you are yourself and
alone for ever."[83] Each contact leads to "the sheer fiery purity
of a purer isolation, a more exultant singleness".[84] The highest
reality for each being is in its purity of singleness and in its
perfect integrity; and all communion, all love, all contacts are
only a means to the attainment of this perfected singleness of
the individual being.

There is, thus, a dual movement—the movement towards
isolation and the movement towards community, towards
contact and away from contact. And both are necessary.
Lawrence, in his writings of different periods, emphasised the
one thing or the other, depending on the immediate experiences
he was going through; and a superficial reading might suggest
that he contradicts himself. But there is really no contradiction.
Man finds his fulfilment through contact with other beings and
with his surroundings. There are, however, times when an
individual must be alone, must possess his own soul in silence.[85]
This, in turn, prepares the individual for further new contacts.
"One has to be an absolute individual, separate as a seed fallen
out of the pod. Then a *volte-face*, and a new start."[86]

Lawrence, in his own life, felt these dual urges very acutely.
At times he was so disappointed with people, or with events,
that he was impelled to find whatever comfort he could in his

[82] *Collected Letters*, I, p. 60.   [83] *Phoenix*, p. 634.   [84] *Ibid.*
[85] *Poems*, III, p. 27.   [86] *Collected Letters*, II, p. 753.

own isolation. At other times he felt the full force of the truth that an individual cut off from his connexions with other people is next to nothing, since his very individuality depends on his relation to others. Thus we find him writing in September 1917 in a letter to Koteliansky:

> I have learnt to be unsocial entirely, a single thing to myself. I hate being squashed into humanity, like a strawberry boiled with all the other strawberries into jam. God above, leave me single and separate and unthinkably distinguished from all the rest: let me be a paradisal being, but *never* a human being: . . . Henceforth I deal in single, sheer beings—nothing human, only the star-singleness of paradisal souls.[87]

But Lawrence, fully aware of what he was saying, added characteristically: "This is the latest sort of swank: also true." He knew that what he was saying was true to his feelings at that time, in those circumstances: "also true". A year later he wrote in the same vein to Katherine Mansfield, saying he was beginning to despair altogether about human relationships —"I feel one may just as well turn into a sort of lone wolf, and have done with it."[88] In his essay "The Education of the People" written during the same period Lawrence said:

> *Noli me tangere.* It is our motto as it is the motto of a wild wolf or deer. I want about me a clear, cool space across which nobody trespasses. I want to remain intact within my own natural isolation, save at those moments when I am drawn to a rare and significant intimacy. The horrible personal promiscuity of our life is extremely ugly and distasteful.[89]

Writing at a different time, in a different frame of mind, Lawrence no longer accepts that "Noli me tangere" can be our motto. He now complains that we have all become hopeless little absolutes to ourselves, and insists that this egocentric absoluteness of the individual must be broken. Man, he says, can have the opportunity to be himself only when he falls back into his true relation with others: "Men must get back into *touch*. And to do so they must forfeit the vanity and the *noli me tangere* of their absoluteness . . . and fall again into true

---

[87] *Op. cit.*, I, p. 525.   [88] *Op. cit.*, I, p. 566.   [89] *Phoenix*, p. 649.

relatedness."[90]   Without this "true relatedness" no one can hope to be a whole or complete individual.   And today we are not whole as human beings because we know only a small fraction of the vital relationships we might have had.   We live, says Lawrence, in an age which believes in stripping away all relationships.   So we strip them away, like an onion, until we come to blank nothingness, emptiness.   Most men have today come to a knowledge of their own complete emptiness.   They had set out wanting badly to be "themselves", and have ended up in being next to nothing.

> What are you, when you've asserted your grand independence, broken all the ties, or "bonds", and reduced yourself to a "pure" individuality?   What are you?
>
> You may imagine you are something very grand, since few individuals even approximate to this independence without falling into deadly egoism and conceit: and emptiness.   The real danger is, reduced to your own single merits and cut off from the most vital human contacts, the danger is that you are left just simply next to nothing. . . . In absolute isolation, I doubt if any individual amounts to much; or if any soul is worth saving, or even having. . . . So that everything, even individuality itself, depends on relationship. . . .[91]

Without real contact, then, we remain more or less non-entities.   At the same time all contacts must leave the single being intact: there should be contact, but no mixing or merging:

> The central law of all organic life is that each organism is intrinsically isolate and single in itself.
>
> The moment its isolation breaks down, and there comes an actual mixing and confusion, death sets in. . . . But the secondary law of all organic life is that each organism only lives through contact with other matter, assimilation, and contact with other life, which means assimilation of new vibrations, non-material. Each individual organism is vivified by intimate contact with fellow organisms: up to a certain point.[92]

"Up to a certain point" because though men live by love, when love—spiritual or sensual—is carried too far, it leads only to death.   The first law of life is that each organism is isolate in

[90] *Op. cit.*, p. 382.   [91] *Op. cit.*, pp. 189-91.   [92] *S.C.A.L.*, p. 62.

itself and must return to its isolation. But isolation, too, beyond a certain point amounts to suicide. "Neither man nor woman should sacrifice individuality to love, nor love to individuality."[93] Love, as a desire for relation with other things, is balanced against the opposite desire of maintaining the integrity of the individual self. To yield entirely to love is to be absorbed by it; the individual must hold his own, or he ceases to be an individual. There is no fulfilment in love itself, even though it is reached *through* love. The central fulfilment for a man is that he "possesses his own soul in strength within him, deep and alone. The deep, rich aloneness, reached and perfected through love."[94] Love, though a great emotion, is only one of the emotions, and "no emotion is supreme, or exclusively worth living for. *All* emotions go to the achieving of a living relationship between a human being and the other human being or creature or thing he becomes purely related to."[95]

No contact or relationship, however, can be perfect. All relationships have their limits set by the singleness of the soul in each person or being. Perfect relationships just cannot be. "Each soul is alone, and the aloneness of each soul is a double barrier to perfect relationship between two beings."[96] To say that Lawrence's central focus is on "man's ontological solitude, [on] the discrete particularity of man as individual separated from other finite individuals by the qualitative, ontological gulf that separates finite creatures from one another",[97] is merely to put in more abstruse terms Lawrence's emphasis on the singleness of each individual soul. Everyone of us has to learn to live from the centre of his or her own responsibility only. This, however, does not mean what is commonly known as individualism; the so-called individualism is in Lawrence's view just cheap egoism, "every self-conscious little ego assuming unbounded rights to display his self-consciousness".[98] Most modern men and women don't even have any individuality left in them:

[93] *S.L.C.*, p. 94.   [94] *Fantasia*, p. 120.
[95] *Phoenix*, p. 529.   [96] *S.C.A.L.*, p. 135.
[97] Nathan A. Scott, Jr., *Rehearsals of Discomposure*, p. 132.
[98] *Phoenix*, p. 637.

Individualism! Read the advertisements! "Jew-jew's hats give a man that individual touch he so much desires. No man could lack individuality in Poppem's pyjamas." Poor devil! If he was left to his own skin, where would he be![99]

We have all of us to be both "starrily single" and "starrily self-responsible". Each individual should act spontaneously from the promptings of his own soul. "Each being," says Lawrence, "is, at his purest, a law unto himself, single, unique, a Godhead, a fountain from the unknown."[1] Eliseo Vivas describes this belief of Lawrence as the most deplorable of all the false and pernicious theories that Lawrence propounded, because he thinks "the autocracy of the dominant impulse of the moment" is all that Lawrence meant by man's standing alone and being the judge of himself, absolutely.[2] This falsifies Lawrence's views in two ways. Lawrence does not present the "ideal" of man's being a "law unto himself" as an absolute; he adds that when it has served its purpose and becomes "ancient, . . . then it can be dispatched".[3] Moreover, the individual acting in pure singleness, Lawrence explains in *Fantasia of the Unconscious*, acts from his whole self, not from impulse alone: "we cannot live purely by impulse. . . . We must live by all three, ideal, impulse, and tradition . . . ".[4]

Man comes to a state of "star-like maturity" only when he has passed through three distinct phases of life and its human relationships. First, the unison with family, and the simple, sexless friendships. Next the powerful sex relation with a woman culminating in marriage. And finally the unison of comrades in collective activity for the creation of the future, of a new era of life. The one phase, however, does not annul the other, it only fulfils the other:

Marriage is the great step beyond friendship, and family, and nationality, but it does not supersede these. Marriage should only give repose and perfection to the great previous bonds and relationships. A wife or husband who sets about to annul the old, pre-marriage affections and connections ruins the foundations of marriage. And so with the last, extremest love,

---

[99] *S.L.C.*, p. 104.   [1] *Phoenix*, p. 216.   [2] *Vivas*, p. 56.
[3] *Phoenix*, p. 216.   [4] *Fantasia*, p. 131.

the love of comrades. The ultimate comradeship which sets about to destroy marriage destroys its own *raison d'être*.[5]

The relationship between child and parents, according to Lawrence, should be spontaneous and non-ideal in nature: it should not be based on love alone. Parental love is not a mere emotion: it is a responsibility and a living purpose. If a child provokes anger, to deny it this anger is to interfere with its natural growth and development. The child should be given spontaneous love and tenderness as well as spontaneous anger and wrath. The relation of parents to the child should be a "continuous interplay of shadow and light", an ever-changing relationship.

The great danger, as Lawrence realised, of the present-day form of idealism—the idealism of love and of the spirit—is that it encourages the growth of false, unnaturally adult relations between parents and children. Intense parental love awakens the child prematurely, and a bond of adult love—not of sex but of higher spiritual love[6]—comes to be established between parent and child. This, however, is fatal—a sort of spiritual incest. For a time the relation works very well. The mother offers, not to her husband as she should, but to her son (or the father to the daughter) the perfect mature flower of married love, sexually asking nothing of the beloved, except that he shall be himself, and accept the gift of her love. The son, of course, finds all this wonderful, and gets on swimmingly for a time— until he is confronted with his own sexual needs. He is linked up already with his mother in the best ideal love he will ever know, for no woman is likely to offer to a husband, a stranger, "that beautiful and glamorous submission" which she gives to her son, her father or her brother. "And so, the charming young girl who adores her father, or one of her brothers, is sought in marriage by the attractive young man who loves his mother devotedly. And a pretty business the marriage is."[7] Love bonds within the family form quickly and without the

---

[5] *S.M.*, p. 262.

[6] Lawrence regarded any sensual response between parent and child as highly improbable: "Myself, I believe that biologically there is a radical sex-aversion between parent and child, at the deeper sexual centres." (*Fantasia*, pp. 118-19.)

[7] *Fantasia*, p. 125.

shocks and ruptures inevitable between strangers; so this kind of love appears the best, the intensest, the highest.

> You will not easily get a man to believe that his carnal love for the woman he has made his wife is as high a love as that he felt for his mother or sister.
> The cream is licked off from life before the boy or the girl is twenty. Afterwards—repetition, disillusion, and barrenness.[8]

The responsibility for this is on the parents, on their inability to come to rest within themselves, to possess their own souls in quiet and fullness, and to leave the child alone. Since the goal of a child's development is the attainment of mature, perfect singleness, the parents must not interfere with his harmonious growth, but should leave him "alone, within his own soul's inviolability".[9]

The relationship which Lawrence explores most fully in his novels from the start is that of man to woman. "I'll do my life work, sticking up for the love between man and woman,"[10] he wrote in a letter in December 1912. In April 1913 he wrote to Edward Garnett:

> I can only write what I feel pretty strongly about: and that, at present, is the relation between men and women. After all, it is *the* problem of today, the establishment of a new relation, or the readjustment of the old one, between men and women.[11]

A week later he wrote to his friend A. W. McLeod that he felt sure England could get out of "her present atrophy" only through a readjustment between men and women. Lawrence believed the source of all life and knowledge to be in man and woman, and the source of all living in the interchange, the meeting and mingling, of the two. The events of the First World War confirmed him in his belief, and he wrote to Lady Cynthia Asquith in November 1916, affirming his faith in the creative nature of man-woman relationship, and reiterating his disbelief in the soldier spirit which he saw as fatal, and leading only to an endless process of death: "The whole crux of life now lies in the relation between man and woman, between Adam and Eve. In this relation we live or die."[12]

[8] *Ibid.* [9] *Phoenix*, p. 639. [10] *Collected Letters*, I, p. 172.
[11] *Op. cit.*, p. 200. [12] *Op. cit.* I, p. 484.

There is hardly any man living, Lawrence says in "We Need One Another", who can exist at all cheerfully without a relationship to some particular woman; and there is hardly a woman on earth who can live cheerfully without some intimate relationship to a man. Men and women have their true being only when they are related, in contact: they are not separate entities in themselves. Man is connected with woman for ever in an unanalysable, complicated life-flow, even if it is only a mere flow in the air:

> It is not only man and wife: the woman facing me in the train, the girl I buy cigarettes from, all send forth to me a stream, a spray, a vapour of female life that enters my blood and my soul, and makes me me. And back again, I send the stream of male life, which soothes and satisfies and builds up the woman.[13]

This spontaneous life-flow, however, is becoming rarer every day, and what we have in its place is the spurious form of love derived from the head—mere fatal love-will and benevolence; and instead of the warm "blood-sex" we have today the nervous, disintegrative sort of sex. But it is not sex-in-the-head which establishes the living and vitalising connexion between man and woman: it is the true blood contact, the contact of positive sex, which takes place without any interference from the upper centres of consciousness. Nearly all modern sex is purely a matter of nerves, cold and bloodless, and therefore destructive rather than vitalising.

> It is quite true, sex today is all mental: intellectual reactions reflected down on to physical process: and that is repulsive, *häslich und widerlich.*[14]

We must, warns Lawrence, get back the phallic sex, or we are all lost. Sex is the pivot of a man's life. Every man makes the supreme effort to "clasp as a hub the woman who shall be the axle, compelling him to true motion without aberration".[15] From a woman man gets the necessary sense of stability; she is like a wall he can back up against.

Lawrence saw the relationship of man to woman as the

---

[13] *Phoenix*, p. 198.   [14] *Collected Letters*, II, p. 1048.   [15] *Phoenix*, p. 444.

central fact in actual human life—the relations to other men and women, parents, friends, all coming after this.

> The great relationship, for humanity, will always be the relation between man and woman. The relation between man and man, woman and woman, parent and child, will always be subsidiary.
>
> And the relation between man and woman will change for ever, and will for ever be the new central clue to human life. It is the *relation itself* which is the quick and the central clue to life, not the man, nor the woman, nor the children that result from the relationship, as a contingency.[16]

Lawrence calls children a "contingency" because he holds that the emergence of man and woman into their greater, purer selves is the main function of a sex relationship; and it is only that which cannot be fulfilled in the two individuals which trickles down as the seed of a new life: "It is not in the children that the new takes place: it is in the mature, consummated men and women."[17] Love itself is not a goal; it is only a travelling towards the goal. In the act of love that which is female in man is given to the woman, that which is male in her draws into the man. The man is singled out into a purer maleness, the woman into a purer femaleness. This in turn brings a realisation of the otherness of the other being, and an accompanying sense of freedom.

Love between man and woman, when it is whole, is both sacred and profane, spiritual as well as sensual. To Lawrence it is the greatest and most complete passion the world will ever see, because it is dual, of two opposing kinds. In sacred love, which is selfless, the lover seeks perfect communion of oneness with the beloved; in profane love he seeks to wrest his own from her. In the fierce passion of sensuality men and women are burnt into essentiality, into sheer separate distinction. Profane love is a destructive fire, but it is only through the "friction of intense destructive flames of sensual love" that we are purified into singleness, into our own unique, gem-like separateness of being.

All whole love between man and woman is dual: but not all love between man and woman is whole. It may be all

[16] *Op. cit.*, p. 531.　　　　[17] *S.M.*, p. 104.

gentle merging into oneness, with no separateness or otherness
discovered, no singleness won. This is the sacred or spiritual
love, which is only half of love. On the other hand love may
be all a battle of sensual gratification, producing gem-like
beings, like Tristan and Isolde, "he pure male singled and
separated out in superb jewel-like isolation of arrogant manhood, she purely woman, a lily balanced in rocking pride of
beauty and perfume of womanhood".[18] This is the profane
love which ends in piercing tragedy when the two beings so
singled out are torn finally apart by death. Neither the passion
for oneness nor the passion for distinct separateness is in itself
enough. It is only when two beings are "unutterably distinguished, and in unutterable conjunction",[19] when there is a
dual passion for separation and for unison, that love is complete.
Hence there must be the sweet love of communion and the
proud love of sensual fulfilment, both together in one love.

We live today in an age of individuality. The treasure of
treasures to each man or woman is his or her own individuality
which, we hope, "will flourish like a salamander in the flame
of love and passion. Which it well may: but for the fact that
there are two salamanders in the same flame, and they fight
till the flame goes out."[20] We start with "true love", and end
with a terrific struggle and conflict—the inevitable result of
two opposing egos trying to snatch an intensified individuality
out of the mutual flame. Now love, as a relationship of unison,
inevitably means the sinking of individuality, to some extent.
"One can't worship love and individuality in the same
breath."[21] Love is a mutual relationship which Lawrence
likens to a flame between wax and air: when either wax or air
insists on having its own way too much, the flame goes out and
the unison disappears. At the same time if either yields to the
other entirely the result is a guttering mess. As long as each
party in the relationship seeks its own in the other, and is
denied, some fight is inevitable. When each of the two parties
seeks its own absolutely then it is a fight to the death. This is
true of what we call "passion". On the other hand when of
the two parties one yields utterly to the other, this is called

---

[18] *Phoenix*, p. 154.   [19] *Poems*, I, p. 261.
[20] *S.L.C.*, pp. 82-3.   [21] *Op. cit.*, p. 83.

sacrifice, and it also means death. But there is also the third thing, "which is neither sacrifice nor fight to the death: when each seeks only the true relatedness to the other".[22] The man remains true to his manhood, the woman to her own womanhood, and the relationship is allowed to work out of itself. What is needed is some sort of balance between love and individuality, arrived at by sacrificing a portion of each.

The aim in man-woman relationship, then, is the attainment of a balance between love and individuality, between spiritual and sensual consummation. It is only when a man is fulfilled in the flesh as well as in the spirit, when he has known the extreme of enjoyment and the ultimate of suffering, both, that his soul is made absolute, immortal. And then, within the fulfilled soul, is established the divine relation between the two infinities which Lawrence calls the Holy Spirit. The Infinite is twofold: the Father and the Son, the Dark and the Light, the senses and the mind, the soul and the spirit, the Eagle and the Dove, the Tiger and the Lamb; and the Holy Ghost is the relation established between the two infinities, between the two natures of God. One may know the Son and deny the Father, or know the Father and deny the Son, but that which one may never deny is the Holy Spirit which relates the dual Infinities into one Whole.

The two Infinities are related, but they are not identical. They are the direct opposites, one of the other, and exist only in this opposition. It is "in the tension of opposites [that] all things have their being".[23] Law and Love, Flesh and Spirit, Father and Son, are eternally in conflict. The primary law of all the universe is the law of dual attraction and repulsion, a law of polarity. Duality, indeed, extends through everything. "There is a great polarity in life itself. Life itself is dual."[24] Lawrence gives as further instances of this duality the antinomy between Male-Female, Change-Stability, Doing-Being, Action-Feeling, Utterance-Emotion, Lion-Unicorn, Day-Night, Light-Darkness, etc. Darkness and Light can never be reconciled, nor can one win over the other. The two opposites exist by virtue of their inter-opposition. "Remove the opposition and there is collapse, a sudden crumbling into universal nothing-

[22] *Phoenix*, p. 531.   [23] *Op. cit.*, p. 67.   [24] *Fantasia*, p. 147.

ness."[25]   The law of dual poles applies equally to the human psyche: the division in our psyche sets our spiritual being against our sensual being.   We are divided in ourselves, against ourselves.   That is our cross.   Man is made up of a dual consciousness, and the two halves are in opposition to each other.   There is a basic hostility in all of us between the physical and the mental, the blood and the spirit: "Mind-consciousness extinguishes blood-consciousness and consumes the blood",[26] because there is a fundamental antagonism between the mental cognitive mode and the physical or sexual mode of consciousness.   The principle of dualism, thus, reigns even within us: "every man as long as he remains alive is in himself a multitude of conflicting men."[27]   But the Holy Ghost is the reconciler; it is neither love nor hatred, for it surpasses both love and hatred.   It is the supreme relation, between Father and Son—not a relation of love, which is specific and relative, but an absolute relation of opposition and attraction both.   Lawrence, in a letter to Eleanor Farjeon, said it was a blasphemy to suggest that the Holy Spirit is Love:

> Can you not see that if the relation between Father and Son, in the Christian theology, were only *love,* then how could they even feel love unless they were separate and different, and if they are divinely different, does not this imply that they are divine opposites, and hence the relation *implied* is that of eternal opposition, the relation *stated* is eternal attraction, love?[28]

In the Holy Ghost we have our oneness of being, our totality of consciousness.   Mind, and conservative psyche, and the incalculable soul, these three are a trinity of powers in every human being: but the Holy Ghost is soul and mind and psyche transfigured into oneness.   It is our real self, "the deepest part of our consciousness / wherein we know ourself for what we are . . .",[29] and if we go counter to this, we naturally destroy the most essential self in us.   The sin against the Holy Ghost, the Balancer, is unforgivable because once the balance is destroyed, the soul is broken and our being becomes inchoate.

---

[25] *R.D.P.*, p. 6.   [26] *S.C.A.L.*, p. 80.   [27] *Op. cit.*, p. 9.
[28] *Collected Letters*, I, p. 369.   [29] *Poems*, III, p. 51.

Lawrence has also other names for this supreme relation between two opposites. It is the evening star at the dividing of the day and night, but itself neither day nor night. It is the Crown for which the Lion and the Unicorn are eternally fighting. It is the lovely rose-blossom which contains and transcends us. It is the music which comes when cymbals clash one upon the other, absolute and timeless. It is the rainbow which comes when night clashes on day; the iridescence, absolute beyond day or night, "which is darkness at once and light, the two-in-one".[30] True consummation is in perfect relatedness, or in equilibrium "in the sense the Greeks *originally* meant it". No equilibrium, however, can ever be quite perfect. In actual life there is no perfect consummation possible. "If two people can be just together fairly often, so that the presence of each is a sort of balance to the other, that is the basis of perfect relationship. There must be true separateness as well."[31] The most desirable man-woman relationship is that of polarisation or equilibrium between two clarified, single beings who have both of them accomplished the sweetness of their own soul's possession. But this equilibrium can be attained only through a prolonged conflict. For the man and woman of today even sex has become a mental relation and a mere means for self-seeking; not a desire for meeting, but for seeking his or her own in the other, always and inevitably. It has therefore become necessary to go through an "awful process" of bitter conflict till one is gradually rid of "one's self-consciousness and sex-in-the-head",[32] and the self becomes whole again. In our egoism we seek, not consummation or union in positive desire, but only frictional reduction in sensual experience. Love, then, is no longer love, it becomes a battle of wills. Just as the relationship Lawrence's novels explore most fully is the man-woman relationship, the conflict Lawrence depicts in them most extensively as well as successfully is that in the relationship of man to woman. Even though widely different interpretations have been given to the presentation of this conflict in the novels, a number of Lawrence critics have pointed to the primary importance of conflict in

---

[30] *R.D.P.*, p. 16.   [31] *S.C.A.L.*, p. 136.   [32] *Fantasia*, p. 135.

Lawrence's depiction of human relations.[33] Bonamy Dobrée,
writing in 1929, remarked that in telling with profounder
implications the old story of sex-antagonism Lawrence consistently showed his men and women "involved in a continual
conflict, a battering and tearing of each other . . .".[34] Stephen
Potter in his book on Lawrence observed that it is conflict
which Lawrence best describes, and that even though his first
essay was called "The Crown", "his subject is not really the
Crown, the prize, but the antagonists who are fighting for it".[35]
In Graham Hough's judgement, no one has excelled Lawrence
in presenting the irrational fluxes and revulsions of feeling
experienced by two people of different sexes living together:
"Lawrence has most uncomfortably brought out the element of
hate that is inextricably entwined with a normal love. There
is something shocking in the nakedness and intensity with
which he presents it."[36] Anthony Beal takes it to be "axiomatic
that no Lawrence marriage should be free from strife—and
strife does not mean nagging and petty irritations, but a battle
of wills".[37] David Daiches holds nearly the same view.
Marriage, he says, was for Lawrence always a fight; and the
tensions, the love-hate interactions, the central part of the
marriage relationship. Daiches thinks Lawrence built his
views of the proper relations between the sexes on his own
relations with Frieda characterised by "endless alternations of
bitter quarrelling and loving reconciliation, of anger and
affection".[38] But he is not sure how far such a marriage
represents the *norm* of an adequate marital relationship. For
Lawrence, he thinks, it clearly did.

---

[33] A recent study of Lawrence by H. M. Daleski (*The Forked Flame*, London,
1965) approaches the novels by way of Lawrence's ideas on duality, and seeks to
understand (with partial success) his development as a novelist by relating
it to the artistic expression of a lifelong conflict between "male" and "female"
elements in Lawrence's own nature.

[34] *The Lamp and the Lute*, (1929), p. 98.

[35] *D. H. Lawrence: A First Study*, London (1930), p. 152. This accords with
Lawrence's own statement of the theme in the essay: "Now they are at it, they
have forgotten all about the crown. The lion and the unicorn were fighting, it is
no question any more of the crown". (*R.D.P.*, pp. 1-2.)

[36] Hough, p. 64.

[37] A. Beal, *D. H. Lawrence*, Edinburgh (1961), p. 32.

[38] Daiches, p. 147.

For Lawrence the crockery-throwing view of love was inevitable and true; but we will not be bullied into conceding its normality, its desirability, its centrality, which is what Lawrence is trying to make us concede.[39]

Such a view, however, can be very misleading. Lawrence does present conflict as essential and inevitable in most marriage relationships: but to conclude from this that he advocates its "desirability" is to judge a little too hastily: what the novels reveal is by no means what Lawrence recommends. On the contrary, Lawrence says:

> The sexes are not by nature pitted against one another in hostility. It only happens so, in certain periods: when man loses his unconscious faith in himself, and woman loses her faith in him, unconsciously and then consciously. It is not biological sex struggle. Not at all. Sex is the great uniter, the great unifier. Only in periods of the collapse of instinctive life-assurance in men does sex become a great weapon and divider.[40]

Sex becomes a divider and the fight between man and woman begins when men become merely personal, things in themselves, cut off from the living world around them. Then man, having lost his instinctive belief in his own life-flow, cannot even love really, and the fight becomes unavoidable. But no woman can get a man's love by fighting him for it. No man ever loves a woman until she has left off fighting him. And she will leave off fighting only when man "finds his strength and his rooted belief in himself".[41]

As to Lawrence's views on the nature of his own relations with Frieda, one has only to read some of the relevant letters to realise that far from glorifying the bitter conflicts of adjustment they had to go through, he only stresses the pity—and the tragic inevitability—of it. Soon after he had met her, Lawrence wrote to Frieda that they would never fight with each other, but always help.[42] But fight they did. A month later he wrote to Edward Garnett, referring to quarrels between him and Frieda, that "the real tragedy is in the war which is waged between people who love each other . . .".[43] The conflict was

[39] *Op. cit.*, pp. 161-2.   [40] *Phoenix*, p. 197.   [41] *Op. cit.*, p. 199.
[42] *Collected Letters*, I, p. 116.   [43] *Op. cit.*, p. 132.

regrettable but unavoidable. In October 1916, Lawrence wrote to Middleton Murry,

> Frieda and I have finished the long and bloody fight at last, and are at one. It is a fight one has to fight—the old Adam to be killed in me, the old Eve in her—then a new Adam and a new Eve. Till the fight is finished, it is only honourable to fight. But, oh dear, it is very horrible and agonising.[44]

So if Lawrence drew on his own experience with Frieda in depicting the relations between the sexes, these experiences form the basis not of the "proper relations" but of actual relations between men and women. "Crockery-throwing" is, of course, only the outward expression of a deeper tension in the relationship. Its manifestations are bound to be different in different cases—with some people it is just silent hostility. But Lawrence held the love-hate relationship, in its essentials, to be valid for most modern marriages. He never holds up a combat of wills between two persons as "the norm of an adequate marriage relationship". He finds the electric atmosphere of wills hateful. "If it's *got* to be a battle of wills", he wrote in a letter to Mabel Luhan, "I'll fight the devil himself as long as the necessity lasts. But it's not my idea of life."[45] He believed that one ought to remove the fight from the field of one's personal relationships, and "put it in the impersonal field of combat with this fixed and rotten society".[46] His letter to his mother-in-law, in which he expressed his exasperation at Frieda's insistence on nothing but "love", is to be understood in this context:

> Oh, mother-in-law, you understand, as my mother finally understood, that a man doesn't want, doesn't ask for love from his wife, but for strength, strength, strength. To fight, to fight, to fight, and to fight again. And one needs courage and strength and weapons. And the stupid woman keeps on saying love, love, love, and writes of love. To the devil with love! Give me strength, battle-strength, weapon-strength, fighting-strength, give me this, you woman!
>
> England is so quiet: writes Frieda. Shame on you that you ask for peace today. I don't want peace. I go around the

---

[44] *Op. cit.*, p. 479.　　[45] *Collected Letters*, II, p. 756.　　[46] *Op. cit.*, p. 915.

world fighting. Pfui! Pfui! In the grave I find my peace. First let me fight and win through.[47]

A man must be a good husband to his wife, for in marriage man has his consummation and being: but the final consummation for man lies beyond marriage. Having fulfilled himself deeply in marriage, he must undertake the sacred responsibility for the next purposive step into the future by giving himself to some passionate, constructive—or even some purposive destructive—activity. The desire to work for humanity is "every man's ultimate desire and need".[48] The essentially religious or creative motive is the first motive for man's activity; the sexual motive comes second. Even greater than the sex impulse is "the desire of the human male to build a world: . . . to build up out of his own self and his own belief and his own effort something wonderful".[49] It is not woman who claims the highest in man: it is man's own religious soul that drives him on beyond woman, to his supreme activity. In the day-time man must follow his own soul's great impulse: but he must also in his hour give himself up to his woman and her world of love, emotion, and sympathy. The night goal of deep, sensual individualism is the woman's. A man should give himself up to his woman for a time and be a perfect answer to her deep sexual call, but he must not give up his purpose. Even a sex union cannot be successful unless the greater hope of purposive activity fires the soul of the man all the time. It is when the sex passion submits to the great purposive passion that there is fullness. But no great purposive passion can endure for any length of time unless it is based upon the true sexual fulfilment of the vast majority of individuals concerned.

> It cuts both ways. Assert sex as the predominant fulfilment, and you get the collapse of living purpose in man. You get anarchy. Assert *purposiveness* as the one supreme and pure activity of life, and you drift into barren sterility, like our business life of today, and our political life. . . . You have got to base your great purposive activity upon the intense sexual fulfilment of all your individuals.[50]

---

[47] *Op. cit.*, pp. 763-4. [48] *Collected Letters*, I, p. 318.
[49] *Fantasia*, p. 12. [50] *Op. cit.*, p. 108.

The great purposive inspiration must always be present, because sex as an end in itself inevitably leads to disaster and tragedy. "When sex is the starting and the returning point both, then the only issue is death. . . . Death is the only pure, beautiful conclusion of a great passion."[51] But an automatic ideal purpose which has no roots in the deep passionate sex is a greater disaster still: it is not even a tragedy, only a slow humiliation and sterility. Better a great passion and then death rather than a false or faked purpose. The best thing, of course, is for a man to fulfil himself deeply in marriage and then be prepared for "new responsibilities ahead, new unison in effort and conflict, the effort to make, with other men, a little new way into the future . . .".[52]

The ultimate relation of comradeship, on which the future of mankind depends, is the final progression from marriage. Acting from his profoundest centres, man acts womanless. The relationship now is with other men: the sacred and inviolable relation of friendship between man and man in the great move ahead. Marriage and deathless friendship are "the two great creative passions, separate, apart, but complementary: the one pivotal, the other adventurous: the one, marriage, the centre of human life; and the other, the leap ahead".[53] Men must always go ahead of their women to fulfil their ultimate desire for great purposive collective activity. A new connexion is now established between men who are bent on the same activity in the creation of a new world. This purposive union is, obviously, not based on sex. It is actually a movement in the opposite direction. It has been suggested that Lawrence "never . . . seems to have understood man-to-man relationships at all well".[54] Perhaps this is so. And the significance of his attempts at some sort of ritualised *Blutbrüderschaft*, both in life and in fiction, is not made as clear as one wishes it had been. Lawrence, nevertheless, does explain at length the essential nature and basis of such a relationship both in his letters and his expository writings. It is, to begin with, not a personal but a purposive relationship between fearless, honourable, and self-responsible men. In a letter to

---

[51] *Op. cit.*, p. 191.   [52] *Op. cit.*, p. 135.
[53] *Phoenix*, p. 665.   [54] Hough, p. 234.

Katherine Mansfield Lawrence explained how Middleton Murry irritated and falsified him by his insistence on a personal relationship, whereas to Lawrence the one basis of friendship between him and Murry could be the desire to create "a new, good, common life, the germ of a new social life together". He wrote:

> One thing I know, I am tired of this insistence on the *personal* element; personal truth, personal reality. It is very stale and profitless. I want some new non-personal activity, which is at the same time a genuine vital activity. And I want relations which are not purely personal, based on purely personal qualities; but relations based upon some unanimous accord in truth or belief, and a harmony of *purpose*, rather than of personality. I am weary of personality. It remains now whether Murry is still based upon the personal hypothesis: because if he is, then our ways are different. I don't want a purely personal relation with him; he is a man, therefore our relation should be based on *purpose*; not upon that which we *are*, but upon that which we wish to bring to pass. . . . trying to create a new life, a new common life, a new complete tree of life from the roots that are within us. I am weary to death of these dead, dry leaves of personalities which flap in every wind.[55]

The only way of true relationship between men is for them to meet in some common belief: but Lawrence wished this belief could also be physical and not merely mental. He wanted the expansion of friendship and brotherhood into a full relationship where there could also be physical and passional meeting "on some third holy ground", as there used to be in the old dances and rituals in the old fights between men.[56]

As in the case of man-woman relationship, man's relation to man is dual: there is the desire for fellowship and communion, but there is also the urge towards keen resistance and isolation. Man must act in concert with man creatively; in this lies his greatest happiness. But he must also "act separately and distinctly, apart from every other man, single and self-responsible",[57] moving for himself without reference to anyone else. Man is first and foremost a single, isolated individual: but he is also part of a concordant humanity, and the very

---

[55] *Collected Letters*, I, p. 395.   [56] *Collected Letters*, II, p. 941.
[57] *Phoenix*, p. 156.

accomplishing of his individuality depends on his fulfilment in social life. If an individual is completely isolated he is in effect deprived of his life, for life consists in the interaction between man and his fellow beings. Lawrence regretted deeply that he, in his own life, could not have any cordial or fundamental contact with society or other people. There are references in a number of his letters and other writings to what he called the frustration of his societal instinct. Time and again he expressed his desire and need to abandon his meaningless and devastating isolation and be connected with some few people in something. In one of his letters to E. Brewster Lawrence said it had always been his steady desire that he should live in contact with a few people and "spin new threads".[58] In another letter to Dr Trigant Burrow he wrote:

> What ails me is the absolute frustration of my primeval societal instinct. . . . I think societal instinct much deeper than sex instinct—and societal repression much more devastating. There is no repression of the sexual individual comparable to the repression of the societal man in me, by the individual ego, my own and everybody else's.[59]

This ego which stands in the way of men's togetherness must be broken so that a relation of spontaneous equilibrium is established. No two persons are exactly alike, and there is bound to be some inequality. But there should be no *sense* of inequality when they meet. "There is *never* either any equality or any inequality between me and my neighbour. Each of us is himself and as such is single, alone in the universe, and not to be compared."[60] All men have their place in a community, as the stars, great and small, fall into their place in the sky—the small as perfect as the great because each is in its own place. The great ones, none the less, are great, and the small ones small.

Are the great ones amongst men to be the leaders, and are the small ones destined to follow? Lawrence seems, with the passage of time, to shift his position on this. In 1915, writing to Lady Ottoline Morrell, Lawrence gave the warning: "We

[58] E. and A. Brewster, *D. H. Lawrence: Reminiscences and Correspondence*, London (1934), p. 73.
[59] *Collected Letters*, II, pp. 989–90.   [60] *Phoenix*, p. 603.

must go very, very carefully at first. The great serpent to destroy, is the will to Power: the desire for one man to have some dominion over his fellow-men. Let us have *no* personal influence, if possible—. . . no 'Follow me'—but only 'Behold'."[61] In *The Fantasia of the Unconscious* (1923), however, Lawrence begins to talk of a relation of "service and leadership, obedience and pure authority. Men have got to choose their leaders, and obey them to the death."[62] By 1928 he was back at the original position when he wrote to Witter Bynner that "the leader of men is a back number . . . the leader-cum-follower relationship is a bore. And the new relationship will be some sort of tenderness, sensitive, between men and men and men and women, and not the one up one down, lead on I follow, *ich dien* sort of business."[63]

Another change which came about with time was in Lawrence's estimate of the relative importance of man's various relationships. As years passed, he increasingly came round to the view that man's first relation is with the cosmos: the vivid and nourishing relation with the living universe around him. Man, he came to believe, is connected "religiously" with the universe prior to his relation with other human beings. No man is fully himself until he is "opened in the bloom of pure relationship" to the entire living cosmos. A man is great according as his relation to the living universe is vast and vital. Man's relation to woman and to other men is certainly very important: but this is not everything: "One would think, to read modern books, that the life of any tuppenny bank-clerk was more important than sun, moon and stars."[64] This has happened because man, in his conceit, has made himself the measure of the universe. Beyond his vital relation with other human beings man also had, in the great ages in the past, a vital relation with animals, reptiles, flowers, trees, waterfalls, clouds, rainbows, and, beyond that, "with sun and moon, the living night and the living day". All man's relationships are only an approach, nearer and nearer, to his last consummation with the cosmic life—with the sun and the moon and the stars: "Degree after degree after degree widens out the

---

[61] *Collected Letters*, I, p. 312.
[62] *Fantasia*, p. 179.
[63] *Collected Letters*, II, p. 1045.
[64] *R.D.P.*, p. 230.

relation between man and his universe, till it reaches the sun and the night."[65]   In "The Proper Study" Lawrence wrote that there was, for the time being, nothing more of importance to be said on the subject of man's relation to woman, to other men, or the whole environment of men.   "You can't get any more literature out of that.   Because any new book must needs be a new stride."[66]   And the next stride takes us where the greatest relation of every man and woman is to "the great God of the End".   But the word "God", Lawrence felt, was somehow tainted.   What he meant by it was some eternal life-flame, or some invisible flow in the depths of the universe which sustains and renews all living things.   We must all get in touch with the vivid life of the cosmos by bringing to life again the great range of responses which have fallen dead in us.   It will probably take a long time, but a start must be made.   The more we interpose machinery between us and the naked forces of the elements, the more we numb and atrophy our senses. The machine, "the eunuch of eunuchs", emasculates us all in the end by depriving us of our vitalising contact with the dynamic universe.   We do not realise how much we lose by our "labour-saving devices".   Of the two evils, in Lawrence's opinion, it would be much the lesser to lose every bit of machinery than to have, as we have, too much of it.   Lawrence is not against the machine itself which is a perfect, mathematically and scientifically correct instrument, and which must be used to save us unnecessary labour.   "Now there is a railing against the machine, as if it were an evil thing.   And the thinkers talk about the return to the medieval system of handicrafts.   Which is absurd."[67]   What Lawrence is against is the misuse of the machine whereby we ourselves become mechanical and cut off our vital relation with the living universe by trying to "conquer" it.   In sowing the seed, for instance, man has his contact with earth, with sun and rain, and this contact must not be broken.   In his awareness of the springing of the corn, man remains in touch with the wonder of creation and recreation following the mystery of death and the cold grave. At the time of the reaping and the harvest he feels the rich touch of cosmos in his contact with earth and sun, and the joy

[65] *Ibid.*   [66] *Phoenix*, p. 722.   [67] *Op. cit.* p. 426.

of his contact with other harvesters. We cannot get away from the rhythm of the cosmos without bitterly impoverishing our lives. Vitally, the human race is dying because it has cut itself off from the great sources of nourishment and renewal which flow eternally in the universe.

> We have lost the cosmos, by coming out of responsive connection with it, and this is our chief tragedy. What is our petty little love of nature—Nature!!—compared to the ancient magnificent living with the cosmos, and being honoured by the cosmos.[68]

The cosmos is a vast living body of which we are a part. But if we unnaturally resist our connexion with the sun and the moon and the planets and the great stars, they destroy us instead of strengthening us. The sun can rot as well as ripe. Many neurotic people, as a matter of fact, become more and more neurotic, the browner and "healthier" they become by sun-bathing. We have lost the sun, and have found in its place "a few miserable thought-forms. A ball of blazing gas! With spots! He browns you!"[69] We can't get the sun in us by "lying naked like pigs on a beach. The very sun that is bronzing us is inwardly disintegrating us—as we know later."[70] The sun is a great source of blood vitality and would stream strength into us if we would let it. But the only way we can get the sun is by going forth—as Juliet in the story "Sun" does— in some sort of worship, worship that is felt in the blood:

> It was not just taking sunbaths. It was much more than that. Something deep inside her unfolded and relaxed, and she was given. By some mysterious power inside her, deeper than her known consciousness and will, she was put into connection with the sun, and the stream flowed of itself, from her womb. She herself, her conscious self, was secondary, a secondary person, almost an onlooker. The true Juliet was this dark flow from her deep body to the sun.[71]

The same with the moon. The moon, according to Lawrence, is not the mere dead lump of the astronomist. When we describe the moon as dead, we—"poor worms with spectacles

---

[68] *Apocalypse*, pp. 68-9.   [69] *Phoenix*, p. 299.   [70] *Apocalypse*, p. 76.
[71] *The Complete Short Stories* (Phoenix Edition), II, p. 535.

and telescopes and thought-forms"[72]—are only describing the
deadness in ourselves. We have lost the moon; and rather
than soothe and heal our nerves as it could, it only "stares down
on us and whips us with nervous whips". Beware, Lawrence
warns, of the spite of Cybele, beware of the vindictiveness of
horned Astarte:

> Now this may sound nonsense, but that is merely because we
> are fools. There is an eternal vital correspondence between our
> blood and the sun: there is an eternal vital correspondence
> between our nerves and the moon. If we get out of contact and
> harmony with the sun and moon, then both turn into great
> dragons of destruction against us.[73]

Modern men and women who complain of being lonely have
lost their living connexion with the cosmos. It is nothing
human or personal they are short of. What they lack is cosmic
life. And this they must get back, even for the sake of restoring
the life-flow in their human relationships.

> That is what is the matter with us. We are bleeding at the
> roots, because we are cut off from the earth and sun and stars,
> and love is a grinning mockery, because, poor blossom, we
> plucked it from its stem on the tree of Life, and expected it to
> keep on blooming in our civilised vase on the table.[74]

All these relationships, in varying degrees, form the subject
of Lawrence's novels. Not men or women, but their living,
changing relations to the "circumambient universe" is his
theme. Lawrence found in the novel a perfect medium for
revealing "the changing rainbow of our living relationships".[75]
The job of a novelist is to reveal true and vivid relationships.
The novel is "the highest form of human expression so far
attained"[76] because, if it is art at all, there will be nothing in it
which is absolute: everything will be relative to everything
else. The novel is the "highest example of subtle inter-
relatedness that man has discovered" because in a novel everything is true only in its own time, place, and circumstance;
and if one tries "to nail anything down, in the novel, either it
kills the novel, or the novel gets up and walks away with the

[72] *Phoenix*, p. 300.   [73] *Apocalypse*, p. 73.   [74] *S.L.C.*, p. 251.
[75] *Phoenix*, p. 532.   [76] *S.L.C.*, p. 64.

nail".[77] There may be didactic bits in a novel, but they are not the novel. The greatness of the novel is that it "won't *let* you tell didactic lies, and put them over".[78] The novelist should never "put his thumb in the pan" in favour of any idea or purpose or emotion because by doing so he prevents the establishment of a pure relatedness. It is only when all things are given full play in a novel that there emerges the wholeness of man and woman, "man alive, and live woman". In a novel the characters should not be good or bad according to some pattern: they should live. And characters in a novel live only in their relation to all other things:

> The man in the novel must be 'quick'. And this means one thing, among a host of unknown meaning: it means he must have a quick relatedness to all other things in the novel: snow, bed-bugs, sunshine, the phallus, trains, silk hats, cats, sorrow, people, food, diphtheria, fuchsias, stars, ideas, God, tooth-paste, lightning, and toilet paper. He must be in quick relation to all these things. What he says and does must be relative to them all.[79]

The novel can help us develop an instinct for life because in it we can plainly see when "the man goes dead, the woman goes inert". The novel, properly handled, can "inform and lead into new places the flow of our sympathetic consciousness, and can lead our sympathy away in recoil from things gone dead".[80] The novel can help us live as nothing else can because it deals with the whole man alive, and is thus superior to poetry, philosophy, or science, which deal only with different bits of man alive. As Lawrence puts it in his essay "Why the Novel Matters",

> To be alive, to be man alive, to be whole man alive: that is the point. And at its best, the novel, and the novel supremely, can help you. It can help you not to be dead man in life.[81]

This, then, is Lawrence's primary concern in his novels: to help us live, by revealing to us our life as a series of living, changing relationships with all the conflicts inherent in them. All his novels are, essentially, imaginative explorations of life

---

[77] *Phoenix*, p. 528.   [78] *S.L.C.*, p. 65.   [79] *Op. cit.*, p. 71.
[80] *Lady Chatterley's Lover*, p. 92.   [81] *Phoenix*, pp. 537-8.

in its various relationships. "Relatedness" is the clue to the understanding of a Lawrence novel. In judging Lawrence as a novelist, the first thing to consider is: To what extent does he succeed in depicting these relations artistically in his novels; how far does he himself live up to the standards he lays down for the novelist? Any approach to Lawrence which ignores this is bound to be inadequate. Attempts have been made to consider Lawrence as a symbolist, as a nihilistic writer, as a psychological novelist, and as a social realist. There is some justification for this, because there obviously is, in Lawrence's novels, some use of symbolism, a definite strain of nihilism, a certain amount of psychoanalytic writing, and much excellently done social realism. But all these are subordinate to Lawrence's main purpose, which is to reveal to us "the changing rainbow of our living relationships".

An exclusive concern with either symbolism in the novels or with psychoanalysis, inevitably leads to criticism which is either too limited to be of much value, or wrong-headed and misleading. Daniel A. Weiss's book, *Oedipus in Nottingham: D. H. Lawrence*, is, notwithstanding the author's protestations to the contrary, not much more than a "case study" of a writer named D. H. Lawrence whose work, with some inconsistencies, turns out for the author to be an illustration of a clinical theory, and is therefore explicable as such. He himself sums up his thesis thus: "In short, *Sons and Lovers* is a coin whose reverse is the remainder of Lawrence's work."[82] J. I. M. Stewart says something to the same effect in suggesting that when Lawrence's novels become battle-grounds of two conflicting ways of consciousness, he is only re-creating the "bitter parental quarrels which he had witnessed as a child" and which "conditioned" the whole of his subsequent life to the extent of his "reproducing his father's stupid violence".[83]

Kingsley Widmer's book on Lawrence's shorter fiction, *The Art of Perversity*, sets out to "explore and partly affirm the perversity that gives much of Lawrence's work its distinctive being".[84] Lawrence's negative ways, Widmer explains, also

[82] *Oedipus in Nottingham*, p. 14.
[83] *Eight Modern Writers*, Oxford (1963), p. 485.
[84] *The Art of Perversity*, p. vii.

provide the affirmations. He, therefore, considers Lawrence's nihilism a fortunate characteristic, and sees in Lawrence's perversity the effort to turn pessimistic knowledge into something positive and meaningful. Widmer's book is useful in that it directs attention to violence, hatred, alienation, and heresy in Lawrence's writing: but his view tends to be too much one-sided and leads him occasionally to wrong interpretations of Lawrence's work: "the onus of misreading" Lawrence, it would appear, lies not only on those who "fail to reckon fully with the perversity";[85] it might lie equally on those who reckon only with the perversity in Lawrence's writings.

F. R. Leavis's *D. H. Lawrence: Novelist* is, in spite of its limitations, still one of the best books on Lawrence. It has been often pointed out how Leavis is concerned more with refuting T. S. Eliot's criticism than with justifying his own liberal praise of Lawrence which, at last, begins to sound over-insistent rather than convincing. What Leavis has done, it must be admitted, had to be done by someone in order to win recognition for Lawrence's genius, and there is every reason to be grateful to him for that. But one cannot help thinking that a price had to be paid for it, for Leavis often loses his sense of perspective and is—owing, one imagines, to the specific nature of the task he had undertaken—led to lay stress on what is insignificant or of second importance in Lawrence. He describes Lawrence as "incomparably the greatest writer in English of our time . . . one of the greatest English writers of any time"; calls him "one of the greatest of all novelists" gifted with "the most profoundly original kind of genius". He is convinced that Lawrence is "the great creative genius of our age, and one of the greatest figures in English literature".[86] But instead of demonstrating this by giving close attention to what is most significant in Lawrence, he digresses, in vindicating Lawrence's "supreme intelligence", to remark rather petulantly, though not unjustifiably, that if Eliot finds Lawrence incapable of thinking, it is a failure of intelligence in Eliot himself.[87] Or he finds it necessary to defend Lawrence against the charge that he lacked a sense of humour by asserting that "no sensitive and highly vital man was ever less given" to anger

[85] *Op. cit.*, p. 210.   [86] Leavis, pp. 18, 30, 147, 303.   [87] *Op. cit.*, p. 27.

than Lawrence, that Lawrence was plainly "one of the great masters of comedy".[88] However, Leavis's main stress in the book, which "carries on from *The Great Tradition*" is on winning for Lawrence his place as "one of the major novelists of the English tradition". Lawrence, he insists, "*was* brought up in the environment of a living and central tradition",[89] the social-cultural tradition of Congregationalism; and his attitude towards life was "the product of a fine and mature civilization, the sanctions, the valuations and the pieties of which speak through the individual".[90] Dr Leavis is, of course, answering Eliot's criticism of Lawrence: but in doing so he—whether he realises it or not—seriously limits Lawrence's achievement. Lawrence is surely not "the greatest kind of creative writer" Leavis claims he is, *because* he belongs to the "same ethical and religious tradition as George Eliot",[91] or some similar reason—though it is possible that Dr Leavis thinks so, as one is led to suspect from his recent review of *The Collected Letters of D. H. Lawrence* in which he seems to suggest that no one not thoroughly familiar with "England to which Lawrence . . . so essentially belonged"[92] can ever hope to understand Lawrence. Leavis has been criticised, overtly or implicitly, by other critics for trying to fit Lawrence's achievement into a narrow tradition. Julian Moynahan thinks Lawrence continues, and modifies, not any moral tradition of the English novel, but its literary tradition beginning with Defoe and Richardson. Eugene Goodheart, on the other hand, criticises Leavis for myopically isolating Lawrence's achievement from its wider European—historical and cultural—context. But whether we place Lawrence in a moral or a literary, English or European tradition—and he *is* in a way connected with all these traditions which he both borrows from and enriches—there is something essential and unique in Lawrence which cannot be understood or appreciated by looking at him as a novelist in any literary or moral tradition. It would be quite wrong to assert that Lawrence belongs to no tradition: but at the same time there

---

[88] *Op. cit.*, p. 13.   [89] *Op. cit.*, p. 308.
[90] *Op. cit.*, p. 75.   [91] *Op. cit.*, p. 104.
[92] F. R. Leavis, " 'Lawrence Scholarship' and Lawrence", *The Sewanee Review*, LXXI, i (1963), p. 27.

is little use in laying stress on this because it does not help us see any more clearly what is central and of primary importance in his work.

Equally little is to be gained by making too much of social realism in Lawrence's novels. There are certainly passages in Lawrence's novels remarkable for their realism, and many warning voices have been raised against ignoring this aspect of Lawrence's art. But it is not as a social historian that Lawrence is to have his place among the great novelists of the world. Lawrence is interested not so much in what is or has been, as in what can be; not so much in the actual human reality as in the human possibility. And even social reality is depicted in the novels as the revelation of human relationships at a particular time.[93] This has been generally recognised by those who have commented on this aspect of Lawrence's work. Thus Arnold Kettle who believes that *The Rainbow* is "far more securely rooted in reality, far more concretely based in the actual human, social issues of twentieth-century England than many readers recognize", also points out that at its best the novel is "a revelation of the nature of personal relationships in twentieth-century England of incomparable power and insight".[94] Dr Leavis who sees in Lawrence a great successor to George Eliot as "a recorder of essential English history"[95] also realises that it is only by presenting the problems and situations of individual men and women that Lawrence makes his diagnosis of modern society and civilisation. David Daiches rightly remarks that for Lawrence problems of civilisation must always be "focused through problems of personal relationships, for civilisation is judged by the kind and qualities of human relationships it makes possible".[96]

One point on which most critics of Lawrence are agreed is the preponderance of the autobiographical element in his writings. His work is considered to be more closely and more

---

[93] As Lawrence says of Van Gogh's sunflowers, the painting "does not represent the sunflower itself"; it reveals the vivid relation between the painter as man and the sunflower at a certain moment of time: "It is neither man-in-the-mirror nor flower-in-the-mirror . . .". (*Phoenix*, p. 527.)

[94] *An Introduction to the English Novel*, II, pp. 129-30.

[95] Leavis, p. 107.   [96] Daiches, p. 146.

obviously related to his life than is the case with most other writers. His novels, it has been argued, constantly spill over into his personal life and can hardly be explained without reference to it. He is supposed to be always present in his novels in one form or another. According to one extreme view "he is not only himself, he is it all—man, woman, earth, stone, sky and the elements as well—and child, bird, beasts and flowers —it is all he".[97]

Lawrence's novels certainly—one might even say inevitably —are autobiographical in the sense that they tell the story of his life in the fullest sense, including the story of his imaginative life. In fact in an important way they are valuable *because* they are autobiographical in this sense. What Lawrence said of *Women in Love* is by and large true of nearly all his novels: they are all "a record of the writer's own desires, aspirations and struggles; in a word, a record of the profoundest experiences in the self".[98] This record of Lawrence's changing, developing self—his "life-and-thought-adventure"—is important for us because, and in as much as, the essential circumstances and experiences of his personal life are also "circumstances of the human condition at the contemporary moment".[99] Lawrence's experiences described imaginatively in the novels—including the failures, the exaggerations, the conflicts, the doubts and uncertainties—have an immediate and profound relevance for the rest of humanity to the extent that "by discovering what Lawrence was, we discover what we are".[1] But the novels, of course, cannot be identified with life: they are not simply self-revelations but the artistic presentation of a life-experience. Lawrence's work has been called a "continuous spiritual autobiography . . . the record, in an imaginative drama, of an unremitting exploration of life".[2] Stephen Spender believes all Lawrence's work is a documentation of his attempts to discover "a new and better relationship between the sexes, and

[97] Knud Merrild, *A Poet and Two Painters*, London (1938), p. 89.

[98] Foreword to *Women in Love*, (Modern Library), p. x.

[99] Eugene Goodheart, *The Utopian Vision of D. H. Lawrence*, Chicago (1963), p. 140.

[1] J. M. Murry, *Love, Freedom and Society*, London (1957), p. 123.

[2] J. M. Murry in *A D. H. Lawrence Miscellany*, ed. H. T. Moore, Carbondale, Ill. (1959), p. 3.

new and better ways of living".[3] Spender, however, adds that
Lawrence himself and not his work is the subject of the experiment. This is not strictly true, for Lawrence does use his
creative work, particularly the novels, as an aid in discovering
"new and better" relationships. Lawrence's habit of putting
everything of himself in the books has its reasons. He often puts
forward his own tentative ideas through various characters in
the novels in order to test them imaginatively. Over and over
in his fiction he "brings to the bar of imaginative judgement his
dearest theoretical convictions".[4] As a result, some of the
beliefs are given up, some qualified, and some get crystallised
as inferences or deductions. Writing for Lawrence was
indeed "a technique for exploring experience".[5] An attack
on his own ideas is typical of Lawrence the novelist because
that is his way of testing them. Anthony West criticises
Lawrence for using some of his novels as workshops for hammer-
ing out new ideas.[6] J. I. M. Stewart goes further by saying
that Lawrence's sole concern in the novels lies in "dramatizing
and analysing his own intractable problems",[7] while Daiches
suggests that the very functioning of Lawrence's artistic
imagination was "oddly bound up with the way in which he
saw his own problems of adjustment and relationship . . .".[8]
But Daiches does not consider Lawrence's direct presence a
weakness in the novels, for he acknowledges that paradoxically
enough Lawrence's "fierce personal involvement can produce
work of genuine artistic power".[9]

The novels are Lawrence's "profoundest spiritual explorations", the record of his "spiritual odyssey";[10] and so they
always end on a note of uncertainty, looking ahead to the next
stage. The ending of one novel gives an intimation of what is
to come in the next, for the novels follow a consistent course
and mark stages in the development of Lawrence's mind. In
Kangaroo where Lawrence insists that a novel, in order to be

---

[3] *The Destructive Element*, p. 181.
[4] Mark Schorer, "Fiction with a Great Burden", *The Kenyon Review*, XIV
(Winter 1952), p. 164.
[5] Mary Freeman, *D. H. Lawrence: A Basic Study of His Ideas*, New York (1955),
p. 3.
[6] West, p. 108.   [7] *Eight Modern Writers*, p. 536.   [8] Daiches, p. 150.
[9] *Op. cit.*, p. 178.   [10] A. Beal, *D. H. Lawrence*, pp. 99, 100.

complete, should not only be a record of emotional adventures but also a "thought-adventure", we read about Richard Lovat Somers, the hero of the novel:

> "I am a fool," said Richard Lovat, which was the most frequent discovery he made. It came, moreover, every time with a new shock of surprise and chagrin. Every time he climbed a new mountain range and looked over, he saw, not only a new world, but a big anticipatory fool on this side of it, namely himself.[11]

It is this constant exploration and discovery in the novels which makes them the central and most significant part of Lawrence's achievement. His short stories, which are more impersonal, are generally better "realized" and have a superior artistic organisation. Some critics have, therefore, been led to the conclusion that Lawrence's best work is to be found in his shorter pieces. "It is apparent," one critic writes, "that Lawrence's most notable artistic successes often occurred in the short story or the novella . . .".[12] Daiches also finds Lawrence's "most perfect work" in the short stories which he sees as having the qualities "of precision and power, of delicacy and urgency".[13] Some of the short stories are, no doubt, remarkably good and, being concise, have a greater thematic unity than is evident in the novels which nevertheless have a large and complex artistic structure of their own. But the stories, precisely because they are more rounded-off and finished, do not represent the most essential in Lawrence: it is only in the novels, which always break new ground, that Lawrence's creative imagination finds its best expression. It is above all the novels, with all their doubts and questionings, which explore and present Lawrence's deepest insights.

The instruments for this exploration in the novels are the characters. It, however, needs to be emphasised that Lawrence projects his views in a novel through many characters, and not only through the hero or through any Lawrence-like figure. Such figures—Birkin, for instance, in *Women in Love*, or Somers in *Kangaroo*—are, moreover, not mere mouthpieces, but are

---

[11] *Kangaroo*, p. 285.   [12] Frederick R. Karl, in *Miscellany*, p. 273.
[13] Daiches, p. 142.

integral to the novel and are subjected to its criticism equally with other characters. There is, naturally, some artistic-imaginative appropriateness in Lawrence's distribution of the views he wants to put to the test in a novel. So that some of the characters seem to express a large proportion of ideas Lawrence came to accept later on. There are, however, other characters, too, through whom Lawrence projects himself and his own ideas. But since these characters are severely criticised in the course of the novel, hardly anybody seems to have recognised that Lawrence even through these characters, is putting to the test aspects of his own "profound experiences in the self". One thing which seems to have caused a great deal of misunderstanding of Lawrence's purpose was his habit of drawing fictional characters with remarkable resemblances in outward appearance to certain living persons. Again, in appropriate imaginative contexts, he sometimes reproduced in the novels more or less exactly some actual situation, or setting, or dialogue. Lawrence was, of course, writing novels—using his gifts of a remarkable memory and an extraordinarily acute sense of observation in order to project an imaginative experience. It was not his purpose as novelist to draw life-like portraits or to caricature people he had known. But that is precisely what those who found themselves in his books thought he was doing. The publication of his very first novel, *The White Peacock*, brought with it threats of libel action. This went on as other novels appeared. Lawrence's friends and acquaintances—not to mention the well-known instances of his having used his intimate family circle: father, mother, brothers, sisters, and wife, in the novels—"discovered" themselves portrayed in his books and were either puzzled and shocked, or were mortally offended and threatened legal action. Jessie Chambers, Middleton Murry, Philip Heseltine, Lady Ottoline Morrell, Mabel Dodge Luhan—to mention only a few in a long list—all bitterly complained that they had not been represented truly in the novels, that Lawrence had "distorted" facts. Lawrence was, however, writing fiction, and it was only to the imaginative world of his own creation that he was obliged to be true. But the fact of Lawrence's being a creative writer has not yet been sufficiently recognised. Even those sympathetic to Lawrence have failed to see the complex relation between reality and its imaginative expression in his work. When Richard Aldington blames Lawrence for drawing "satirical portraits which for hatred, vindictiveness and cruelty are hard to match in literature",[14] he only betrays his own insufficient understanding of Lawrence's genius as a novelist. When Harry T. Moore in his biography of Lawrence, *The Intelligent Heart,* speaks of Lawrence's "meanness" and "cruelty"[15] in portraying his friend-benefactors satirically in the novels, one can only say that if biographers were to suspend their hasty literary judgements for the while that they are telling a life story, how much better it would be for the story that they are telling!

Lawrence did use his friends and acquaintances as material for his novels, but always with some creative purpose. His real interest lay not in the outward "personality" of the characters but in their inner life. As Compton Mackenzie, one of Lawrence's "victims"—he was used by Lawrence in the story "The Man Who Loved Islands"—is reported to have remarked, Lawrence "had a trick of describing a person's setting and background vividly, and then putting into the setting an ectoplasm entirely of his own creation".[16] This led to frequent complaints of distortion and falsification by the "originals" of Lawrence's characters, who did not realise that Lawrence was not simply transcribing facts from life, that generally a number of living persons went into the creation of a single character. When Lady Ottoline Morrell objected to the publication of *Women in Love* because she saw in Hermione Roddice a recognisable and unflattering portrait of herself, Lawrence wrote to his literary agent, J. B. Pinker:

> My dear Pinker: Really, the world has gone completely dotty! Hermione is not much more like Ottoline Morrell than Queen Victoria, the house they claim as theirs is a Georgian house in Derbyshire I know very well—etc. Ottoline flatters herself. There *is* a hint of her in the character of Hermione: but so there is a hint of a million women, if it comes to that.[17]

---

[14] *Portrait of a Genius But . . .*, London (1950), p. 290.
[15] *The Intelligent Heart,* p. 201.
[16] Harry T. Moore, *The Life and Works of D. H. Lawrence,* p. 198.
[17] *Collected Letters,* I, p. 502.

Tracing the "originals" of Lawrence's characters, or relating incidents in the novels to actual events on which these are based, can be a very interesting pastime for a Lawrence scholar. As a matter of fact one can get all the flavour of literary gossip if one reads certain episodes in some of the novels with the originals in mind. To a certain extent some background material can be of real help in coming to a clearer understanding of Lawrence's fiction. Comparing what is reported in a novel to what was actually said in a situation, or drawing a parallel between a character in a novel and an actual person, can in some cases throw considerable light on a particular scene or conversation or relationship which is otherwise obscure: but to pass literary or aesthetic judgements on the basis of hearsay or conjecture or even accepted biographical fact is quite another matter. Investigation into the genesis of a great work of art is a much more arduous and exacting task than critics, ordinarily, are prepared to impose on themselves.

One final point needs to be clarified before proceeding to an examination of the novels themselves as revelations of various relationships and of the conflicts which inhere in these relationships. The life of man, says Lawrence, is a "long endless venture into consciousness down an ever-dangerous valley of days".[18] The role of art in this venture is to reveal to man his unknown self which lies deep in the passional soul, not having been yet admitted into the consciousness. It is the job of an artist to penetrate "the very sources of human passion and motive".[19] In a letter addressed to an American journalist, Kyle Crichton, who had sent one of his stories to Lawrence for his comment, Lawrence explained what he thought an artist ought to do with his material:

> I read your story at once and will say my say at once. . . . You are too journalistic, too much concerned with facts. You don't concern yourself with the *human inside* at all, only with the inside of steel works. It's the sort of consciousness the working man has: but at the same time he's got a passionate sub-conscious. And it's the *sub-conscious* which makes the story;

---

[18] *Phoenix*, p. 732.   [19] *Op. cit.*, p. 263.

otherwise you have journalism. Now you want to be an artist,
so you've got to use the artists' faculty of making the sub-
conscious conscious.[20]

To make the sub-conscious conscious, to make articulate the
sub-conscious communication between people, to present
unfamiliar and un-understood states of mind—that is what a
distinctively Lawrentian piece of writing attempts to do.
Lawrence, through his creative art, shed light on dark and
unexplored areas of the human mind and thus succeeded in
extending the limits of man's consciousness.[21] His genius
consists, above all, in his having brought to the level of
consciousness and having revealed to us in his novels the sub-
conscious conflicts involved in different human relationships.

Lawrence made an important statement about the nature
of his artistic purpose in his foreword to *Women in Love*. "Any
man of real individuality", he wrote, "tries to know and to
understand what is happening, even in himself, as he goes
along. This struggle for verbal consciousness should not be
left out in art. It is a very great part of life. . . . It is the
passionate struggle into conscious being."[22] Lawrence's novels
record this passionate struggle into conscious being. Writing a
novel was for him a thought-adventure, an exploration of the
unconscious. A novel, he believed, should reveal what people
are, "inside themselves".[23] But Lawrence did not understand
by this what some of his contemporaries understood by revealing a character from the inside. He repudiated "the modern
serious novel" of his time, in which he found nothing but
"self-consciousness picked into such fine bits that the bits are
most of them invisible".[24] The characters in such a novel, he
said, are absorbedly concerned only with one thing: what they
feel and do not feel, and "how they react to every moral button";
and the readers of the novel are as frenziedly absorbed in
applying "the author's discoveries to their own reactions:

[20] *Collected Letters*, II, p. 851.
[21] Lawrence is, of course, not the only one among modern novelists to have
tried to explore the murky depths of the unconscious. What distinguishes his
work is the revelation in it of the subconscious forces governing the ever-changing
relationships depicted.
[22] *Women in Love* (Modern Library), n.d., p. x.
[23] *Collected Letters*, II, p. 1047.   [24] *Phoenix*, p. 518.

'That's me! That's exactly it! I am just finding myself in the book!'' Lawrence found this extreme of self-consciousness utterly childish.

> "Did I feel a twinge in my little toe, or didn't I?" asks every character of Mr. Joyce or of Miss Richardson or M. Proust. Is my aura a blend of frankincense and orange pekoe and boot-blacking, or is it myrrh and bacon-fat and Shetland tweed? The audience round the death-bed gapes for the answer. And when, in a sepulchral tone, the answer comes at length, after hundreds of pages: "It is none of these, it is abysmal chloro-coryambasis," the audience quivers all over, and murmurs: "That's just how I feel myself."[25]

The novel, Lawrence urged, must grow up, and present "new, really new feelings, a whole line of new emotion"[26] instead of inventing new sensations in the old line. It must put away all childish things like:

> "Do I love the girl, or don't I?"—"Am I pure and sweet, or am I not?"—"Do I unbutton my right glove first, or my left?" —"Did my mother ruin my life by refusing to drink the cocoa which my bride had boiled for her?" These questions and their answers don't really interest me any more, though the world still goes on sawing over them. . . . The purely emotional and self-analytical stunts are played out in me. I'm finished. I'm deaf to the whole band. But I am neither *blasé* nor cynical. I'm just interested in something else.[27]

Lawrence was interested in feelings which are going to carry us through into the next epoch; he was interested in "What next?" He, therefore, wanted the novel to break a way through, like a hole in the wall, in order to discover a new world outside. Lawrence's own novels embody his vision of life, revealed in terms of man's living relationships to his circumambient universe; and in the following chapters all the novels—from *The White Peacock* to *Lady Chatterley's Lover*—are examined primarily as artistic-imaginative revelations of these relationships and conflicts in these relationships.

[25] *Op. cit.*, p. 517.   [26] *Op. cit.*, p. 520.   [27] *Op. cit.*, pp. 519-20.

E

II

The Early Statement

LAWRENCE wrote his first novel *The White Peacock* five or six times before it was published in its final form in 1911. He had been tussling away, he tells us, for four years, getting it out "in inchoate bits, from the underground of my consciousness".[1] Jessie Chambers has recorded how Lawrence told her he wanted to try writing a novel on the pattern of George Eliot's novels:

> "The usual plan is to take two couples and develop their relationships," he said. "Most of George Eliot's are on that plan. Anyhow I don't want a plot, I should be bored with it. I shall try two couples for a start.[2]

Another thing he told her was that while in the novels of "Fielding and the others" the action had been outside, George Eliot "started putting all the action inside".[3] He himself wondered which was right, and concluded by saying that there ought to be a bit of both. Two or three things clearly emerge from this. Lawrence, it can be seen, was trying from the very start to go deep into the "underground of [his] consciousness" in order to write fiction. Secondly, he was not interested in any conventional plot as such in the novel: his interest lay in developing the relationships of his characters, letting the plot take care of itself. Also, he wanted to combine a certain amount of realistic writing with a description of what goes on inside the minds of the characters. His correspondence of the period also reveals how little he cared about the pedantic rules or principles of artistic creation commonly accepted by novelists and critics at the time. Writing in 1908 to Blanche

[1] *Assorted Articles*, London (1930), p. 149.
[2] E. T. (Jessie [Chambers] Wood), *D. H. Lawrence: A Personal Record*, London (1935), p. 103.
[3] *Op. cit.*, p. 105.

Jennings, with whom he was to exchange a number of letters discussing his first novel, he said:

> I wish you . . . to read and criticise some writing of mine that purports to be a novel. . . . I would not ask you to criticise it so much as a work of art . . . applying to it the tests of artistic principles, and such-like jargon— . . . but I would like you to tell me frankly whether it is bright, entertaining and convincing—or the reverse.[4]

Lawrence was confident that in *Laetitia*, as the novel was then called, there were some fine scenes and "exquisite passages" such as he was not going to write again. He was prepared to "declare in the teeth of all the jabbering critics in the world" that his novel contained some beautiful writing— by which, however, he did not mean "good English" or any such thing, for he had realised early that he must deliberately flaw his English if he was to be "anything but a stilted, starched parson".[5] He was sure his novel had "some real good stuff", even though the narrative was not naturalistic enough to satisfy those who only cared about "whether such people could really exist, and live like other folk in the midst of neighbours, chapels and mothers-in-law". Lawrence himself was not bothered by this; social realism was not his main aim: "I don't care a damn," he commented, "whether they live or whether they don't."[6] His purpose was to explore human relationships imaginatively so as to reveal the limitations or failures in them, and also to hint at their possibilities.

Lawrence had set out with the idea of taking two couples and working out their relationships. In a way there *are* two couples whose relations, before and after marriage, seem to have been developed in the course of the novel: Lettie and Leslie, George and Meg. A closer look at the novel, however, reveals that essentially there is only one relationship round which the entire novel moves—that of George and Lettie; and that all other characters and relationships are meant, by way of comparison or contrast, to be direct or indirect comments on this relationship. Viewed thus, the appearance of the father (Beardsall) and of the gamekeeper (Annable) in the narrative

---

4 *Collected Letters*, I, pp. 4-5.   5 *Op. cit.*, p. 12.   6 *Op. cit.*, p. 14.

can be seen to be an integral part of the novel's design, and their tales no longer remain irrelevant episodes introduced for their own sake, as some have thought.

The White Peacock, one reader of the novel suggests,[7] attempts to reconcile the fundamental dualism in Lawrence's own mind. Even though the dark-light, above-below, air-earth, spirit-flesh, God-devil, bird-serpent oppositions are not quite as "firmly established in the book" as this critic seeks to make out, the novel certainly is concerned with the conflict between culture and primitivism, "between ideality and reality, . . . between life as transcendence, escaping into the skies, and life as immanence, rooted in the world".[8] Man's higher religious needs are acknowledged, but equal emphasis is laid on man's continuing to be related to earth and to the life of nature around him. The struggle is for man's wholeness, attained through adequate, satisfactory relationships. The main narrative, reinforced by thematically related episodes, dramatises how various characters fail to attain wholeness of being through the reconciliation of their basic dual needs.

George, an earth-bound young farmer, is shown in the opening pages of the novel to be leading a self-satisfied animal existence. His sister, Emily, who compares him to "a fatted calf",[9] thinks he is callous and brutal.[10] Lettie who is fond of him, though also aware of his limitations, refers to him as "my Taurus",[11] "Mon Taureau",[12] and tells him that all he has learnt to like in life is a good dinner, a warm hearth and a lazy evening. But George is at the same time striving to "educate" himself. He is fond of reading, and through his association with his friend Cyril (the first person narrator of the tale) and Lettie, he is awakened to consciousness. Lettie, in the chapter entitled "A Vendor of Visions", tries to wake him up to another existence by talking to him of music and painting, and of death and suffering—not all of which he understands. She tells him, "You are blind; you are only half-born; you are gross with good living and heavy sleeping. You are a piano which will only play a dozen common notes. Sunset is nothing to you—it

---

[7] Robert E. Gajdusek, "A Reading of *The White Peacock*", in *Miscellany*, p. 189.
[8] *Op. cit.*, p. 198.   [9] *W.P.* (Phoenix Edition), p. 5.   [10] *Op. cit.*, p. 13.
[11] *Op. cit.*, p. 19.   [12] *Op. cit.*, p. 20.

merely happens anywhere. Oh, but you make me feel as if I'd like to make you suffer".[13]   Lettie feels George never really grows up, like bulbs which spend all summer getting fat and fleshy, but never wakening the germ of a flower. "Things don't flower", she tells him, "if they're overfed. You have to suffer before you blossom in this life."[14]   His friendship with Cyril acquaints him with new subjects—chemistry, botany, psychology.   Cyril tells him, while they both work on the farm through the still mornings, of life, of sex and its origins; of Schopenhauer and William James.   They talk a great deal of poetry and of metaphysics.   George rapidly makes all these ideas part of himself.

In course of time all this makes him dissatisfied with his existence and he comes to feel "like a toad in a hole".[15]   He feels he cannot change because everything around him keeps the same: but he comes to be acutely aware of the truth in Lettie's remark: "You're like a bit out of those coloured marble mosaics in the hall, you have to fit in your own set, fit into your own pattern, because you're put there from the first.   But you don't want to be like a fixed bit of a mosaic—you want to fuse into life, and melt and mix with the rest of folk, to have some things burned out of you . . .".[16]   George, however, remains passive in the face of this realisation, merely "dreaming fulfilments", never trying to do anything to "make things happen".[17]   So he lingers on in his role of "a lazy animal", looking a picture of content—"solid, healthy, easy-moving content",[18] as Lettie puts it.   This sense of contentment, however, is there only on the surface.   Underneath, George is coming to realise that work and sleep and comfort make only half a life: "I might as well be Flower, the mare",[19] he declares in a conversation over supper one day.   Living in the same place he feels like a bit of the old building walking, his old feelings sticking to him "like the lichens on the walls".[20]   But his problem is not a simple one of moving away from the old place. He rightly dreads what he calls the "slow crumbling away from my foundations",[21] for as soon as his connexion with the land is

---

[13] *Op. cit.*, p. 27.   [14] *Ibid.*   [15] *Op. cit.*, p. 64.
[16] *Ibid.*   [17] *Op. cit.*, p. 65.   [18] *Op. cit.*, p. 94.
[19] *Op. cit.*, p. 186.   [20] *Op. cit.*, p. 199.   [21] *Op. cit.*, p. 234.

broken, he begins to decay. The process of uprootedness is graphically represented in the novel when George points out to Cyril a sycamore which—even though it keeps on growing—is spoiled, its "fine balance of leaves" gone, because its leading shoot was broken off when the tree was young. George, when he has broken away from the land, has a similar experience. "I seem thrown off my balance", he tells Cyril.[22] He now feels cut off from everything, and experiences a sense of loneliness "like a vacuum . . . all loose in the middle of a space of darkness".[23] All connexions broken, he declines steadily, drinking hard, until at the end he is completely alienated:

> Like a tree that is falling, going soft and pale and rotten, clammy with small fungi, he stood leaning against the gate, while the dim afternoon drifted with a flow of thick sweet sunshine past him, not touching him.[24]

George's problem has been the complex one of responding to the demands of his awakening consciousness while remaining at the same time rooted in his connexion with the soil, of answering the needs both of his spirit and of his flesh. The failure of his relationship with Lettie is, in the main, attributable to a failure of will in him, a failure to accept the responsibilities of consciousness.

Lettie's constant references to George in the opening pages of the novel as "bos-bovis; an ox",[25] a "primitive man",[26] and her reminders to him that he only loves food and comfort and knows practically nothing, are meant to provoke George into taking the initiative and acting for himself. But as soon as he begins to understand and tries to act, Lettie draws back in panic. She admires his "physical beauty, as if he were some great firm bud of life",[27] but believes in feminine passivity and, instead of responding to his feelings, expects to be held and kept by him. When George, however, proves slow and Lettie becomes apprehensive that he "would for ever hang fire",[28] she "pulls down the small gold grapes" and chooses a life of comfort and respectability by getting engaged to Leslie. Cyril,

---

[22] *Op. cit.*, p. 285. [23] *Op. cit.*, p. 284. [24] *Op. cit.*, p. 321.
[25] *Op. cit.*, p. 15. [26] *Op. cit.*, p. 26. [27] *Op. cit.*, p. 48.
[28] *Op. cit.*, p. 116.

too, now tells George: "You should have gripped her before and kept her."[29] Lettie's explanation to George for her action is that she couldn't help it, that she was expected to act the way she did, "and you're bound to do what people expect you to do".[30] George is, understandably, not satisfied by this piece of reasoning and finds himself in a fix. He feels that Lettie, having started him off, has left him at a loose end, and he blames her for it: "You played with me, and showed me heaps of things. . . . You have awakened my life—I imagined things that I couldn't have done."[31] In an inspired moment the realisation dawns on George that he wants Lettie more than anything, that he must have her, and so decides to ask her to marry him. But even after he has found out that "it doesn't do to go on dreaming", he lingers on and misses his chance of asking Lettie, occasioning Cyril's comment: "He has not asked her, the idiot".[32] Cyril tells George later on that he should have insisted and made his own destiny. George, we are told, did not have the courage to risk himself; and even when he is challenged by Lettie to make the struggle to "shape things", he is unable to rouse himself to decide the question of his own and her future. Lettie sums up the situation for him in these words:

> "The threads of my life were untwined; they drifted about like floating threads of gossamer; and you didn't put out your hand to take them and twist them up into the chord with yours. Now another has caught them up, and the chord of my life is being twisted, and I cannot wrench it free and untwine it again—I can't."[33]

When Lettie is married to Leslie, George decides to get married to the "soft and warm" Meg, a woman of great physical charm. Her love for George is generous. He finds her easy and lovely, "full of soothing and comfort . . . trust and lovingness",[34] and he is "incredibly happy" for a time in his amused indulgence of his voluptuous but uneducated wife. This, however, does not last very long. He finds after a few years that he has no longer the peace and quiet he used to have while he worked on the farm. He cannot even find time to

[29] *Op. cit.*, p. 90. [30] *Op. cit.*, p. 121. [31] *Op. cit.*, p. 117.
[32] *Op. cit.*, p. 90. [33] *Op. cit.*, p. 214. [34] *Op. cit.*, p. 235.

read. Now "it's the kids all day, and the kids all night".[35]
Meg finds her fulfilment in the children, performing her role
as mother to perfection. Bathing her baby she droops her head
"with the grace of a Madonna",[36] and her movements are
"lovely, accurate and exquisite, like an old song perfectly
sung". George finds himself excluded from all this. "Meg
never found any pleasure in me", he remarks bitterly to Cyril,
"as she does in the kids."[37] Cyril's reflexion that a woman is
"so ready to disclaim the body of a man's love" applies to Meg,
Emily, and Lettie alike: "She yields him her own soft beauty
with so much gentle patience and regret; she clings to his
neck, to his head and his cheeks, fondling them for the soul's
meaning that is there and shrinking from his passionate limbs
and his body."[38] It is this sense of triumphant completeness
and self-sufficiency of the mother-and-child world from which
the man is left out "alone and ineffectual", which occasions the
judgment in the novel that

> A woman who has her child in her arms is a tower of strength,
> a beautiful, unassailable tower of strength that may in its turn
> stand quietly dealing death.[39]

No wonder that George discovers marriage to be "more of a
duel than a duet" in which one party wins and takes the other
"captive, slave, servant—". In the marital duel Meg wins the
victory over her husband (as do Emily and Lettie over *their*
husbands) because she has the children on her side. As time
passes, she becomes more authoritative, and as she moves about
the room in her house she seems "to dominate everything,
particularly her husband".[40]

George had decided to marry Meg because he had "built
on Lettie", and when Lettie was gone he was at a dead loss
having nothing definite to shape his life to. "I have looked to
marriage," he confesses to Cyril, "to set me busy on my house
of life, something whole and complete, of which it will supply
the design. I must marry or be in a lost lane."[41] Having
severed himself from his roots in the soil, he dreads "the

[35] *Op. cit.*, p. 267.   [36] *Op. cit.*, p. 273.   [37] *Op. cit.*, p. 274.
[38] *Ibid.*   [39] *Op. cit.*, p. 289.   [40] *Op. cit.*, p. 308.
[41] *Op. cit.*, p. 235.

complete darkness" of his "solitariness", and needs Lettie, who had made him "conscious", for a light. All that Lettie succeeds in doing, however, is to cause a split in him, graphically represented in the novel by the "fine parting" she makes in his hair. George has been left to choose either vitality *or* idealism, the life of the senses *or* that of the spirit, whereas a "whole and complete" life would have been possible for him only when the needs of both his physical body and his awakened consciousness had been satisfied.

In order to underline the fact that George's problem has no simple and easy solution Lawrence introduces into the narrative the episodes of the father and of the gamekeeper, Annable. These incidents illustrate the complexity of situations like the one in which George is placed. If George had not been roused to consciousness by Lettie and Cyril, would that have been a satisfactory situation? The answer given by the story of the father is in the negative; whereas the story of the gamekeeper points out that renouncing deliberately the responsibilities of consciousness is no way out, either.

Answering the criticism that the incident of the father Beardsall was not quite relevant to the narrative, Lawrence wrote to Blanche Jennings: "The Father incident is not unnecessary—there is a point; there are heaps of points, I told you there would be, but you have not bothered to find them."[42] The point, however, is not—as Richard Aldington[43] and some others have thought—that Lawrence wanted to express his dislike for his own father by making the father in the novel die of drink. The character of Frank Beardsall is in fact presented with much sympathy and understanding. He is shown to have suffered more than his wife. He saves money and leaves behind as much as four thousand pounds for his wife and children. The old woman at whose house he dies ("He wor a rum feller", she says) and the doctor (who calls him "a jolly decent fellow—generous, open-handed") both speak well of him. There is even a suggestion that he was not liked just because other people "couldn't get to the bottom of him". His wife, when he is dead, realises that she was at fault in having set the children against him while he needed them, just because her

[42] *Collected Letters*, I, p. 27.   [43] Introduction to *W.P.*, p. viii.

"illusion of him", her "romance" was shattered soon after marriage. The death of Frank Beardsall has a significance in that it brings a new consciousness to Cyril and Lettie, making them reflect on "the unanswered cry of failure" in the relationship of their parents.

The story of the gamekeeper has been judged to be "entirely irrelevant", "incorporated into the book for no reason at all".[44] But the reason is fairly obvious. Lawrence himself, defending Annable's presence in the book, is said to have told Jessie Chambers, "He *has* to be there. Don't you see why? He makes a sort of balance. Otherwise it's too much one thing, too much *me*."[45] But there is a more important reason: Annable's life-story is an illuminating comment on the possibilities of relationship between George and Lettie. There are many parallels between George and Annable, Lady Crystabel and Lettie. Annable is Lady Crystabel's animal, "son animal—son boeuf"; Lettie calls George "bos-bovis; an ox". The Lady views Annable "in an aesthetic light" ("I was Greek statues for her", he relates to Cyril); Lettie finds George "picturesque . . . quite fit for an Idyll". Lady Crystabel begins "to get souly"; Lettie is also referred to in the novel as one of the "souly sort". Both of them are said to live life at second hand. More than all this it is the peacock symbol which relates Lettie and Lady Crystabel.

One day while Cyril and the gamekeeper are standing in the churchyard, a peacock comes flapping up the terraces and perches on the neck of "an old bowed angel". The bird bends its voluptuous neck, peers about, then lifts up its head and yells.

> The sound tore the dark sanctuary of twilight. The old grey grass seemed to stir, and I could fancy the smothered primroses and violets beneath it waking and gasping for fear.
> The keeper looked at me and smiled. He nodded his head towards the peacock, saying:
> "Hark at that damned thing!"
> Again the bird lifted its crested head and gave a cry, at the same time turning awkwardly on its ugly legs, so that it showed us the full wealth of its tail glimmering like a stream of coloured stars over the sunken face of the angel.

---

[44] West, p. 96.   [45] E. T., *D. H. Lawrence*, p. 117.

"The proud fool!—look at it! Perched on an angel, too, as if it were a pedestal for vanity. That's the soul of a woman—or it's the devil."

He was silent for a time, and we watched the great bird moving uneasily before us in the twilight.

"That's the very soul of a lady," he said, "the very, very soul. Damn the thing, to perch on that old angel. I should like to wring its neck."

Again the bird screamed, and shifted awkwardly on its legs . . .[46]

Annable picks up a piece of sod and flings it at the bird. When the peacock flaps away down the terraces, Annable exclaims, "Just look! the miserable brute has dirtied that angel. A woman to the end, I tell you, all vanity and screech and defilement."[47]

The identification between Lady Crystabel and the peacock is obvious enough in the passage, and when a little later Annable remarks that it wasn't all Lady Crystabel's fault, and Cyril suggests, "A white peacock, we will say", the gamekeeper laughs and says, "Yes, she was fair enough." The "white" in the novel's title, as one critic rightly remarks, indicates a moral quality ("spotless"; "without blemish"), but is meant to be pejorative "for the purity suggested by the equivocal adjective is really an avoidance of life".[48] Lettie, too, is guilty of avoiding life[49] and has a number of peacock characteristics. The parallel is made quite explicit at one point where Lettie's "splendour" is compared to that of a peacock:

> Lettie stood between the firelight and the dusky lamp-glow, tall and warm between the lights. As she turned laughing to the two men, she let her cloak slide over her white shoulder and fall with silk splendour of a peacock's gorgeous blue over the arm of the large settee. There she stood with her white hand upon the peacock of her cloak, where it tumbled against her dull orange dress. She knew her own splendour, and she drew up her throat laughing and brilliant with triumph.[50]

---

[46] *W.P.*, p. 147.   [47] *Op. cit.*, p. 148.

[48] William A. Fahey, "Lawrence's *The White Peacock*", *The Explicator*, xvii, iii (Dec. 1958), Item 17.

[49] The epithet "white" is used for her frequently. "A white violet, is she?" Cyril says of her.   [50] *W.P.*, p. 251.

Lettie had been drawn to Leslie not only because of his social position; there was also the attraction of his fine physique "suggestive of much animal vigour".[51]   But marriage based on sexual response alone, Lawrence wrote to Blanche Jennings discussing his novel, means a sacrifice of one's finer, nobler feelings:

> Most people marry with their souls vibrating to the note of sexual love—and the sex notes may run into beautiful aesthetics, poetry and pictures and romance.   But love is much finer, I think, when not only the sex group of chords is attuned, but the great harmonies, and the little harmonies, of what we call religious feeling (read it widely) and ordinary sympathetic feeling.   After marriage, most folks begin to slacken off the chords of their nature, and confine themselves to a little range. It is a great shame.   Laetitia, you see, responded, and that very weakly, to Leslie, only in the sex melody.[52]

Lettie's life with Leslie requires that she fold round herself and him "the snug curtain of the present" while they sit like children playing behind the hangings of an old bed.   "She shut out all distant outlooks, as an Arab unfolds his tent and conquers the mystery and space of the desert.   So she lived gleefully in a little tent of present pleasures and fancies."[53] Only occasionally does she peep out of the tent into the outer space.   Then she sits poring over books and feels discontented. Lettie, however, gradually subsides into "a small indoor existence with artificial light and padded upholstery".[54]   She decides to abandon the charge of herself to serve her children, taking pride in the fact that she is a "wonderful mother".

> Having reached that point in a woman's career when most, perhaps all, of the things in life seem worthless and insipid, she had determined to put up with it, to ignore her own self, to empty her own potentialities into the vessel of another or others, and to live her life at second-hand.   This peculiar abnegation of self is the resource of a woman for the escaping of the responsibilities of her own development.   Like a nun, she puts over her living face a veil, as a sign that the woman no longer exists for herself: she is the servant of God, of some man,

---

[51] *Op. cit.*, p. 44.   [52] *Collected Letters*, I, p. 23.
[53] *W.P.*, p. 144.   [54] *Op. cit.*, p. 287.

of her children, or maybe of some cause. As a servant, she is no longer responsible for herself, which would make her terrified and lonely. Service is light and easy. To be responsible for the good progress of one's life is terrifying. It is the most insufferable form of loneliness, and the heaviest of responsibilities.[55]

"To be responsible for the good progress of one's life" is indeed the heaviest of responsibilities. No character in the novel succeeds in facing the responsibilities of his or her own development. Not Annable, certainly—for he virtually goes back on his development, hating all signs of culture, and holding civilisation to be "the painted fungus of rottenness".[56] He is, as he says himself, "like a good house, built and finished, and left to tumble down again with nobody to live in it".[57] He has come to believe in the motto: "Be a good animal, true to your animal instinct". His advice to all is: Be a good animal; do as the animals do. In the novel, "demon", "devil", "devil of the woods", and "Pan" are the words used to refer to him. Another significant association of his is with the snowdrops. His appearance "like some malicious Pan" just as Lettie is reflecting on how the "mysterious" snowdrops seem to her "something out of an old religion that we have lost", is not fortuitous. Lettie thinks that the snowdrops "belong to some knowledge we have lost, that I have lost and that I need".[58] What she—together with all of us—has lost and needs is what the character of the gamekeeper serves to emphasise in the novel. But the animal-like existence of the gamekeeper is, in itself, no more "whole and complete" life than the second-hand living of the novel's white peacocks. Annable is by no means what Graham Hough unwittingly suggests he is—"the first bearer of the Lawrentian philosophy";[59] for belief "only in the physical" and scorn for "all spirituality" is no tenet of the Lawrentian creed.

The relationship which undergoes the least development in the course of the novel is that of Cyril and Emily. Emily is in certain ways an early portrait of Miriam of *Sons and Lovers*. In *The White Peacock* she is a timid, suffering, defenceless girl who

---

[55] *Op. cit.*, p. 280. [56] *Op. cit.*, p. 145. [57] *Op. cit.*, p. 148.
[58] *Op. cit.*, p. 129. [59] Hough, p. 30.

undergoes a sudden transformation towards the end of the book. Much that we learn about her comes to us by way of judgements passed on her by Cyril. We are told that she is an "intensely serious girl",[60] who finds the animal vigour and gusto of her brother George loathsome and disgusting. Her "earnest, troublesome soul" is plainly visible in her sad, still eyes. "You are like Burne-Jones' damsels", Cyril tells her, "Troublesome shadows are always crowding across your eyes and you cherish them."[61] Her eyes and the tones of her voice proclaim that for her sorrows alone are real:

> Some people, instead of bringing with them clouds of glory, trail clouds of sorrow; they are born with "the gift of sorrow"; . . . Emily had the gift of sorrow.[62]

She is, we learn, extravagantly emotional, "quivers with feeling", has a "brooding and defenceless" nature, and lacks self-confidence. Then we are abruptly told near the end of the story that Emily has been able to "clothe" her sensitiveness, and that her soft, vulnerable eyes—"like naked life, naked defenceless protoplasm"[63]—are no longer the soulful eyes which used to make Cyril feel "nervous and irascible". She has now acquired "a new self-confidence", and when she is married she rules, with her quiet self-assurance, her "rejoiced husband and servant".[64] One is led to suspect that what is being said about Emily is not without a touch of irony, for like Lettie she has "found her place" in the home, having "escaped from the torture of strange, complex modern life".[65] Like Lettie and Meg, again, she is moved to ecstasy when she is absorbedly playing the mother to a child. Cyril, once, watches her while she baths her brother's little baby:

> A distinct, glowing atmosphere seemed suddenly to burst out around her and the child, leaving me outside. The moment before she had been very near to me, her eyes searching mine, her spirit clinging timidly about me. Now I was put away, quite alone, neglected, forgotten, outside the glow which surrounded the woman and the baby.[66]

---

[60] *W.P.*, p. 13. [61] *Op. cit.*, p. 68. [62] *Op. cit.*, p. 69.
[63] *Op. cit.*, p. 268. [64] *Op. cit.*, p. 320. [65] *Op. cit.*, p. 316.
[66] *Op. cit.*, p. 274.

To the extent that Cyril is a self-portrait, it is a portrait of the self Lawrence had outgrown when he wrote the novel. He is, of course, not the "young fool . . . and a frightful bore" that Lawrence calls him in some of his letters of the period: but he is a naïve, lonely, introverted youth who has not yet succeeded in finding his place in the world. All his efforts to relate himself to people and things around him prove futile and he, like George, is left alone as the book ends. The most serious attempt he makes in the novel is to establish a relation of friendship with George. It is Cyril's talks (about science, poetry, metaphysics) with George—while they are working together, harvesting corn—which bring "the first crop of intimacy" between them to fruition.[67] Their friendship is now at "its mystical best".[68] Cyril is haunted by a sense of his "rooted loneliness",[69] and yearns vaguely for some sort of companionship. His heart, "heavy with vague longing" for contact, makes him turn to the life of nature around him, but his failure to relate himself to his surroundings makes him wonder: "What did I want that I turned thus from one thing to another?"[70] The realisation is brought home to him when, walking after rain through the wet fields one day, he discovers a lark's nest.

> I perceived the yellow beaks, the bulging eyelids of two tiny larks, . . . The two little specks of birds lay side by side, beak to beak, their tiny bodies rising and falling in quick unison. I gently put down my fingers to touch them; they were warm; gratifying to find them warm, in the midst of so much cold and wet. . . . In my heart of heart, I longed for someone to nestle against, someone who would come between me and the coldness and the wetness of the surroundings.[71]

Just before this, George and Cyril have sat huddled together under a sack, watching the rain fall "like a grey striped curtain" and listening to the swish of the raindrops which fall all about them:

> . . . we felt the chill of the rain, and drew ourselves together in silence. He smoked his pipe, and I lit a cigarette. The rain continued; all the little pebbles and the red earth glistened in

---

[67] *Op. cit.*, p. 58.   [68] *Op. cit.*, p. 88.   [69] *Op. cit.*, p. 126.
[70] *Op. cit.*, p. 220.   [71] *Op. cit.*, p. 219.

> the grey gloom. We sat together, speaking occasionally. It was at these times we formed the almost passionate attachment which later years slowly wore away.[72]

Critics have tended to make too much of the homosexual suggestions in the relationship. The relationship is surely *meant* to be non-sexual (though different in nature from the "purposive" relation Lawrence was to depict later on between Birkin and Gerald in *Women in Love* or Aaron and Lilly in *Aaron's Rod*). Even the obviously suspect towel-rubbing scene comes as a brief interlude between scenes of mowing on the field where George's father, George and Cyril are busy trying to "get in hay without hired assistance". But passages like the following two do suggest, especially when read out of context, the presence of unconscious homosexual tendencies in Cyril—though whether these are to be attributed to immaturity in Cyril or in the author is not quite clear:

> George was sitting by the fire, reading. He looked up as I entered, and I loved him when he looked up at me, and as he lingered on his quiet "Hullo!" His eyes were beautifully eloquent—as eloquent as a kiss.

> [George] saw that I had forgotten to continue my rubbing, and laughing he took hold of me and began to rub me briskly, as if I were a child, or rather, a woman he loved and did not fear. I left myself quite limply in his hands, and, to get a better grip of me, he put his arms round me and pressed me against him, and the sweetness of the touch of our naked bodies one against the other was superb. It satisfied in some measure the vague, indecipherable yearning of my soul; and it was the same with him. When he had rubbed me all warm, he let me go, and we looked at each other with eyes full of still laughter, and our love was perfect for a moment, more perfect than any love I have known since, either for man or woman.[73]

The emphasis in the relationship finally is on a kind of male friendship whereby George and Cyril work together, sing, recite verses, and talk of books, and life seems "full of glamour"[74] to both of them. But it needs to be said that Lawrence is not

[72] *Op. cit.*, p. 218.   [73] *Op. cit.*, p. 222.   [74] *Op. cit.*, p. 224.

as explicit about the nature of the relationship as one wishes he had been.

The White Peacock is, on the whole, not a successful novel. The impression it leaves on the reader is a very diffuse one. It is more a generalised statement than a working out of the conflicts latent in the relationships it deals with tentatively. Most of the themes and conflicts vaguely suggested here were developed and powerfully presented by Lawrence in his subsequent novels. Neither his vision nor his style has yet the sharpness and intensity which are the distinctive features of his later novels.

The Trespasser, Lawrence's second novel, concentrates mainly on depicting the basic conflict of the flesh and the spirit as manifested in the relations between men and women. It is well known that the narrative is to a certain extent based on part-manuscript of Helen Corke's novel which she was to publish later under the title *Neutral Ground* (1933). The basis of the story in Lawrence's own experience with Helen Corke, is however, no less important. *The Trespasser*, as Michael C. Sharpe has suggested, is a deeply personal novel in as much as both the original of Siegmund, the novel's hero, and Lawrence himself "had unsuccessfully loved the same woman, and he saw their failure as resulting from a deep-rooted disorder in sexual relations".[75] Lawrence's acquaintance with Helen Corke and with Rachel Anand Taylor helped him recognise the true nature and the extent of the problem of what Mrs Taylor had called "The Dreaming Woman"—the type of woman "who, though vividly alive spiritually and mentally, denies the natural instincts of physical love and motherhood".[76] Speaking of his personal involvement in the novel, Lawrence said in a letter to Edward Garnett that he could not regard *The Trespasser* at ease because it was so much his own naked self:

> I give myself away so much, and write what is my most palpitant, sensitive self, that I loathe the book, because it will betray me to a parcel of fools. Which is what any deeply personal or lyrical writer feels, I guess.[77]

---

[75] "The Genesis of D. H. Lawrence's *The Trespasser*", *Essays in Criticism*, XI, p. 34. [76] *Op. cit.*, p. 37. [77] *Collected Letters*, I, p. 94.

F

Siegmund, who has suppressed his soul for years trying to do his duty to his wife and children, decides to break free and to have at least a few days purely for his own joy by spending a short holiday with his pupil Helena on the Isle of Wight. This decision has not been an easy one, as for him it means "a severing of blood-ties, a sort of new birth".[78] It is "one of the crises of his life", a moment of deep inner conflict. The domestic life he has led so far is summed up by "a broken, coarse comb, a child crying because her hair was lugged, a wife who had let her hair go till now, when she had got into a temper to see the job through; and then the teddy-bear, pathetically cocking a black worsted nose . . .".[79] Either he himself must go under and continue leading an existence he hates, or—if he breaks free—his children who are so dear to him must suffer. Having agreed, however, to spend the holiday with Helena, he finally resolves to do so.

Siegmund sets out on his five-day adventure hoping he has escaped at least for the time being the conflict which has been tormenting him. But he only flees from one conflict to be caught up in a different one. When he tries to give expression to his sense of tragedy, telling Helena "how his life was wrenched from its roots",[80] he finds that she does not at all understand him.[81] Wanting to "blind himself with her, to blaze up all his past and future in a passion worth years of living",[82] he soon discovers that Helena only wants tenderness and "dream love" and hates the passionate male in him. All that Siegmund and Helena do on the island for five days serves to bring out more than anything else the utter incompatibility of their natures. Their disharmony, as one critic has remarked, "is not a matter of misunderstanding or intellectual adjustment or arbitration of negotiable differences but a cleavage of temperament, for which there is no cure".[83]

---

[78] *The Trespasser*, p. 9.   [79] *Op. cit.*, pp. 10-11.

[80] *Op. cit.*, p. 18.

[81] There are over a dozen explicit comments in the narrative on how either Helena or Siegmund completely fails to understand the other. See pp. 18, 20, 25-7, 28, 38, 58, 77, 82, 87, 100, 109, 111, etc.

[82] *The Trespasser*, p. 18.

[83] Leo Gurko, "*The Trespasser*, D. H. Lawrence's Neglected Novel", *College English*, XXIV, i (Oct. 1962), p. 31.

Helena neither loves nor needs the real Siegmund. The Siegmund she loves is only a projection of her own soul. With her "the dream is always more than actuality".[84] Consequently her dream of Siegmund means more to her than Siegmund himself. To the real man in him, whose dreams are "melted in his blood", she is very cruel:

> His dreams were the flowers of his blood. Hers were more detached and inhuman. For centuries a certain type of woman has been rejecting the 'animal' in humanity, till now her dreams are abstract, and full of fantasy, and her blood runs in bondage, and her kindness is full of cruelty.[85]

The value of all things for Helena lies in the fancy they evoke. Actual people she finds "vulgar, ugly and stupid, as a rule".[86] So she habitually clothes everything in fancy, seeing flowers sometimes as "fairies' telephones", sometimes as "tiny children in pinafores".[87] The rippling sunlight on the sea is to her the Rhine maidens spreading their bright hair to the sun. This is her favourite way of thinking. Even death is to her just one of her symbols, "the death of which the sagas talk— something grand, and sweeping, and dark".[88] Helena is essentially the same type of woman as Lawrence's "latest love" of whom he wrote in 1910 to Blanche Jennings:

> She . . . covers herself with a woolly fluff of romance. . . . She refuses to see that a man is a male, that kisses are the merest preludes and anticipations, that love is largely a physical sympathy that is soon satisfied and satiated . . . she is all sham and superficial in her outlook, and I can't change her.[89]

Siegmund, too, cannot change Helena. In a moment of passion when their lips seem to meet and fuse together in "the long, supreme kiss, in which man and woman have one being"[90] Siegmund becomes a "tense vivid body of flesh, without a mind": his blood, alive and conscious, runs towards her: but Helena does not have the man's brightness and vividness of blood, and is already exhausted when she draws away her lips.

---

[84] *The Trespasser*, p. 23.   [85] *Ibid.*   [86] *Op. cit.*, p. 34.
[87] *Op. cit.*, p. 99.   [88] *Op. cit.*, p. 36.   [89] *Collected Letters*, I, p. 59.
[90] *The Trespasser*, p. 23.

Her desire is "accomplished in a real kiss": she belongs to "that class of 'dreaming women' with whom passion exhausts itself at the mouth".[91] Helena sinks away from Siegmund's caresses, subtly drawing back from him. He is much too sensitive not to sense this: his heart sinks at her withdrawal and the caress goes out of his mouth even while it remains on her throat. The situation is paralleled in Lawrence's story of the same period, "The Witch *à la Mode*", where Coutts sees Winifred after the first genuine kiss "swooning on her unnatural ebb of passion" as if "already she had had enough.[92] The attraction-repulsion, love-hate relationship between Coutts and Winifred is repeated in *The Trespasser*. In the evening when Helena enters the room, Siegmund's eyes seek her "as sparks lighting on the tinder":[93] but seeing her eyes "only moist with tenderness" his look instantly changes. The "gloom of tenderness" in her eyes does not let him reveal the passion burning in him. He finds he cannot even look at her. He tries to be tender towards her and to answer "her dream love",[94] but cannot put out the fire inside him. Helena wants his caresses and tenderness; he can only turn away, remaining aloof and intractable. The look of weariness and suffering in his curiously searching but disappointed eyes troubles her. "What is it, dear?" she is finally driven to ask. "You", he replies.

Against her will Helena yields to the importuning of "his whole body . . . burning and surging with desire":

> He sat in the chair beside her, leaning forward, his hands hanging like two scarlet flowers listless in the fire glow, near to her, as she knelt on the hearth, with head bowed down. One of the flowers awoke and spread towards her. It asked for her mutely. She was fascinated, scarcely able to move.
>
> "Come," he pleaded softly.
>
> She turned, lifted her hands to him. The lace fell back, and her arms, bare to the shoulder, shone rosily. He saw her breasts raised towards him. Her face was bent between her arms as she looked up at him afraid. Lit by the firelight, in her white, clinging dress, cowering between her uplifted arms, she seemed to be offering him herself to sacrifice.

---

[91] *Ibid.*
[93] *The Trespasser*, p. 25.
[92] *The Complete Short Stories*, I, p. 61.
[94] *Ibid.*

In an instant he was kneeling, and she was lying on his shoulder, abandoned to him. There was a good deal of sorrow in his joy.[95]

Siegmund's stillness and peace afterwards make Helena wonder how he, who was a burning volcano a short while ago, could now be "like the sea . . . musing by itself". This is the Siegmund of her dreams, created by her. But in her thrill there is also a quiver of pain because just when Siegmund comes nearest to her dream-image of him, he is also beyond her and does not need her.

Siegmund's joy, in turn, is mixed with sorrow because Helena, instead of responding to his body's passion, seems only to offer herself as a sacrifice. Bathing in a rock-pool the next morning and seeing his handsome body's reflexion in the water he wonders why Helena, who should rejoice in him, rejects him as if he were "a baboon under [his] clothing",[96] and "thinks ten thousand times more of that little pool, with a bit of pink anemone and some yellow weed, than of me".[97]

Helena loves "the trifles and the toys" in life and is, like a child, indifferent to the consequences. Life is to her either beautiful, fantastic, or inscrutable; or else mean and vulgar, below consideration. Siegmund, too, can play with the delicious warm surface of life, but he is always aware of the relentless mass of cold beneath. This is his experience of Helena, too. The smooth, warm, delightful sand on the shore reminds him of Helena: but he soon discovers the "deep weight of cold" underneath the surface. Helena is like the seashore, "the deep mass of cold, that the softness and warmth merely floated upon".[98]

Corresponding to Siegmund's dual experience of Helena, the latter feels she encounters two different Siegmunds. There is the Siegmund of her dreams, who belongs to the world of "the curling splash of retreat of the little sleepy waves",[99] and whose soul she wants to listen to. But there is also the Siegmund with a powerfully thudding heart, the strange and insistent man whom she does not understand.

[95] *Op. cit.*, pp. 27-8.
[97] *Ibid.*
[99] *Op. cit.*, p. 38.
[96] *Op. cit.*, p. 32.
[98] *Op. cit.*, p. 47.

Presently she laid her head on his breast, and remained so, watching the sea, and listening to his heart-beats. The throb was strong and deep. It seemed to go through the whole island and the whole afternoon, and it fascinated her: so deep, unheard, with its great expulsions of life. Had the world a heart? Was there also deep in the world a great God thudding out waves of life, like a great heart, unconscious? It frightened her. This was the God she knew not, as she knew not this Siegmund.[1]

This Siegmund with a strong heart beating powerfully, "silent and strange in a tide of passion", is a great deal like the brute sea which flings Helena about in "a game of terror". The roaring thud of the waves reminds her of Siegmund's beating heart, and she remembers how much she "hates the brute in him".[2] It is not that Helena is not glad to have Siegmund love her. For a moment or two when Siegmund kisses her, her whole body is filled with a "hot flush like wine, . . . most exquisite, as if she were nothing but a soft flame of fire against him".[3] But it is not actually his passion that she wants: she only desires that he should want her madly. She wants, on the one hand, to possess all of him, and, on the other, to sacrifice herself to him, to "make herself a burning altar to him".[4] She kisses the sad and dejected Siegmund, clasps him fervently till his roused passion burns away all his heaviness and he seems "tipped with life". Now Helena is satisfied that Siegmund wants her, and she wants no more. The urgent knocking of his heart on her breast gives her both a sense of triumph and a thrill of dread and excitement—dread, because she finds Siegmund's passion so incomprehensible.

How he came to be so concentratedly urgent she could not understand. It seemed an unreasonable, an incomprehensible obsession to her. Yet she was glad, and she smiled in her heart, feeling triumphant and restored. Yet again, dimly, she wondered where was the Siegmund of ten minutes ago, and her heart lifted slightly with yearning, to sink with a dismay. This Siegmund was so incomprehensible.[5]

---

[1] *Ibid.*   [2] *Op. cit.*, p. 41.   [3] *Op. cit.*, p. 58.
[4] *Op. cit.*, p. 45.   [5] *Op. cit.*, p. 58.

The Siegmund she understands is the one whose soul she can gather, in all her benignity and compassion, to "the bosom of her nurture"—not merely as Helena, but in her role as a personification of the great motherhood of women, as "Hawwa —Eve—Mother!"[6]

Meanwhile Siegmund, reviewing the time spent with Helena, struggles "to diagnose his case of splendour and sickness".[7] He concludes that he has "drunk life too hot", and that living too intensely kills one, more or less. Looking at the carved figure of Christ on a cross, he seeks to draw a parallel between his tragedy and Christ's—even though he knows that his own tragedy is small, futile, and despicable in comparison. Life seems to him to be treating him in the same manner as it had treated "the Master":

> "Thirty years of earnest love; three years' life like a passionate ecstasy—and it was finished. He was very great and very wonderful. I am very insignificant, and shall go out ignobly. But we are the same; love, the brief ecstasy, and the end. . . ."[8]

Siegmund's "brief ecstasy" with Helena foreshadows his end. As Hampson, who is really only a "sort of Doppelgänger",[9] tells Siegmund, he has acquired a liking for intensity in life, for vivid soul experience which he cannot now do without. But this is fatal for him, as it is like feeding one's normal flame with oxygen. He does not have the dispassionate intellect which could control him and economise. So he rushes unimpeded towards his doom:

> "The best sort of women—the most interesting—are the worst for us," Hampson resumed. "By instinct they aim at suppressing the gross and animal in us. Then they are supersensitive—refined a bit beyond humanity. We, who are as little gross as need be, become their instruments. . . . The ordinary woman is, alone, a great potential force, an accumulator, if you like, charged from the source of life. In us her force becomes evident.
>
> "She can't live without us, but she destroys us. These deep, interesting women don't want *us*; they want the flowers of the

---

6 *Op. cit.*, p. 61.　　7 *Op. cit.*, p. 63.
8 *Op. cit.*, p. 65.　　9 *Op. cit.*, p. 72.

spirit they can gather of us. We, as natural men, are more or less degrading to them and to their love of us; therefore they destroy the natural man in us—that is, us altogether."[10]

Like Lettie in *The White Peacock* Helena wants "the Mist Spirit" of her fancy to draw a curtain round her and Siegmund so that she can remain in her own "fine world" without having to think of "the outside" which she dreads. But Siegmund, the painful need for self-revelation upon him, tears open "the heavy gold mist-curtain" by starting to tell her the story of his marriage with Beatrice. As they walk in silence afterwards it slowly dawns on Helena that love, after all, forms only an episode in man's life. It is her hour of disillusion. Looking at Siegmund walking ahead of her, she shudders to realise that her dream-image of him is completely shattered. She now knows that the Siegmund who had seemed to radiate joy into her surroundings was only a projection of her own soul. In such a frame of mind his voice sounds to her stupid, his arms round her hurt in their "brute embrace". She feels utterly alone now. His heart beating against her no longer thrills her: she finds his physical self hateful and repulsive. She grows frantic and struggles to get free of his embrace. Siegmund, pushed away thus, is stunned. Even when, a little later, Helena repents and he has her in his arms, he cannot find any comfort in it: in spirit he is quite alone, seeking "courage and faith for his own soul".[11] Helena, sensing that his spirit ignores her, is afraid she might lose him. With "Madonna love" she tries to soothe him, kissing him delicately with fond, reassuring kisses. Her pity, however, cannot console Siegmund now. He has come to realise that Helena, who gives herself to her fancies only, does not really need him: "she only wants me to explore me like a rock-pool, and to bathe in me".[12] As long as she had confused him with her god, she had accepted him as her ideal lover. Now she has found out the real Siegmund and rejected him. His sense of humiliation, this "spear in the side of his tortured self-respect"[13] prompts him to analyse the cause of his failure. He concludes that all his life he has been pushed this way and that like a fool because he has not been masterful,

---

[10] *Op. cit.*, pp. 69-70.   [11] *Op. cit.*, p. 86.
[12] *Op. cit.*, p. 100.   [13] *Op. cit.*, p. 101.

because he has always given way and has never been able to compel anything for fear of hurting. With Helena, he thinks, he has failed as a lover because he is so "timid of compulsion": "I ought to have had her in love sufficiently to keep her these few days."[14]

While Siegmund is on his way back to London he is painfully aware that he is merely moving from one scene of failure to another—an earlier one, with his family. Thinking of his future, he comes to the conclusion that he can no longer go on living with his wife. He must, therefore, provide for her, and himself live separately. But can he live alone? He realises that in fact he cannot:

> "I shall want Helena; I shall remember the children. If I have the one, I shall be damned by the thought of the other. This bruise on my mind will never get better. Helena says she would never come to me; but she would, out of pity for me. I know she would.
> "But then, what then? Beatrice and the children in the country, and me not looking after the children. . . ."[15]

Siegmund cannot see any way out of the dilemma. When, on his return home, he is rejected by his wife and his children, he finds there is nothing he can really turn to. Death alone remains as a way out of the conflict. He feels he is like a limb out of joint from the body of life. He can neither break with Helena and return to a degrading life at home, nor leave his children to go to Helena. The only thing which remains possible is "to depart, . . . to cut himself off from life". This, it occurs to him, would be shirking the responsibility of himself; but not finding himself strong enough to face and fight through the conflicts he cannot possibly evade any longer, he commits suicide by hanging himself.

The novel does not end here: but the suicide brings to a conclusion the "Saga of Siegmund". Whatever the novel gains by concentrating its gaze on just one aspect of man-woman relationship is, however, not enough to compensate for the loss of a wider perspective of the relationship as a whole. There is also a certain amount of repetitiveness, and the language tends

---

[14] *Op. cit.*, p. 103.   [15] *Op. cit.*, p. 118.

at places to be strained and artificial. But above all, Lawrence's handling and presentation of the situation is not yet mature. No subsequent novel of Lawrence has the kind of definite conclusion, with little wider significance, that *The Trespasser* has. Instead, the next novel, *Sons and Lovers*, forms more or less the first—and necessarily inconclusive—chapter in a long and continuous story of the modern man's quest for wholeness of being. Essentially it is the story of all sensitive and thinking men and women in search of a better and more meaningful life, in as much as Lawrence's imaginative genius could reconstruct it.

III

Son as Lover

"*Sons and Lovers* is supposed, technically, to have no construction. The world is full of technical fools."[1] Lawrence wrote this in a letter to E. H. and Achsah Brewster eight years after the novel's publication. He had worked hard at his novel, "pruning it and shaping it and filling it in", and was impatient at the charge that the novel lacked form. He was fully convinced that his novel was "a unified whole",[2] though he granted that it might be found at first a bit difficult to grasp as a whole. In November 1912, some months before the novel was published, he wrote to Edward Garnett:

> I tell you it has got form—*form*: haven't I made it patiently, out of sweat as well as blood. It follows this idea: a woman of character and refinement goes into the lower class, and has no satisfaction in her own life. She has had a passion for her husband, so the children are born of passion, and have heaps of vitality. But as her sons grow up she selects them as lovers—first the eldest, then the second. These sons are *urged* into life by their reciprocal love of their mother—urged on and on. But when they come to manhood, they can't love, because their mother is the strongest power in their lives, and holds them. . . . As soon as the young men come into contact with women, there's a split. William gives his sex to a fribble, and his mother holds his soul. But the split kills him, because he doesn't know where he is. The next son gets a woman who fights for his soul—fights his mother. The son loves the mother —all the sons hate and are jealous of the father. The battle goes on between the mother and the girl, with the son as object. The mother gradually proves stronger, because of the tie of blood. The son decides to leave his soul in his mother's hands,

---

[1] *Collected Letters*, II, p. 651.   [2] *Collected Letters*, I, p. 191.

and, like his elder brother go for passion. He gets passion.
Then the split begins to tell again. But, almost unconsciously,
the mother realises what is the matter, and begins to die. He
is left in the end naked of everything, with the drift towards
death. . . . Now tell me if I haven't worked out my theme, like
life, but always my theme. . . . If *you* can't see the development
—which is slow, like growth—I can.[3]

Lawrence is obviously defending here the form and construction
of his novel, not giving a critical appreciation of it—though
many critics appear to have assumed that he was. They quote
Lawrence's own dictum[4]—"Never trust the artist, trust the
tale"—against him, arguing that there is a discrepancy between
"the drift towards death" in the letter to Garnett and the
actual ending of the novel. Paul's movement towards the
"faintly humming, glowing town" at the end, they maintain,
contradicts Lawrence's "summary" of the novel. It must, one
imagines, have given a great deal of satisfaction to these critics
to think that they have caught out Lawrence here: but there is
in fact no contradiction between Lawrence's statement in the
letter and the conclusion of the novel. The "drift towards
death" is unmistakably there. Paul's decision to turn against it
("But no, he would not give in.") in no way cancels out the
drift; on the contrary it acknowledges implicitly that such a
drift is there. As Lawrence, answering the question why he
left Paul so derelict, so "stripped of everything" at the end, is
reported to have said, "Ah, but he had his courage left."[5]
Paul has enough strength and courage left in him to turn
towards "the city's gold phosphorescence". But there is no
indication in the novel that at the end Paul has all of a sudden
left his mother finally behind, though there is no doubt a
definite hint that he is on his way to becoming a man in his own
right by casting off his dependence on his mother. That the
book ends with Paul's determined move towards attaining his
own "wholeness of being", and not with any sudden transformation of him, is also indicated by the poems Lawrence

[3] *Op. cit.*, pp. 160-1.

[4] Mr Hough, for some reason, gives it to Dr Leavis: "Never trust the author,
trust the tale, as Dr Leavis puts it". (Hough, p. 51.)

[5] H. J. Forman, "With D. H. Lawrence in Sicily", *The New York Book Review
and Magazine* (27 Aug. 1922), p. 12. Reprinted in Nehls, II (1958), p. 109.

wrote at the death of his mother,[6] especially "The Virgin Mother":

> I kiss you good-bye, my darling,
> Our ways are different now;
> You are a seed in the night-time,
> I am a man to plough
> The difficult glebe of the future
> For the seed to endow.
>
> Is the last word now uttered?
> Is the farewell said?
> Spare me the strength to leave you
> Now you are dead.
> I must go, but my soul lies helpless
> Beside your bed.[7]

Paul, like Lawrence, knows he must turn away from the direction which leads to darkness and death, and yet his attachment to his mother has been so strong that a part of him seems to have died with his mother. *Sons and Lovers*, however, is not a novel about the Oedipus complex or mother fixation of the Freudians. Lawrence had heard of Freud before he wrote the final draft of the novel, but he never subscribed to any theories of Freudianism—which he took to be a branch of medical science, interesting in many respects, but quite often wrong and limited in its approach. Referring to one of the reviews of *Sons and Lovers*, published in a journal of psychoanalysis, Lawrence remarked in a letter to Barbara Low:

> You know I think 'complexes' are vicious half-statements of the Freudians: sort of can't see wood for trees. When you've said *Mutter*-complex, you've said nothing— . . . a complex is not simply a sex relation: far from it.—My poor book: it was, as art, a fairly complete truth: so they carve a half lie out of it, and say '*Voila*'. Swine![8]

Lawrence's protest was against distortion of the total meaning of his novel. "Father complex, mother complex, incest dreams:

[6] Such a comparison between a situation in fiction and one in actual life, though in general of limited validity, is made permissible in the present case by Lawrence's own statement that parts of *Sons and Lovers* dealing with Paul's relations with his parents are almost pure autobiography.

[7] *Poems*, I, pp. 84-5. [8] *Collected Letters*, I, p. 475.

pah, when we've had the little excitement out of them we shall forget them as we have forgotten so many other catch-words", he wrote later in *Fantasia*.[9] But he was not unaware of the element of truth in the findings of psychoanalysis. He recognised, and stressed, that even a relation of intense pure sympathy or sacred love between parent and child "inevitably involves us in a conclusion of incest"—though to distinguish his views from those of the Freudians he calls it "spiritual incest", which he nevertheless describes as even more dangerous than sensual incest because it is less instinctively repugnant. Lawrence had written in his foreword to *Sons and Lovers* that it is in the Flesh, in Woman, that we have our knowledge of God the Father, the Unknowable. "In her we go back to the Father . . . blind and unconscious." Every woman demands that her man, having done his day's work, should come to her with joy and be renewed, "be re-born of her", so that he can go forth again the next morning with his new strength:

> But if the man does not come home to a woman . . . to be warmed, and restored, and nourished, . . . then she shall expel him from the house. . . . For in the flesh of the woman does God exact Himself. And out of the flesh of the woman does He demand: 'Carry this of Me forth to utterance.' And if the man deny, or be too weak, then shall the woman find another man, of greater strength. And if, because of the Word, which is the Law, she do not find another man, nor he another woman, then shall they both be destroyed. For he, to get that rest, and warmth, and nourishment which he should have had from her, his woman, must consume his own flesh, and so destroy himself: whether with wine, or other kindling. And she, either her surplus shall wear away her flesh, in sickness, or in lighting up and illuminating old dead Words, or she shall spend it in fighting with her man to make him take her, or she shall turn to her son, and say, 'Be you my Go-between.'
>
> But the man who is the go-between from Woman to Production is the lover of that woman. And if that woman be his mother, then is he her lover in part only; he carries for her, but is never received into her for his confirmation and renewal, and so wastes himself away in the flesh. The old son-lover was Oedipus. The name of the new one is legion. And if a son-

---

[9] *Fantasia*, p. 126.

lover take a wife, then is she not his wife, she is only his bed. And his life will be torn in twain, and his wife in her despair shall hope for sons, that she may have her lover in her hour.[10]

These views were further elaborated in *Fantasia* where Lawrence explains how an exaggerated and intense spiritual love from the parents leads to a painfully false relation between parents and children. By establishing a dynamic relation with the child in the second plane of consciousness, the parents—because of their monomania for love and more love—do "what it is vicious for any parent to do".[11] They unwittingly establish a bond of adult love with the child—not of sex, because Lawrence held that biologically there is a radical sex-aversion between parent and child at the deeper sensual centres, but of sacred, spiritual love. . Even this relation of pure love between parent and child, however, is fatal because it inevitably arouses in the child the centres of sex which cannot then find response from the sensual body of any other person. Parents, instead of helping the child's growth into manhood so that he would in his time "possess his own soul in strength within him, deep and alone",[12] make it impossible for him to grow. When a woman has attained her fulfilment through love, "deep sensual love, and exquisite sensitive communion", she should make the great resolution to come to rest within herself, living in peace and equilibrium with her husband. Instead, her craving for more love makes her look round for a new sort of lover, one who will "understand" her; and as often as not she turns to her son. In him she provokes what she wants:

> He is a medium to her, she provokes from him her own answer. So she throws herself into a last great love for her son, a final and fatal devotion, that which would have been the richness and strength of her husband and is poison to the boy.[13]

Mother-supported, mother-stimulated, the son "gets on swimmingly" for a time, until he is faced with his own sexual needs. What is he to do with his sensual, sexual self? "And if a son-lover take a wife, then is she not his wife, she is only his bed. And his life will be torn in twain . . .". He is already linked

---

[10] *Letters*, pp. 100-2.   [11] *Fantasia*, p. 117.
[12] *Op. cit.*, p. 120.   [13] *Op. cit.*, p. 122.

up with his mother in an ideal love, "the best that he will ever know", because love within the family involves no shocks or ruptures inevitable between strangers, and therefore seems the best and highest. The intense non-sexual parent-child love has forestalled the great love experience which should lie in the future: "The cream is licked off from life before the boy or the girl is twenty. Afterwards—repetition, disillusion, and barrenness."[14]

Sons and Lovers, like all other novels of Lawrence, is primarily an enquiry into human relationships. At one stage in the novel Paul, commenting on a picture in his sketch-book, says: "it's more shimmery, as if I'd painted the shimmering protoplasm in the leaves and everywhere, and not the stiffness of the shape. That seems dead to me. Only this shimmeriness is the real living."[15] Paul's intent is to reproduce not the "dead crust" of the shape that leaves have, but the shimmer which reveals them in relation to their surroundings. Lawrence's focus in the novel, similarly, is not on the stiff shape or outline of his characters but on the actual shimmer of life as expressed in the relationships between these characters, and also in their relation to the living universe around them.[16] David Daiches, discussing *Sons and Lovers*, has remarked: "Insistently, like a drum beat in the background of the novel, runs the question: 'What is, what ought to be, what can be, the most vital relation between man and woman'."[17] This, in itself, is certainly quite right—though it is, of course, true of other novels of Lawrence, too: but what is important to bear in mind is that such a statement leaves out the novel's preoccupation with the parent-child relationship which is what, after all, the novel is basically about: about sons and lovers, or more precisely about sons as lovers.

Eliseo Vivas has found that "in *Sons and Lovers* Lawrence's intention and the intention of the novel are disparate".[18] Lawrence, he thinks, wants us to believe that both Miriam and Morel were at fault and that Mrs Morel was a loving mother

[14] *Op. cit.*, p. 125.

[15] *Sons and Lovers* (Phoenix Edition), p. 152.

[16] Alfred Kazin makes a similar point in his perceptive article "Sons, Lovers and Mothers", published in *Partisan Review*, XXIX, iii (Summer 1962).

[17] Daiches, p. 145.   [18] *Vivas*, p. 180.

and wife made unhappy by an uncouth, drinking husband. Neither Paul nor Lawrence, he goes on, can see that Mrs Morel is not a good mother. We are not told what sources of information about Lawrence's intentions (apart from those realised in the novel itself) Mr Vivas has available to him. But as far as Lawrence's expressed intentions are concerned—as in his foreword to *Sons and Lovers* and other writings of the period —the novel was largely inspired by the "tragedy of thousands of young men"[19] whose lives, he found, were being ruined by the possessive love of their mothers.[20] The novel itself is, of course, an artistic depiction of a complex situation. It shows Paul involved in a series of unsatisfactory relationships, which are presented with all the perplexities, pain and conflict which they give rise to. Paul himself is as much to blame for the failures in relationships as any other character. In *Sons and Lovers* there is, as Graham Hough has put it, no spectator character who stands apart from the action of the novel to serve as a vehicle for the novelist's point of view: "No one is right. . . . All the main characters—Paul, Miriam, Mrs Morel, Clara Dawes—make extremely penetrating remarks on each other. All are blind to much that is going on around them."[21] The technique used is to give the actual process of living, with all its doubts, gropings, and uncertainties. If the actors in a scene are bewildered, are unaware of what is happening to them, then "the writing refrains from going beyond their actual awareness; yet the material for a fuller understanding is there".[22]

Part 1 of the novel begins with the early married life of Paul's parents. His mother had met Morel at a Christmas party when she was twenty-three. She was a puritan, and a high-minded and stern idealist whose life had been cramped by "thought and spirit". Morel with his natural joyous manner

---

[19] *Collected Letters*, 1, p. 161.

[20] Lawrence is later (in 1922) reported to have said that he wished he had done his father "more justice" in *Sons and Lovers*. Many have supposed this to mean that Lawrence, by implication, admitted to having condoned his mother's faults in the novel. But this conclusion is mistaken. Lawrence who had by then come to see his father in a different light, recognising his "unquenchable fire and relish for living", only wished he had not as a child accepted his mother's judgment of their father unquestioningly. See E. and A. Brewster, *D. H. Lawrence*, pp. 254-5

[21] Hough, p. 51.   [22] *Op. cit.*, p. 45.

and his rare, ringing laughter seems to her so different and wonderful. She is fascinated by "the dusky, golden softness of this man's sensuous flame of life".[23] They get married, and "for three months she was perfectly happy: for six months she was very happy".[24] As Paul tells Miriam later on in the novel, Mrs Morel during this time gets real joy and satisfaction in her life with her husband. She has a passion for him which binds them together, and she remains grateful to him even afterwards for the big and intense experience which, as it were, fertilised her soul so that she could go on to develop and mature. Even though they begin to drift apart after a brief harmonious life together, Mrs Morel has already had "what one *must have*, . . . the real, real flame of feeling through another person".[25]

Mrs Morel discovers some unpaid bills in the pocket of her husband's coat, and finds out all the lies he has told her to deceive her. She begins to despise Morel, who, it seems to her, "lacked principle". A fearful and long-lasting battle begins between husband and wife whose natures are utterly different. His nature is purely sensuous—which she had found so fascinating when she had first met him. Now with her puritanical instinct she strives to make him moral, religious. Like a fanatic she tortures him, drives him out of his mind by forcing him against his will to face things and fulfil his obligations. "She could not be content with the little he might be; she would have him the much that he ought to be. So, in seeking to make him nobler than he could be, she destroyed him."[26] Morel, in his turn, often comes home drunk. On one such occasion he turns his pregnant wife out into the cold night and bolts the door; another time he hits her with a drawer, making her bleed profusely. Afterwards, however, he suffers a great deal, especially because he does not express his regret to her, while his conscience inflicts on him the punishment which eats "into his spirit like rust"[27] and which he can only alleviate by drinking. Stephen Spender has quoted Lawrence's subsequent judgement about his parents' quarrels from an unpublished document in the library of the University of Cincinnati. Here,

[23] *Sons and Lovers*, p. 10.   [24] *Op. cit.*, p. 11.
[25] *Op. cit.*, p. 317.   [26] *Op. cit.*, p. 16.
[27] *Op. cit.*, p. 41.

writing four years before his death, Lawrence summed up the situation thus:

> My mother fought with deadly hostility against my father, all her life. He was not hostile, till provoked, then he too was a devil. But my mother began it. She seemed to begrudge his very existence. . . .[28]

In the novel itself Lawrence does not make any such judgement by trying to put the blame either on Morel or on Mrs Morel—though he provides enough material for us to see that they are both to blame. He only shows them, time and again, involved in a relationship full of conflict when "each forgot everything save the hatred of the other and the battle between them".[29] In this "deadlock of passion" Mrs Morel proves stronger, and Morel gradually gets alienated from the life of the family. With Paul's birth, she resolves to leave him alone, taking him to be just an inevitable part of her circumstances, and to turn for love and life to her children instead of to him. He, half-regretfully but relentlessly cast off by his wife, is reduced to "more or less a husk"[30] now. Mrs Morel, moreover, has the children on her side, and they together shut him out from all their affairs, treating him as "an outsider".[31] There are now only moments when he enters again into the life of his own people; this is when he is engaged in some domestic work—cobbling the boots, or mending the kettle, or making the fuses—and when the children enjoy attending on him. For the rest the bloody battle between husband and wife rages on. When the family move to another house, the shrieking of the wind-swept ash tree in front of it comes to symbolise for the children "the anguish of the home discord".[32] They hear the loud shouts of their father, come home nearly drunk, then the sharp replies of their mother, followed by the banging of their father's fist on the table, and finally everything is "drowned in a piercing medley of shrieks and cries from the great, wind-swept ash-tree. . . . The wind came through the tree fiercer and fiercer. All the chords of the great harp hummed, whistled,

---

[28] *The Creative Element*, London (1953), p. 96.
[29] *Sons and Lovers*, p. 22.   [30] *Op. cit.*, p. 46.
[31] *Op. cit.*, p. 64.   [32] *Op. cit.*, p. 59.

and shrieked. And then came the horror of the sudden silence, silence everywhere, outside and downstairs. What was it? Was it a silence of blood? What had he done?"[33] Lawrence has recorded the same experience in his poem "Discord in Childhood":

> Outside the house an ash-tree hung its terrible whips,
> And at night when the wind rose, the lash of the tree
> Shrieked and slashed the wind, as a ship's
> Weird rigging in a storm shrieks hideously.

> Within the house two voices arose, a slender lash
> Whistling she-delirious rage, and the dreadful sound
> Of a male thong booming and bruising, until it had
>   drowned
> The other voice in a silence of blood, 'neath the noise of
>   the ash.[34]

The unforgivable sin of Mrs Morel is her dragging the children into these quarrels. Her feeling of resentment against her husband is transmitted to the children who are thus unnecessarily implicated in the conflict, sharing her troubles and pain, and hating their father. "She never suffered alone any more: the children suffered with her."[35] Lawrence, giving his judgement on the situation several years later, wrote in *Fantasia*: "It is despicable for any one parent to accept a child's sympathy against the other parent. And the one who *received* the sympathy is always more contemptible than the one who is hated."[36] In the novel itself this does not come out as sharply as that, but the criticism of Mrs Morel in pitting her children against their father is clearly implied.

Having cast off her husband, Mrs Morel turns first to her eldest son, William. Even while he is at school her thoughts are turned to him. He is a very capable boy, "the smartest lad in the school". In her eyes he is already a young man, "full of vigour, making the world glow again for her".[37] He wins prizes in sports so that his mother might feel pleased and be proud of him.

[33] *Op. cit.*, p. 60.
[34] *Poems*, i, pp. 6-7.
[35] *Sons and Lovers*, p. 61.
[36] *Fantasia*, p. 93.
[37] *Sons and Lovers*, p. 47.

When he was twelve he won a first prize in a race: an inkstand
of glass, shaped like an anvil. It stood proudly on the dresser,
and gave Mrs. Morel a keen pleasure. The boy only ran for
her. He flew home with his anvil, breathless, with a "Look,
mother!" That was the first real tribute to herself. She took
it like a queen.[38]

She lives her life now through her son, and jealously guards this
arrangement against all risks to which it is open. She dis-
approves of William's going to dances, and of the girls he meets
there. When he gets a place in London at a very good salary,
she is more hurt at the thought of his going away than glad at
his success. As the day of William's departure draws nearer,
her heart grows dreary with despair. "She loved him so much!
More than that, she hoped in him so much. Almost she lived
by him."[39] When William, finally, goes away to London to
start a new life, she begins to think of him as "her knight who
wore *her* favour in the battle".[40] She has the satisfaction that
her sons, who are derived from her, are going into the world to
do what *she* wants: "their works also would be hers".[41]

William, who has been brought up on his reciprocal love
for his mother, discovers when he begins courting a girl in
London that he is in some way still held by Mrs Morel. He is
an intelligent young man, fond of reading, who has till now
been used to having all his thoughts sifted through his mother's
mind. So he is disconcerted to find that Miss Western—
"Gipsy" or "Gyp" as he calls her—is not at all serious like his
mother, that she cannot really think, and understands in fact
nothing but love-making and chatter. "You know," he tells
his mother, "Gyp's shallow. Nothing goes deep with her."[42]
He wants companionship from her; she, however, responds by
asking him to be "the billing and twittering lover". He is
puzzled and begins to fret, feeling uneasy within himself. But
he cannot give her up because for some things he feels he
couldn't do without her. "You know, mother," he confides to
Mrs Morel on one of his visits home, "when I am away from
her I don't care for her a bit. . . . But then, when I'm with her
in the evenings I am awfully fond of her."[43] His inability to

[38] *Op. cit.*, p. 52.   [39] *Op. cit.*, p. 55.   [40] *Op. cit.*, p. 79.
[41] *Op. cit.*, p. 101.   [42] *Op. cit.*, p. 133.   [43] *Op. cit.*, p. 120.

make a total commitment in love causes a split in him. His face comes to be "stamped with conflict and despair",[44] while his refusal to oblige his mother by breaking with the girl leads to a conflict between him and Mrs Morel whose "heart was heavy now as it had never been. . . . Now her soul felt lamed in itself. It was her hope that was struck."[45] William, fatally divided within himself, begins to waste away: his letters from London come to have a feverish tone; he seems "unnatural and intense", and it is not long before the split kills him.

With the death of her son, and with him of all her hopes, Mrs Morel becomes indifferent to everything going on around her. She "could not be presuaded, after this, to talk and to take her old bright interest in life".[46] She recovers from this state of apathy only when Paul falls dangerously ill with pneumonia. Then the realisation comes to her: "I should have watched the living, not the dead."[47] Paul's illness, in a way, saves his mother.

Paul had been an unwanted child. But Mrs Morel had decided early in one of those "still moments when the small frets vanish, and the beauty of things stands out, and she had the peace and strength to see herself"[48] that having brought the child into the world unloved, she must make up for it by loving him intensely. Paul gets implicated in the life of his mother even earlier than William had done. Even while he is a small boy his soul seems always attentive to her, and—seeing suffering and disillusion on her face—he determines to do what he can to let her have "her life's fulfilment".[49] He feels he would much rather die than cause disappointment to his mother. When William goes off to London Mrs Morel chooses him as her companion. She feels excited "like a woman accepting a love-token"[50] when Paul brings flowers for her. She talks to him of all things that occupy her mind; and he listens to her eagerly, sharing her trouble in order to lighten it. Gradually she comes to share almost everything with him, though more unconsciously than consciously. When Paul goes for an interview to a firm making surgical appliances in Nottingham, she

---

[44] *Op. cit.*, p. 131.　　[45] *Op. cit.*, p. 132.　　[46] *Op. cit.*, p. 139.
[47] *Op. cit.*, p. 140.　　[48] *Op. cit.*, p. 36.　　[49] *Op. cit.*, p. 66.
[50] *Op. cit.*, p. 68.

accompanies him and the two walk down the station street "feeling the excitement of lovers having an adventure together".[51] Paul, in turn, does everything for his mother, tells her everything; and she listens to his story feeling as if it were her own life. "The two shared lives."[52] It is only with William's death, however, that Mrs Morel's life roots itself in Paul and the two are "knitted together in perfect harmony".[53] Paul is urged on in life by his mother, drawing his life-warmth and strength from her, unconsciously. Her influence makes him patient and "quietly determined" in his work; her mere presence rouses him to his soul's intensity: "I can do my best things when you sit there in your rocking-chair, mother," he tells her.[54] When two of Paul's paintings win first prize awards in an exhibition Mrs Morel is beside herself with joy. Her own life seems to her to take on a new meaning. In her son's achievements "she was to see herself fulfilled".[55] Paul, too, feels satisfied in having been able to do something for her, if only a trifle: "All his work was hers."[56] Again, later, when one of Paul's pictures gets a first prize and is sold for twenty guineas, she takes it to be not just her son's but her own triumph. "Didn't I say we should do it!" she keeps on repeating, "I knew we should do it."[57] It is always: *we* should do it.

This relationship works very well for a time. It is when Paul grows into manhood and seeks to establish an independent adult relationship with Miriam that the struggle begins. Mrs Morel dislikes Miriam, and fights against her when she finds Paul being drawn away by the girl who, she can see, is "one of the deep sort". When Paul is late in coming home on any particular day she frets and gets angry. "She is one of those," she broods about Miriam, "who will want to suck a man's soul out till he has none of his own left. . . . She will never let [Paul] become a man; she never will."[58] Mrs Morel is not jealous of Paul's development. She, of course, wishes him the best in life. Ironically, however, what she says of Miriam's influence on her son—that in trying to absorb all of him she would never

[51] *Op. cit.*, p. 91. [52] *Op. cit.*, p. 114. [53] *Op. cit.*, p. 141.
[54] *Op. cit.*, p. 158. [55] *Op. cit.*, p. 183. [56] *Op. cit.*, p. 184.
[57] *Op. cit.*, p. 253. [58] *Op. cit.*, p. 160.

let him be a man on his own feet—is equally true of her own relationship with him. She is right in thinking that Miriam is "not like ordinary girls"[59] and that her love for Paul would leave "no room, not a bit of room" for herself: but she is not aware that as long as she *herself* lives her life through Paul and remains "the chief thing to him, the only supreme thing", there is no possibility of his realising himself. In forcing his sympathy for herself by telling him how she "never had a husband—not really—", she prevents his growth into maturity —for thus she remains "the strongest tie in his life . . . the pivot and pole of his life, from which he could not escape".[60] Lawrence gave his verdict later in *Fantasia*:[61]

> In becoming the object of great emotional stress for her son, the mother also becomes an object of poignancy, of anguish, of arrest, to her son. She arrests him from finding his proper fulfilment on the sensual plane.

This is precisely what Mrs Morel does to Paul. He gives up his struggle to free himself from her inhibiting influence by drawing away from Miriam. The peace he thus temporarily attains is, however, "the bitter peace of resignation". Coming back to his mother, Paul has the dubious satisfaction of self-sacrifice in having been faithful to her. "She loved him first; he loved her first."[62] Wherever he goes her soul goes with him; whatever he does her soul stands by to help him. She cannot bear that he should be with Miriam, so she determines she "would fight to keep Paul".[63]

For Paul, however, his mother's love alone is not enough. His new young life urges him toward something else and he is mad with restlessness. Mrs Morel, seeing this, only wishes Miriam could somehow "take this new life of his", giving satisfaction to his body—and leave the soul to her. Paul himself, caught in this conflict of two women, fights them both, but in the process begins to waste away. In desperation he turns to Miriam again, but comes up against the obstacle of his "physical bondage": he shrinks from any physical contact with her. Looking round, he finds a good many of the nicest men

[59] *Op. cit.*, p. 213. [60] *Op. cit.*, p. 222. [61] *Fantasia*, p. 165.
[62] *Sons and Lovers*, p. 222. [63] *Ibid.*

he knows to be like himself—bound in by their own virginity which they cannot break out of.

> Being the sons of mothers whose husbands had blundered rather brutally through their feminine sanctities, they were themselves too diffident and shy. They could easier deny themselves than incur any reproach from a woman; for a woman was like their mother, and they were full of the sense of their mother.[64]

Mrs Morel's astonishment, when she sees Paul again going frequently to Miriam, soon gives way to a feeling of bitterness: but she recognises the uselessness of any interference. There comes to be a coldness between mother and son. He hardly tells her anything now. The bitter, gloomy, irritable Paul reminds her of William just before his death, and she begins "to give up at last; she had finished. She was in the way."[65]

Paul, having decided to force the issue with Miriam, realises after a week of passion with her that it has been a failure. He again feels lonely and sick, and for a time spends most of his time in the company of men. Mrs Morel is frankly relieved to learn that Paul has nearly broken off with Miriam. She does not mind when Paul starts going out with Clara because in comparison with her she finds herself easily the stronger. Paul, nevertheless, now has a "life apart from her— his sexual life".[66] Of this he tells nothing to her and consequently there comes to be a distance between them. Unknowingly, Paul begins to resist his mother's influence. She still keeps his soul, but this only makes Paul hate her at times and to pull at her bondage.

> His life wanted to free itself of her. It was like a circle where life turned back on itself, and got no farther. She bore him, loved him, kept him, and his love turned back into her, so that he could not be free to go forward with his own life, really love another woman.[67]

He had made an attempt with Miriam, but had found he could not really love her. Now he and Clara are passionately in love, as far as passion goes, but their love is never complete. He loves her when he sees her "just as *the woman*", but when she

---

[64] *Op. cit.*, p. 279. [65] *Op. cit.*, p. 289.
[66] *Op. cit.*, p. 345. [67] *Ibid.*

begins to talk as a person he hardly ever listens to her. He feels
he could never belong to her, or to any other woman, never
give himself to them in marriage. "You know, mother," he
tells Mrs Morel, "I think there must be something the matter
with me, that I *can't* love."[68] The women he loves do not
hold him, and he sometimes has a strong sense of guilt that he
wrongs them. They all seem to want *him* and he "can't ever
give it them". To his mother's suggestion that he probably
hasn't yet met the right woman, his blunt rejoinder is: "And
I never shall meet the right woman while you live."[69] Mrs
Morel feels "as if she were done". She and Paul begin to avoid
each other. A constant sickness keeps on gnawing at his heart;
while she is now "ill, distant, quiet, shadowy".[70] Shortly
afterwards Paul learns that his mother has cancer. He attends
to his ill mother, knowing that she is going to die and that the
bond which has till now held them together must snap. Sitting
in the kitchen, smoking, one day, he discovers one of his
mother's grey hairs as he brushes some grey ash off his coat.
He holds it up and it drifts into the chimney. Making a
meaningful gesture he lets go and the long grey hair floats and
is gone into the blackness of the chimney.

His mother's death, nevertheless, comes as a blow to Paul.
He feels all crumpled up and lonely, and draws himself
together smaller and smaller:

> His mother had really supported his life. He had loved her;
> they two had, in fact, faced the world together. Now she was
> gone, and for ever behind him was the gap in life, the tear in
> the veil, through which his life seemed to drift slowly, as if he
> were drawn towards death.[71]

Paul cuts himself off from life more and more, feeling un-
substantial and shadowy. He wants someone to help him: but
he is prepared to go on alone if nobody would help. Clara
goes away with Dawes to Sheffield. There is scarcely any bond
between Paul and his father who now goes to live with a family
of friends. "There was nothing left."[72] Everything seems to
have gone smash for Paul. Things lose all their reality for him:

[68] *Op. cit.*, p. 350.   [69] *Op. cit.*, p. 351.   [70] *Op. cit.*, p. 368.
[71] *Op. cit.*, p. 407.   [72] *Op. cit.*, p. 410.

> The first snowdrops came. He saw the tiny drop-pearls among the grey. They would have given him the liveliest emotion at one time. Now they were there, but they did not seem to mean anything.[73]

The only real thing remaining to him is the thick darkness at night, "whole and comprehensible and restful", to which he can abandon himself. He knows that he is destroying himself, so he keeps on struggling against this drift towards death. "So the weeks went on. Always alone, his soul oscillated, first on the side of death, then on the side of life, doggedly."[74] Something—the drift towards darkness and death—separates him from other people: he cannot "get into touch". He feels he has no part in the life of the world around him. "Whatever spot he stood on, there he stood alone."[75] His soul, he feels, is with his mother still: but there is also his body, like a tiny spark which "the immense dark silence" seems to be pressing into extinction, into nothing "and yet not nothing". Just when he is on the verge of giving in, wishing his mother would have him alongside with her, he turns abruptly away.

> But no, he would not give in. Turning sharply, he walked towards the city's gold phosphorescence. His fists were shut, his mouth set fast. He would not take that direction, to the darkness, to follow her. He walked towards the faintly humming, glowing town, quickly.[76]

Paul's relationship with Miriam is complicated by a number of factors. It is not only he who is held by his mother when he meets Miriam: she, too, is by no means free from the possessive influence of *her* mother, Mrs Leivers, whose children had been born "almost leaving her out of count" and whom she could not let go "because she never had possessed them".[77] Both Paul and Miriam are bound in by their virginity; both, initially, live on a high plane of abstraction, circumscribed by their ideas of "purity" and spirituality. In all that happens between them it is not easy to say which of the two is to blame more. A superficial reading of the novel might leave the impression that it is Miriam, with her abnormal spiritual

[73] *Ibid.* [74] *Op. cit.*, p. 412. [75] *Op. cit.*, p. 419.
[76] *Op. cit.*, p. 420. [77] *Op. cit.*, p. 279.

intensity, who is responsible for the failure of their relationship. But this is probably because Paul does most of the talking in the book. A little care in reading, however, shows that Paul is equally guilty. Lawrence is here, as Graham Hough rightly points out, portraying the relationship mainly from the inside, *i.e.* presenting it as his own relation with Jessie Chambers had appeared to him *at the time*. If he has any delusions about it, he portrays them, too: but he also puts into the picture their grounds and causes:

> Paul thinks he is a clear-headed, rational creature, irritated by the obscure complexities of Miriam's nature. But in fact he is in a far more complex emotional tangle than she; and the matter for such a reading of the situation is presented quite fully at the same time as his own quite different view. This is not a common achievement—to give the false judgement of a participant in a situation, to give it almost entirely through his eyes, yet to incorporate in it the grounds of a true judgement.[78]

Lawrence was, of course, by no means the first to make use of such a "point of view" in fiction: but it presents considerable difficulties to those readers who, not expecting it in a Lawrence novel, fail to take account of it.

Miriam is a romantic girl whose spirit seems to be always "dreaming in a land far away and magical". Like Emily in *The White Peacock* and Helena in *The Trespasser*, she is cut off from ordinary life by her religious intensity which makes the world for her "either a nunnery garden or a paradise, where sin and knowledge were not, or else an ugly, cruel thing".[79] She can rarely get into human relations with people. Her friend, her companion, her lover is Nature—probably because, as Lawrence says in his essay ". . . Love was Once a Little Boy", in one's love for nature everything comes so easy: there is nothing to oppose one's egoism. Nature, flowers, babies "are so lovable because they can't answer back".[80] Miriam madly wants her little brother to let her swathe him in love. Her intensity leaves no emotion on the normal plane. At the same time she is "gripped stiff" inside, and can never let herself go, or abandon herself to anything.

[78] Hough, p. 47.   [79] *Sons and Lovers*, p. 148.   [80] *S.L.C.*, p. 89.

The relationship of Paul and Miriam starts in an "atmosphere of subtle intimacy" born of their "common feeling for something in Nature". Paul is also drawn to Miriam because of the intensity to which she rouses him; in contact with her he gains insight into his work, and his vision goes deeper. They are both late in maturing, psychically even more than physically, and neither of them is conscious that there is any love growing between them. She is exceedingly sensitive, and the slightest grossness makes her recoil. So their intimacy goes on "in an utterly blanched and chaste fashion. It could never be mentioned that the mare was in foal."[81] They have holy communions over rose bushes, when the flowers seem to "kindle something in their souls", or they share mystic experiences in "shadowy religious places", their souls responding to each other—until Miriam discovers a serpent in the Eden of her pure, spiritual relationship with Paul, and then the conflict begins. Realising with shame and torment that she loves not only soul-communions with Paul but also Paul himself, she prays to God to keep her from loving him if she "ought not to love him". Then seeing the anomaly in her prayer—for if love was God's gift, how could it be wrong to love!—she decides to be "God's sacrifice" by loving Paul "as Christ would, who died for the souls of men".[82] Prayer is essential to her because it saves her from thinking and deciding for herself: real independence and self-responsibility are terrifying to her, as they are to so many.

Paul all this while is completely unaware that his attachment to Miriam amounts to anything more than a platonic friendship. "He was a fool who did not know what was happening to himself."[83] Their intimacy has been so abstract, "such a matter of the soul, all thought and weary struggle into consciousness" that he cannot think of themselves as lovers. When he is with Miriam all his natural fire of love is "transmitted into the fine stream of thought".[84] She, too, likes him best when he is wrestling with his own soul, "passionate in his desire for understanding". Then, having reduced him to the level of abstraction, if she puts her arm in his, it causes him

[81] *Sons and Lovers*, p. 162.   [82] *Op. cit.*, p. 172.
[83] *Op. cit.*, pp. 172-3.   [84] *Op. cit.*, p. 173.

almost torture: "It caused a violent conflict in him. . . . His consciousness seemed to split. The place where she was touching him ran hot with friction. He was one internecine battle, and he became cruel to her because of it."[85]

Returning home with Miriam from the seashore one evening, Paul suddenly becomes aware of an enormous orange moon staring at them from the rim of the sandhills. He stands still, looking at it, his blood seeming "to burst into flame" so that he can hardly breathe. He stands perfectly still, his heart beating heavily with desire: but he cannot get across to Miriam. She is only deeply moved and religious—her "best state" against which he is impotent. He himself is not clearly aware that what he wants at the moment is "to crush her on his breast to ease the ache there". The fact that he might want her as a man wants a woman has in him been suppressed into a shame. When she shrinks away from such a thought, he too winces to the depth of his soul. "And now this 'purity' prevented even their first love-kiss. It was as if she could scarcely stand the shock of physical love, even a passionate kiss, and then he was too shrinking and sensitive to give it."[86]

Paul puts the blame on Miriam for forcing him to be so spiritual, and hates her for making him in some way despise himself. In fact both of them are struggling at the same time to liberate themselves from the hold of "purity". His efforts are the more prominent because he is more vocal, and because the novel is more about him; she does not speak out but wonders all the same that if he does not really want to be spiritual with her why doesn't he be otherwise.[87] When she looks at him challengingly, he finds there is something which prevents him from kissing her. His own explanation is that it is the naked soul "in her great dark eyes" which comes in the way; it does not occur to him that he himself is as yet incapable of any but the spiritual-abstract relation which he has with her. He thinks he wants to give passion and tenderness to her, whereas she wants not him but only "the soul out of his body":

> He went on in his dead fashion:
> "If only you could want *me*, and not what I can reel off for you!"

---

[85] *Op. cit.*, p. 173.   [86] *Op. cit.*, p. 179.   [87] *Op. cit.*, p. 188.

"I!" she cried bitterly—"I! Why, when would you let me
take you?"

"Then it's my fault," he said, and, gathering himself
together, he got up and began to talk trivialities. He felt
insubstantial. In a vague way he hated her for it. And he
knew he was as much to blame himself. This, however, did
not prevent his hating her.[88]

One reason why Paul hates her is his awareness of the inadequacy in himself. He realises that her love is "too good for
him. . . . His own love was at fault, not hers."[89] He also
knows that before he can kiss her he will have to "drive something out of himself". Finding that their friendship neither
stays there nor gets anywhere else, he suggests to her that they
break off. "I can only give friendship," he tells her, "it's all
I'm capable of—it's a flaw in my make up. . . . Let's have
done."[90] Actually he is at this time incapable of giving her
anything. His deepest love is for his mother, to whom he has
gone back during this period, and he cannot give it to Miriam.
At the same time he cannot even love her physically "as a man
ought to love his wife", because sex has become so complicated
in him that it is for him a detached thing quite apart from actual
women: a woman is to him still much like his own mother,
and he is "full of the sense of [his] mother".[91] Looking at
Miriam singing "like a nun singing to heaven", or like "one
who sings beside a Boticelli Madonna, so spiritual",[92] he wishes
he could always be gentle and tender with her, "breathing
with her the atmosphere of reverie and religious dreams". She
seems to him to have "an eternal maidenhood" about her, and
he is afraid of hurting her.

Miriam herself does not believe she would ever have Paul:
but she is prepared to sacrifice herself for his sake. She only
sees "tragedy, sorrow and sacrifice ahead".[93] But she feels
she holds "the keys to his soul",[94] and vows to defend and keep
all the best of himself that Paul brings to her. He fights against
her persistently because of her desire to "absorb" him, to have
all his soul—which he cannot give her. She takes him one day

[88] *Op. cit.*, p. 194.   [89] *Op. cit.*, pp. 207-8.   [90] *Op. cit.*, p. 220.
[91] *Op. cit.*, p. 279.   [92] *Ibid.*   [93] *Op. cit.*, p. 215.
[94] *Op. cit.*, p. 223.

to the back garden to show him some daffodils, goes down on
her knees before a cluster and begins caressing the flowers with
her cheeks and mouth and brow, sipping them with fervid
kisses.[95] Paul, in anger and irritation, asks her why she cannot
have more restraint but must always be fondling things:

> "Can you never like things without clutching them as if
> you wanted to pull the heart out of them? . . . You wheedle the
> soul out of things. . . . You are always begging things to love
> you, as if you were a beggar for love. . . . You don't want to
> love—your eternal and abnormal craving is to be loved. You
> aren't positive, you're negative. You absorb, absorb, as if
> you must fill yourself with love, because you've got a shortage
> somewhere."[96]

Paul says all this mechanically, as if his fretted soul, "run hot
by thwarted passion, jetted off these sayings like sparks from
electricity". He has not the faintest notion of what he is
saying. Probably he is merely repeating what he has heard his
mother say about Miriam. What he says of her tendency to
"absorb" is, nevertheless, true; and this provides the "ground
for strife" between them. Miriam thinks Paul has desires for

---

[95] There are also a number of other scenes with flowers in the novel. It is
easy to notice the presence of flowers in various significant scenes and conclude
that they have a "symbolic" or "ritualistic" importance; but what precisely this
significance is, is difficult to say. Mark Spilka, who has commented in detail on
these floral scenes, holds that characters in the novel are judged again and again
by their relations with flowers. The most important of such revealing scenes, he
says, is the one which takes place between Paul and his rival sweethearts, Miriam
and Clara. But it is doubtful if one can attach the kind of significance he claims
for this and other similar scenes. The key to revelation, according to him, is in
the formula "How to Pick Flowers". (*The Love Ethic of D. H. Lawrence*, p. 53.)
But this surely is the view held by Miriam ["It is the spirit you pluck them in that
matters", (238) she says], whose attitude towards flowers Spilka unequivocally
condemns. Lawrence's own views are given in his essay "Nottingham and the
Mining Countryside" where he says:
> Now the love of flowers is a very misleading thing. Most women love flowers
> as possessions and as trimmings. They can't look at a flower, and wonder a
> moment, and pass on. If they see a flower that arrests their attention, they
> must at once pick it, pluck it. Possession! A possession! Something added
> on to *me*! And most of the so-called love of flowers today is merely this
> reaching out of possession and egoism: something I've *got*; something that
> embellishes *me*. (*Phoenix*, p. 137.)
That this is Miriam's attitude probably no one would dispute. But that Paul's
own attitude is very different is, to say the least, doubtful.
[96] *Sons and Lovers*, p. 218.

"higher" as well as "lower" things, but is confident that the desires which she arbitrarily calls "higher" would ultimately win. To put this to the test she arranges a meeting between him and Clara Dawes. The three of them go for a walk, and Miriam exults to see that she and Paul can still commune over flowers, enjoying the field of cowslips together, while Clara remains disconsolate, away. But Paul is getting more and more dissatisfied with his relation to Miriam, and when they are with Clara there is generally "a triangle of antagonism"[97] between them. Miriam is pained to find that Paul is capable of choosing the lesser in place of the higher. There follows "a long battle between him and her". Having been unfaithful to his "higher" self, he feels ashamed, then again rebels. "Those were the ever-recurring conditions."[98] She is his conscience still, but a conscience which is becoming too much for him now. He cannot just leave her because she does in a way hold what is best in him. The trouble, however, is that she takes no account of the rest of him "which was three-quarters". So he writes a letter to her saying he can give her only spirit-love, not embodied passion: "See, you are a nun. I have given you what I would give a holy nun—as a mystic monk to a mystic nun. . . . In all our relations no body enters."[99] He then goes on to tell her that if people marry they must live together as affectionate humans, not as two souls; and concludes that love in the common sense of the term is not possible between them. This brings to an end the first phase of his relationship with Miriam.

Paul, now twenty-three, is still a virgin. His sex-instinct, over-refined by Miriam, now grows particularly strong: and when he is in the company of Clara he finds a new self arising in him, "warning him that sooner or later he would have to ask one woman or another".[1] He would like to marry Miriam if only he could get over the obstacle of his "physical bondage": but he shrinks from all physical contact with her. There is, he thinks, a kind of overstrong virginity in both of them which they cannot break through: perhaps in his love for her there is "a strong desire battling with a still stronger shyness and virginity".[2] But Paul realises that if he is to overcome this

[97] *Op. cit.*, p. 249. [98] *Op. cit.*, p. 251. [99] *Ibid.*
[1] *Op. cit.*, p. 232. [2] *Op. cit.*, p. 278.

H

virginity, which has become a positive force in him, he must make an attempt with Miriam to deliberately break through. So he tells her that they have been "too fierce" in their "purity". Some sort of perversity in their souls, he suggests to her, "makes us not want, get away from, the very thing we want. We have to fight against that."[3] Miriam acquiesces, ready to let him "have what he liked of her". At first, while kissing her, the full gaze of love in her eyes watching him makes him feel "sacrificed to her purity". But in the darkness where he cannot see her but only feel her, his passion floods him and he asks her, "Sometime you will have me?" She is reluctant: but seeing he is disappointed, she clenches her body stiff and forces out of her shut teeth the words: "You *shall* have me." She has resolved that "she would submit religiously to the sacrifice".[4]

Paul now courts Miriam like a lover, but she never lets him leave himself "to the great hunger and impersonality of passion; he must be brought back to a deliberate, reflective creature. As if from a swoon of passion she called him back to the littleness, the personal relationship."[5] He wants his person to be left alone, but she insists on his looking at her with eyes full of tender love. "His eyes full of the dark, impersonal fire of desire, did not belong to her." The thick-voiced, oblivious Paul seems a stranger to her. She relinquishes herself to him, but as if in sacrifice with something of horror in it. Making love to her, Paul is unaware of her as a person: she is to him then only a woman.

> Later it began to rain. The pine-trees smelled very strong. Paul lay with his head on the ground, on the dead pine needles, listening to the sharp hiss of the rain—a steady, keen noise. His heart was down, very heavy. Now he realized that she had not been with him all the time, that her soul had stood apart, in a sort of horror. He was physically at rest, but no more. Very dreary at heart, very sad, and very tender, his fingers wandered over her face pitifully. Now again she loved him deeply. He was tender and beautiful.[6]

---

[3] *Op. cit.*, p. 282. [4] *Op. cit.*, p. 287.
[5] *Op. cit.*, p. 284. [6] *Op. cit.*, p. 286.

Miriam, like Helena in *The Trespasser*, fails to see that what she finds "tender and beautiful" is what has come out purified through the fire of passion at which she looks with such horror. Paul experiences a state of identification with "the great Being". For him it is a moment in eternity, when he feels "along with everything". He tells Miriam: "To be rid of our individuality, which is our will, which is our effort—to live effortless, a kind of curious sleep—that is very beautiful, I think; that is our after-life, our immortality."[7]

Paul's experience is valid enough, and an essential requisite for human fulfilment. But it is an experience in one direction only and therefore needs to be complemented by the experience of "higher", positive, creative love—for the fire of passion, in itself, only destroys and does not create. For one day Paul loves Miriam utterly, "to the last fibre of his being": but this never comes again, and his sense of failure grows stronger with the passage of time. He visits her when she is staying alone at her grandmother's cottage. They have the little house all to themselves:

> He never forgot seeing her as she lay on the bed. . . . And then he wanted her, but as he went forward to her, her hands lifted in a little pleading movement, and he looked at her face and stopped.[8]

Miriam lies there as if she has given herself up to sacrifice, "like a creature awaiting immolation". His blood falls back[9] and he asks her if she is sure she wants him. She answers "Yes", feeling she is doing something for him. He shuts his eyes and his blood beats back again. But afterwards there is a dull pain in his soul. This goes on: Paul wears Miriam out with passion, but has always to put her out of count and act from the brute strength of his own feelings. Within a week Paul knows that "it would never be a success between them".[10] That the relationship of Paul and Miriam should end in

---

[7] *Op. cit.*, pp. 287-8.   [8] *Op. cit.*, p. 289.

[9] Lawrence has presented the same situation and experience in his poem "Lotus and Frost" (*Poems*, I, pp. 96-7) also, where the lotus lilies of desire rise to the surface, but a "look of hatred" on them by the woman makes all the blossoms shut in pain and all the buds "sink over to die unopened".

[10] *Sons and Lovers*, p. 292.

failure was inevitable. At first they only meet at the high plane of abstraction, having soul communions and working for "understanding" between them. Then Paul, having yielded his soul to his mother, wants to make his love for Miriam entirely an affair of the body (as he does later with Clara, and fails again). He wants only "the impersonality of passion", which is merely one half of love; whereas Miriam, though admitting under Paul's influence that physical passion between lovers is right, wants only the pure communion of spiritual love, only merging and absorption, with "no separateness discovered, . . . no otherness admitted"[11]—which is the other half of love. For their love to have been whole there needed to be the sweet love of communion *and* the fierce love of sensual fulfilment, both together in one love. Of this, as things stand, neither of the two is capable.

Even after they have broken off Miriam is confident that Paul, having had his "baptism of fire in passion" with Clara, will ultimately return to give his life into her hands—for then, she thinks, he "would want to be owned, so that he could work".[12] In a state of despair and loneliness after his mother's death, Paul does turn to her. In this condition, when he feels weak and helpless, he would, if Miriam were to have the courage and strength to claim him, let her "take him and relieve him of the responsibility of himself".[13] But Miriam, much too ready to sacrifice herself for him, cannot take the initiative to claim his body and soul for herself. "Or was it a mate she wanted? Or did she want a Christ in him?" reflects Paul. It is the end between them: she is unutterably bitter that he has rejected her sacrifice; he is left with the "hate and misery of another failure".

Paul's relationship with Clara is partly like William's relation to Gypsy, and partly like his own relationship with Miriam in its later stages. As far as *his* role in the relationship is concerned, there is hardly any difference in his affairs with Miriam and with Clara. It has been generally supposed that

---

[11] *Phoenix*, p. 154.   [12] *Sons and Lovers*, p. 318.
[13] Paul, at the time, blames her for not doing so. But why should he expect Miriam to be responsible for him? Lawrence surely wants to convey the extent of despair into which Paul has fallen. He has, of course, to learn to be self-responsible before he can attain maturity.

Paul seeks to establish a spiritual relation with Miriam, and a sensual one with Clara. This is, however, a gross over-simplification of what actually happens in the novel. Just before he breaks with Miriam, Paul, on his side, has a purely physical—and *thereby* unsatisfactory—relationship with her. It is not just that Miriam is unable to respond to him sexually; it is equally that he himself is obliged, under his mother's influence, to leave his soul altogether out of the relationship. With Clara, too, the unsatisfactoriness in the relation comes in because Paul never gets into touch with her as an individual— she is for him merely a woman, indiscriminate representative of womanhood, useful for the gratification of his sexual needs.

Paul's relation with Clara Dawes begins as "perfectly honourable" friendship between man and woman, "such as any civilized persons might have".[14] He is not conscious of any sexual feelings connected with her. But the nature of their future relationship is already defined in an early scene which suggestively gives intimations of what is to come. Paul, Miriam, and Clara, going for a walk, see a great bay horse in the distance.

> The big red beast seemed to dance romantically through that dimness of green hazel drift, away there where the air was shadowy, as if it were in the past, among the fading bluebells that might have bloomed for Diedre or Iseult.[15]

Both the powerful stallion and the bluebells in their connexion with Iseult, convey suggestions of a dark, primeval world of passions. Clara, the emancipated suffragette, who has not yet been sexually awakened despite her marriage, at first approaches the stallion "half-fascinated, half-contemptuous"; a little later she is just fascinated by it; then she goes forward to stroke its neck in acceptance, and, finally, calls it "a beauty". Her cautious, hesitant approach is again emphasised when they actually come to the edge of the dark wood where the bluebells have flowed over into the open field. Paul thinks for a moment how terrified the wild men of old tribes must have been—both those who burst into open spaces from the dark woods and those who tip-toed into the unfamiliar darkness of the forests from

---

[14] *Sons and Lovers*, p. 276. [15] *Op. cit.*, p. 233.

the open—and remarks to Clara that she looks like one of the open space sort, apprehensive of going into the darkness of the woods.

Clara's own explanation why she had separated from her husband is that she "went to sleep" as she grew to be a woman and Baxter never managed to wake her up, never got at her; and when he tried to be brutal to her and to bully her because he hadn't got her, she left him. Paul, however, suspects that she herself is to blame in some way; that when Baxter turned out to be different from what she had imagined him to be, she made him feel as if he were nothing—which "knocked him to peices". When things did not work out well she became "the *femme incomprise*" and left him because she was only half-alive with him, the other half dormant, deadened. "And the dormant woman was the *femme incomprise*, and she had to be awakened."[16] It is Paul who effects this awakening in her. Together they have "the baptism of fire in passion". Having known the "immensity of passion", they feel like Adam and Eve when they lost their innocence and realised the magnificence of the power which "drove them out of Paradise and across the great night and the great day of humanity".[17] It is to both of them "an initiation and a satisfaction", and they let themselves be carried by the tremendous heave of the magnificent power which overwhelms them and with which they feel identified:

> All the while the peewits were screaming in the field. When he came to, he wondered what was near his eyes, curving and strong with life in the dark, and what voice it was speaking. Then he realized it was the grass, and the peewit was calling. The warmth was Clara's breathing heaving. He lifted his head and looked into her eyes. They were dark and shining and strange, life wild at the source staring into his life, stranger to him, yet meeting him; and he put his face on her throat, afraid. What was she? A strong, strange, wild life, that breathed with his in the darkness through this hour. It was all so much bigger than themselves that he was hushed. They had met, and included in their meeting the thrust of the manifold grass stems, the cry of the peewit, the wheel of the stars.[18]

---

[16] *Op. cit.*, p. 317.   [17] *Op. cit.*, p. 354.   [18] *Op. cit.*, p. 353.

This is a beautiful experience, a "verification" for both Paul and Clara: but it is not sufficient in itself to form the basis of a satisfactory relationship. It scarcely brings them nearer each other. Clara, in some way, is left unsatisfied: she feels she doesn't really get to Paul, never has him fully. There is some big, vital part in him she has no hold over: but she never actually tries to get it, or even to know what it is. He, too, is aware that these experiences with Clara are to him completely impersonal—something that happens because of her without his being related to her. "It was as if they had been blind agents of a great force."[19]

Paul and Clara love each other passionately, as far as it is a question of passion: but their love does not go deep enough. William's experience with Gyp is also Paul's experience with Clara: he loves her when he is with her and sees her "as *the woman*", but in daytime forgets of her existence completely. Clara feels bitter that he should come to her in his need to satisfy his "naked hunger ... strong and blind and ruthless in its primitiveness", but should take no account of her at other times. She complains to him that he seems to love her only at night, not in the daytime; and he feels "guilty under the accusation". Even the act of love, where Paul thinks they fulfil each other, comes to leave Clara more and more dissatisfied. She feels that he isn't all there with her, that he doesn't really want *her*, but something just for himself. "But is it *me* you want, or is it *It*?" she says to him.[20] And he again feels guilty under the accusation that he leaves Clara out of count and takes her simply as he would take any woman. He only knows that when he starts love-making, the emotion is always strong enough to carry with it reason, soul, blood—everything in a great sweep. For such moments when he carries her away, right away, Clara too is grateful to him. But such an experience fails her too often, and they rarely reach the height of the time when the peewits had called: "often they realized it had been a failure, not what they had wanted".[21] Each evening that they are together makes a split between them. All efforts they make to get near to each other only lead to a greater distance between the two. They know well that they would have to part sooner or later.

[19] *Op. cit.*, p. 354.   [20] *Op. cit.*, p. 363.   [21] *Op. cit.*, p. 364.

"Together they had received the baptism of life, each through the other: but now their missions were separate."[22]　Clara goes back to live with her husband in Sheffield and Paul "scarcely saw her again".

Sons and Lovers is mainly the story of Paul Morel's development; and Lawrence tells this story by unfolding to us the history of his changing relationships—in particular, his relationship with his mother and with Miriam Leivers and Clara Dawes.　The depiction of Paul's struggle to understand and face the conflicts in these relationships not only takes up the major part of the narrative but also gives it "form", of which Lawrence spoke in his letter defending the construction of the novel.　In one sense *Sons and Lovers* is a unique success: it is probably the only important novel in English which takes for its main theme a situation which Lawrence believed to be a fairly representative one, for his day.　"It's the tragedy of thousands of young men in England", he wrote to Edward Garnett when he had completed his novel.　It is surely possible to dispute the *extent* to which such a situation obtains in actual life—where a boy or a girl find themselves unable to fall in love because of the possessive love of a parent; and, of course, there is little possibility of the circumstances presented in the novel duplicating themselves exactly.　But—and one does not need to be a psychologist to perceive this—there is no doubt that excessive parental love tends to inhibit the growth of children, making it extremely difficult for some of them to adjust themselves, when they grow up, to the demands of their adult lives, especially their sex lives.　*Sons and Lovers* presents this argument dramatically in a most effective and convincing manner.　It impresses on the reader the long-term risks involved in too intimate—even if non-libidinous—family relationships which appear to flourish so very well in the short run.　If such a relationship as Mrs Morel's with Paul only prevents the son from finding proper fulfilment in life, then— the novel suggests—we must look closely into our ideas about parent-child relationship in order to ensure that every child has the opportunity of a free and full development.

The sections of the novel which deal with Paul's love affairs

[22] *Op. cit.*, p. 361.

with Miriam and Clara depict the successes and the failures, the harmonies and the conflicts in the relationships with remarkable accuracy and power. But the technique used here, though it probably lends to the narrative a greater feel of life-as-it-is-actually-lived, has prevented many from grasping their significance in the total scheme of the novel. Paul's inability to establish a satisfactory relationship with either Miriam or Clara should be seen to be directly related to the excessive attachment between him and Mrs Morel. It must also be said that the achievement of *Sons and Lovers* in this part of the book is overshadowed by Lawrence's far more brilliant and outstanding achievement in his next two novels—*The Rainbow* and *Women in Love*—where he draws with a rare beauty and incomparable power possibly the best imaginatively realised picture in the English language of the conflict-ridden relations between men and women in search of a satisfying, harmonious, and meaningful life together.

IV

There Must be a New World

LAWRENCE's letter to Edward Garnett about characterisation in *The Rainbow* has been so frequently quoted and so variously commented on that there is an obvious risk of many a reader being misled by his vague familiarity with it into believing that he has understood its meaning and significance. The letter is, no doubt, a very important declaration of Lawrence's concerning his aim and method in novel-writing, and must be read in full together with his other comments on the subject. One or two points, however, must be made clear, as their implications are not at once obvious, and as they have been completely misunderstood by many who have attempted lengthy explanations of them.

Having stated that he takes a different attitude towards his characters—which necessitates a different attitude in the reader, too—Lawrence goes on to say:

> ... somehow—that which is physic—non-human, in humanity, is more interesting to me than the old-fashioned human element —which causes one to conceive a character in a certain moral scheme and make him consistent. The certain moral scheme is what I object to ... it is the inhuman will, call it physiology, or like Marinetti—physiology of matter, that fascinates me. I don't so much care about what the woman *feels*—in the ordinary usage of the word. That presumes an *ego* to feel with. I only care about what the woman *is*—what she IS—inhumanly, physiologically, materially—according to the use of the word: but for me, what she *is* as a phenomenon (or as representing some greater, inhuman will), instead of what she feels according to the human conception. ... You mustn't look in my novel for the old stable *ego*—of the character. There is another *ego*, according to whose action the individual is unrecognizable, and passes through, as it were, allotropic states which it needs

a deeper sense than any we've been used to exercise, to discover are states of the same single radically unchanged element. (Like as diamond and coal are the same pure single element of carbon. The ordinary novel would trace the history of the diamond—but I say, 'Diamond, what! This is carbon.' And my diamond might be coal or soot, and my theme is carbon.)[1]

In any discussion of the above statement it is absolutely necessary to bear in mind (a) the special use Lawrence makes of words like "ego", "human element", and "inhuman will", and (b) the stress he lays on his concern with what a character *is*.

The "ego", according to Lawrence, is the sum total of what we *conceive* ourselves to be. And that which a man conceives himself to be is far different from his real self, his essential and unique nature which cannot be analysed or explained, but which can be experienced in every single instance. What we imagine ourselves to be is denoted by the term "personality"— the mental-subjective self. A personality, as distinct from a character, is a self-conscious *I am*. Most of us today are reduced to mere "personalities". Man in his self-consciousness has made a picture of himself and now lives more or less from that picture, from without inwards. Men and women have come to live automatically according to some image—" 'A good little girl'—'a brave boy'—'a noble woman'—'a strong man'—'a productive society'—'a progressive humanity'—it is all the picture."[2] The ordinary novel takes this "human element" in humanity for its subject. But the little conscious ego or the mental concept which we falsely call ourselves—"that doll-like entity . . . made in ridiculous likeness"[3] of a person—is not all of a human being. Life is lived not just at the social, conventional level. Beneath the daily, superficial self of a character lies the real, essential self. As Will Brangwen in *The Rainbow* comes to realise after his marriage with Anna, "things are not what they seem" outwardly.

> It was as if the surface of the world had been broken away entire: Ilkeston, streets, church, people, work, rule-of-the-day, all intact; and yet peeled away into unreality, leaving here exposed the inside, the reality: one's own being, strange

---

[1] *Collected Letters*, I, pp. 281-2.   [2] *Phoenix*, p. 380.   [3] *S.L.C.*, p. 103.

feelings and passions and yearnings and beliefs and aspirations, suddenly become present, revealed, the permanent bedrock, knitted one rock with the woman one loved. It was confounding.[4]

Again, after the birth of his daughter Ursula, he learns to recognise and to submit to "the awful, obliterated sources which were the origin of his living tissue. He was not what he conceived himself to be! Then he was what he was, unknown, potent, dark."[5]

A character in *The Rainbow*, says Lawrence, passes through, as it were, allotropic states which are, nevertheless, the states of the "same single radically unchanged element". The implication—and much criticism has floundered here—is *not* that all characters are ultimately, in their essence, the same[6]—which would in fact be the exact opposite of Lawrence's repeatedly proclaimed belief in the uniqueness of each individual. What Lawrence is saying here—in defence, we must remember, of his novel's "psychology"—is that unless a reader is prepared to bring to his reading of this novel "a deeper sense than we've been used to exercise", he might fail to recognise a character when it passes through very different phases of life experience. In his essay on "The Novel" Lawrence defines character as "the flame of a man, which burns brighter or dimmer, bluer or yellower or redder, rising or sinking or flaring according to the draughts of circumstance and the changing air of life, *changing itself continually*, *yet remaining one single*, *separate flame*, flickering in a strange world".[7] Towards the end of *The Rainbow* Ursula, looking back at her past, realises that in all the varied phases of her life she has been so different, and yet always the same Ursula Brangwen. What she really, positively is, she even now does not know:

[4] *The Rainbow* (Phoenix Edition), p. 146.

[5] *Op. cit.*, p. 208.

[6] Even Julian Moynahan who is otherwise highly appreciative of Lawrence's achievement in *The Rainbow* completely confuses the issue when he says: "If the essence of a character is carbon, then the essence of all characters is carbon, and you cannot write a novel about carbon and nothing but carbon". (Moynahan, pp. 41-2.) See also A. Huxley's: "Most of us are more interested in diamonds and coal than in undifferentiated carbon, however vividly described". (Introduction to *Letters*.)

[7] *S.L.C.*, p. 75. (Italics added.)

That which she was, positively, was dark and unrevealed, it could not come forth. . . . This world in which she lived was like a circle lighted by a lamp. This lighted area, lit up by man's completest consciousness, she thought was all the world: that here all was disclosed for ever. Yet all the time, within the darkness she had been aware of points of light, like the eyes of wild beasts, gleaming, penetrating, vanishing. And her soul had acknowledged in a great heave of terror only the outer darkness. This inner circle of light in which she lived and moved, wherein the trains rushed and the factories ground out their machine-produce and the plants and animals worked by the light of science and knowledge, suddenly it seemed like the area under an arc-lamp, wherein the moths and children played in the security of blinding light, not even knowing there was any darkness, because they stayed in the light.[8]

The "lighted area", the "inner circle of light", is all that the ordinary novelist sees. This is the world of "humanity": "men clotting together into social masses in order to limit their individual liabilities".[9] The "diamond" whose history the ordinary novel traces is the character conceived in a dull, old, dead moral scheme and made at all costs consistent to it. But if characters in a novel keep on behaving according to some fixed pattern, they cease to live and "the novel falls dead". However, when Lawrence says, "Diamond, what! This is carbon. And my diamond might be coal or soot, and my theme is carbon", the inference to be drawn, again, is *not* that he does not write at all about the life of his characters at the social, conventional level. He obviously does, and at great length. Only, he is not content with seeing life at this level or depicting his characters as mere personalities;[10] his vision goes deeper to the level of "carbon"—which he claims to be his distinctive theme. It was not just the artist's vanity which led him to state that he believed his novel was "great—so new, so really a stratum deeper than I think anybody has ever gone in a novel".[11] In addition to what an ordinary novel does, Lawrence's novels —from *The Rainbow* onwards—seek to realise the "non-human" quality of life. "Damn humanity," he writes in one of his letters, "let me have a bit of inhuman or non-human truth, that

[8] *The Rainbow*, pp. 437-8. [9] *S.L.C.*, p. 71.
[10] Unless, of course, they are just that. [11] *Collected Letters*, I, p. 193.

our fuzzy emotions can't alter."[12]   He says he does not care
for what a woman *feels* with her ego, only for what she *is*.[13]   His
interest is not in emotions or personal feelings and attachments,
which are merely expressive—and whose expression has, moreover, become mechanical—but in the tremendous unknown
forces of life, coming into us unseen and "driving us, forcing us,
destroying us if we do not submit to be swept away".[14]   It is by
revealing to us these dark, unknown forces in operation that
Lawrence hopes to show his characters as they "inhumanly,
physiologically, materially" are.   Behind all living characters
stands the felt but unnamed and unknown flame, and if the
novelist makes his characters "too personal, too human", the
flame dies out and what we are then left with is "something
awfully lifelike, and as lifeless as most people are".[15]   Earl
Brewster reports Lawrence's remark to him that "it is not the
incidents which befall a character that are important, but
what that character is".[16]   And a character in a Lawrence novel
is what it is only in relation to other characters and to its
surroundings.   Lawrence's main interest, thus, lay not in ego-
determined personalities, or in their fixed, socially-determined
relations, but in the living, changing relationships of essential
individual beings below the level of their fully conscious selves.
Lawrence, concluding his letter, warns Garnett that he should
not expect *The Rainbow* to develop along conventional lines, but
should look for the action of the ordinarily-unrecognised vital
instincts and impulses, those great unseen forces which give
shape both to the characters and to the novel as a whole:

> You must not say my novel is shaky—it is not perfect, because
> I am not expert in what I want to do.   But it is the real thing,
> say what you like.   And I shall get my reception; if not now,
> then before long.   Again I say, don't look for the development

---

[12] *Op. cit.*, p. 491.

[13] It is worthwhile recalling here Lawrence's letter of 17 Jan. 1913 to Ernest
Collings: "I conceive a man's body as a kind of flame, like a candle flame, forever
upright and yet flowing: and the intellect is just the light that is shed on the things
around.   And I am not so much concerned with the things around—which is
really mind—but with the mystery of the flame forever flowing, coming God
knows how from out of practically nowhere, and being *itself*, whatever there is
around it, that it lights up".   (*Collected Letters*, I, p. 180.)

[14] *Collected Letters*, I, p. 291.   [15] *S.L.C.*, p. 69.   [16] *D. H. Lawrence*, p. 13.

of the novel to follow the lines of certain characters: the characters fall into the form of some other rhythmic form, as when one draws a fiddle-bow across a fine tray delicately sanded, the sand takes lines unknown.[17]

The rules of construction followed by the "traditional" novel can have hardly any relevance in making a judgement about such a work. So when Arnold Bennett criticised *The Rainbow* for lacking construction, Lawrence wrote to his literary agent J. B. Pinker:

> Tell Arnold Bennett that all rules of construction hold good only for novels which are copies of other novels. A book which is not a copy of other books has its own construction, and what he calls faults, he being an old imitator, I call characteristics. I shall repeat till I am grey—when they have as good a work to show, they may make their pronouncements *ex cathedra*. Till then, let them learn decent respect.[18]

What is *The Rainbow* about? What makes it a great novel? Why has it been generally regarded, with *Women in Love*, as Lawrence's most significant work? There is no short and simple answer to these questions. With rich and complex works of art like *The Rainbow* there cannot be any short and simple answers. Lawrence himself, commenting at different times, laid stress on one or the other aspect of the novel's intention.[19] Something, however, must be said about what the novel is primarily not and was not intended to be. To begin with, Lawrence does not offer *The Rainbow* as a record of English social history. This is not to deny the book its value as a chronicle: but any claim made for the novel's greatness based on its accurate documentation of certain social conditions is a claim based on the novel's incidentals. F. R. Leavis thinks Lawrence is unsurpassed—even incomparable—as a social historian among novelists, and points to "the incomparable wealth" of *The Rainbow* "as social and cultural history".[20] His

---

[17] *Collected Letters*, I, p. 282.   [18] *Op. cit.*, p. 399.

[19] While it is necessary to make a distinction (as Eliseo Vivas does) between the "intention" of a novel and that of a novelist—for the two are not necessarily the same—I have come across no evidence to suggest that Lawrence failed to realise his "intention" in any of his novels.

[20] Leavis, p. 134.

discussion of the novel as "a study of contemporary civilization" is excellent. But by restricting his attention to the novel's achievement as a record of "the history of civilization in England", he misses much of the essential meaning of the work. Marvin Mudrick qualifies the status of *The Rainbow* as "a brilliant record of English manners and morals" by stressing the novel's basic assumption that "the relationship between husband and wife is the central fact of human existence".[21] Some of the conclusions Mudrick arrives at are questionable, but he is certainly right in seeing the question of human relationships as the key issue in the novel. Writing to Edward Garnett in April 1913, Lawrence had declared that *the problem* of the day was the establishment of a new relation between men and women. It is primarily these relationships of men and women, with all their tensions and conflicts—as well as the relations of parents and children, and of men and women to the life of nature around them—which Lawrence presents with his inimitable power in *The Rainbow*.

Secondly, *The Rainbow* does *not* offer sex as a solution to the problems of the modern man. On the contrary, it affirms that sex is not and cannot be the answer to the issues raised by the complexity of modern civilisation. It is entirely misleading to say that Lawrence thought "the only hope for man" in the present industrial-technological era lay in the "fullest possible realization of the sexual impulse".[22] Julian Moynahan, rightly seeing "the redemption" offered by the novel in "maximum relatedness in mysterious association with maximum individuation",[23] nevertheless shows confusion in thinking when he makes the claim that the theme of *The Rainbow* is "salvation" attained through "the crucial relation . . . between a man and a woman in marital and sexual experience".[24] The central argument of the novel, in fact, is that whatever limited salvation the earlier generations might have found in their sex lives, for Ursula, the modern woman, sexual experience alone offers no salvation at all. The relation of man to woman remains the central fact in actual human life, but sexual consummation, by itself, cannot lead to complete fulfilment. In sex is only half our fulfilment;

---

[21] *Miscellany*, p. 61.   [22] Mudrick in *Miscellany*, p. 70.
[23] Moynahan, pp. 46-7.   [24] *Op. cit.*, p. 43.

and when sex becomes an end in itself, Lawrence later on wrote in *Fantasia*, the only result can be disaster and death. Asked about the message of *The Rainbow*, Lawrence wrote in a letter:

> I don't know myself what it is: except that the older world is done for, toppling on top of us: and that it's no use the men looking to the women for salvation, nor the women looking to sensuous satisfaction for their fulfilment. There must be a new world.[25]

In another letter written at the time that Lawrence was correcting the proofs of *The Rainbow* he had said:

> Whatever else it is, it is the voyage of discovery towards the real and eternal and unknown land.[26]

The novel, then, is concerned with giving an account of this journey towards the "new world", the "unknown land". Ursula is given a glimpse of the Rainbow at the end of the book, but the bulk of the narrative only describes the Flood, the deluge which precedes its appearance. *The Rainbow*, in this sense, is a destructive work, though not purely destructive. Lawrence called it "destructive-consummating", referring to the novel's "working up to the dark sensual or Dionysic or Aphrodisic ecstasy".[27] There is a great consummation in this sensual ecstasy, even if it is a "consummation in death". And, at the same time, the frictional, destructive, dark sensuality is also the way towards self-realisation, towards the discovery of one's single, separate self. Lawrence in his letter of 22 Apr. 1914 described the theme of *The Wedding Ring* (as the novel was then called) as: "woman becoming individual, self-responsible, taking her own initiative." Whatever else Ursula's experiences have meant to her, they have revealed to her that beneath her outward, conscious, social self she has another true and real self. One critic, A. L. Clements, has very convincingly argued[28] that the quest for the self is the central and unifying theme of *The Rainbow*. He however, under-estimates the importance of

---

[25] *Collected Letters*, I, p. 422.   [26] *Letters*, p. 240.
[27] *Collected Letters*, I, p. 519.
[28] "The Quest for the Self: D. H. Lawrence's *The Rainbow*", *Thoth* (Univ. of Syracuse) III (Spring 1962), pp. 90-100.

I

human relationships in the novel, and mistakenly sets up the quest for selfhood against the subject of relationships. The two themes are really closely related and interdependent: the "quest for the self" is carried on by a character in a Lawrence novel by entering into various relationships; and having found "the self" there is nothing an individual can do with it except keep it in a living relationship with the "circumambient universe".

> My source and issue is in two infinities, I am founded in the two infinities. But absolute is the rainbow that goes between: the iris of my very being.[29]

The quotation is from Lawrence's essay "The Crown" written soon after the completion of *The Rainbow*. The two infinities referred to are the infinity of the past (or the Pagan infinity) and the infinity of the future (or the Christian infinity). A man must know both eternities in order to achieve consummate being. His fulfilment is dual: in flesh and in spirit, in darkness and in light. In order to attain "wholeness of being", man must find fulfilment in two directions, represented in fictional terms in the first few pages of *The Rainbow* by "the teeming life of creation" on the Marsh Farm in which the men are immersed, and "the activity of man in the world at large" to which the women on the Farm aspire. In a way, the development of the entire novel is suggested in its very first paragraph which deals with the life of the Brangwens on the Marsh farm: whenever one of the Brangwen men working in the fields lifts his head from his work he sees on a hill two miles away the church-tower at Ilkeston; so that even when he turns again to the horizontal land he is aware of "something standing above him and beyond him in the distance". It is this "something unknown", as yet above and beyond the Brangwens, which must be added on to their life for it to be complete. (The women on the farm already yearn for this "finer, more vivid circle of life"—if not for themselves, then for their children.) The horizontal of the land (the life of "blood-intimacy") and the vertical of the church tower ("the higher form of being") must be brought together in the complete arch of the rainbow.

[29] *R.D.P.*, p. 27.

The Brangwen men live in close relationship to the land on which they work. They feel "the pulse and body of the soil"; they know "the intercourse between heaven and earth"; their bodies are "impregnated with the day, cattle and earth and vegetation and the sky". And this life with all its interrelations is enough for them. But the women on the Marsh Farm want another and higher form of life than this, for which they look out from the "heated, blind intercourse of farm-life" to the spoken world beyond "where men moved dominant and creative, having turned their back on the pulsing heat of creation, and with this behind them, were set out to discover what was beyond".[30] Their eyes are fixed on the battle being waged on the edge of "the unknown", on men fighting "outwards to knowledge". They, too, crave "to know", and thus to achieve a higher form of being.

Life on the Marsh Farm is brought nearer to the unknown life beyond when a canal is constructed across the farm's meadows and, a short time afterwards, a colliery sunk on the other side of the canal. The "invasion" becomes complete when the Midland Railway comes down the valley, bringing prosperity to the Brangwens, and making them almost tradesmen. As they work in the fields now the shrill whistle of the trains re-echoes through their hearts "with fearsome pleasure, announcing the far-off come near and imminent":

> As they drove home from town, the farmers of the land met the blackened colliers trooping from the pit-mouth. As they gathered the harvest, the west wind brought a faint, sulphurous smell of pit-refuse burning. As they pulled the turnips in November, the sharp clink-clink-clink-clink-clink of empty trucks shunting on the line, vibrated in their hearts with the fact of other activity going on beyond them.[31]

The Brangwens still live a more or less protected life. The Alfred Brangwen of this period is able to lead a relatively simple, uncomplicated existence with his wife: the two are "very separate beings", knowing nothing of each other, yet vitally connected and living in their separate ways from one root. It is when their youngest child Tom is growing up that conflicts

---

[30] *The Rainbow*, p. 3.   [31] *Op. cit.*, p. 7.

and complexities begin to appear because of his contacts with
the "unknown" world, the "beyond".

Tom is sent forcibly to a grammar school by his mother
whose aspiration is that he should grow up to be a gentleman.
He, however, knows his own limitations and has the fore-
knowledge that he would be a failure from the first. He is
more sensuously developed than other boys, more refined in
instinct; his feelings are more discriminating. But when it
comes to mental things, he is at a disadvantage. So he is glad
when he leaves school to return home. Back on the farm he is
in his own again and grows up "very fresh and alert, with zest
for every moment of life". Once, he gets drunk in a public
house and goes upstairs with a prostitute. He is then nineteen.
The experience proves to be "so nothing, so dribbling and
functional" that it comes as a shock to him. Also, woman so
far has been to him "the symbol of that further life which com-
prised religion and love and morality". Now the disillusion of
his first carnal contact with woman strengthens his "innate
desire to find in a woman the embodiment of all his inarticulate,
powerful religious impulses".[32]

One Whitsuntide while Tom, now twenty-four, is out with
two other young fellows, he meets a handsome, reckless girl
neglected for an afternoon by the man who had brought her out.
He glows with pleasure when his "most glorious adventure"
with this girl turns out to be quite different from his first
experience with the prostitute. Later on he meets and talks to
the man also, a middle-aged foreigner, and the "fine" contact
with the "exquisite graciousness" of the stranger sets his whole
being in a whirl. He becomes conscious that there is still so
much outside his knowledge, and wonders whether life really
is as he has so far known it. Of the two experiences—with the
girl, and with the foreigner—it is the meeting with the middle-
aged stranger which seems to him the more significant. After
this encounter he dreams day and night of an intimacy with
subtle-mannered, fine-textured people—which, somehow, also
includes "the satisfaction of a voluptuous woman". He is
already on the look-out for a Lydia Lensky; so that when he
actually meets her it is for him, as it were, the fulfilment of a

---

[32] *Op. cit.*, p. 14.

dream. For the time being, however, he takes recourse to drink and solitude in order to suppress his consciousness that he really wants something more than the world of Cossethay and Ilkeston can offer: it is a very strong root which holds him to the Farm, and yet he knows that he does not really belong to the "commonplace unreality" around him.

Then, one day, as he is returning with a load of seed from Cossethay, he sees Lydia walk past him. "That's her", he says involuntarily, "a pain of joy" running through him. The mere sight of her transports him to a "far world, not Cossethay, a far world . . . beyond reality" (*i.e.* beyond the reality of Cossethay and Ilkeston). He already feels curiously certain about her, as if she were destined to him. And when he learns that she is the widow of a Polish doctor, a foreigner ("she belonged to somewhere else"), it is with "profound satisfaction" that he receives the news.

> A swift change had taken place on the earth for him, as if a new creation were fulfilled, in which he had real existence. Things had all been stark, unreal, barren, mere nullities before. Now they were actualities that he could handle.[33]

He does not yet clearly know what he wants. Then, as he is working alone on the land, "the facts and material of his daily life fell away, leaving the kernel of his purpose clean". It now comes upon him that he must marry Lydia. He feels he is only fragmentary, something incomplete, and that unless she comes to him he would remain as a nothingness: "without her he was nothing. . . . But with her, he would be real . . . she would bring him completeness and perfection."[34]

Tom is drawn to Lydia because of her foreignness. But just because she is such a stranger for him he cannot get definitely into touch with her. He finds he knows her so little. It is only after their marriage that in his moments of overwhelming passion Tom can let himself go from past and future and is reduced to the moment with her. Then they are together in "an elemental embrace" beyond their superficial differences. But afterwards he finds she is still foreign and unknown to him, and living in contact with her seems to him like living in

---

[33] *Op. cit.*, p. 26.   [34] *Op. cit.*, p. 35.

contact with "the unknown, the unaccountable and incalculable".[35] This fills him with rage and antagonism at times, and he walks about for days stiffened with resistance to her. Then suddenly, as if out of nowhere,[36] there comes to be a connexion between them. The tension, the bond, bursts and the flood of passion breaks forward "into a tremendous, magnificent rush". This hour, too, passes away, and again there is severance between them.

> But no matter. They had had their hour, and should it chime again, they were ready for it, ready to renew the game at the point where it was left off, on the edge of the outer darkness, when the secrets within the woman are game for the man, hunted doggedly, when the secrets of the woman are the man's adventure, and they both give themselves to the adventure.
>   She was with child, and there was again the silence and distance between them. She did not want him nor his secrets nor his game, he was deposed, he was cast out. He seethed with fury at the small, ugly-mouthed woman who had nothing to do with him. Sometimes his anger broke on her, but she did not cry. She turned on him like a tiger, and there was battle.[37]

The battle goes on between them. As the months of her pregnancy go by, Lydia begins to leave him more and more alone, becomes less and less aware of him until he feels his existence is annulled. Then he wants to break her into acknowledgement of him, into awareness of him. He, finally, gives up and turns to his step-child Anna for sympathy and love.

When Tom Brangwen sees his wife happily absorbed in nursing his newly-born son, a pain goes over him "like a thin flame", for he perceives that he must subdue himself in his approach to her. He wants once again the exchange of love and passion such as he has had at first with her. She comes to him and it seems that it is once again going to be as it was before: but her passion dies down before he wants it to die

---

[35] *Op. cit.*, p. 55.
[36] We are reminded of the tremendous, unknown forces of life coming into us unseen—representing the "non-human quality of life" of Lawrence's letter to Garnett.
[37] *The Rainbow*, p. 58.

down. He wants to go on, whereas she can take no more. So he has to learn the bitter lesson to abate himself.

> She could only want him in her own way, and to her own measure. And she had spent much life before he found her as she was, the woman who could take him and give him fulfilment. She had taken him and given him fulfilment. She still could do so, in her own times and ways. But he must control himself, measure himself to her.
>
> He wanted to give her all his love, all his passion, all his essential energy. But it could not be. He must find other things than her, other centres of living.[38]

But Brangwen, instead of turning his current of life to some creative purpose, instead of developing his consciousness towards a "higher form of being", forms another centre of love in the child, Anna, and also begins to drink heavily now and again. Only once—after his meeting with Mrs Forbes, his brother Alfred's mistress—does he return home despising himself for his own poor way of life. He realises that in spite of his marriage to a "lady" he has remained a prisoner to the life on the farm, sitting safe and easy and unadventurous: "He was a clod-hopper and a boor, dull, stuck in the mud." More than ever he wishes to clamber out, to "this visionary polite world". But when he gets back to the Marsh, he sees how fixed everything is; and as the excitement of the visit begins to pass off, he subsides again into his restricted life with his wife and Anna. His relation with Lydia is not altogether satisfactory. She complains to him bitterly that he either leaves her alone, or takes her like cattle, quickly, to forget her again. When she tries to make it up with him, he is drawn to her, and yet is unable to let himself go. Something in him shrinks from yielding to her, resists the relaxing towards her, opposes the mingling with her, even while he most desires it. He is afraid of "the awful unknown" in her. Gradually, however, the tension within him relaxes, and he yields himself to "the subterranean force of his desire" to be with her, to mingle with her in order to find himself in her.

> Their coming together now, after two years of married life, was much more wonderful to them than it had been before.

[38] *Op. cit.*, p. 78.

> It was the entry into another circle of existence, it was the
> baptism of another life, it was the complete confirmation. . . .
> She was the doorway to him, he to her. At last they had thrown
> open the doors, each to the other, and had stood in the door-
> ways facing each other, whilst the light flooded out from behind
> on to each of their faces, it was the transfiguration, glorification,
> the admission.[39]

He does not know her, as a "person", any better or any more
precisely now than he did before. He does not understand her
foreign nature, or her foreign speech. "But he knew her, he
knew her meaning, without understanding":

> What did it matter, that Anna Lensky was born of Lydia and
> Paul? God was her father and her mother. He had passed
> through the married pair without fully making Himself known
> to them.
>   Now he was declared to Brangwen and to Lydia Brangwen,
> as they stood together. When at last they had joined hands,
> the house was finished, and the Lord took up his abode. And
> they were glad. . . .
>   Anna's soul was put at peace between them. She looked
> from one to the other, and she saw them established to her
> safety, and she was free. She played between the pillar of fire
> and the pillar of cloud in confidence, having the assurance on
> her right hand and the assurance on her left. She was no
> longer called upon to uphold with her childish might the
> broken end of the arch. Her father and her mother now met
> to the span of the heavens, and she, the child, was free to play
> in the space beneath, between.[40]

Love between Tom and Lydia, as far as love goes, is undoubtedly a success. It brings fulfilment to their lives—though
not complete fulfilment. The flesh is fulfilled but the spirit is
not. Lydia, reminiscing after the death of Tom Brangwen, feels
grateful to him because through him she had "come to her own
self". Tom, too, is proud of the sensual consummation he has
had with his wife. But when, just before Anna's marriage, he
looks back at his life as a whole he is not satisfied: he feels there
is something missing in his life.

<hr/>

[39] *Op. cit.*, p. 91.   [40] *Op. cit.*, pp. 91-2.

Was his life nothing? Had he nothing to show, no work? He did not count his work, anybody could have done it. What had he known, but the long, marital embrace with his wife! Curious, that this was what his life amounted to! At any rate, it was something, it was eternal. He would say so to anybody and be proud of it. He lay with his wife in his arms, and she was still his fulfilment, just the same as ever. And that was the be-all and the end-all. Yes, and he was proud of it.

But the bitterness, underneath, that there still remained an unsatisfied Tom Brangwen, who suffered agony because a girl cared nothing for him. He loved his sons—he had them also. But it was the further, the creative life with the girl, he wanted as well.[41]

Tom had first turned to Anna when Lydia, pregnant with his first son, had started ignoring him, leaving him more and more alone. He had then found his "chiefest source of solace" in the child to whom he had appealed with all his power for affection. The growth of the bond of love between father and child is admirably described by Lawrence, especially in the beautifully rendered scene in which Tom takes little Anna— clamouring blindly, insistently, for her mother who is in labour at the time—to the barn where, watched by the child, he feeds the cows, and then the two sit still listening to the snuffing and breathing of the cows for a long time. As Anna grows up she comes to depend more and more on her father who stands "like a rock" between her and the world. Then the time comes when this relationship has to come to an end. At eighteen Anna, in love with Will, wants a life of her own. But Tom cannot bear it that she should want to go away from him, leaving a void, "an unendurable emptiness in him".[42] He feels bitter that he should be isolated from her, with a generation between them:

> The child who clung to him wanted her child-husband. As was natural. And from him, Brangwen, she wanted help, so that her life might be properly fitted out. But love she did not want. Why should there be love between them, between the stout, middle-aged man and this child? How could there be anything between them, but mere human willingness to help each other? He was her guardian, no more.[43]

---

[41] *Op. cit.*, pp. 124-5. [42] *Op. cit.*, p. 115. [43] *Op. cit.*, pp. 123-4.

Anna now wants to be rid of her dependence on her parents and to get away from the atmosphere of rich, inarticulate Brangwen intimacy of her home. And she lays hold of Will as a means of escape to a different world. "In him the bounds of her experience were transgressed: he was the hole in the wall, beyond which the sunshine blazed on an outside world."[44]

The relationship between Will and Anna, however, is not going to be an easy one because of the radical difference in their natures. A hasty reading of the novel might suggest that Will, with his love for Gothic arches and church architecture, belongs to the "daylight" world of purposive activity and higher consciousness, while Anna tends to immerse herself in a life of procreation and domesticity. But in fact the case is just the reverse. Will only seeks a dark emotional experience in the church, shunning the world of man's activity, whereas Anna, like the Brangwen women of the first chapter, clings to "the worship of the human knowledge" and to her belief in the "omnipotence of the human mind".[45] As long as they stick to their positions rigidly a continuous battle between them is inevitable. The early sheaf-gathering scene[46] enacts synoptically the entire story of their future relationship, suggesting the conflicts of adjustment implicit in their different, opposed natures, and foretelling how for a long time Anna, Anna Victrix, will be "always first", Will following a little way behind, until they finally meet.

Anna's very first impressions of Will are meaningful: he reminds her, significantly, of "some animal, some mysterious animal that lived in the darkness under the leaves and never came out, but which lived vividly, swift and intense".[47] Will is "only half-articulate".[48] The church—the church building —has an irresistible attraction for him, but the church teaching

[44] *Op. cit.*, p. 109.

[45] *Op. cit.*, p. 169. That this will not take her very far, and that in spite of her higher aspirations she will, like Lettie in *The White Peacock*, end up in a life of prolific domesticity, is also hinted at in Lawrence's description of her appearance at her wedding, reminiscent of the import of similar passages in his first novel: "Oh, a vain white peacock of a bride perching herself on the top of the wall and giving her hand to the bridegroom on the other side, to be helped down. The vanity of her white, slim, daintily-stepping feet, and her arched neck". (*The Rainbow*, p. 132.)

[46] *The Rainbow*, pp. 116-20.   [47] *Op. cit.*, p. 102.   [48] *Op. cit.*, p. 108.

in itself means nothing to him. "In church he wanted a dark, nameless emotion, the emotion of all the great mysteries of passion."[49] What matters to him is the feeling that Church arouses in him; what really counts is his dark emotional experience of the Infinite, of the Absolute. He attaches little importance to his social life, his life among men: his "dark, inhuman" soul cares nothing for humanity. He prefers things he cannot understand with the mind. Anna is bitter against him because he lets his mind sleep: "That which was human, belonged to mankind, he would not exert."[50] When she forces him to question his belief in some of his passionately held "unquestioned concepts", he feels she is destroying him:

> Did he believe the water turned to wine at Cana? She would drive him to the thing as a historical fact: so much rain-water—look at it—can it become grape-juice, wine? For an instant he saw with the clear eyes of the mind and said no, his clear mind, answering her for a moment, rejected the idea. And immediately his whole soul was crying in a mad, inchoate hatred against this violation of himself. . . . Very well, it was not true, the water had not turned into wine. The water had not turned into wine. But for all that he would live in his soul as if the water *had* turned into wine. For truth of fact, it had not. But for his soul, it had.[51]

Blind "as a subterranean thing" he just ignores the human mind and runs after his "dark-souled" desires. This infuriates Anna and she fights him off. But that is by no means the only source of conflict between them.

Just after their marriage Will and Anna have some blissful days together in their cottage, away from all the world. They live "buried like a seed in darkness", having shed the hard rind of worldly knowledge and experience. In the chapter "Anna Victrix" we have an account of Will and Anna living at the level of "carbon"—both of them "very quick and alive, lit up from the other world".[52] Will is occasionally troubled in his orderly, conventional mind at their having abandoned "the established rule of things" so completely: he feels, for a time,

[49] *Op. cit.*, p. 155.   [50] *Op. cit.*, p. 168.
[51] *Op. cit.*, pp. 168-9.   [52] *Op. cit.*, p. 145.

that one ought to be "a decent social being". But Anna, "like an expert skittle-player", scatters all his qualms and "smaller beliefs", and he is both astonished and delighted to see his "Tablets of Stone [go] bounding and bumping and splintering down the hill, dislodged for ever."[53] The old things, the existence on the surface, the life of "houses, factories, trams, the discarded rind"—nothing matters any more. All that counts is that he should love Anna and she should love him, and that they should "live kindled to one another". They find themselves "at the heart of eternity", complete beyond the touch of time or change, barely aware of the world of human activity going on somewhere in the far distance. Anna is the first to come out of this trance. Being less inhibited she comes to her fulness more quickly, and is sooner ready to return to the outside world. She announces one day that she is going to give a tea-party. Will's heart sinks: it appears to him that in returning from their "timeless universe" to the "dead world" again she is only forfeiting the perfect reality with him for that which is shallow and worthless. "She would admit the outside world again, she would throw away the living fruit for the rind. He began to hate this in her."[54] Anna, in return, despises him for hanging on to her in his almost childish dependence on her. His hovering near her, wanting always to be with her, irritates her beyond bearing. She resists him because he seems to her a dark, almost evil thing, pursuing her, hanging on to her. She suggests to him that he ought to be doing some work. But his soul only grows the blacker: "the darkness of his soul was thorough".[55] He remains wrapped in his own tense, black will, completely unaware of her. For him she has, as it were, ceased to exist. Then one day while he is at his work it strikes him that Anna, whom he has only seen triumphant before, might be hurt. His heart is suddenly "torn with compassion", and he goes back to her, his heart aflame with love for her. They are reconciled, but this does not bring them any closer to each other. He does not understand that he has acquiesced. There is no real understanding between them because it is only he who has yielded, given way. The sense of hostility now appears in their sexual relations, too. She loves and caresses him, until

[53] *Op. cit.*, p. 146.   [54] *Op. cit.*, pp. 147-8.   [55] *Op. cit.*, p. 148.

he is roused "like a hawk", keen and instant and without any tenderness.

> He came to her fierce and hard, like a hawk striking and taking her. He was no mystic any more, she was his aim and object, his prey. And she was carried off, and he was satisfied, or satiated at last.
>
> Then immediately she began to retaliate on him. She too was a hawk. If she imitated the pathetic plover running plaintive to him, that was part of the game. When he, satisfied, moved with a proud, insolent slouch of the body and a half-contemptuous drop of the head, unaware of her, ignoring her very existence, after taking his fill of her and getting his satisfaction of her, her soul roused, its pinions became like steel, and she struck at him. When he sat on his perch glancing sharply round with solitary pride, pride eminent and fierce, she dashed at him and threw him from his station savagely, she goaded him from his keen dignity of a male, she harassed him from his unperturbed pride, till he was mad with rage, his light brown eyes burned with fury, they saw her now, like flames of anger they flared at her and recognised her as the enemy.
>
> Very good, she was the enemy, very good. As he prowled round her, she watched him. As he struck at her, she struck back.[56]

Neither of them is fully aware why there is "such a battle between them".[57] Anna senses in Will a desire to interfere with her, to impose himself on her: he is "the outsider", "the stranger", representing something alien and "unknown" against which she must defend herself by clinging fiercely to her known self. More and more she comes to realise that her husband is a blind thing, without knowledge, "a dark opposite" to her; that they are actually "opposites, not complements". It is only when the flood of passion carries them away that they love each other to transport again. Then he loves her for her very strangeness to him, "for the wonder of her soul which was different from his soul";[58] and she, instead of dreading it, loves "the touch of the unknown" about him.

[56] *Op. cit.*, p. 159.   [57] *Op. cit.*, p. 162.
[58] *Op. cit.*, p. 161.

So it went on continually, the recurrence of love and conflict between them. One day it seemed as if everything was shattered, all life spoiled, ruined, desolate and laid waste. The next day it was all marvellous again, just marvellous. . . . They fought an unknown battle, unconsciously. Still they were in love with each other, the passion was there. But the passion was consumed in a battle. And the deep, fierce unnamed battle went on.[59]

The battle is by no means abated when Anna informs her husband that she is going to have a baby. She now seems fulfilled, separate, "sufficient in her half of the world", and Will cannot bear to know that he is left alone, cut off from her. He wants her, needs her to come to him and complete him, make him whole. He is obsessed by a sense of his own limitation. Her need for the moment is fulfilled: she is complete in herself: but he has not yet had his fulfilment. He is ashamed of his helpless need of her, but must turn to her because he cannot come to his fulfilment without her. She, however, does not want his "bitter-corrosive love" now. She wants to enjoy the "vagueness and innocence of pregnancy": but it seems to her that he is all the time trying to force his will on her. She wants to be at peace with him and longs to give him love, pure love. Will, however, does not want the "flowery handfuls of innocent love" that she has to offer. He is not satisfied yet: his heart is still all raging desire, his soul "a black torment of unfulfilment". He insists on having from her the satisfaction and peace which she has had from him. "He had given her fulfilment. Let her rise up and do her part."[60] He is cruel to her. Anna feels he wants to destroy her; and she decides to avenge herself. It is in this state that she, big with child, dances naked in her bedroom the dance of his nullification. The sight of the naked pregnant woman "dancing his non-existence" does obliterate him. He is tormented for the rest of his life by the vision of her as "a strange, exalted thing having no connection with himself."[61] Next, it is Will's turn to exert his "dark and beastly will" towards her destruction. Anna finds her life "sinking under the grip of his physical will", and she turns fiercely on him to fight him: "What horrible hold did he want to have

[59] *Op. cit.*, pp. 163-5.　　[60] *Op. cit.*, p. 179.　　[61] *Op. cit.*, p. 181.

over her body? Why did he want to drag her down, and kill her spirit? Why did he want to deny her spirit? Why did he deny her spirituality, hold her for a body only?"[62]

Anna hates Will for depending on her so utterly. He himself desperately wants to be able to leave her. He is aware that for his own soul's sake, for his manhood's sake, he must be able to leave her. But he finds that he cannot. "And upon what could he stand, save upon a woman? Was he then like the old man of the seas, impotent to move save upon the back of another life? Was he impotent, or a cripple, or a defective, or a fragment?"[63] His problem is that he must have a woman, and having a woman he must also be free of her. He finds Anna persistently, ruthlessly pushing him away from her. She refuses to sleep with him any more because, she says, he destroys her sleep. It is only after a long struggle that something gives way in him and he relaxes. He recognises at length his own limitation and gives in—to Anna Victrix. The battle between them, for the time being, is over:

> He could be alone now. He had just learned what it was to be able to be alone. It was right and peaceful. She had given him a new, deeper freedom. The world might be a welter of uncertainty, but he was himself now. He had come into his own existence. He was born for a second time, born at last unto himself, out of the vast body of humanity. Now at last he had a separate identity, he existed alone, even if he were not quite alone. Before he had only existed in so far as he had relations with another being. Now he had an absolute self— as well as a relative self. . . . She had given him to himself.[64]

With this newly-gained certainty in his soul Will is content to live with and for the sake of Anna only. The great mass of activity in which mankind is engaged still means nothing to him. His mind is, nevertheless, vaguely troubled by a sense of something more, something further that needs to be added on to his life.

The birth of her baby, Ursula, means much to Anna, yet she does not feel quite fulfilled. She still strains her eyes "to something beyond", and she can see a long way off a faint, gleaming horizon and a rainbow like an archway above it.

[62] *Op. cit.*, p. 182.   [63] *Op. cit.*, p. 184.   [64] *Op. cit.*, p. 187.

She sees "the hope, the promise" in the rainbow, yet she is not sure that she should be travelling further towards it. She is a rich woman enjoying her riches, and is quite willing to postpone "all adventure into unknown realities". She consoles herself with the thought that if her soul has found no utterance, at least her womb has.

> With satisfaction she relinquished the adventure to the unknown. She was bearing her children.
>   There was another child coming, and Anna lapsed into vague content. If she were not the wayfarer to the unknown, if she were arrived now, settled in her builded house, a rich woman, still her doors opened under the arch of the rainbow, her threshold reflected the passing of the sun and moon, the great travellers, her house was full of the echo of journeying.[65]

The essential difference in the natures of Will and Anna is also brought out in their respective experiences in Lincoln Cathedral. Anna, with her husband, goes to visit her uncle, Baron Skrebensky. The atmosphere of freedom there, which leaves each person detached and isolated, makes her acutely aware of how "the curious enveloping Brangwen intimacy" has been stifling her. She now wants to get back to her old, sharp, detached self. It is immediately after this visit that they go to Lincoln Cathedral.

For Will it means looking forward to a great experience. He is highly excited in anticipation of the consummation he is going to have in the "perfect womb" of the Cathedral. His experience of consummation, when he is there, is no doubt genuine—as even the quality of prose in the chapter would testify: but essentially it is of the same order, of the same kind, as the consummation he has had during his early married life with Anna. A comparison of the descriptions of Will's experience with Anna and his experience in the Cathedral also bears this out. Coming to the Cathedral Will finds himself "on the brink of the unrevealed"; when approaching Anna he has the consciousness of coming to something "strange" and "unknown". The Church is "like a seed in silence"; during their honeymoon Will and Anna live in a remote world "buried like

[65] *Op. cit.*, p. 193.

a seed in darkness".[66] The Cathedral seems to Will to be "away from time, always outside of time"; Will and Anna, as they lie close together, feel they are "beyond the touch of time and change". All this—as well as the repetitive use of words like gloom, seed, womb, darkness, dark, in the chapter—clearly suggests that Will in "his passionate intercourse with the cathedral"[67] is looking for the same kind of satisfaction which he had found earlier in his ecstatic sensual experience with Anna. Lawrence's exposition "Of Being and Not-Being" in his "Study of Thomas Hardy" is a closely relevant and helpful comment on "The Cathedral" chapter in *The Rainbow*. Every man, says Lawrence, seeks in woman that which is stable, eternal, immutable. But should the woman, for some reason, fail him, he then must search elsewhere than in woman for the attributes of Immutability, Permanence, Eternality. And he can do so by attempting to create and define in his conscious-ness the object of his desire, or, by making conscious "his desire to find a symbol"[68] which is available to him at will for his own complete satisfaction. For Will Brangwen the Cathedral is such a symbol, as it was, according to Lawrence, for all Europe during the medieval period when the collective, stupendous aspiration of the people found a concrete embodiment in the cathedrals, in the kind of architecture "whose essence is in utter stability".[69] Will's experience of Lincoln Cathedral—where "before" and "after" are folded together, and all is "contained in oneness"—is a response to the static, absolute quality of its architecture.[70] However, in the details of these cathedrals there was also present the denial of Oneness which the whole proclaimed. The little figures, the gargoyles, the imps, "from their obscurity, jeered their mockery of the Absolute".[71] It is these little figures which save Anna—who, too, is overcome with wonder and awe—from being swept "in the tide of passion" towards the Infinite. These sly little faces suggest to her that however much there might be inside the Cathedral, there is a good deal that has been left out of "the great concept

---

[66] *Op. cit.*, p. 141.   [67] *Op. cit.*, p. 201.
[68] *Phoenix*, p. 446.   [69] *Op. cit.*, pp. 453-4.
[70] See *The Rainbow*, pp. 198-201, for Lawrence's beautiful rendering of Will's and Anna's experience in Lincoln Cathedral.
[71] *Phoenix*, p. 454.

K

of the church".[72] Will is bitterly angry when Anna successfully mocks at his transports and ecstasies over the Cathedral. She has destroyed "another of his vital illusions": he can no longer "satisfy his blind passion" for cathedrals as they represent an absolute no more. He is still alive to the "dark, mysterious world of reality" inside them, but now it is only a world within a world.

> He listened to the thrushes in the gardens and heard a note which the cathedrals did not include: something free and careless and joyous. He crossed a field that was all yellow with dandelions, on his way to work, and the bath of yellow glowing was something at once so sumptuous and so fresh, that he was glad he was away from his shadowy cathedral.
> There was life outside the Church. There was much that the Church did not include. . . . Still he loved the Church. As a symbol he loved it. He tended it for what it tried to represent, rather than for what it did represent.[73]

What it tries and fails to represent is the Absolute. The Church itself, he knows, is incomplete and does not fulfil anything in him; yet he continues in his devotion to it because he is aware of some limit to himself: some inadequacy, something undeveloped, unformed in his very being prevents him from having his fulfilment. He remains lapsed in his connexion with Anna. She is the daytime, the daylight, the "upper world"; to him belongs the darkness of the dark, sensuous underworld. All his daytime activity is a kind of sleep, whereas her effort all the time is "to be free, to belong to the day".[74] However, over Anna, in the course of time, comes the trance of motherhood, and she begins to live merely in her own "violent fruitfulness". The outside, public life comes to mean nothing to her; no sense of duty or responsibility troubles her any more. This goes on until, one day, she perceives "a new turn of affairs". Will returns home very late, a strange man with a queer, absolved look on his face. He has just left a small, common girl casually picked up at the music-hall in Nottingham and is for the time being scarcely aware of Anna. She knows instantly that "her old, established supremacy" must come to an end. But if she cannot influence him in the old way, she

---

[72] *The Rainbow*, p. 201.   [73] *Op. cit.*, p. 203.   [74] *Op. cit.*, p. 214.

decides, she would at least be level with him in the new. If he
is going to be absolved from his "good" self, she too can throw
love and responsibility overboard. If he is the sensual male
seeking his pleasure, she would be the female ready to take
hers, in her own way. So they both, in one motion, abandon
the moral position to merely seek gratification pure and simple.

> He was quite ousted from himself, and sensually transported
> by that which he discovered in her. He was another man
> revelling over her. There was no tenderness, no love between
> them any more, only the maddening, sensuous lust for discovery
> and the insatiable, exorbitant gratification in the sensual
> beauties of her body. . . . He lived in a passion of sensual
> discovery with her for some time—it was a duel: no love, no
> words, no kisses even, only the maddening perception of beauty
> consummate, absolute through touch.[75]

In the "darkness and death" of their sensual experience there
is no conscious intimacy, no tenderness of love. Their love has
become a sensuality "violent and extreme as death". It is all
mere lust, "a passion of death".[76] But this destructive Dionysic
or Aphrodisic ecstasy, deathly in itself, has a highly important
place in a total marriage relationship—for it is only through the
fierce passion of sensuality that one is purified into singleness
and separateness of being. Will had not so far been liberated
into his pure "otherness" of being. Now, having at last been
reduced to his single self through a satisfactory sensual consummation with Anna, he can begin "to find himself free to
attend to the outside life as well". His fulfilled intimate life
sets another man in him free. He now turns with interest to
public life in order to see what part he can take in it. He wants
to be "unanimous with the whole of purposive mankind".
For the first time, he begins to take some real interest in public
affairs. He has "at length, from his profound sensual activity,
developed a real purposive self".[77] When there is a talk of
starting night schools and handicraft classes, it appears to him
"supremely desirable" that he himself should be teaching
carpentry and wood-carving to the village boys. He is very
happy and keen in his new public spirit. Actually, his creative
energies find full release only many years later when his

[75] *Op. cit.*, p. 233.   [76] *Op. cit.*, p. 234.   [77] *Op. cit.*, p. 235.

daughters, Ursula and Gudrun, are grown up. Then he is able to make his way towards individual expression and individual form. He begins modelling in clay, producing really beautiful reproductions; then turns to painting; takes up jewellery; and later on beaten and chiselled metal work. Finally he finds some kind of escape from the "hot, dusky enclosure" of his family life by taking up the job of Art and Handiwork Instructor for the County. His achievement, limited and belated, is still more than Tom Brangwen's.

One could say that love between Will and Anna is not as successful as it was in the first generation between Tom and Lydia. But this is true only in the sense that whereas the elder Brangwen and the Polish woman could readily reconcile themselves to the contentment offered by their "long marital embrace", when we come to the story of Will and Anna we are made to feel that there are many yearnings and aspirations which have remained unsatisfied. (And this will be even more so in the next generation with Ursula whose quest for complete fulfilment will be the most difficult of all.) But considering what is actually achieved in the relationship, the story of the second generation is certainly the richer; for even though the sense of failure is stronger, it is so only in the context of the more ambitious fulfilment sought.

Like Tom Brangwen Will had turned early to his daughter, finding that his relation with his wife, lost in her "violent trance of motherhood", had left him unfulfilled, unready for fulfilment. The bond between Will and Ursula grows rapidly into a passionate attachment to each other. The child turns towards the father "like a quivering needle" for all things in her life. But Will's love for his daughter is too intense: he comes too near to her. She is "wakened too soon" from the transient unconsciousness of childhood. It is only after a hard struggle and many shocks that Ursula is able to free herself from this excessively demanding love of her father. She has never had much feeling for her mother, and she does not like being at home with its "babies and muddled domesticity"—except on Sundays when for her "a visionary world" comes to pass. When she hears in the church: "The sons of God saw the daughters of men that they were fair: and they took them

wives of all which they chose", the words sound to her like a
voice coming from another world, stirring her deeply. She
wonders who these "Sons of God" were, and whether they
would have found her fair and taken her to wife. She imagines
that these sons of God had really known no expulsion, no
ignominy of the fall; and so utterly does she desire that the
sons of God should come to the daughters of men that she comes
to believe more in her desire and its fulfilment than in the
obvious facts of life. This dream, this vision remains with her
a long time; and she not only decides that "one of the Sons of
God" should in time come to her and "take her to wife", she
even succeeds for a time in creating one such in her lover,
Anton Skrebensky—until she is finally disillusioned and realises
that it is "not for her to create, but to recognize a man created
by God".[78]

As Ursula moves from girlhood towards womanhood, the
cloud of self-responsibility gradually gathers upon her. The
Sunday world of "absolute truth and living mystery" gives way
to the week-day world of acts and deeds. The glorious play-
world of religion becomes unreal, "a tale, a myth, an illusion",
having little relevance to the life as she actually knows it. And
she has come to see by now that "that which one cannot
experience in daily life is not true for oneself". Her task now
is to learn the week-day life. She feels she must go out somewhere, must "become something"; and the thought of it
makes her afraid, troubled.

> Why, oh why must one grow up, why must one inherit this
> heavy, numbing responsibility of living an undiscovered life?
> Out of the nothingness and the undifferentiated mass, to make
> something of herself! But what? In the obscurity and path-
> lessness to take a direction! But whither? How take even one
> step? And yet how stand still? This was torment indeed, to
> inherit the responsibility of one's own life. . . . How to act, that
> was the question? Whither to go, how to become oneself? One
> was not oneself, one was merely a half-stated question. How
> to become oneself, how to know the question and the answer
> of oneself, when one was merely an unfixed something-nothing,
> blowing about like the winds of heaven, undefined, unstated.[79]

---

[78] *Op. cit.*, p. 493.   [79] *Op. cit.*, pp. 281-2.

It is during this period of self-searching that Ursula meets Anton Skrebensky for the first time, and she lays hold of him at once as one of her dreams. "Here was one such as those Sons of God who saw the daughters of men, that they were fair."[80]   Skrebensky seems to bring to her "a strong sense of the outer world", "a sense of distances and large masses of humanity". But from the very beginning there are also indications that their relationship, even at its very best, is going to be no more than an inadequate, incomplete affair, and that Skrebensky is far from being the door into the unknown that Ursula for a time supposes him to be.

Love between Anton and Ursula begins as a kind of daring and reckless game of "magnificent self-assertion". Neither of them can hope to get out of their relation of passion alone anything more than "his or her own maximum self, in contra-distinction to all the rest of life".[81]   But once begun the game of passion goes on.   Then Anton, his leave over, goes back to the army, and Ursula spends most of her time "running on by herself", dreaming of him and waiting for him to come back. Skrebensky is, however, gradually changing—becoming more and more a part of "the established order of things" and letting his life in the army override and kill his "intrinsic self".   So when Ursula sees him again at her uncle Fred's wedding he is already found wanting when she questions him on hat he really thinks of his life in the Engineers.   A strange, distracted feeling, "a sense of potent unrealities" comes over her as Anton fails to give any satisfactory reply when she asks him what, in the event of a war, he would be fighting for.   When her persistence finally drives him to the admission that he would fight in order to do his "duty by the nation", her bitter retort is: "It seems to me as if you weren't anybody—as if there weren't anybody there, where you are.   Are you anybody, really?   You seem like nothing to me."   The long conversation in the novel[82] should be read in its entirety, as no summary of it will be found to be adequate.   What clearly emerges from their verbal exchanges is that Ursula and Skrebensky represent two radically different points of view.   One can safely assume that among the readers of *The Rainbow* there have been and will

[80] *Op. cit.*, p. 290.   [81] *Op. cit.*, p. 301.   [82] *Op. cit.*, pp. 308-9.

be people who would give their support and approval to the ideas expressed by Anton. But to Ursula's way of thinking an individual who merely exists in readiness for when he is needed by the nation or society, is no longer an individual; he, as it were, in himself does not exist: he is a nothingness. Immediately following on this discussion comes the short but significant episode with the bargee. In contrast to Skrebensky who seems to Ursula to create deadness and sterility around her, the bargee gives her a pleasant, warm feeling, making her perceive the richness of her own life. Even Anton is not without envy for the grimy, lean man for his ability to worship and have communion with both the body and the spirit of Ursula together—whereas he himself, he feels, can never desire a woman in this manner. "Why did he never really want a woman, not with the whole of him: never loved, never worshipped, only just physically wanted her."[83] He knows quite well that his love for Ursula amounts to no more than mere physical desire. He is incapable of a full commitment in love because his soul is already paralysed, dead: he exists only in as much as he represents "the great, established, extant Idea of life". He, however, has his senses which need to be gratified; so he decides "he would want [Ursula] with his body, let his soul do as it would".[84] The description of his experience with Ursula which follows—in which he is completely annihilated, reduced to nothing by her—is essentially an account of his unsuccessful attempt, with the subtle power of his will, to compel her, to possess her. The entire scene appropriately takes place under a full moon, associated in Lawrence's writings with Aphrodite, the queen of the senses, the goddess of destruction whose "white cold fire consumes and does not create".[85] Ursula finds that Skrebensky stands in the way of her communion with the great white moon. She feels the persistent, inert burden of him overcoming her life and energy, and she is filled with a rage to tear things asunder. "Her hands felt destructive, like metal blades of destruction."[86] Anton, seeing her cold and hard "as the moon itself", exerts all his power to

---

[83] *Op. cit.*, p. 315. [84] *Ibid.*
[85] D. H. Lawrence, *Twilight in Italy*, Pocket Edition (1954), p. 60.
[86] *The Rainbow*, p. 318.

bear her down, to overcome her. His will is set to achieving just one aim: "If he could only compel her. . . . If he could only set a bond round her and compel her. . . . Then he would have her, he would enjoy her. How he would enjoy her, when she was caught."[87] But in spite of all his efforts she remains intact: hard and bright "as a piece of moonlight", cold and unmoved "as a pillar of salt". Then, looking at him, at his "shadowy, unreal, wavering presence", she is suddenly seized with a desire to lay hold of him and "make him into nothing". So when Anton, in his obstinacy, persists in his efforts to overcome her "salt-burning body", she lets him try what he can do:

> She took him in the kiss, hard her kiss seized upon him, hard and fierce and burning corrosive as the moonlight. She seemed to be destroying him. He was reeling, summoning all his strength to keep his kiss upon her, to keep himself in the kiss.
> But hard and fierce she had fastened upon him, cold as the moon and burning as a fierce salt. Till gradually his warm, soft iron yielded, yielded, and she was there fierce, corrosive, seething with his destruction, seething like some cruel, corrosive salt around the last substance of his being, destroying him, destroying him in the kiss. And her soul crystallised with triumph, and his soul was dissolved with agony and annihilation. So she held him there, the victim, consumed, annihilated. She had triumphed: he was not any more.[88]

This is how Ursula's deeper and darker self, not her conscious self, has responded to the "love" Skrebensky has to offer. But she herself is afraid of "that other burning, corrosive self" concealed beneath her kind and loving self. She does not trust the true and sure response of her own "pure being" to Skrebensky's wilful sensuality. When she comes to herself, when "a sort of daytime consciousness" comes back to her, she wants to forget all that has happened. In the daily, commonplace world she is a nice, kind girl (her "diamond" self) with yearnings for goodness and affection. She is slowly overcome with horror at the madness—as she now sees it—at the "horrible thing" which had possessed her:

[87] *Op. cit.*, pp. 318-9.   [88] *Op. cit.*, p. 320.

She was seized with a frenzied desire that what had been should never be remembered, never be thought of, never be for one moment allowed possible. She denied it with all her might. With all her might she turned away from it. She was good, she was loving. Her heart was warm, her blood was dark and warm and soft. She laid her hand caressively on Anton's shoulder.

"Isn't it lovely?" she said, softly, coaxingly, caressingly. And she began to caress him to life again. For he was dead. And she intended that he should never know, never become aware of what had been. She would bring him back from the dead without leaving him one trace of fact to remember his annihilation by.

She exerted all her ordinary, warm self, she touched him, she did him homage of loving awareness. And gradually he came back to her, another man. She was soft and winning and caressing. She was his servant, his adoring slave. And she restored the whole shell of him. She restored the whole form and figure of him. But the core was gone. His pride was bolstered up, his blood ran once more in pride. But there was no core to him: as a distinct male he had no core. His triumphant, flaming, over-weening heart of the intrinsic male would never beat again. He would be subject now, reciprocal, never the indomitable thing with a core of over-weening, unabateable fire. She had abated that fire, she had broken him.[89]

Shortly afterwards war is declared with the Boers in S. Africa and Skrebensky gets busy making preparations to go. He is wholly given over to the performance of his duties now, giving no thought to his unfulfilled self, to "the soul that aspired and had true hope of self-effectuation".[90] He comes to disregard his relationship with Ursula, taking it to be of little importance. In the "great scheme of man's elaborate civilization", he believes, neither individual men and women nor their connexions or intimacies matter. The unit, the person, has no significance except in so far as he represents the whole. "What did a man matter personally? He was just a brick in the whole great social fabric, the nation, the modern humanity."[91] The whole form must be preserved at all cost, for nothing can—at

[89] *Op. cit.*, pp. 320-1.   [90] *Op. cit.*, p. 326.   [91] *Ibid.*

least no personal reason can—justify its rupture. He decides he must fill his place in the unquestionably important Whole to the best of his ability, no matter if his own soul—the soul of one individual—remains dead, still-born within him.

> The good of the greatest number was all that mattered. That which was the greatest good for them all, collectively, was the greatest good for the individual. And so, every man must give himself to support the state, and so labour for the greatest good of all. One might make improvements in the state, perhaps, but always with a view to preserving it intact.
>
> No highest good of the community, however, would give him the vital fulfilment of his soul. He knew this. But he did not consider the soul of the individual sufficiently important. He believed a man was important in so far as he represented all humanity.
>
> He could not see, it was not born in him to see, that the highest good of the community as it stands is no longer the highest good of even the average individual. He thought that, because the community represents millions of people, therefore it must be millions of times more important than any individual, forgetting that the community is an abstraction from the many, and is not the many themselves. Now when the statement of the abstract good for the community has become a formula lacking in all inspiration or value to the average intelligence, then the "common good" becomes a general nuisance, representing the vulgar, conservative materialism at a low level.[92]

Skrebensky is aware that the highest good of the greatest number primarily means the material welfare of all classes in the community: good wages, equal opportunities, good conditions of living. He does not really care about his own material prosperity. But he is unable to see that what he considers unimportant for himself cannot be worthy of every sacrifice on behalf of other people. He knows his duty is very plain: to keep in mind "the material, the immediate welfare of every man, that's all". So there comes over Skrebensky "a sort of nullity, which more and more terrified Ursula".[93] Skrebensky, however, goes away to S. Africa, and Ursula is left alone with

[92] *Op. cit.*, pp. 326-7. [93] *Op. cit.*, p. 327.

her burden of self-responsibility. But in fact she has no well-defined self so far: she is yet "a wavering, undefined sensibility only, without form or being".[94] Her contact with Skrebensky has left her strangely overwrought and abnormally sensitive. Her sexual life, in this state, "flamed into a kind of disease within her".[95] When Skrebensky is gone, there springs up a "queer awareness", then an "unspoken intimacy" between her and her class-mistress, Miss Inger: "The two women became intimate. Their lives seemed suddenly to fuse into one, inseparable."[96] But as this Lesbian affair progresses a heavy clogged sense of deadness begins to gather on Ursula. Instead of the fine intensity which she wants, her contact with Winifred Inger gives her a feeling of moist clay cleaving to her because it has no life of its own. "The fine, unquenchable flame of the younger girl would consent no more to mingle with the perverted life of the elder woman." So Ursula, with an instinctive sureness of judgment, arranges a meeting between her mistress and her uncle Tom—which finally leads to their marriage. As it turns out, the perversity and the clayey grossness in Miss Inger is matched by the "dark corruption" and the repellent "sense of putrescence" in the colliery-manager. As soon as he sees the woman, he knows that "they were akin".[97] His life, as Ursula perceives with horror, is entirely dedicated to the running of "the great machine": the pit has come to be his "great mistress", his *raison d'être*. He cynically reviles the state of things brought about by the "monster of the colliery". But in spite of all his criticism and condemnation he still wants the great machine, for it is in serving the machine that he has the only happy moments of his life. Ursula, filled with revulsion for Winifred as well as for her Uncle Tom, decides to get away and be rid of them both for ever. However, during the few months of her intimacy with her school-mistress, and in her two weeks' stay at her Uncle's, Ursula has developed very rapidly. She is even more fixed now in her desire for "complete social independence". After Skrebensky's departure she had realised that there was the "mysterious man's world to be adventured upon, the world of daily work and duty, and existence as a

[94] *Op. cit.*, p. 334.
[95] *Op. cit.*, p. 332.
[96] *Op. cit.*, p. 340.
[97] *Op. cit.*, p. 348.

working member of the community".[98] Now she resolves to give a practical shape to her plan for making a conquest of this world—the world of man, of which the Brangwen women of Chapter 1 had dreamed. She gets a job as a teacher in a school. The story of Ursula's teaching experience has been judged to be unrelated to the main theme of the novel. Thus Marvin Mudrick remarks that "the career of Ursula as a teacher, however interesting it may be in its own right, is recorded at too much length and with too little relevance to the theme of the novel".[99] J. I. M. Stewart, similarly, speaks of the "long, brilliant, but thematically irrelevant account of [Ursula's] experiences while teaching".[1] The connexion between Ursula's experiences at school and the theme of the novel is, however, quite obvious. The first chapter of the book shows us the women on the Farm yearning for "knowledge" and for participation in "the activity of man in the world at large". Neither Lydia nor Anna (in spite of her aspirations) manages to do that. It is only Ursula, in the third generation, who succeeds in transcending "the close, physical, limited life of herded domesticity".[2] As she posts the completed application forms for a teaching job, she feels she has established a connexion with "the outer, greater world of activity, the man-made world".[3]

Ursula begins her work as a teacher dreaming of how she would make her pupils love her by her kindness and personal approach to them. "She would make everything personal and vivid, she would give herself, she would give, give, give all her great stores of wealth to her children, she would make them so happy, and they would prefer her to any teacher on the face of the earth."[4] Her dreams are, however, shattered on her very first day in school. She had left her home hoping to be independent, free; the school turns out to be just another prison. She had set out in quest of her true, real self—only to find that she must alter herself to suit some hard, concrete, vicious thing called "reality".

In the school, as Ursula soon comes to see, it is power alone

[98] *Op. cit.*, p. 333.
[99] *Miscellany*, p. 76.
[1] *Eight Modern Writers*, p. 507.
[2] *The Rainbow*, p. 353.
[3] *Op. cit.*, p. 360.
[4] *Op. cit.*, p. 367.

that matters. If she is to succeed, she must put her actual self out of count and become a mere instrument, using her will to reduce the class of "fifty collective children" to an automatic state of obedience. A personal relationship with each child is out of the question, as they seem to her a collective, inhuman thing rather than individual children. "They were so many, that they were not children. They were a squadron."[5] Ursula, with her sensitive soul, is ill-equipped for the task of compelling the children by imposing her will on them. She cannot manage her class. And even though she does not give in, she is all the time haunted by the thought that she is never really a success. "She did not believe that she could ever teach that great, brutish class, in that brutal school: ever, ever."[6] And yet if she fails here it would, she knows, be an implicit admission that "the man's world" has been too strong for her, that she has been unable to take her place in it. That would mean her going ahead in life without "having freed herself of man's world, never having achieved the freedom of the great world of responsible work".[7] So she resolves to be distant and impersonal with the children, to be no more than "Standard Five teacher" at school: "It was an agony to the impulsive, bright girl of seventeen to become distant and official, having no personal relationship with the children. For a few days . . . she succeeded, and had some success with the class. But it was a state not natural to her, and she began to relax."[8] It is only after two incidents involving boys jeering at her in public and throwing stones at her that a decisive change takes place in her soul:

> Never more, and never more would she give herself as individual to her class. Never would she, Ursula Brangwen, the girl she was, the person she was, come into contact with those boys. She would be Standard Five teacher, as far away personally from her class as if she had never set foot in St. Philip's school. She would just obliterate them all, and keep herself apart, take them as scholars only. . . . She, as teacher, must bring them all as scholars, into subjection. And this she was going to do. . . . She was going to fight and subdue.[9]

[5] *Op. cit.*, p. 376.   [6] *Op. cit.*, p. 391.   [7] *Ibid.*
[8] *Op. cit.*, p. 393.   [9] *Op. cit.*, pp. 395-6.

Ursula succeeds finally in imposing order on her class, though not before she has paid a price "out of her own soul" for it. She has taken her place in the "world of work and man's convention". Having "put in her tiny brick to the fabric man was building, she had qualified herself as co-builder".[10]

In leaving her home and earning her own living Ursula had made a determined move towards freeing herself. But having more freedom, she only becomes more acutely aware of so much more she must meet and surpass before she can stand free and come to her "real, individual self". Besides her desire to read and enrich herself with great, beautiful books, and to meet big, free people, she is also aware of some other want which she cannot as yet give a name to. For a time she is attracted to Anthony Schofield, brother of a fellow school-teacher. But when he makes a proposal of marriage to her, she finds that she cannot accept it. She likes Anthony well enough, but the kind of life he has to offer is precisely the life she has left behind at home.

> All her life, at intervals, she returned to the thought of him and of that which he offered. But she was a traveller, she was a traveller on the face of the earth, and he was an isolated creature living in the fulfilment of his own senses.
>
> She could not help it, that she was a traveller. She knew Anthony, that he was not one. But oh, ultimately and finally, she must go on and on, seeking the goal that she knew she did draw nearer to.[11]

The goal which she feels she is drawing nearer to is not at all clearly defined in her mind. All she knows is that having arrived in the world of man's activity she has come not to any "finer, more vivid circle of life", but to the deadness and grossness of a mechanical existence which she must reject. Her experiences of Winifred Inger, her uncle Tom and the life in his pits, even school-teaching[12]—all have left in her mouth "the ash and grit of disillusion, of falsity",[13] which she must

---

[10] *Op. cit.*, p. 425. [11] *Op. cit.*, p. 417.
[12] What Ursula accomplishes during her school-teaching days is just adding her tiny brick to "the fabric man was building"—the same "great social fabric", devotion to which had reduced Skrebensky to nullity in her eyes.
[13] *The Rainbow*, p. 437.

spit out. She, next, enters college with high hopes. But even here the whole thing turns out to be a sham, spurious; and a harsh disillusion comes over her again.

> What good was this place, this college? What good was Anglo-Saxon, when one only learned it in order to answer examination questions, in order that one should have a higher commercial value later on? She was sick with this long service at the inner commercial shrine. Yet what else was there? Was life all this, and this only? Everywhere, everything was debased to the same service. Everything went to produce vulgar things, to encumber material life.[14]

When Ursula, in this state of utter disillusion, hears of Skrebensky's coming to meet her, it is not at all surprising to see her turn to him once again, wishing to find in him "the new life, the reality". As she looks back at her past he seems to her like "the gleaming dawn, yellow, radiant, of a long, grey, ashy day. The memory of him was like the thought of the first radiant hours of morning. And here was the blank grey ashiness of later daytime."[15] But when she actually meets him she only sees, with a cold sense of despair, the soulless man "made up of a set of habitual actions and decisions". When he tells her of his acceptance of an appointment in India, her fears about his "always side-tracking his own soul" are confirmed. She already knows that if he is going to India then that is not her road. But she also loves him, loves "the body of him". He seems to want something of her. She can feel "the dark, heavy fixity of his animal desire".[16] It is this dumb desire of his which has brought him to her. And she decides she must accept him and have her satisfaction, even if this means abandoning her quest for the time being:

He was her lover, though good and evil should cease. Her will never relaxed, though her heart and soul must be imprisoned and silenced. . . . Her heart and her soul were shut away fast down below, hidden. She was free of them. She was to have her satisfaction.[17]

---

[14] *Op. cit.*, pp. 435-6.   [15] *Op. cit.*, p. 438.
[16] *Op. cit.*, p. 443.   [17] *Op. cit.*, p. 444.

Having pushed "her heart and soul" out of the way, she spends the next few weeks immersed in the dark richness of her "sensual sub-consciousness". Skrebensky, too, having no "civic self" to maintain for the time being, feels free to be his individual self. For the days that he is with Ursula he is no longer "the young man of the world", and the two meet in a "superb consummation" which makes them both "absolute and happy and calm". Then he suggests to Ursula, "I suppose we ought to get married". But this she cannot accept, for she knows that if he married he would once again "assume his social self". In making their connexion public they would be putting it within range of all those things which had nullified him, and from which he is entirely dissociated for the moment. As his social wife she would become almost a "material symbol", whereas their present dark, vivid, fluid relationship is far richer than any relation on the level of conventional life could be. So they live blissfully in their own world of ever-changing reality for some weeks. Then, suddenly—like Anna's desire for giving a tea-party—comes over Ursula the irresistible desire to go away. "She must be gone at once." They go to Paris, then to Rouen where the old streets, the Cathedral and "the monumental peace" of the town seem to Skrebensky to take her away from him. He can see that she "followed after something that was not him".[18] Here for the first time he has "a cold feeling of death", his first taste of "the bitterness of ecstasy". It was inevitable that their destructive, consuming passion should bring to them the "sense of death towards which they were wandering".

When Ursula goes away Anton finds himself surrounded by "an ashen-dry, cold world of rigidity, dead walls and mechanical traffic". He feels her absence "destroyed his being", because he *has* no real individual being of his own: he has never let his soul develop, and, parted from Ursula, is no more than "a cold surface of consciousness". His relationship with her has left him utterly dependent on her, a "mere attribute of her". He has never discovered his pure, separate, proud individuality; he has not even learnt the lesson Will had to

[18] *Op. cit.*, p. 455.

learn: that he must be able to stand alone. His passion for Ursula has always contained "a developing germ of death":

> After each contact, her anguished desire for him or for that which she never had from him was stronger, her love was more hopeless. After each contact his mad dependence on her was deepened, his hope of standing strong and taking her in his own strength was weakened.[19]

What Ursula "never had from him" is nowhere clearly stated in the book. When questioned she can only say that she cannot take love, personal gratification, to be an end in itself, that she wants something more, something "impersonal" which Skrebensky cannot give her. "He seemed added up, finished. She knew him all round, not on any side did he lead into the unknown."[20] The only alternative to being Mrs Skrebensky that she can see is entering the bondage of teaching once more, which she heartily detests. At the same time she cannot reconcile herself to the thought of marriage and living with Skrebensky amid the European population in India. He already seems to her something of the past, finite, "that which is known".[21] As she looks forward to the unexplored future she cannot see any place for him in it. In her need she had created him for the time being, and he was with her in her desire during the weeks of passionate ecstasy: but he had "never become finally real". When she puts him to the test in the course of their short stay on the Lincolnshire coast, he finally breaks down—once again watched by a great incandescent moon:

> . . . there in the great flare of light, she clinched hold of him, hard, as if suddenly she had the strength of destruction, she fastened her arms round him and tightened him in her grip, whilst her mouth sought his in a hard, rending, ever-increasing kiss, till his body was powerless in her grip, his heart melted in fear from the fierce, beaked, harpy's kiss. The water washed again over their feet, but she took no notice. She seemed unaware, she seemed to be pressing in her beaked mouth till she had the heart of him. Then, at last, she drew away and looked at him—looked at him. He knew what she wanted. He took her by the hand and led her across the foreshore, back

---

[19] *Op. cit.*, p. 462.   [20] *Op. cit.*, p. 473.   [21] *Op. cit.*, p. 493.

L

to the sandhills. She went silently. He felt as if the ordeal of proof was upon him, for life or death. He led her to a dark hollow.

"No, here," she said, going out to the slope full under the moonshine. She lay motionless, with wide-open eyes looking at the moon. He came direct to her, without preliminaries. She held him pinned down at the chest, awful. The fight, the struggle for consummation was terrible. It lasted till it was agony to his soul, till he succumbed, till he gave way as if dead, lay with his face buried, partly in her hair, partly in the sand, motionless, as if he would be motionless now for ever, hidden away in the dark, buried, only that, and no more.[22]

This extreme experience of "burning, salty passion" leaves them both more dead than living. They can no longer delude themselves. "It had been a failure", Ursula now confesses to him—referring to their relationship as a whole, not to the scene on the dunes by the sea. Skrebensky, still clinging to the life of his body, tries to save himself by keeping himself occupied with the things of the moment, by "adhering to the trivial present". He cannot bear to even think of Ursula who represents for him "the challenge of his own soul".[23] So he quietly marries his colonel's daughter and goes away to India.

Ursula returns home very "faint, dim, closed up"—having for a time lost interest in everything. Then the conflict in her mind is suddenly revived when she realises with a shock that she is probably with child by Skrebensky. Her soul is sick: the child seems to her the seal set on her own nullity. But her flesh is thrilled. She thinks of marrying Skrebensky and living simply as a good, dutiful wife to him. She tries to persuade herself that she was only being wicked and arrogant in wanting to have some fantastic fulfilment in her life. For a time she comes to think that her mother—who had learnt to ignore her unsatisfied yearnings and to accept the given life—was right; that she herself, in insisting on creating life to fit herself, has been arrogant and conceited. She makes herself believe that she has now at last discovered her real self. "For what had a woman but to submit? What was her flesh but for child-bearing, her strength for her children and her husband, the

---

[22] *Op. cit.*, p. 479.   [23] *Op. cit.*, p. 482.

giver of life? At last she was a woman."[24]   Her self-deception, however, does not last long, for the reassertion of the dark unknown forces of life within her—symbolised in her encounter with the powerful horses—brings the conflict again to the fore-front.   Her going out for a walk in the "chaos of rain" outside, a long way from the house which she fears might suffocate her, is not unlike her coming out of the stifling intimacy of her home into the turmoil of the world.   Then, very wet and "far enveloped in the rain", she decides she must "beat her way back through all this fluctuation, back to stability and security".[25]   This is more or less what she has done in deciding to get married to Skrebensky.   But she has not reckoned with her profound unconscious, with the "tremendous unknown forces of life" which she now encounters in the shape of horses looming in the rain.   As she pursues her way back, the horses draw near.   She wants to avoid them.   "She did not want to lift her face to them.   She did not want to know they were there. ... What were they? ...   She did not know, she did not look."[26] But the horses block her way, burst before her, and re-gather in the distance waiting for her approach.   For a moment she thinks she has succeeded in avoiding them.

> They were behind her.   The way was open before her, to the gate in the high hedge in the near distance, so she could pass into the smaller, cultivated field, and so out to the high-road and the ordered world of man.   Her way was clear.[27]

But the horses are "up against her"; they have been only awaiting their chance.   So, as she moves forward with small steps, they gallop down the path and thunder past her, swerving and crashing by to her left hand.   Then they gather themselves into a knot once more.   Ursula finally succeeds in getting away by climbing into the boughs of an oak tree and dropping on the other side of the hedge.   She barely manages to get back home, and is very ill for a fortnight.   During her illness she reflects on the unreality, the falsity of her connexion with Skrebensky, and wonders what still binds her to him.   The answer at long last comes that it is the child.   Nevertheless she does not want

[24] *Op. cit.*, p. 485.   [25] *Op. cit.*, p. 486.
[26] *Op. cit.*, pp. 486-7.   [27] *Op. cit.*, p. 488.

to be bound by Skrebensky and his world. Hence the conflict. "She fought and fought all through her illness to be free of him and his world, to put it aside, into its place. Yet ever anew it gained ascendancy over her, it laid new hold on her."[28] Gradually the resolve forms itself in her that she must break out of the shell of unreality surrounding her:

> And again, to her feverish brain, came the vivid reality of acorns in February lying on the floor of a wood with their shells burst and discarded and the kernel issued naked to put itself forth. She was the naked, clear kernel thrusting forth the clear, powerful shoot, and the world was a bygone winter, discarded, her mother and father and Anton and college and all her friends, all cast off like a year that has gone by, whilst the kernel was free and naked and striving to take new root, to create a new knowledge of Eternity in the flux of Time. And the kernel was the only reality; the rest was cast off into oblivion.[29]

Ursula has landed alone on the shores of an unexplored, undiscovered world. Skrebensky belongs to the world she has cast off. So when his telegram comes that he is married she is not disappointed. She now knows that she could not have created in him the man of her own desire. "It was not for her to create, but to recognise a man created by God. The man should come from the Infinite and she should hail him."[30]

As she grows better she tends to see, influenced by the experience of her own rebirth, signs of new germination beneath the husks of other people also. She can still see the unliving, stiffened bodies of the colliers and the terrible corruption spreading over the face of the land: but it is also given to her to see the faint iridescence in the sky steadily forming itself into a vast rainbow.

> And the rainbow stood on the earth. She knew that the sordid people who crept hard-scaled and separate on the face of the world's corruption were living still, that the rainbow was arched in their blood and would quiver to life in their spirit, that they would cast off their horny covering of disintegration, that new, clean, naked bodies would issue to a new germination,

---

[28] *Op. cit.*, p. 491. [29] *Op. cit.*, p. 492. [30] *Op. cit.*, p. 493.

to a new growth, rising to the light and the wind and the clean rain of heaven. She saw in the rainbow the earth's new architecture, the old, brittle corruption of houses and factories swept away, the world built up in a living fabric of Truth, fitting to the over-arching heaven.[31]

What Ursula sees in the rainbow is a hope for the future, a promise of fulfilment—for herself and for the rest of mankind—in a new world. The hard, brittle world of corruption and falsity she has come out into holds no possibility for such a fulfilment. And she has learnt by now that sensual satisfaction alone will not do. So she, with the author's concurrence, rests her hope in the belief that "there must be a new world".

Lawrence had plans of his own as to how this new world could be brought about. His experience during the First World War was to leave him a bitterly disillusioned man in many respects: but he continued to stand firmly by his belief in man's imperative need for collective purpose activity—though he was no longer sure what shape this could take. Just after the completion of *The Rainbow*, however, he had some radical but impracticable schemes which he fondly hoped could be immediately effected. Lawrence's correspondence of the period—especially his letters to Bertrand Russell which have been so unjustifiably (and without explanation) run down even by his own 'champions'[32]—reveals the same passionate concern for the destruction of the old world and the creation of a new one which we find at the end of *The Rainbow*. In February 1915 Lawrence wrote to Russell iterating his belief that as long as men were enclosed within the "hard, unliving, impervious shell" of a money-oriented society, they could not even begin to live; that "the shell, the form, the whole frame" must, as a first step, be smashed:

> I write to say to you that we *must* start a solid basis of freedom of actual living—not only of thinking. We *must* provide another standard than the pecuniary standard, to measure *all* daily life by. We must be free of the economic

---

[31] *Op. cit.*, p. 495.
[32] Richard Aldington, for instance—whom J. I. M. Stewart describes as Lawrence's "most sympathetic and perceptive critic"—calls these letters "not only absurd, but even ignominious". (Foreword to Nehls, III (1959), XIV.)

question.   Economic life must be the means to actual life:
We must make it so at once.

 There must be a revolution in the state.   It shall begin by
the nationalising of all industries and means of communication,
and of the land—in one fell blow.   Then a man shall have his
wages whether he is sick or well or old—if anything prevents
his working, he shall have his wages just the same.   So we shall
not live in fear of the wolf—no man amongst us, and no woman,
shall have any fear of the wolf at the door, for all the wolves
are dead.[33]

Then Lawrence, with almost incredible naïveté goes on to add:
"Which practically solves the whole economic question for the
present."   Two months later he wrote to E. M. Forster that
he wished somebody would "make a league" with him to war
against "the fussy Mammon, that pretends to be a tame pet
now, and so devours us in our sleep".[34]   To Lady Ottoline
Morrell he complained that Russell was more concerned with
having his own "personal fling at the world" than in uniting
for a purpose.   "And individuals do not *vitally* concern me any
more.   Only a *purpose* vitally concerns me, not individuals."[35]
In his letter of 16 Aug. 1915, written to Lady Cynthia Asquith,
he went further by saying that Russell was betraying the "real
truth": "Russell says I cherish illusions, that there *is* no such
spirit as I like to imagine, the spirit of unanimity in truth,
among mankind.   He says that is fiction."[36]   Lawrence himself
at this time was interested in associating only with those who
were prepared to act in "a new unanimity" to bring about
"an immediate destruction—and reconstructive revolution in
actual life, England, now".[37]   Another letter written from
Littlehampton during the same month is strikingly reminiscent of the concluding page or two of *The Rainbow*.   By
September doubts begin to appear in his mind and he is not
very hopeful that his idea of forming a little nucleus of living
people would be a success:

 Perhaps by Christmas we shall have some little footing, and I
can be reconciled to all my friends, and we can unite in a bigger
effort, a bigger paper, and Russell give his lectures, and we

---

[33] *Collected Letters*, I, pp. 316-17. [34] *Letters*, p. 224. [35] *Op. cit.*, p. 243.
[36] *Collected Letters*, I, p. 362. [37] *Op. cit.*, p. 363.

can have good Club Meetings. Perhaps—God knows. And perhaps, everything will fizzle out.[38]

The "bigger paper" implies a reference to the short-lived *Signature* which Lawrence hoped might prove the seed of a great change in life and set in a new era. He admitted that in expecting so much he was perhaps being too self-important, but nevertheless decided he must do his best: "It is no good if everybody leaves the doing to everybody else."[39]

A note of despair is already discernible in the letters written in the beginning of 1916. Lawrence feels he is unable to do anything for the moment. The world seems to him like a ship going down: but he is determined not to sink with the ship: he would rather live a life apart than submit to the falsehood of the times. The only hope he could see in the interim lay in "a nucleus of love between a man and a woman",[40] and the company of a few friends, if possible. And he had, of course, the world of his creative work, his art, besides. Even in his moments of utter revulsion against "the horrible mass of humanity" he continued to believe in the value of his creative writing, for "a work of art is an act of faith, as Michael Angelo says, and one goes on writing to the unseen witnesses".[41] In his letter of 15 February, addressed to Ottoline Morrell, he wrote:

> I feel quite anti-social, against this social whole as it exists. I wish one could be a pirate or a highwayman in these days. But my way of shooting them with noiseless bullets that explode in their souls, these social people of today, perhaps it is more satisfying. But I feel like an outlaw. All my work is a shot at their very innermost strength, these banded people of today.[42]

He had, moreover, not lost hope altogether. There must be at least some other people, he felt sure, who shared his faith in the "little hard flame of truth" which goes on burning inside one in spite of everything:

> Still I know that there are some other people, who have the same abstraction, who live finally by the central truth, and by

---

[38] *Letters*, p. 257. [39] *Op. cit.*, p. 259. [40] *Collected Letters*, I, p. 415.
[41] *Op. cit.*, p. 449. [42] *Op. cit.*, pp. 428-9.

nothing of the loathsome outer world. And in the end, I hope we can add our spirit together, unite in essential truthfulness, and create a new well-shapen life out of the smashed mess of the old order—I do believe we can, in time. But we have to give ourselves time—heaven knows how long.[43]

The realisation that it might take a long time to create "a new order of life" did not, however, prevent Lawrence's desire to "start something afresh" asserting itself intermittently. In January 1917 he wrote, "I want to get into contact with something new."[44] And a few weeks later: "I feel like starting something somewhere: but hardly know yet where to begin."[45] One opening available to him as a writer was to communicate with the rest of mankind through his art. In his next novel, *Women in Love*, are implicit the results of his experiences during the war years.[46] Writing a foreword to it in September 1919, he remarked:

We are now in a period of crisis. Every man who is acutely alive is acutely wrestling with his own soul. The people that bring forth the new passion, the new idea, this people will endure. Those others, that fix themselves in the old idea, will perish with the new life strangled unborn within them. Men must speak out to one another.[47]

Women in Love was his own way of speaking out, at the time.

[43] *Letters*, p. 368. [44] *Op. cit.*, p. 395. [45] *Op. cit.*, p. 403.
[46] These results, however, find explicit expression only some years later in "The Nightmare" chapter in *Kangaroo*.
[47] *Women in Love* (Modern Library), n.d., p. x.

V

Dies Irae

The novel is more or less a sequel to *The Rainbow*, and I think I'll call it *Noah's Ark*.[1]

What I really have to say: Thinking about the title *Women in Love*. If you care to change it to *Day of Wrath*, I am willing.
Dies irae, dies illa
Solvet saeclum in favilla.
That for the motto.[2]

To what extent is *Women in Love* really a sequel to *The Rainbow*? The apparent connexion between the two novels is slight; and it has been suggested that only the names Ursula and Gudrun Brangwen are carried over from the earlier novel. F. R. Leavis, for instance, takes the view that *Women in Love* has "no organic connection with *The Rainbow*;[3] another commentary on the novel also advises the reader to treat the two novels separately for the reason that the character of Ursula undergoes a change and "any effort by the reader to fuse the two Ursulas in his reading of *Women in Love* would lead to difficulties".[4] Yet Lawrence himself wanted the reader to assume in the Ursula of *Women in Love* the experience she acquires in the previous novel. The character of Ursula, thus, not only does not present any difficulties, it can be understood even better when seen in its process of development. It is well known that Lawrence had originally conceived of a single work to be called *The Sisters*, and that this was later divided into two books we now know as *The Rainbow* and *Women in Love*.[5] Now, even at an early stage when the novel

---

[1] *Collected Letters*, I, p. 533.   [2] *Op. cit.*, p. 631.   [3] Leavis, p. 96.
[4] W. W. Robson, "D. H. Lawrence and *Women in Love*", in *The Modern Age*, Harmondsworth (Penguin), 1961, p. 288.
[5] "I am going to split the book into two volumes: it was so unwieldy. It needs to be in two volumes." (*Collected Letters*, I, p. 306.)

was envisaged as *The Sisters*, Lawrence insisted that according to his "scheme of the novel" he "*must* have Ella [as Ursula was then called] get some experience before she meets her Mr. Birkin".[6] This experience was later incorporated in *The Rainbow*, and Lawrence continued to think of *Women in Love* as its continuation. In his foreword to *Women in Love* he wrote: "This book is a potential sequel to *The Rainbow*"; and there are several references in his letters to the same effect.[7] The eagerness with which he welcomed the suggestion that the two novels be called *Women in Love*, Vol. i and ii cannot be explained merely in terms of the exigencies of publication—though that aspect, no doubt, had its importance. "*The Rainbow* and *Women in Love* are really an organic artistic whole", he wrote to Martin Secker. "I cannot but think it would be well to issue them as *Women in Love*, Vol. I and Vol. II."[8] All this is not to deny that there is a difference of tone and emphasis in the two novels as finally published. Lawrence himself, while describing *Women in Love* as a sequel to *The Rainbow*, did not overlook the fact that in some respects it was also "very different":[9] he characterised the earlier novel as "destructive-consummating": but *Women in Love*, he said, was "purely destructive" as it contained "the results in one's soul of the war".[10] *Women in Love* can be said to be more inward-looking: "At present,"Lawrence wrote in 1916, "my real world is the world of my inner soul, which reflects on to the novel I write".[11] He had concluded *The Rainbow* on a note of hope in a regenerated society; the solution sought in *Women in Love* is no longer social: whatever fulfilment the characters achieve is reached through their individual relationships. Lawrence's predicament is not unlike that of Birkin in the novel's discarded "Prologue" chapter which shows him reflecting on "the winter that has come upon mankind":

> And Birkin was just coming to a knowledge of the essential futility of all attempt at social unanimity in constructiveness. In the winter, there can only be unanimity of disintegration,

---

[6] *Collected Letters*, i, p. 263.
[7] *Op. cit.*, pp. 471, 495, 519, 533.
[8] *Op. cit.*, p. 615.
[9] *Op. cit.*, p. 495.
[10] *Op. cit.*, p. 519.
[11] *Op. cit.*, p. 453.

the leaves fall unanimously, the plants die down. . . . How to get away from this process of reduction . . . which was universal though unacknowledged, this was the unconscious problem which tortured Birkin day and night. . . . In the world the autumn was setting in. What should a man add himself on to?—to science, to social reform, to aestheticism, to sensational-ism? The whole world's constructive activity was a fiction, a lie, to hide the great process of decomposition, which had set in. What then to adhere to?[12]

The vision revealed in *Women in Love* is, however, not altogether despairing—for while on the one hand the novel is "so end-of-the-world" and terrifying, on the other hand, as the author himself has observed, "it is, it must be, the beginning of a new world too".[13] What Birkin finally comes to "adhere to" is his perfected relationship with Ursula. Even though he is aware that this in itself is not everything and cannot be a substitute for "unanimous . . . constructive activity", his immediate need is to obtain complete fulfilment in marriage. As Lawrence says in his poem "Manifesto",

> . . . only fulfilment will do,
> real fulfilment, nothing short.
> It is our ratification,
> our heaven as a matter of fact.
> Immortality, the heaven, is only a projection
> of this strange but actual fulfilment,
> here in the flesh.[14]

This fulfilment in the flesh is, however, possible only through a prolonged conflict leading to the emergence of two beings who are "unutterably distinguished and in unutterable conjunc-tion".[15] Also, corresponding to the conflict in the relations between individuals is the conflict that goes on within each individual. All these conflicts in themselves form the complex structure of the novel; and it is the depiction of these conflicts which gives us the clue to its form as well as its meaning. The tense atmosphere of the entire novel is admirably intimated in its very first pages which show the two sisters—Ursula and

[12] D. H. Lawrence, "Prologue to *Women in Love*", *Texas Quarterly*, VI, i (1963), p. 103.
[13] *Collected Letters*, I, p. 482.   [14] *Poems*, I, p. 258.   [15] *Op. cit.*, p. 261.

Gudrun—talking "as their thoughts stray through their minds".[16] They look at each other, laugh and feel frightened;[17] talking amiably, they become at moments "almost hostile";[18] they hold themselves "tense";[19] cause a "constraint" over each other;[20] and thus betray "the tension of the situation".[21] This ambivalence of theirs is carried over into the later part of the novel, and in their other relationships. Ursula, for instance, persists a long time in her ambivalent attitude towards Birkin. She draws back "even though her desire sent her forward" towards him;[22] she finds him "horrible. And yet she was fascinated";[23] he appears to her "so attractive and so repulsive at once".[24] It is, of course, not the mere statement that there is some sense of opposition, or that the characters in the story experience a tension in their relationships, which makes *Women in Love* the great novel it is; it is the translation of this conflict into dramatic terms which makes it a work of art of the highest order. Lawrence's supreme achievement lies in his having succeeded in communicating the ever-changing living relationships of his characters through the action of the novel itself.

Women in Love is primarily, though not exclusively, a novel about man-woman relationship which Lawrence—when he began writing *The Sisters*—regarded as "*the* problem of today". He wrote to Edward Garnett, "I can only write what I feel pretty strongly about: and that, at present, is the relation between men and women."[25] In *Women in Love* he goes straight to the matter, and his exploration of the novel's theme begins on its very first page with Gudrun's question to Ursula, "don't you *really want* to get married?" To her further question whether she thinks one needs the *experience* of having been married, Ursula's rejoinder is that rather than an experience, marriage is more likely to be the end of experience. This

---

[16] The apparently casual talk is, however, loaded with significance—as Leavis and others have pointed out. See also George H. Ford's Introduction to " 'The Wedding' Chapter of D. H. Lawrence's *Women in Love*", *Texas Studies in Literature and Language*, VI, ii (1964), p. 136.

[17] *Women in Love*, p. 2.   [18] *Op. cit.*, p. 3.   [19] *Op. cit.*, p. 7.
[20] *Ibid.*   [21] *Op. cit.*, p. 5.   [22] *Op. cit.*, p. 178.
[23] *Op. cit.*, p. 432.   [24] *Ibid.*
[25] *Collected Letters*, I, p. 200.

questioning of the institution of marriage is further underlined in the chapter "In the Train" where Birkin, after a tense pause in a conversation with Gerald, suddenly looks "straight and overpowering" into the eyes of the other man, and asks him, "What do you think is the aim and object of your life, Gerald?" and, without listening to the reply, goes on: "Do you think to live is the be-all and end-all of life?" He himself, Birkin explains, wants the "finality of love". Gerald cannot quite make it out.

> "I don't believe a woman, and nothing but a woman, will ever make my life," said Gerald.
> "Not the centre and core of it—the love between you and a woman?" asked Birkin.
> Gerald's eyes narrowed with a queer dangerous smile as he watched the other man.
> "I never quite feel it that way," he said.
> "You don't? Then wherein does life centre, for you?"
> "I don't know—that is what I want somebody to tell me. As far as I can make out, it doesn't centre at all. It is artificially held *together* by the social mechanism."
> Birkin pondered as if he would crack something.
> "I know," he said, "it just doesn't centre. The old ideals are dead as nails—nothing there. It seems to me there remains only this perfect union with a woman—sort of ultimate marriage—and there isn't anything else."
> "And you mean if there isn't the woman, there's nothing?" said Gerald.
> "Pretty well that—seeing there's no God."[26]

This, then, is Birkin's "aim and object" in life. Seeing that there is no God, and that the old ideals are dead as nails, he wants to make this "ultimate marriage" with a woman the centre and core of his life. The rest of the novel is substantially a working out of Birkin's attempt, and Gerald's failure, to realise this immediate aim.

Birkin is, in many ways, the central figure in the novel, and the reader, at one stage or another, tends to judge all other characters with reference to him. He expresses many of Lawrence's own formulated views. But whether he is a virtual

---

[26] *Women in Love*, pp. 50-1.

self-portrait of Lawrence or not, he is primarily a character in
the novel and therefore subject to the criticism of the work as a
whole. W. W. Robson is quite right in his remark about Birkin
that "if his peculiarities are Lawrence's own, they are presented
by Lawrence quite objectively": but he takes a rather superficial, though not uncommon, view when he goes on to suggest
that Lawrence had intended for him some kind of "standard-
supplying role in the book".[27] Birkin's views, even if they are
to be identified with Lawrence's own, are submitted to the
criticism of the novel. The author shows him to be irritable,
high-strung and self-willed; his Salvator Mundi touch is felt
by others to be despicable; his abstract, far-fetched expressions,
which he utters with a certain Sunday-school stiffness, often
make him look ridiculous. Lawrence, one is left in no doubt,
has done it all on purpose: this is his way of laughing at
himself:

> . . . the Holy Ghost . . . within us . . . prompts us to . . . laugh
> when we must laugh, particularly at ourselves, for in deadly
> earnestness there is always something a bit ridiculous. The
> Holy Ghost bids us never to be too deadly in our earnestness,
> always to laugh in time, at ourselves and everything.
> Particularly at our sublimities. Everything has its hour of
> ridicule—everything.[28]

In the novel we are introduced to Birkin by Ursula. He is a
school inspector of the county—one of the "various men of
capacity" with whom Hermione Roddice, "the most remarkable woman in the Midlands", has "various intimacies of mind
and soul".[29] They have been lovers for several years, but he is
now trying to leave her. The more Hermione strives to bring
him to her, the more he fights her back. She, however, needs

[27] *The Modern Age*, p. 290.
[28] *S.C.A.L.*, pp. 69-70. Anaïs Nin is quite right when she remarks that
Lawrence is "above all an artist since he can stand off from and observe critically
even his most passionate feelings and convictions"; and that if he has created
Birkin who carries the burden of Lawrence's earnestness—even his "ridiculous
exaltations"—he has also created the characters "who *answer Birkin*, . . . and
who put him in the wrong". (*D. H. Lawrence: An Unprofessional Study*, London
(1961), pp. 100-2.) See also Leavis, p. 176; and Robert L. Chamberlain,
"Pussum, Minette, and the Africo-Nordic Symbol in Lawrence's *Women in Love*",
P.M.L.A., LXXVIII (1963), 412.
[29] *Women in Love*, p. 10.

him desperately to complete her lack of natural sufficiency; and she still has confidence in her strength to keep him. Without him, she feels, she will never be able to fill the "terrible void", the "deficiency of being" within her.

Hermione is an intellectual woman of the new school, "nerve-worn with consciousness".[30] She moves among the foremost in the world of culture and of intellect: she is "a Kulturträger, a medium for the culture of ideas".[31] Her self is all in her head. She can never be spontaneous. She always wants to *know*: it is an obsession with her. She is intelligent enough to be able to recognise her own lack of spontaneity, and even mocks at deliberateness and self-consciousness. "Aren't we exchanging the substance for the shadow", she says, "aren't we forfeiting life for this dead quality of knowledge? And what does it mean to me after all? What does all this knowing mean to me? It means nothing!"[32] Actually, it means everything to her: it is all her life. Her awareness of her "incapacity to be spontaneous" does not help her to be any more spontaneous. Birkin, who can see through her pose, tells her that even her so-called desire for "pure sensation and 'passion' " is merely the worst and last form of intellectualism:[33] "Passion and instincts—you want them hard enough, but through your head, your consciousness. It all takes place in your head, under that skull of yours."[34] She is "a leaf of the old great tree of knowledge".[35] But the tree is withering, and she knows it. So she must fight for withered truths, with a "devastating cynicism at the bottom of her". And she fights with a persistent, almost insane *will*. If only we could learn to use our will, she believes, we could do everything: "The will can cure anything and put anything right. That I am convinced of. . . ."[36]

She wants to impose her will on all she comes in contact with. Her blood runs sharp if she is thwarted even in a trifling matter. She must have power—especially over any male being. She

---

[30] *Ibid.*   [31] *Ibid.*   [32] *Op. cit.*, p. 35.

[33] Birkin is not against the mind or intellect as such. In fact he thinks most people have "too little" mind to be able to know how to make use of it. He believes, as Lawrence himself did, that mental consciousness is an invaluable instrument for the achievement of "spontaneity" and "wholeness of being".

[34] *Women in Love*, p. 35.   [35] *Op. cit.*, p. 284.   [36] *Op. cit.*, p. 131.

talks to the stag in the park, wanting to wheedle and fondle it because "he was male, so she must exert some kind of power over him".[37] She puts cream before a cat but holds "the cat's head with her long, slow, white fingers, not letting him drink, holding him in her power".[38] Ursula is quite right when she tells Birkin that all that Hermione wants is petty, immediate power.[39]

Birkin, in fact, knows it already—only too well. He is aware that Hermione's "love" for him is not a passion at all but a bullying will: she only wants to have him in her power. He tells her that she hasn't got any real body, "any dark sensual body of life"; that she has only her will and her conceit of consciousness", and her "lust for power, to *know*".[40] Her will has gone completely over to the mental consciousness and is working for the destruction of her "blood-being".

What Hermione represents is an "extravagance of spiritual *will*",[41] an intellectual form of bullying. Lawrence defines bullying as the desire to superimpose one's will upon another person, and he characterises it as "most fatal, most hateful of all things".[42] Birkin thinks likewise and so fights Hermione back. Hermione knows that a split between them is coming, and her hatred of him is "subconscious and intense". At the same time she is "stimulated above all things by this conflict with him".[43]

The split finally comes one day when Birkin, having spoken his mind, feels "violent waves of hatred and loathing of all he said coming out of her".[44] He afterwards feels sorry and goes to her boudoir to make it up with her. Finding her sitting at her table writing letters, he takes up a large volume and sits down with his back to her. But she cannot go on with her writing any longer. Her whole mind is turned into "a chaos, darkness breaking in upon it, and her self struggling to gain control with her will . . .":

> And then she realized that his presence was the wall, his presence was destroying her. Unless she could break out, she

---

[37] *Op. cit.*, p. 80.   [38] *Op. cit.*, p. 292.   [39] *Op. cit.*, p. 299.
[40] *Op. cit.*, p. 35.   [41] *Fantasia*, p. 36.   [42] *Op. cit.*, p. 47.
[43] *Women in Love*, p. 81.   [44] *Op. cit.*, p. 97.

must die most fearfully, walled up in horror. . . . She was aware of him sitting silently there, an unthinkable evil obstruction. . . .

A terrible voluptuous thrill ran down her arms—she was going to . . . have her consummation of voluptuous ecstasy at last. It was coming! In utmost terror and agony, she knew it was upon her now, in extremity of bliss. Her hand closed on a blue, beautiful ball of lapis lazuli that stood on her desk for a paper-weight. She rolled it round in her hand as she rose silently. Her heart was a pure flame in her breast, she was purely unconscious in ecstasy. She moved towards him and stood behind him for a moment in ecstasy. He, closed within the spell, remained motionless and unconscious.

Then swiftly, in a flame that drenched down her body like fluid lightning and gave her a perfect, unutterable consummation, unutterable satisfaction, she brought down the ball of jewel stone with all her force, crash on his head.[45]

Her fingers, however, are in the way and deaden the blow. She lifts her arm high, her hand clasping the ball of lapis lazuli, to aim a second blow. But Birkin hurriedly covers his head with a thick volume, and the blow comes down, "almost breaking his neck, and shattering his heart". Birkin is shattered but his soul is unafraid and unsurprised. He leaves her standing and goes away.[46] Hermione, enraged by Birkin's obstinate refusal to surrender himself to her will, gives the conflict between them a violent shape. But having pushed the conflict to its extreme she also unwittingly liberates him from her influence.

Birkin, however, escapes from conflict with one woman, only to be involved soon afterwards in conflict with another. Ursula, we are told in the first chapter, has been wanting to know Birkin who "piqued her, attracted her and annoyed her . . . something kept her from him as well as attracted her to him".[47] She meets him next in the chapter "An Island".

[45] *Op. cit.*, pp. 97-8.

[46] The scene of Hermione's "murderous attack" on Birkin, George H. Ford remarks, has baffled many readers. And there is some truth in his observation that both her violence and Birkin's reaction to it become clearer when seen in the light of the "unpublished" "Prologue" chapter of the novel which gives a "full account of the earlier stages of this frustrating affair". (*Texas Quarterly*, VI, i, p. 97.) But even in the book as published, Hermione's violence does not come to us as a surprise because we are made to feel all along that her frictional relationship with Birkin has been heading towards some such "consummation".

[47] *Women in Love*, p. 15.

M

They get talking, "rousing each other to a fine passion of opposition".[48] Birkin expounds to her his views on love and humanity. Love, he says, is just one of the emotions like all the others, which one feels or does not feel, according to circumstance. It is only a part of any human relationship, and not an absolute. Ursula does not agree, and sneers at him. She, nevertheless, once again finds him both attractive and detestable; and this "duality in feeling" which he creates in her makes "a fine hate of him quicken in her bowels".[49]

The clash of ideas between Birkin and Ursula is not without significance; and it must find its way to a resolution. "The little conflict into which they had fallen had torn their consciousness and left them like two impersonal forces, there in contact."[50] Ursula realises that she is in a way strictly hostile to Birkin and yet is held by some bond to him. There has started "a fight to the death between them—or to new life: though in what the conflict lay, no one could say".[51]

What Birkin wants of Ursula is something beyond love, something more than love. Love, he says, gives out in the last issues. He, like Lawrence himself, believes that there is no fulfilment in love itself. Fulfilment, indeed, must come *through* love, through a perfected harmony between the lover and the beloved: but this communion, wonderful as it is, is by no means itself the fulfilment. In fact, the very attainment of this harmony is dependent on the "clarified singleness of each being, a singleness equilibrised, polarised in one by the counterposing singleness of the other".[52] Fulfilment lies in "deep rich aloneness", in the "fulness of self-possession".[53]

This stark, impersonal, isolated being within each of us, Birkin holds, does not and cannot meet and mingle. He, therefore, does not believe in the mere merging of two beings into oneness. The alternative he puts forward is that of "true relatedness": the man remains true to his nature, the woman to hers; both maintain their individual identity and let the relationship work of itself. What he is looking for, he tells Ursula, is a sort of "mystic balance" with her:

[48] *Op. cit.*, p. 118.   [49] *Op. cit.*, p. 122.
[50] *Op. cit.*, p. 124.   [51] *Op. cit.*, p. 135.
[52] *Fantasia*, p. 219.   [53] *Op. cit.*, p. 120.

What I want is a strange conjunction with you— . . . not
meeting and mingling; but . . . an equilibrium, a pure balance
of two single beings—as the stars balance each other.[54]

Ursula finds this far-fetched talk about equilibrium and the
stars rather ridiculous. She feels that if what Birkin says were
really true, he should not have the need to drag in the stars.
She mockingly compares him to Mars and tells him that what
he wants of her is to be his satellite. "There—there—you've
given yourself away! You want a satellite, Mars and his
satellite!"[55] She is convinced that Birkin wants her to
surrender to him her individuality, to yield to him her very
identity; and she is naturally reluctant "to give the sort of
submission he insists on".[56] Her protest against Birkin's desire
(as she understands it) to bully and dominate her takes the form
of her hatred of him. Her whole nature seems "sharpened and
intensified into a pure dart of hate".[57] Ursula does not completely understand why she has come to hate Birkin so. She
is none the less overcome by, possessed by, this "poignant
hatred" of him. Her hatred is, however, different from
Hermione's. She does not hate Birkin for this or that. She
does not want to do anything to him. Her hate is "pure and
gem-like". All that she wants is not to have any connexion
with him.

Birkin, meanwhile, has been lying ill and meditating on his
future. He realises that his life is in some way bound up with
Ursula's: but he cannot accept the sentimental, romantic love
Ursula has to offer. He knows quite well what such love ends
up in. The thought of living in "the horrible privacy of
domestic and connubial satisfaction" appears repulsive to him.

The hot narrow intimacy between man and wife was abhorrent.
The way they shut their doors, these married people, and shut
themselves into their own exclusive alliance with each other,
even in love, disgusted him. It was a whole community of
mistrustful couples insulated in private houses or private rooms,
always in couples, and no further life, no further immediate,
no disinterested relationship admitted: a kaleidoscope of

---

[54] *Women in Love*, p. 139.
[55] *Op. cit.*, p. 142.
[56] *Op. cit.*, p. 285.
[57] *Op. cit.*, p. 190.

couples, disjointed, separatist, meaningless entities of married couples.[58]

Marriage in this sense seems hateful to him, and he rejects it definitely. Later in the novel Birkin again defines marriage of this kind as "a sort of tacit hunting in couples: the world all in couples, each couple in its own little house, watching its own little interests, and stewing in its own little privacy. . . ."[59] This time he is talking to Gerald, to whom he explains that though he does believe in a permanent union between a man and a woman, he cannot take it to be the last word; and that the love-and-marriage ideal must be taken down from its pedestal.

Ursula, however, still sticks to this ideal. She wants "unspeakable intimacies".[60] She wants to have Birkin utterly, completely—to have him as her own. She makes, we are told, great professions to herself of her willingness to warm his footsoles between her breasts, but only on condition that he gives himself up to her absolutely. She believes in an absolute surrender to love. "She believed that love far surpassed the individual."[61]

Birkin cannot agree to this. He cannot grant that love is everything. To him the individual is more than love or than any relationship. He wants "to be single in himself, the woman single in herself".[62] But it appears to him that women always have a passion for possession; they always want to have, to own, to control, to dominate. He finds possession at the hands of "Woman, the Great Mother of everything" intolerable. He had found it so in the case of Hermione who even through her humbleness and subservience had wanted to claim him as her own. And Ursula, he feels, wants the same— only perhaps in a different way.[63]

---

[58] *Op. cit.*, p. 191.   [59] *Op. cit.*, p. 344.   [60] *Op. cit.*, p. 257.
[61] *Op. cit.*, p. 258.   [62] *Op. cit.*, p. 191.

[63] A helpful gloss on the subject is to be found in one of Lawrence's letters to Katherine Mansfield, where he says that "at certain periods the man has a desire and a tendency to return into the woman, make her his goal and end, find his justification in her. In this way he casts himself as it were into her womb, and she, the Magna Mater, receives him with gratification. . . . It is awfully hard, once the sex relation has gone this way, to recover. If we don't recover, we die". (*Collected Letters*, I, p. 565.)

It filled him with almost insane fury, this calm assumption of the Magna Mater, that all was hers, because she had borne it. Man was hers because she had borne him. A Mater Dolorosa, she had borne him, a Magna Mater, she now claimed him again, soul and body, sex, meaning, and all. He had a horror of the Magna Mater, she was detestable.[64]

Why should a man, he argues with himself, be considered a broken-off fragment of a woman; why should men and women consider themselves as broken fragments of one whole? Perhaps there was a time—before sex was—when beings were mixed. Then the process of singling away into individuality started. The womanly drew to one side, the manly to the other. This polarisation, Birkin thinks, has been imperfect till now; it is for us now to achieve the "pure duality of opposition".[65] It is not true then, he concludes, that men and women are broken fragments of one whole. "Rather we are the singling into purity and clear being, of things that were mixed. Rather the sex is that which remains in us of the mixed, the unresolved."[66]

In all this Birkin's "meditations" are remarkably similar to Lawrence's own. In his essay on "Love" he says:

We are not clear, we are mixed and mingled. I am in the beloved also and she is in me. Which should not be, for this is confusion and chaos. Therefore I will gather myself complete and free from the beloved, she shall single herself out in utter contradistinction to me. . . . In the pure passion of oneness, in the pure passion for distinctness and separateness, a dual passion of unutterable separation and lovely conjunction of the two, the new configuration takes place . . .[67]

It is with some such thoughts in mind that Birkin goes to France for a time, and is, on his return, watched by Ursula while he throws stone after stone in frenzied persistence to break the image of the moon reflected in the pond.

Ursula sets out one evening towards Willey Water. There, walking among the trees in the still, "clear as crystal" night, far away from any human beings, she finds a sort of "magic peace". But she starts violently as she perceives something on

---

[64] *Women in Love*, p. 192.
[66] *Op. cit.*, p. 192.
[65] *Op. cit.*, p. 193.
[67] *Phoenix*, pp. 153-4.

her right, between the tree trunks—"a great presence, watching her, dodging her". It is only the moon, risen through the thin trees. She swerves down to the steep bank above the pond, looking at the water that is "perfect in its stillness, floating a moon upon it". She notices a shadow moving by the water. It is Birkin. He does not know she is there. So she comes quite close to him without his being aware of it. He is talking disconnectedly to himself: "Cybele—curse her! The accursed Syria Dea! Does one begrudge it her? What else is there—?"[68] Ursula finds it all so ridiculous she wants to laugh loudly. Birkin, meanwhile, stands staring at the water; then stoops, picks up a stone and throws it sharply at the pond. The bright moon leaps and sways, all distorted. Birkin stoops and finds another stone.

> Then again there was a burst of sound, and a burst of brilliant light, the moon had exploded on the water, and was flying asunder in flakes of white and dangerous fire. Rapidly, like white birds, the fires all broken rose across the pond, fleeing in clamorous confusion, battling with the flock of dark waves that were forcing their way in. The furthest waves of light, fleeing out, seemed to be clamouring against the shore for escape, the waves of darkness came in heavily, running under towards the centre. But at the centre, the heart of all, was still a vivid, incandescent quivering of a white moon not quite destroyed, a white body of fire writhing and striving and not even now broken open, not yet violated.[69]

The moon gradually draws itself together. Birkin stands and watches till the pond is almost calm, the moon "almost serene." Then he looks for more stones and starts throwing them one after the other at the pond.

> The moon leapt up white and burst through the air. Darts of bright light shot asunder, darkness swept over the centre. There was no moon, only a battlefield of broken lights and shadows, running close together. Shadows, dark and heavy, struck again and again across the place where the heart of the moon had been, obliterating it altogether. The white fragments pulsed up and down, and could not find where to go,

---

[68] *Women in Love*, p. 238.   [69] *Op. cit.*, p. 239.

apart and brilliant on the water like the petals of a rose that a wind has blown far and wide.

Yet again, they were flickering their way to the centre, finding the path blindly, enviously. And again, all was still, as Birkin and Ursula watched. The waters were loud on the shore. . . . And he was not satisfied. Like a madness, he must go on. He got large stones, and threw them, one after the other, at the white-burning centre of the moon, till there was nothing but a rocking of hollow noise, and a pond surged up, no moon any more, only a few broken flakes tangled and glittering broadcast in the darkness, without aim or meaning, a darkened confusion . . .[70]

Ursula, who has been sitting in the dark, motionless and spent, feels his "invisible tenacity" and is dazed. When the moon becomes whole again she is afraid Birkin would stone it again. So she slips from her seat and comes down to him saying, "You won't throw stones at it any more, will you?" Birkin replies that he wanted to see if he could "make it be quite gone off the pond".

"Yes, it was horrible, really. Why should you hate the moon? It hasn't done you any harm, has it?"
"Was it hate?" he said.
And they were silent for a few minutes.[71]

The passage has been very often quoted and commented upon. It was perhaps J. Middleton Murry who first pointed out that Birkin is here trying to destroy Aphrodite[72]—though that is also made quite obvious by Lawrence's other references to the moon. In *Fantasia of the Unconscious* Lawrence equates moon with "sea-born Aphrodite, mother and bitter goddess".[73] In his introduction to Frederick Carter's *The Dragon of the Apocalypse* he tells us that men in the past "called the moon Artemis, or Cybele, or Astarte".[74] Graham Hough remarks that Birkin's mythology, in calling the moon Cybele or Syria Dea, is "a little rusty".[75] Eliseo Vivas, defending Lawrence

---

[70] *Op. cit.*, pp. 239-40.   [71] *Op. cit.*, p. 241.
[72] *Son of Woman*, p. 118. His interpretation of the chapter "Moony" is, however, quite mistaken and unconvincing. See Harry T. Moore's rejoinder in *The Life and Works of D. H. Lawrence*, p. 122.
[73] *Fantasia*, p. 181.   [74] *Phoenix*, p. 300.   [75] Hough, p. 79.

against "Mr. Hough [who] observes that Lawrence's mythology is a little rusty",[76] traces the mythological identifications of Cybele with the terrible goddess Aphrodite who was served by sodomistic eunuch priests. He, then, concludes that in this scene "Birkin is expressing the ancient and deep-rooted fear some men have felt towards women."[77] All this, besides being vague and inaccurate, is quite unnecessary, as we know from the novel itself what is going on in Birkin's mind. When we see him last in the novel he is already meditating on the instinct of maternal possessiveness he finds in Hermione and Ursula. In cursing the Mother Goddess Cybele, he is rejecting the egocentric possessiveness of "the Great Mother", the "calm assumption of the Magna Mater".[78]

And yet he is not quite sure that one should "begrudge it her", for "what else is there—?"[79] It is this conflict in his mind which the symbolic scene, above all, conveys. Graham Hough is right in describing the scene as "a characteristic piece of Lawrentian writing in that it is powerful in itself, purely descriptively; and in having as well a second layer of significance . . .".[80] Eliseo Vivas calls the device used by Lawrence here "the constitutive symbol"—a symbol "whose referend cannot be fully exhausted by explication, because that to which it refers is symbolised not only *through* it but *in it*".[81] This is not very different from Lawrence's own definition of symbols as organic units of consciousness which can never be explained away because their value is not simply a mental one.[82] Such scenes as the shattering of the image of the moon, or the rabbit scene, are important, says Eliseo Vivas, in that they gather the significance of preceding events and illuminate the scenes or situations that follow.[83] This is certainly so: but perhaps that is not their only or even their chief value. Their primary

---

[76] Vivas, p. 259. Graham Hough, actually, says Birkin's mythology, not Lawrence's, is a bit rusty: but in the given context the distinction is not very material.

[77] Vivas, p. 260. For an anthropological interpretation, see Paul B. Newman, "D. H. Lawrence and the Golden Bough", *The Kansas Magazine* (1962), pp. 79 ff.

[78] *Women in Love*, p. 192.   [79] *Op. cit.*, p. 238.

[80] Hough, p. 78. However, cf. Daiches, pp. 170-1. Daiches is of the opinion that the often admired scene is "too *voulu*", and that the symbol in it "remains imposed and wilful".

[81] Vivas, p. 208.   [82] *Phoenix*, p. 295.   [83] Vivas, p. 281.

function in the novel—apart from the sheer beauty and power of description in them rendered with such immediacy—is that they deepen our understanding of what is going on, in a way which could not have been possible by any other means. These scenes—whether constitutive symbols, semiotic symbols, or just symbolic scenes—serve, above all, to mark significant stages in the development of conflict in the novel.

The conflict going on in the mind of Birkin is stated in descriptive terms later in the same chapter. Ursula, Birkin realises, cannot bring herself to drop her "frightened apprehensive self-insistence".[84] And he himself, too, has "his idea and his will".[85] As long as either of them "insists to the other", there can, he knows, be no accord. What after all, he reflects, does he want? He is not quite sure whether he is looking in Ursula for just "an idea of what he wanted", or for "the interpretation of a profound yearning".[86] If the latter, how is it that he is always talking about sensual fulfilment. The two, he confesses, do not agree very well. In a subsequent chapter, "Excurse", Birkin again admits that he is "so spiritual on the one hand, and in some strange way, degraded on the other. . . . He knew that his spirituality was concomitant of a process of depravity, a sort of pleasure in self-destruction".[87] The discarded "Prologue" chapter makes an explicit, discursive statement on the subject. There we are told of Birkin's inability to love any woman completely with a "living, creative love": "The incapacity to desire any woman, positively, with body and soul, this was a real torture, a deep torture indeed." He certainly *wants* to love: but "between wanting to love, and loving, is the whole difference between life and death". His problem is not one of understanding or of conviction. He knows his thoughts and reactions thoroughly well: but "self-knowledge is not everything"; and no man "by taking thought, can add one cubit to his stature. He can but know his own height and limitation". His fundamental desire is to be able to love completely, "in one and the same act: both body and soul at once, stuck into a complete oneness in contact with a complete woman". That, he knows, is the only way he can

[84] *Women in Love*, p. 243.
[86] *Ibid.*
[85] *Op. cit.*, p. 245.
[87] *Op. cit.*, pp. 300-1.

keep his integrity of being; so he cannot consent to sacrifice
one half of himself to the other. "He would not sacrifice the
sensual to the spiritual half of himself, and he could not
sacrifice the spiritual to the sensual half." At the same time
he is unable to obtain fulfilment in both: "the two halves
reacted from each other". It is always a case of one or the
other, of spirit *or* of senses—"and each, alone, was deadly".[88]

In the chapter "Moony" we see Birkin reflecting on "the
death of the creative spirit" and the "lapse from pure integral
being" which he finds "imminent in himself". He knows that
when the relation between "the senses" and "the outspoken
mind" breaks—leaving the experience all in one sort—the only
result can be the death of "the happy creative being". He is
reminded of an African statuette of a woman with a long
elegant body on short legs; of her diminished beetle face and
unexpectedly heavy protuberant buttocks below her slim
loins. This figure represents for him the quintessence of purely
sensual, purely unspiritual knowledge—"knowledge through
the senses, knowledge arrested and ending in the senses, mystic
knowledge in disintegration and dissolution . . .".[89] This is one
way of fulfilment: the long African process of purely sensual
understanding, of "knowledge in the mystery of dissolution".[90]
While the Africans, Birkin thinks, had fulfilled themselves
through sun-destruction, the white races, having the Arctic
north behind them, would "fulfil a mystery of ice-destructive
knowledge, snow-abstract annihilation".[91] Both the African
process (symbolised by the statuette) and the Northern (of
frost-knowledge: represented by Gerlad, "an omen of the
universal dissolution into whiteness and snow") are, however,
a denial of the creative life, of "the goodness, the holiness, the
desire for creation and productive happiness",[92] and are
therefore finally rejected by Birkin.[93] He chooses the way of

---

[88] *Texas Quarterly*, VI, i, pp. 104-8.   [89] *Women in Love*, pp. 245-6.
[90] *Op. cit.*, p. 246.   [91] *Ibid.*
[92] *Op. cit.*, p. 245.
[93] In the Western industrial society, Julian Moynahan comments, "the same
relation between mind and feeling has broken; desire for feeling has lapsed,
leaving the single impulse to production, disembodied progressive industrial
know-how, knowledge arrested in system-making. It is equally a knowledge in
disintegration and dissolution". (Moynahan, p. 80.) *Cf.* Robert L. Chamberlain,
in *P.M.L.A.* (Sept. 1963), pp. 415-16: "the African and Northern progressions

freedom, the "paradisal entry into pure, single being, the individual soul taking precedence over love and desire for union . . .".[94] This "lovely state of free proud singleness" accepts the obligations of love: but even while it loves and yields, it never forfeits its own proud individual singleness. Hermione's spiritual intimacy and Ursula's emotional-physical intimacy are neither of them acceptable to Birkin:

> Fusion, fusion, this horrible fusion of two beings, which every woman and most men insisted on, was it not nauseous and horrible anyhow, whether it was a fusion of the spirit or of the emotional body? Hermione saw herself as the perfect Idea, to which all men must come: and Ursula was the perfect Womb, the bath of birth, to which all men must come! And both were horrible. Why this dreadful all-comprehensiveness, this hateful tyranny? Why not leave the other being free, why try to absorb, or melt, or merge? One might abandon oneself utterly to the *moments*, but not to any other being.[95]

Ursula is still at the stage where she wants to absorb, to merge. She is still at the emotional-personal level. She has not yet had the deep, pure, sensual knowledge of Birkin which should have made her aware of the "other Being" in him.

> He had taken her as he had never been taken himself. He had taken her at the roots of her darkness and shame—like a demon, laughing over the fountain of mystic corruption which was one of the sources of her being, laughing, shrugging, accepting, accepting finally. As for her, when would she so much go beyond herself to accept him at the quick of death?[96]

The passage has baffled many. Its meaning, however, becomes clear when we realise that by "the fountain of mystic corruption" and "the roots of her darkness and shame"

---

are modes of the same process. . . . The two halves of the great cultural contrast which give the novel its most brilliant effects are more than complementary at the level of the individual; they are identical, each by implication encompassing the other. What matters is the break, the rift—not whether the break first manifests itself in a mind sense-enslaved or in a sensuality mind-enslaved. When this break occurs, both mind and senses become victimized by their alienation from each other, enslaved each by impulse towards its antipodes; and then the hopeless shunting begins".

[94] *Women in Love*, p. 247.   [95] *Op. cit.*, p. 301.   [96] *Op. cit.*, p. 296.

Lawrence means "one of the sources" of Ursula's being: her purely sensual being. Birkin has known the "pure, fierce passion of sensuality" with her, which has given him his "sheer separate distinction", by reducing him to "her essential otherness".[97] In the act of love, Lawrence says in his "Study of Thomas Hardy", "that which is mixed in me is given to the female, that which is male in her draws into me, I am complete, I am pure male, she is pure female; . . . I know how perfectly she is not me, how perfectly I am not her, how utterly we are two . . .".[98] Birkin has by now known Ursula as a distinct separate being; but she has not yet discovered him as "one of the sons of God such as were in the beginning of the world". Birkin could very well say, with Lawrence:

> She has not realised yet, that fearful thing, that I am the other,
> She thinks we are all of one piece.
> It is painfully untrue.
>
> I want her to touch me at last, ah, on the root and quick of my darkness . . .
> Then we shall be two and distinct, we shall have each our separate being.
> And that will be pure existence, liberty.
> Till then, we are confused, a mixture, unresolved, unextricated one from the other.
> It is in pure, unutterable resolvedness, distinction of being, that one is free,
> not in mixing, merging, not in similarity.[99]

Ursula in the course of time comes to realise Birkin's "distinction of being". She comes to look upon him as one of the sons of God from the Book of Genesis who saw the daughters of men, that they were fair. Out one evening with Birkin, she feels transported to the dream-world of her childhood as she sees in the distance Southwell Minster—the rigid, dark cathedral her father had loved so much—and the first stars on the sky. Lawrence suggestively evokes the world of his last novel, *The Rainbow*. We are being prepared for the fact that Ursula is going to achieve "the rainbow" which her parents and she

[97] *Phoenix*, p. 154.   [98] *Op. cit.*, p. 468.   [99] "Manifesto", *Poems*, I, p. 260.

herself had failed to achieve in that novel. Soon afterwards, as Birkin stands in the little parlour of an inn looking at her upturned face, she knows that he is "looking down at her, and seeing that she [is] fair".[1] She is drawn to him strangely, and kneeling on the hearthrug before him she puts her arms round his loins. As she traces with her finger-tips the back of his thighs and his loins, she discovers something "more than wonderful, more wonderful than life itself".[2] What she experiences is "neither love nor passion". What she has found at the back and base of the loins is "the source of the deepest life-force, the darkest, the deepest, strangest life-source of the human body".[3]

This talk about "loins" and "darkest sources" irritates many readers. Even Lawrence's sympathetic critics are apologetic about such passages and declare that here Lawrence is seen at his worst. There is some justification for this criticism. Lawrence's style is by no means always perfect; and some of the passages remain obscure even after several readings of the novel. Yet it is difficult to see how Lawrence could have avoided using words like "darkness", "loins", "mystic corruption", "star equilibrium"—when these alone, once their meaning is grasped, appear to be the most appropriate expressions in their context. Again, when he resorts to words like "unutterable", "ineffable", he probably means literally what he says. We should not forget that he was trying to communicate through language experiences which, however crucial and significant, have till now remained inarticulate. His success is not always unqualified. In any case many of his "obscure" passages easily lend themselves to misinterpretations. G. Wilson Knight, for instance, makes the following comment on the passage referred to above:

> There is . . . talk of fingers, loins, back, flanks, downward movement of the hand, electricity and darkness; and the word 'mystic' recurs.[4]

He would, therefore, have us conclude that "frontal, phallic sexuality is surpassed . . ."; and that the "novel describes in

---

[1] *Women in Love*, p. 304.   [2] *Op. cit.*, p. 305.   [3] *Op. cit.*, p. 306.
[4] "Lawrence, Joyce, and Powys", *Essays in Criticism*, xi (1961), p. 406.

imaginative terms certain sexual encounters of an abnormal kind". It is rather puzzling to find that Professor Knight should interpret these lines the way he does, considering that he quotes, in the same essay, from *Fantasia of the Unconscious* in which Lawrence explains that in the loins are located the immensely powerful voluntary centres which are responsible for the individual's knowledge of his distinct, separate existence: his "knowledge of I am I in separation". In *Psychoanalysis and the Unconscious* Lawrence explicitly discusses how searching and exploring the beloved brings back pure objective apprehension, perfect knowledge of the beloved:

> Now this knowledge in itself argues a distinction between the lover and the beloved. . . . For what is the beloved? She is that which I myself am not. . . . In the first mode of upper consciousness there is perfect surpassing of all sense of division between the self and the beloved. In the second mode the very discovery of the features of the beloved contains the full realization of the irreparable, or unsurpassable, gulf.[5]

In the novel itself Birkin is shown waiting for Ursula to take this knowledge of him, knowledge of his otherness.

> Now she would know him, and he too would be liberated. . . . They would give each other this star equilibrium which alone is freedom.[6]

It is only when Ursula comes to realise Birkin's "otherness" that she gains "an essential new being", and is "left quite free . . . free in complete ease, her complete self".[7] It is freedom, they finally agree, that they want: a perfected relation which leaves them both free. But the conflict is not yet over, for while Birkin wants to be free, in a free place, with a few other people, the mention of "a few other people" depresses her. Birkin wants a "further fellowship" which Ursula does not understand.

> "But why?" she insisted. "Why should you hanker after other people? Why should you need them?"
> This hit him right on the quick. His brows knitted.
> "Does it end with just our two selves?" he asked, tense.

---

[5] *Fantasia*, pp. 236-7.   [6] *Women in Love*, p. 311.   [7] *Op. cit.*, p. 306.

"Yes—what more do you want? If anybody likes to come along, let them. But why must you run after them?"

His face was tense and unsatisfied.

"You see," he said, "I always imagine our being really happy with some few other people—a little freedom with people."[8]

Ursula cannot understand why Birkin should need others when he has got her; why he should want to force others—for instance, Gerald—to love him when he does not really want their love. Birkin cannot agree to this.

His face was full of real perplexity.

"Don't I?" he said. "It's the problem I can't solve. I *know* I want a perfect and complete relationship with you: and we've nearly got it—we really have. But beyond that. *Do* I want a real, ultimate friendship with Gerald? Do I want a final, almost extra-human relationship with him—a relationship in the ultimate of me and him—or don't I?"

She looked at him a long time with strange bright eyes, but she did not answer.[9]

Ursula does not answer; but he himself does—at the end of the novel, when Gerald is already dead.

"Did you need Gerald?" she [Ursula] asked one evening.

"Yes," he said.

"Aren't I enough for you?" she asked.

"No," he said. "You are enough for me, as far as a woman is concerned. You are all women to me. But I wanted a man friend, as eternal as you and I are eternal."

"Why aren't I enough?" she asked. "You are enough for me. I don't want anybody else but you. Why isn't it the same with you?"

"Having you, I can live all my life without anybody else, any other sheer intimacy. But to make it complete, really happy, I wanted eternal union with a man too: another kind of love," he said.

"I don't believe it," she said. "It is an obstinacy, a theory, a perversity."

"Well—" he said.

"You can't have two kinds of love. Why should you!"

---

[8] *Op. cit.*, p. 355.   [9] *Ibid.*

"It seems as if I can't," he said, "Yet I wanted it."
"You can't have it, because it is false, impossible," she said.
"I don't believe that," he answered.[10]

The novel ends on this uncertain note. Birkin's predicament
here is Lawrence's own. Lawrence felt that it was not woman
who claimed the highest in man. He saw the ultimate greatest
desire in man as the desire for purposive, creative activity
undertaken in unison with other kindred souls. Frieda, it
appears, knew it well. She says:

> Love is really the key to Lawrence. When I said, like a woman
> does: 'But why do you bother about other people? You have
> me, isn't that enough?' He replied: 'Yes, it's a lot, but it
> isn't everything.'[11]

Birkin's love for Ursula, too, is a lot: but it isn't everything.
It has to be supplemented by a friendship as sacred and
inviolable as his relation with Ursula.[12] Birkin has been wanting such a friendship all along, though he has not always been
conscious of it. From the very beginning the relations of
Birkin and Gerald are shown to be straining towards a resolution. Their talks always bring them to a "deadly nearness of
contact, a strange perilous intimacy".[13] This appears to them
hate at times, and love at others; actually it is both. Even the
hostility between them is very near to love. But they never
admit it. They intend to keep their relationship on the level
of a casual, free-and-easy friendship. Their disbelief in the
possibility of a deep relationship between man and man
prevents the development of their powerful but suppressed
friendliness. Their attempts to keep a distance result in a
peculiar tension of hostility between them, which they sometimes interpret as hatred. Once while travelling together in a
train, Birkin declares to Gerald that he hates him "starrily".
Gerald, in return, confesses that he, too, perhaps hates Birkin

[10] *Op. cit.*, pp. 472-3.
[11] Frieda Lawrence, *The Memoirs and Correspondence*, ed. E. W. Tedlock. London
(1961), pp. 134-5.
[12] See *Phoenix*, p. 665, for Lawrence's views. He later on modified these views
on the nature of man's relation to man, but his belief in man's need for purposive
creative activity remained unchanged to the end.
[13] *Women in Love*, p. 28.

at times, but that he is not acutely aware of it. Yet, in spite of this feeling of hatred, they also experience a curious heart-straining towards each other.

Gerald finds Birkin's company very congenial. He is unconsciously drawn to him; he wants to be "within his sphere of influence";[14] he feels for him what he has never felt for anybody else. Later in the novel, he confesses to Birkin:

> I have gone after women—and have been keen enough over some of them. But I don't believe I've ever felt as much *love* for a woman as I have for you—not *love*. You understand what I mean.[15]

But beyond this, he does not seem to take much notice of him. Birkin appears to him a wonderful spirit, clever, whimsical, delightful. But he cannot take him seriously, for he considers his own understanding much sounder, and his own truths harder and more durable. Birkin, in comparison, seems to him in some way "young, innocent, childlike; so amazingly clever, but incurably innocent".[16] He cannot really believe in him. That is why when Birkin, realising at last that he had been loving Gerald all along even though he had been all along denying it, proposes that they should swear a *Blutbrüderschaft*, Gerald excuses himself by saying, "We'll leave it till I understand it better".[17]

Birkin, when he is faced with the question of a permanent conjunction between two men, recognises that to love a man purely and fully has been a necessity inside himself all his life. When he proposes *Blutbrüderschaft* to Gerald, he has no sloppy emotionalism in mind. There are to be no wounds in the manner of the old German knights: all that is obsolete. What he is suggesting is an *impersonal* relationship which leaves them both free. Gerald, thinking that he himself knows better, puts Birkin off: but they do attain some sort of *Brüderschaft* in the scene where they wrestle together, Birkin trying to teach ju-jitsu to Gerald.[18] The wrestling, both of them acknowledge,

---

[14] *Op. cit.*, p. 51.   [15] *Op. cit.*, p. 268.
[16] *Op. cit.*, p. 198.   [17] *Op. cit.*, p. 199.
[18] Graham Hough says there is "clearly a sexual element in all this which Lawrence was unwilling to acknowledge". (Hough, p. 85.) In fact, what Lawrence is not prepared to accept is not the presence of a sexual element in man

N

has had some deep meaning for them: but it is "an unfinished meaning."[19]

It is an unfinished meaning because Gerald is still limited, still fatally committed to "one form of existence, one knowledge, one activity . . .".[20] He cannot accept Birkin's offer to enter into a bond of pure trust and love with him. He cannot agree with Birkin when the latter says:

> We want something broader. I believe in the *additional* perfect relationship between man and man—additional to marriage . . . but equally important, equally creative, equally sacred, if you like.[21]

This is, Middleton Murry says, more or less what Lawrence said to him. "What he really wanted of me", Murry goes on, "he never put into words, and to this day I am doubtful whether he ever knew".[22] That, in spite of Murry's doubts, Lawrence probably did know what he wanted his relation with Murry to be, is evident from the following two quotations from his letters—the first addressed to Cynthia Asquith, the second to Katherine Mansfield:

> Murry says . . . he believes in what I say, because he believes in me, he might help in the work I set out to do because he would be believing in me. But he would not believe in the work. He would deplore it. He says the whole thing is

---

to man relationship, but its desirability. We find him wondering as early as in 1913 "why nearly every man that approaches greatness tends to homosexuality, whether he admits it or not"—even when all tradition and instinct tell us that "it means extinction of all purposive influences". (*Collected Letters*, I, p. 252.) His own tentative explanation was that man finds his love for man satisfying in that he thereby "projects his own image on another man". In the "unpublished" "Prologue" chapter to *Women in Love*, Birkin, who is puzzling over this problem, is tortured by the thought that the male physique has "a fascination for him". His attraction towards the "perfect and beautiful" specimens among men is actually a desire for identification with them: by seeing them, by apprehending them sensuously, he knows "their very blood"; he wants to *be* those men, to "take the very substance" of them. Yet he is afraid of the attraction he feels for other men as he considers it a "bondage": "For he would never acquiesce to it. He could never acquiesce to his own feelings, his own passion. He could never grant that it should be so, that it was well for him to feel this keen desire to have and to possess the bodies of such men, the passion to bathe in the very substance of such men . . .". (*Texas Quarterly*, VI, i, pp. 108-10.)

[19] *Women in Love*, p. 265.   [20] *Op. cit.*, p. 199.
[21] *Op. cit.*, p. 345.   [22] *Between Two Worlds*, London (1935), p. 412.

personal: that between him and me it is a case of Lawrence
and Murry, not of any union in an *idea*. He thinks the introduction of any idea, particularly of any political idea, highly
dangerous and deplorable. The thing should be left personal,
each man just expressing himself.[23]

. . . I want relations which are not purely personal . . . but
relations based upon some unanimous accord in truth or
belief, and a harmony of *purpose*, rather than of personality.
I am weary of personality. It remains now whether Murry is
still based upon the personal hypothesis: because if he is, then
our ways are different. I don't want a purely personal relation
with him; he is a man, therefore our relation should be based
on *purpose*; not upon that which we *are*, but upon that which
we wish to bring to pass.[24]

In the novel, too, Birkin takes care to explain to Gerald that
what he wants is "an impersonal union that leaves one free".[25]
Gerald would not have it. He is suspicious of Birkin's offer of
impersonal relationship, the nature of which he never really
comes to understand, and which he therefore rejects as immature
and childish. Birkin is aware that Gerald wants to be "*fond* of
him" without taking him seriously. And this makes him go
"hard and cold". The conflict between them, though mute
and subdued, continues till the two men gradually drift apart
and finally revoke one another.[26] The fact that Birkin could
not have Gerald's love does not blind him to his need of it.
"He should have loved me", he tells Ursula at the end of the
novel when Gerald is dead.[27] He remembers how Gerald had
once clutched his hand with a warm, momentous grip of love,
but had let it go after a second—forever. If Gerald had kept
true to the grasp, he should still have been "living in the
spirit" with his friend Birkin.

But Gerald is dead, dead "like bluish, corruptible ice".[28]
His death in the midst of sheer slopes and precipices covered
with snow is not unexpected. We have had intimations of it

---

[23] *Collected Letters*, I, p. 362.

[24] *Op. cit.*, p. 395. See above, p. 39.

[25] *Women in Love*, p. 199. Birkin tells Ursula also that he wants an "almost
extra-human relationship (p. 350) with Gerald.

[26] *Women in Love*, p. 427.   [27] *Op. cit.*, p. 471.   [28] *Ibid.*

through his connexion with the African statuette. But that is
not the only time Gerald is related to ice, snow, frost, cold,
whiteness, the Arctic north. There are recurrent references in
the novel associating him with these. The very first time we
see him in the first chapter, we are told that there is something
"northern about him" which magnetises Gudrun; that his
"northern flesh" glistens like sunshine refracted through
"crystals of ice"; that he looks pure as "an arctic thing".[29]
He is from the beginning fated to destruction through this one
process of cold, abstract knowledge, with his will acting as an
accomplice.

Gerald's story is essentially the story of his will. He has
become almost a slave to it. Will, intellect, abstract ideals—
these have exclusive dominance over him and give his life
point and direction. The assertion of his will brings him time
and again into conflict with whatever he comes in contact:
but he is possessed by a passion to fulfil his will, and he goes on
doing it till he finally breaks down and "immediately [goes] to
sleep".

It is Gerald's will which works in him throughout. There
is an unconscious will, we are to understand, even behind his
accidental killing of his brother in childhood.[30] He exults in
his affair with Minette, the girl he meets with Birkin at the
Pompadour, because he can hold her "in the hollow of his
will";[31] because he knows "she must relinquish herself into his
hands and be subject to him".[32] He enjoys his power over her:
his is the only will that counts; she is just "the passive substance
of his will".[33] His attitude to sex gets so perverted that he
comes to feel "his mind needed acute stimulation, before he
could be physically roused".[34]

Gerald's will to power is almost perfectly exemplified in the
episode where he forces his sensitive Arab mare to stand at the
railway crossing while a train goes by. The incident is first and
foremost exquisite narration. The whole thing, as F. R. Leavis
says, is rendered with shattering immediacy.[35]

The mare does not like the chuffing of the locomotive in the

---

[29] *Op. cit.*, p. 9.   [30] *Op. cit.*, p. 42.   [31] *Op. cit.*, p. 65.
[32] *Ibid.*   [33] *Op. cit.*, p. 72.   [34] *Op. cit.*, p. 225.
[35] Leavis, p. 155.

distance and winces away, as if hurt by the noise: but Gerald pulls her back and holds her head to the gate. The repeated sharp blasts of the chuffing engine make a terrifying noise. The mare, rocking with terror, recoils like a spring let go. But this only provokes Gerald's will into action. With a glistening, half-smiling look on his face, he brings her back. The sharp clanking of the locomotive makes the mare rebound "like a drop of water from hot iron". Gerald, however, sits "glistening and obstinate", and forces the mare back, not letting her get out of "the grasp of his will". But as strong as the pressure of his compulsion is the repulsion of her utter terror, throwing her back away from the railway, so that she spins round on two legs "as if she were in the centre of some whirlwind".[36] A sharpened look comes on Gerald's face and, pressing on her like a sword, he forces the mare round. Meanwhile the eternal trucks rumble on, one after the other "like a disgusting dream that has no end". As the connecting chains grind and squeak, the mare paws and strikes away mechanically: but Gerald has now encompassed her and brings her down as if she were a part of his own physique.

Gerald later explains to Hermione that if the mare is to be of any use to him at all, it must learn to stand noises. To Ursula's objection as to why he should have to inflict unnecessary torture, his answer is that the mare is there for his use, and that if he does not use his animals as he likes, the animals will use him as they like.

> "That's a fact," said Gerald. "A horse has got a will like a man, though it has no *mind*, strictly. And if your will isn't master, then the horse is master of you. And this is a thing I can't help. I can't help being master of the horse."[37]

In this Gerald has the whole-hearted approval of Hermione, another devotee of the will. She is the "feminine counterpart of Gerald".[38] But for the same reason she also dislikes him extremely. Her will cannot gain ascendancy where he is present with *his* will: she feels nullified. Once, while they are

---

[36] *Women in Love*, p. 103.   [37] *Op. cit.*, p. 131.
[38] W. W. Robson, in *The Modern Age*, p. 298.

in a boat, both of them at the same time take it into their heads to look at a drawing in Gudrun's sketch-book. There is an inevitable clash of wills:

> "Let me look," said Gerald, reaching forward for the book. But Hermione ignored him, he must not presume, before she had finished. But he, his will as unthwarted and unflinching as hers, stretched forward till he touched the book. A little shock, a storm of revulsion against him, shook Hermione unconsciously.[39]

Hermione releases the book before he has properly got it, and it tumbles against the side of the boat and falls into water. That is Hermione's chance. "There!" she exclaims triumphantly, with a ring of malevolence in her voice, and proceeds with her apologies which are repeated so many times that both Gerald and Gudrun feel exasperated.

The incident serves to bring Gerald and Gudrun closer. She had once been "tortured with a desire to see him again";[40] had "envied him almost painfully" while he swam in the lake;[41] and had looked at him fascinated "with black-dilated, spellbound eyes"[42] while he sat on his mare. Now she knows that they are associated in "a sort of diabolical free-masonry",[43] and that henceforward she is going to have power over him. There is already a bond established between them.

The bond is ratified in the chapter "The Water Party", where Gudrun, seeing a cluster of Highland cattle, goes in a strange palpitating dance towards them. She is determined not to be frightened: she is confident of some secret power in herself and she is out to test it. "Don't they look charming . . .?" she cries to Ursula in a high voice, "like the scream of a sea gull".[44] Her high, strident voice is her response to the challenge of physical, animal strength. She has already "cried in a strange, high voice, like a gull",[45] on seeing Gerald's indomitable struggle with his strong mare; she will cry again "like the crying of a sea gull, . . . the high note in her voice like a sea gull's cry"[46] when she encounters the frenzied violence of

[39] *Women in Love*, p. 113.   [40] *Op. cit.*, p. 9.   [41] *Op. cit.*, p. 40.
[42] *Op. cit.*, p. 103.   [43] *Op. cit.*, p. 114.   [44] *Op. cit.*, p. 158.
[45] *Op. cit.*, p. 105.   [46] *Op. cit.*, p. 233.

the "most fearfully strong" rabbit. Her whole being revolts at the idea of submission to sheer physical strength.

Gudrun goes forward till she is near enough to be able to touch the wild Scotch bullocks. A terrible shiver of fear and pleasure runs through her body. But she is deprived of her ecstasy because Gerald, thinking it is not safe, shouts and frightens off the cattle. Gudrun gets angry, looks at him with dark eyes of resentment, and then goes after the cattle. Gerald, following, comes up with her:

> She looked at him inscrutably.
> "You think I am afraid of you and your cattle, don't you?" she asked.
> His eyes narrowed dangerously. There was a faint domineering smile on his face.
> "Why should I think that?" he said.
> She was watching him all the time with her dark, dilated, inchoate eyes. She leaned forward and swung round her arm, catching him a light blow on the face with the back of her hand.
> "That's why," she said, mocking.[47]

Gudrun feels an irrepressible desire for violence against Gerald. She shuts off the feelings of fear and dismay which fill her conscious mind. She is already determined not to be afraid. Gerald is stunned and cannot speak for some seconds. "You have struck the first blow", he says at last, forcing the words out in a soft, low voice. "And I shall strike the last", Gudrun retorts involuntarily with confident assurance. Gerald remains silent; he does not contradict her. When Gudrun, after some time, asks him not to be angry with her, he stammers out: "I am not angry with you. I'm in love with you."[48]

Gerald, however, does not really love Gudrun. He has, as he confesses to her later, never loved her, and is never going to love her. Nor does Gudrun ever get to love him. The farthest she gets to is to feel pity for him. "Men and love—there [is] no greater tedium":[49] this, we are informed, is her basic feeling. Love does not interest her except in so far as she can make use of it as an artist. She thinks of Gerald as *bagatelle*; a lover, to her, is mere "fuel for the transport of this

[47] *Op. cit.*, p. 162.   [48] *Op. cit.*, p. 163.   [49] *Op. cit.*, p. 450.

subtle knowledge, for a female art, the art of pure, perfect knowledge in sensuous understanding".[50]   Her ideal is exemplified in women like Cleopatra who "reaped the essential from a man, . . . harvested the ultimate sensation, and threw away the husk".[51]

Both Gerald and Gudrun are presented by Lawrence with a great deal of admiration: but they are, as Birkin points out to Ursula, the flowers of sensuous perfection and thereby also the flowers of dissolution; they belong to the "flowering mystery of the death process".[52]   Their "love", under the domination of sea-born Aphrodite, is destined to end in "universal nothing".[53] Gudrun had once admired and envied Gerald for his perfect mastery over "the pure translucency of the grey, uncreated water".[54]   She learns soon enough, when Gerald fails to rescue his sister from drowning, that he is not infallible even there. Ironically, this comes immediately after he has, for the first time in his life, been able to let himself go, to let his mind be submerged, transfused into the things about him.   While he sits "balanced in separation"[55] with Gudrun in the canoe, he imperceptibly melts "into oneness with the whole".

> It was like pure, perfect sleep, his first great sleep of life.   He had been so insistent, so guarded, all his life.   But here was sleep, and peace, and perfect lapsing out.[56]

Gerald is suddenly brought back to his guarded, insistent self by a confusion of shouting and noise over the water.   Somebody has fallen into the water.   He once again becomes keen and alert and "instrumental".[57]   Gudrun's heart sinks to see his sharp impersonal face.   Later in the novel, Gudrun once again reflects on Gerald's potentialities as a marvellous instrument— this time as an instrument for the reorganisation of the industrial system "with his force of will and his power for comprehending the actual world".[58]   She is aware that if he were confronted with any problem, any hard actual difficulty, he would overcome it.   "He had the faculty of making order out of confusion. Only let him grip hold of a situation, and he would bring to

[50] *Op. cit.*, p. 440.   [51] *Ibid.*   [52] *Op. cit.*, p. 164.
[53] *Ibid.*   [54] *Op. cit.*, p. 39.   [55] *Op. cit.*, p. 169.
[56] *Op. cit.*, p. 170.   [57] *Op. cit.*, p. 171.   [58] *Op. cit.*, p. 407.

pass an inevitable conclusion."[59] To her Gerald appears like a
pure, inhuman, almost superhuman instrument; and at times
his instrumentality strongly appeals to her.

Gerald, indeed, believes in the pure instrumentality of the
individual. "As a man as of a knife: does it cut well? Nothing
else mattered."[60] He has no emotional qualms, and dismisses
all talk of suffering and feeling. The sentimental humani-
tarianism of his father appears to him ridiculous. Everything
in the world, he believes, has its function, and its goodness or
otherwise depends on how well it performs this function. If a
miner is a good miner, he is perfect, complete. He himself,
Gerald thinks, must be a good director of industry and then
he will have fulfilled his life. Gerald arrives on the scene when
there is talk of closing down two of his father's coal-mines
because they have been worked by old, obsolete methods. He
immediately perceives that there is plenty of coal in the seams,
and that what is needed is to put the great industry in order,
to reorganise the great social productive machine. As soon as
he sees the firm, he knows what he has to do: he has a fight to
fight with Matter—"to turn upon the inanimate matter of the
underground, and reduce it to his will".[61] It is not for the
sake of money that Gerald takes over the mines; what he
wants is the pure fulfilment of his own will in his struggle with
"the resistant Matter of the earth".

> And for this fight with matter, one must have perfect instruments
> in perfect organisation, a mechanism so subtle and harmonious
> in its workings that it represents the single mind of man, and
> by its relentless repetition of the given movement, will accom-
> plish a purpose irresistibly, inhumanly.[62]

This inhuman system implies the substitution of the mechanical
principle for the organic. It requires the subordination of
every organic unit to the great mechanical purpose.

Gerald achieves this perfect mechanical organisation. He
succeeds in converting the industry into a "new and terrible
purity".[63] The whole system comes to be so perfect that he
himself is hardly necessary any more; and at times a strange
fear comes over him when he does not know what to do.

[59] *Ibid.*   [60] *Op. cit.*, p. 215.   [61] *Op. cit.*, p. 220.
[62] *Ibid.*   [63] *Op. cit.*, p. 224.

But now he had succeeded—he had finally succeeded. And
once or twice lately, when he was alone in the evening and had
nothing to do, he had suddenly stood up in terror, not knowing
what he was. And he went to the mirror and looked long and
closely at his own face, at his own eyes, seeking for something.
. . . He was afraid that one day he would break down and be
a purely meaningless [bubble] lapping round a darkness.[64]

Gerald, who has believed that every problem can be worked
out, in life as in geometry, now discovers that his will cannot
fill the expanding vacuum inside him. He realises that he will
have to go in some direction, shortly, to find relief. And he
turns to Gudrun. The nature of their relationship is once again
sharply brought out in the chapter "Rabbit". As Gudrun
takes the lusty rabbit Bismarck out of the hutch, holding it by
the ears, it lunges wildly, its body "flying like a spring coiled
and released". Gudrun tries to hold "the black and white
tempest" at arm's length, but the fearfully strong rabbit proves
too much for her and her wrists are badly scored by the claws
of the animal. She is utterly overcome, shaken like a "house
in storm". A heavy rage wells up in her. Her heart is filled
with a fury at the "bestial stupidity"[65] of this struggle. Gerald
comes to her help and takes the rabbit from her: but the
"demoniacal" rabbit makes itself into a ball and lashes out:

> The long, demon-like beast lashed out again, spread on the
> air as if it were flying, looking something like a dragon, then
> closing up again, inconceivably powerful and explosive. The
> man's body, strung to its efforts, vibrated strongly. Then a
> sudden sharp, white-edged wrath came up in him. Swift as
> lightning he drew back and brought his free hand down like a
> hawk on the neck of the rabbit. Simultaneously, there came
> the unearthly abhorrent scream of a rabbit in the fear of death.
> It made one immense writhe, tore his wrists and his sleeves in
> a final convulsion, all its belly flashed white in a whirlwind of
> paws, . . . [Gudrun] looked almost unearthly. The scream of
> the rabbit, after the violent tussle, seemed to have torn the veil
> of her consciousness.[66]

The scene is generally interpreted as a rejection by Gerald and
Gudrun of the "organic life" represented by the rabbit. Yet

[64] *Op. cit.*, pp. 224-5.   [65] *Op. cit.*, p. 232.   [66] *Op. cit.*, p. 233.

what seems to be emphasised in the episode is not the contrast
between the organic life of the rabbit and Gerald's mechanical
attitude to life, but the beastliness and demon-like nature of the
rabbit.   Gerald and Gudrun do not reject what the rabbit
represents to them: they accept it and reciprocate it; they
participate in the beast's animal passion.   One of Lawrence's
poems, "Rabbit Snared in the Night", has the same theme, and
the following extract from it might help to make the nature of
the struggle involved clear:

> Why do you spurt and sprottle
> like that, bunny?
> Why should I want to throttle
> you, bunny?
>
> *I* did not want it,
> this furnace, this draught-maddened fire
> which mounts up my arms
> making them swell with ungovernable strength.
>
> I must be reciprocating *your* vacuous, hideous passion.
> Come, you shall have your desire,
> Since already I am implicated with you
> in your strange lust.[67]

Gerald and Gudrun, too, are implicated in the beast's "strange
lust".   They feel a mutual "hellish recognition".[68]   They are
implicated with each other in "abhorrent mysteries", the
mysteries of purely sensual knowledge.   When Gudrun's heart
is "filled with a fury", and when a "white-edged wrath" comes
upon Gerald, they undergo the same experience.   The un-
earthly scream of the rabbit seems to Gudrun to tear the veil of
her consciousness; and when Gudrun shows a deep red score
on her arm, the long red rip seems to Gerald to be "torn across
his own brain, tearing the surface of his ultimate consciousness".[69]   They, we are to understand, in this manner exchange
an "obscene recognition" of what their future relationship is
to be.

  Gerald soon comes to the conclusion that for him nothing
in the world matters except "somebody to take the edge off

[67] *Poems,* I, pp. 230–2.   [68] *Women in Love,* p. 234.   [69] *Op. cit.,* p. 235.

one's being alone".[70] His loneliness becomes unbearable to him while he sees his father slowly dissolve and disappear in death. In the stress of the ordeal, he loses his hold on outer, daily life. He must somehow fill the hollow void in his soul. In the extremity his instinct leads him to Gudrun. Gerald's love thus begins as a desperate need. He wants Gudrun to complete himself, just as Hermione had wanted Birkin to complete herself. His love is a complete dependence. As he walks with Gudrun one evening to see her back home, he feels like a pair of scales, "the half of which tips down and down into an indefinite void". He slips his arm round her waist to balance her in opposition to himself, and suddenly feels "liberated and perfect, strong and heroic".[71]

After the death of his father Gerald is left completely alone. He cannot bear it: he has no confidence left in his own strength any more. Deeply frightened in his soul, he decides he must "seek reinforcements", and so walks through mud in the dark night to Gudrun[72] to find relief in her:

> Into her he poured all his pent-up darkness and corrosive death, and he was whole again. It was wonderful, marvellous, it was a miracle. This was the ever-recurrent miracle of his life, at the knowledge of which he was lost in an ecstasy of relief and wonder.[73]

Gerald feels his life return to him. He becomes a man again. Gudrun appears to him now "Mother and substance of all life",[74] and he begins to worship her.[75] From now on she is like an end to him. To be with her, to have her, "so soft, her skin like silk, her arms heavy and soft",[76] means for him a great and complete experience—something final. His passion for Gudrun becomes in itself a goal for him. But it is a fatal goal. Sex as an end in itself, says Lawrence, is a disaster:

---

[70] *Op. cit.*, p. 259.   [71] *Op. cit.*, p. 321.

[72] This, as Mark Schorer puts it, is "love *as* death" (the chapter in the novel is entitled "Death and Love"): Gerald "brings the clay of his father's new grave into [Gudrun's] bedroom". ("Women in Love", in *The Achievement of D. H. Lawrence*, ed. Frederick J. Hoffman and Harry T. Moore. Norman, Okla. (1953), p. 171.)

[73] *Women in Love*, p. 337.   [74] *Ibid.*

[75] See footnote on p. 172, quoting Lawrence's letter to Katherine Mansfield.

[76] *Women in Love*, p. 430.

When sex is the starting and the returning point both, then the only issue is death. . . . Death is the only pure, beautiful conclusion of a great passion. Lovers, pure lovers should say "Let it be so". And one is always tempted to say "Let it be so." But no, let it be not so.[77]

Gerald, however, has yielded to the temptation of "Let it be so". His experience with Gudrun, he tells Birkin, withers his consciousness, burns the pith of his mind: "It blasts your soul's eye, and leaves you sightless. Yet you *want* to be sightless, you *want* to be blasted, you don't want it any different." Gerald knows that to exist at all, he must be completely free of Gudrun; he must be self-sufficient as Gudrun is sufficient unto herself; he must leave her if she wants to be left. And yet he cannot leave her, for he has nowhere else to go to, nothing else to fall back on. The alternative, in his case, is to stand by himself in sheer nothingness; and Gerald shudders at the thought. He has entered a *cul-de-sac* and now there is no going on.

> . . . between two particular people, any two people on earth, the range of pure sensual experience is limited. The climax of sensual reaction, once reached in any direction, is reached finally, there is no going on. There is only repetition possible, or the going apart of two protagonists, or the subjugating of the one will to the other, or death.[78]

Gerald cannot go on repeating the experience with Gudrun because she will not have it: his passion now seems awful to her, "tense and ghastly, and impersonal, like a destruction, ultimate".[79] She feels she is being killed by his tearing at "the bud of her heart". He cannot leave her and go away, as this means a retreat into his dreaded state of nothingness. He cannot give in and subjugate his will to hers, for it is by his will alone that he lives. The only way out is a contest of wills, and then death. One of them must triumph over the other. The conflict comes to the surface during their stay among the snow-covered Tyrolese mountains. When Ursula and Birkin go away, Gudrun feels herself "free in her contest with Gerald. . . . Already a vital conflict had set in which frightened them both."[80] In his essay on Edgar Allan Poe, Lawrence says:

[77] *Fantasia*, p. 191.
[79] *Op. cit.*, p. 435.
[78] *Women in Love*, p. 443.
[80] *Op. cit.*, p. 432.

> . . . love pushed to extremes is a battle of wills between the lovers.
>
> Love is become a battle of wills.
>
> Which shall destroy the other of the lovers? Which can hold out longest against the other?[81]

This is precisely the struggle going on between Gerald and Gudrun, superbly evoked in the last chapters of the novel. Sometimes it is Gerald who seems stronger, while Gudrun is almost gone; sometimes it is the reverse. But it is always the eternal see-saw, "one destroyed that the other might exist, one ratified because the other was nulled".[82]

Seeing that Gudrun has come to hate him openly—for "every woman despises a man who has 'fallen' to her; despises him with her tenderest lust"[83]—and that he cannot have her by any other means, he is possessed by an uncontrollable desire to kill her, to strangle every spark of life out of her. That, he thinks, would be a perfect voluptuous consummation. Finding his opportunity one day when he finds Gudrun with the artist Loerke on the blinding slopes of snow, he takes her throat between his hard, powerful hands. As his grip on her throat tightens, a "pure zest of satisfaction" fills his soul. Gudrun's fighting and struggling is only "her reciprocal lustful passion in this embrace", and the more violently she struggles, the greater is his frenzy of delight. Then, suddenly, hearing Loerke's voice, Gerald realises to what depths he is letting himself go, as if he cared about her enough to have her life on his hands. He lets go his grip and drifts up the snow-covered slopes in the gathering twilight, with the only desire to go on and on and then "go to sleep". He stumbles on up the slopes of snow with a small moon shining brilliantly overhead, "a powerful brilliant thing that was always there, unremitting, from which there was no escape".[84] He wants now to come to the end: he has had enough. He moves up higher and higher towards the summit of the slopes till he comes to a half-buried Crucifix, a little Christ under a sloping hood at the top of a pole. It suddenly flashes through Gerald's mind that somebody is going to murder him. He looks round in terror

---

[81] *S.C.A.L.*, p. 65.
[82] *Women in Love*, p. 436.
[83] *S.C.A.L.*, p. 85.
[84] *Women in Love*, p. 464.

at the shadowy slopes of snow, and it dawns on him that there is no escape. He can feel the blow descending, and he wanders unconsciously till he slips and falls down, "and as he fell, something broke in his soul and immediately he went to sleep".[85] That was the inevitable end—the only way out of the conflict left to him.

Women in Love has been judged by many critics to be Lawrence's best novel. Lawrence himself regarded it as "a serious and profound piece of work . . . a much finer work than *The Rainbow*".[86] It is certainly the most complex and the most closely organised of all his novels. And it is perhaps also the most difficult. The kind of attention a reader needs to bring to it is not normally associated with the reading of fiction. There is much in it which acquires its proper significance only on a second or subsequent reading of the book. There are passages in it which are by no means easily understood or explained. Yet some of these are of crucial importance, in that they provide the clue to the meaning of the whole work; and it will not do to dismiss them simply as bad writing. Thus Leavis, who praises *Women in Love* in the highest terms, has very little to say about the Ursula-Birkin relationship, which, nevertheless, forms the core of the novel. No estimate of *Women in Love* as a great work of art can be even nearly complete without a full appreciation of Lawrence's incomparable power to depict, in all their manifestations, the various conflicts in relationships which constitute in themselves the "plot" of the novel.

[85] *Op. cit.*, p. 466.   [86] *Letters*, p. 286.

VI

The Changing Scene

LAWRENCE's next novel, *The Lost Girl*, is an exceptional work in the sense that it is not for the most part a record of his "profoundest experiences in the self". The book was begun as a "pot-boiler" in 1913 under the title *The Insurrection of Miss Houghton* (which was later changed to *A Mixed Marriage*, and finally to *The Lost Girl*). The first two-thirds of the novel is, as Lawrence himself remarks,[1] quite unlike his usual style: it is far more "eventual". After the difficulties he had experienced with the publication of *The Rainbow* and *Women in Love*, he intended this novel to be "quite *unexceptionable*, as far as the censor is concerned".[2] His concern about seeing the book published is also evident in his letter of 7 May 1920 written just after the completion of the novel:

> That bee in my bonnet which you mention, and which I presume means sex, buzzes not over-loud. I think *The Lost Girl* is quite passable, from Mudie's point of view.[3]

The Lost Girl is the story of Alvina Houghton. She gets lost in the course of the novel in more than one sense of the term. "Not morally lost, I assure you", Lawrence wrote in the same letter from which the above quotation is taken. But to the world that the novel depicts she is irretrievably lost. "You're a lost girl!" cries old Miss Pinnegar when Alvina brings Cicio with her to stay the night at Manchester House. "You lost girl!" she says again when she finds Alvina in the company of "strange men" drinking and playing cards on a Sunday evening. "I don't know how ever you'll be saved, after such a sin", Mr May mockingly concurs. But beyond all this, she herself feels "quite, quite lost . . . lost to Woodhouse, to Lancaster, to England—all lost"[4] as she is travelling in a cart

---

[1] *Collected Letters*, I, p. 616.   [2] *Ibid.*
[3] *Op. cit.*, p. 628.   [4] *The Lost Girl* (Phoenix Edition), p. 316.

among the mountains in Italy, on her way to the tiny hamlet of
Califano where she is to live with Cicio. Once there, the
knowledge sinks into her "like ice" that she is utterly lost.

> There is no mistake about it, Alvina was a lost girl. She
> was cut off from everything she belonged to. Ovid isolated
> in Thrace might well lament. The soul itself needs its own
> mysterious nourishment. This nourishment lacking, nothing
> is well.[5]

Alvina Houghton's story begins in Woodhouse, a small
industrial town in the Midlands—Woodhouse which "as a
very condition of its own being, hated any approach to
originality or real taste".[6] During the first long twenty-five
years of her life she is virtually left out of account, overshadowed by her virtuous and high-minded governess Miss
Frost. Miss Frost instructs her thoroughly in "the qualities of
her own true nature", and Alvina believes what she is taught.
For twenty years she remains the demure, refined creature of
her governess's desire. Occasionally, she has fits of boisterous
hilarity, "not quite natural", which make Miss Frost uneasy
because "never, never had she known anything so utterly alien
and incomprehensible and unsympathetic as her own beloved
Vina".[7] Miss Frost, however, dismisses these bursts of hilarious
jeering in Alvina as accidental aberrations on the girl's part
from "her own true nature".[8] But is Alvina's "own true nature"
really what Miss Frost takes it to be? Is the demure, affectionate dove in her truly "her own real self"?

> The mighty question arises upon us, what is one's own real
> self? It certainly is not what we think we are and ought to be.
> Alvina had been bred to think of herself as a delicate, tender,
> chaste creature with unselfish inclinations and a pure, "high"
> mind. But high-mindedness had really come to an end with
> James Houghton, had really reached the point, not only of
> pathetic, but of dry and anti-human, repulsive quixotry. In
> Alvina high-mindedness was already stretched beyond the
> breaking point. Being a woman of some flexibility of temper,
> wrought through generations to a fine, pliant hardness, she

---

[5] *Op. cit.*, p. 324.
[7] *Op. cit.*, p. 21.
[6] *Op. cit.*, p. 5.
[8] *Op. cit.*, p. 22.

flew back. She went right back on high-mindedness. Did she
thereby betray it?

We think not. If we turn over the head of the penny and
look at the tail, we don't thereby deny or betray the head.
We do but adjust it to its own complement. And so with high-
mindedness. It is but one side of the medal—the crowned
reverse. On the obverse the three legs still go kicking the soft-
footed spin of the universe, the dolphin flirts and the crab leers.

So Alvina spun her medal, and her medal came down tails.
Heads or tails? Heads for generations. Then tails. See the
poetic justice.[9]

When Alvina is twenty-three she meets Graham, a dark
little Australian with "very dark eyes, and a body which seemed
to move inside his clothing".[10] Miss Frost, seeing him, declares
that he has dark blood in his veins and that he is not a man to
be trusted. The stress on Graham's "dark" nature is in direct
contrast to the purity and high-mindedness of Miss Frost.
Alvina is strongly attracted by "the darkie"—as Graham is
popularly known—but this attraction is by no means "love".
It is something more primitive: more sensuality than tender
love. Miss Frost tries to wake the girl's loving heart—which
loving heart is certainly not occupied by Graham whom Alvina
finds both fascinating and a trifle repulsive.

> In her periods of lucidity, when she saw as clear as daylight . . .,
> she certainly did not love the little man. She felt him a terrible
> outsider, an inferior, to tell the truth. She wondered how he
> could have the slightest attraction for her. In fact she could
> not understand it at all. . . . And then, most irritating, a
> complete *volte face* in her feelings. The clear-as-daylight mood
> disappeared as daylight is bound to disappear. She found her-
> self in a night where the little man loomed large, terribly large,
> potent and magical, while Miss Frost had dwindled to
> nothingness.[11]

Graham, however, goes away to Australia leaving Alvina
behind in Woodhouse with its "terrible crop of old maids" and
its "blank or common" men. For a time it looks as if she too is
destined to join the ranks of old maids. The young men of her
own class in Woodhouse do not like her because of her "ancient

---

[9] *Op. cit.*, pp. 34-5.   [10] *Op. cit.*, p. 22.   [11] *Op. cit.*, pp. 24-5.

sapience" which goes deeper than they can fathom. But Alvina, we are told by the narrator, is no ordinary girl. Her story is, therefore, not that of an ordinary girl in ordinary circumstances:

> Ordinary people, ordinary fates. But extraordinary people, extraordinary fates. Or else no fate at all. . . . There was no hope for Alvina in the ordinary. If help came, it would have to come from the extraordinary. Hence the extreme peril of her case.[12]

Alvina, not wanting to let her extraordinary points be "worn down by the regular machine-friction of our average and mechanical days",[13] decides to get away from Woodhouse. She shocks everyone in Manchester House by her announcement that she is going to Islington for six months to get training as a maternity nurse. They all hope she is just talking at random, and wait for the usual, tender, shrinking Vina—"the exquisitely sensitive and nervous, loving girl"—to be herself again: but there is no return of such a creature. So "she kissed them all good-bye, brightly and sprightlily, and off she set".[14]

Alvina adjusts herself fairly quickly to her new life amid coarse and vulgar companions, working in the dreadful lying-in hospital. Outwardly, she feels exhilarated and in full swing. Within a short time she picks up the characteristic, hard nurse's laugh, and the nurse's leer, and comes to excel all others in quips and *double-entendres*. But deep inside she is profoundly shocked; and the dreadful things she sees in the hospital, and afterwards, finish her youth and tutelage for ever: "How many infernos deeper than Miss Frost could ever know, did she not travel? the inferno of the human animal, the human organism in its convulsions, the human social beast in its abjection and its degradation."[15] In the course of her training experience she is transformed from a frail, pallid, diffident girl into a rather fat, warm-coloured young woman with a certain bounce. She had lived for so long as a pure, high-minded girl under the "beautiful but unbearable tyranny"[16] of Miss Frost. Now she feels it is time for Miss Frost to die, time for her darling to be gently

---

[12] *Op. cit.*, pp. 86-7.   [13] *Op. cit.*, p. 86.   [14] *Op. cit.*, p. 31.
[15] *Op. cit.*, p. 33.   [16] *Op. cit.*, p. 36.

and softly folded into immortality. "It was time for that perfected flower to be gathered to immortality. A lovely *immortel*. But an obstruction to other, purple and carmine blossoms which were in bud on the stem."[17] However, in spite of this reasoning, "the inflexible stiffness of her backbone" does not yet let her do as she likes. She knows she does not really care about her virginity—even despises it: but her upbringing is as yet too strong a force for her. She dearly wishes she could go the whole length, be wholly committed.

> But sophistry and wishing did her no good. There she was, still isolate. And still there was that in her which would preserve her intact, sophistry and deliberate intention not withstanding. Her time was up. She was returning to Woodhouse virgin as she had left it. In a measure she felt herself beaten. Why? Who knows. But so it was, she felt herself beaten, condemned to go back to what she was before. Fate had been too strong for her and her desires: fate which was not an external association of forces, but which was integral in her own nature. Her own inscrutable nature was her fate: sore against her will.[18]

Back in Manchester House Alvina once more assumes her old quiet, dutiful, affectionate self. Somewhere at the back of her mind is "the fixed idea, the fixed intention of finding love, a man":[19] but as yet this idea is in abeyance. Moreover, Woodhouse men in general are rather afraid of her, as they sense in her a desire for something serious and risky: "Not mere marriage—oh dear, no! But a profound and dangerous inter-relationship."[20] She herself is a "desperate nereid", highly exclusive and selective by nature, and is therefore unable to accept the offers made to her by the common Woodhouse suitors. So day follows day, month follows month, season after season goes by and she grubs away like a housemaid in her father's house, doing the round of shopping, singing in the choir on Sundays, and visiting friends occasionally:

> The trouble with her ship was that it would *not* sail. It rode waterlogged in the rotting port of home. All very well

---

[17] *Op. cit.*, p. 36.
[18] *Op. cit.*, p. 39-40.
[19] *Op. cit.*, p. 50.
[20] *Op. cit.*, p. 63.

to have wild, reckless moods of irony and independence, if you have to pay for them by withering dustily on the shelf.[21]

When she is about twenty-eight, Alvina gets apprehensive, seeing that she is withering towards old-maiddom. Now if she were an ordinary girl (which the author protests she is not), her story would end in either her marrying some dull school-teacher or office clerk, or her finding some work—like teaching the piano, or sitting in the cash-desk of some shop, or acting as a subordinate nurse—and thus having her "independence". "But seriously faced with that treasure, and without the option of refusing it, strange how hideous she found it."[22] Alvina, in short, is not prepared to accept any of these alternatives. Her position is indeed desperate, and any help—if it comes— "would have to come from the extraordinary". However, before that can happen she herself must be in readiness to receive such help: she must stand on her own ground rather than exist merely as a conforming member of the Woodhouse respectability. A decisive step in this direction is taken when she goes on the stage to play the piano for her father's last venture for financial success, popularly known as "Houghton's Endeavour":

> On the whole, Alvina enjoyed the cinema and the life it brought her. She accepted it. And she became somewhat vulgarised in her bearing. She was *déclassée*: she had lost her class altogether. The other daughters of respectable tradesmen avoided her now, or spoke to her only from a distance. . . . Alvina did not care. She rather liked it. She liked being *déclassée*. She liked feeling an outsider. At last she seemed to stand on her own ground.[23]

She gets a good deal of fun out of her work in the Pleasure Palace. She has the opportunity to come into contact with all sorts of artistes of the inferior stage, and finds it amusing to see and know people so different from any that she had known before. "It was so different from Woodhouse, where everything was priced and ticketed." These people do not care a straw "who you were or who you weren't". It is in these circumstances that she meets Cicio for the first time: he is one of the

---

[21] *Op. cit.*, p. 83.   [22] *Op. cit.*, p. 84.   [23] *Op. cit.*, p. 122.

four young men in Madame Rochard's Natcha-Kee-Tawara Troupe which comes to perform at James Houghton's Pleasure Palace.

Cicio—his full name is Francesco Marasca[24]—is, like Graham, the dark opposite of what Alvina was brought up by her high-minded governess to be. He is, as one critic has rightly noted, "consistently presented in a double perspective, corresponding with the heroine's ambivalent responses to the challenge he offers her"; while often it so happens that she is "caught on the horns of a dilemma, making both responses at once".[25] She is, on the one hand, struck by his inferiority to her, his self-consciousness, his stupidity, his "half-loutish, sensual-subjected way of the Italians".[26] He is only half-articulate, "just stupid and bestial",[27] "an uncouth lout"; and there are times when Alvina feels she is "demeaning herself shamefully" in associating with him. But she is also, on the other hand, aware of his "great instinctive good-naturedness". From the very first she feels "convinced of his ultimate good nature. He seemed to her to be the only passionately good-natured man she had ever seen."[28] She cannot help having some "strange vague trust, implicit belief in him". There are moments when she perceives "a dark, mysterious glamour on his face, passionate and remote".[29] Then he appears to her unbearably beautiful: his peculiar southern aloofness, it seems to her, gives him a certain beauty and distinction which she finds bewitching, and which leaves her powerless.

Alvina's responses are, of course, not purely subjective: they correspond to the stimuli provided by widely different traits in Cicio's character. This comes out quite clearly when he tells her about the hardships in his early life in Italy:

> And it seemed, in spite of all, one state was very much the same to him as another, poverty was as much life as affluence. Only

---

[24] Julian Moynahan makes the following interesting and acute, though rather sweeping, comment in this connexion: ". . . Madame Rochard remarks of Cicio's surname, Marasca, that it has a bad sound: 'It sends life down instead of lifting it up'. Alvina's rejoinder—'Why should life always go up?'—is what the novel is all about". (Moynahan, p. 136.)

[25] Moynahan, p. 132.   [26] *The Lost Girl*, p. 164.   [27] *Op. cit.*, p. 185.
[28] *Op. cit.*, p. 146.   [29] *Op. cit.*, p. 167.

he had a sort of jealous idea that it was humiliating to be poor, and so, for vanity's sake, he would have possessions. The countless generations of civilisations behind him had left him an instinct of the world's meaninglessness. Only his little modern education made money and independence an *idée fixe*. Old instinct told him the world was nothing. But modern education, so shallow, was much more efficacious than instinct. It drove him to make a show of himself to the world. Alvina watching him, as if hypnotised, saw his old beauty, formed through civilisation after civilisation; and at the same time she saw his modern vulgarianism and decadence.[30]

It is the conflict within Alvina, caused by her responding simultaneously to both Cicio's positive and negative qualities, which marks throughout her relationship with him. In the world of "daylight consciousness" he holds no attraction for her. The first time that she comes physically close to him and picks up his hand impulsively to kiss it, the silver ring on his finger is a constant reminder to her of his "subjection" and inferiority. However, he strongly appeals to the other, the darker self in her whose existence she barely recognises. His look goes "right into her, beyond her usual self"[31] and finds a response there. In the description of their first sexual experience the word "dark" recurs. Cicio is the "dark southerner" against whom all her defences fail when "suddenly she found herself in the dark":

> If for one moment she could have escaped from that black spell of his beauty, she would have been free. . . . But the spell was on her, of his darkness and unfathomed handsomeness. . . . How she suffered no one can tell. Yet all the time, his lustrous dark beauty, unbearable. . . . And she could have fought, if only the sense of his dark, rich handsomeness had not numbed her like a venom.[32]

Twice again she is shown struggling frenziedly against his "strange mesmeric power" with which he wants to dominate her: but she finds she is powerless to resist the "unknown dark flood of his will". He seems to her dark and insidious and "so beautiful"; and this leaves her numb, submissive, will-less. It is as if "he possessed the sensual secrets" by means of which he

[30] *Op. cit.*, pp. 228-9.   [31] *Op. cit.*, p. 146.   [32] *Op. cit.*, p. 209.

casts a spell on her, so that she is completely swept away by his dark passion. "Now Alvina felt herself swept—she knew not whither—but into a dusky region where men had dark faces and translucent yellow eyes, where all speech was foreign, and life was not her life. It was as if she had fallen from her own world on to another, darker start, where meanings were all changed."[33] In the dusky, unfamiliar region where Alvina has arrived, it is Cicio's will which holds sway, while she herself is quite powerless. As she finds out after her marriage to Cicio, in his dark, mesmeric love there is no tenderness or wonderful intimacy of speech which she had always imagined and craved for. His love "extinguished her. She had to be the quiescent, obscure woman: she felt as if she were veiled."[34] Under his spell one part of her self sinks into extinction, and she comes to live only "in the dim back regions of consciousness". The tender, sensitive, refined, high-minded Alvina was one side of the medal; now the medal is turned over and we see she has gone to the other extreme. The fear, however, is that instead of adjusting the head to its complement, the tail, and thus being her whole self, she might stay lapsed in the present condition. She is aware that she is in a drugged state, but is tempted to remain thus in her "dark, warm coma". For a time she is so completely under the influence of a dark, sweet passivity and indifference that she cannot help concluding it must be evil— that she herself must be evil; and yet she feels she has no power to be otherwise. She suspects—her mind remains "distantly clear" to see what is happening to her—that she is being atavistic in letting herself be absorbed in this state of sensual subjection to Cicio:

> Was it atavism, this strange, sleep-like submission to his being? Perhaps it was. Perhaps it was. But it was also heavy and sweet and rich. Somewhere, she was content.[35]

For Alvina Cicio's "beauty, his dark shadow" has a certain compelling fascination, notwithstanding her awareness that their relation implies her own extinction. When she goes to live with him in Califano, the tiny hamlet near the Italian village of Pescocalascio, we find that she is affected in just the

---

[33] *Op. cit.*, p. 241.   [34] *Op. cit.*, p. 297.   [35] *Ibid.*

same way also by the place he comes from. These last few pages of the book,[36] in addition to being a superb evocation of the spirit of the place, underscore the nature of Alvina's atavistic relationship with Cicio. In going to the "unspeakably lovely" Pescocalascio, she feels she has "gone beyond the world into the pre-world", has reverted to "an old eternity". The grand "pagan twilight of the valleys" steals her soul away. She feels transfigured. But at the same time the mysterious influence of the mountains and valleys seems to be annihilating her. She is enraptured with the "terrific beauty" of the place, but is also horrified by its savage annihilation of her:

> It seems there are places which resist us, which have the power to overthrow our psychic being. It seems as if every country had its potent negative centres, localities which savagely and triumphantly refuse our living culture. And Alvina had struck one of these, here on the edge of the Abruzzi. . . . The terror, the agony, the nostalgia of the heathen past was a constant torture to her mediumistic soul. She did not know what it was. But it was a kind of neuralgia in the very soul, never to be located in the human body, and yet physical. Coming over the brow of a heathy, rocky hillock, and seeing Cicio beyond leaning deep over the plough, in his white shirt-sleeves following the slow, waving, moth-pale oxen across a small track of land turned up in the heathen hollow, her soul would go all faint, she would almost swoon with realisation of the world that had gone before. And Cicio was so silent, there seemed so much dumb magic and anguish in him, as if he were forever afraid of himself and the thing he was. He seemed, in his silence, to *concentrate* upon her so terribly. She believed she would not live.[37]

It is not only Cicio, however, who "concentrates" on Alvina so that she feels she would not live; even more "extinguishing" is the influence of the breathtaking beauty of the place. Both cast a spell on her; and giving in to either means her own destruction. The strangeness and the primitiveness of the life around her appeals strongly to the Englishwoman coming from a more conscious and advanced, even if devitalised, civilisation:

---

[36] These concluding pages bear a close resemblance to the ending of *St. Mawr*, and are charged with the same significance.

[37] *The Lost Girl*, pp. 324-5.

but she soon comes to see that she can never become a part of it, or even endure it for a life-time: "It was impossible for her to become one with it altogether."[38]   Cicio, she concludes, must take her "to America, or England—to America preferably".   In the meantime, however, Italy enters the war, Cicio is called up, and the novel ends in "suspense"—the title of the last chapter—when he promises, before leaving, that he will come back to her and then both of them will go away—to America or somewhere else.   The novel gives no indication of the possibilities in Alvina's future life with Cicio.   But at the point where the novel ends she is surely little more than a lost girl.   In giving up Woodhouse and its values she had also found something—the rich, dark life of her body.   But faced with the prospect of this "lapse of life" in the Abruzzi, where her very soul is starved of its "mysterious nourishment", Alvina is rightly apprehensive.   She is lost in the old pagan world of the past: but if she is to be true to what Lawrence calls elsewhere "the great devious onward-flowing stream of conscious human blood",[39] she must find her way onward, forward, and not remain lapsed in the mysterious world of the past.   *The Lost Girl* leaves Alvina still lost, though not without hope that one day both she and Cicio might be able to find a way out, and save themselves.

In *Aaron's Rod*, as in *The Lost Girl*, the story opens in the English Midlands and then moves on to Italy—though the significance of the change in scene in the two novels cannot be said to be the same.   *Aaron's Rod*, in fact, continues Lawrence's "life and thought adventure" at the point where *Women in Love* had left it, and further explores the theme of man-woman relationship, bringing out its limitations and inadequacies, and defining at length man's need for coming into possession of his own soul, for "his isolate self-responsibility".   It is this central theme which unites many of the apparently unrelated episodes in the novel.   Jim's harangues on love, as well as Lilly's on his relationship with Tanny—no less than Aaron's own experiences with Josephine Ford and the Marchesa del Torre—serve in their different ways to clarify Aaron's feeling of dissatisfaction

[38] *Op. cit.*, p. 330.   [39] *Phoenix*, p. 99.

arising out of the kind of relationship he has had with his wife. Birkin at the end of *Women in Love* leaves Ursula puzzled as to why, having her, he should still want an additional relationship with a man, too. *Aaron's Rod*, elaborating the theme, explains through an imaginatively conceived situation the need for man-to-man relationship, and goes on to experiment with one of the possible forms that such a relationship could assume.

Love, Lawrence believed, is only a travelling, not a goal; it is a process, not an end. There is no fulfilment in love itself, even though it can and should lead to "the fulfilment of single aloneness", to the "central fullness of self-possession."[40] The central fulfilment for a man is that he should possess his own soul within him, "deep and alone". This deep, rich aloneness is reached and perfected through love, and only through love: but love, nevertheless, remains only a means to an end. "One has to learn," Lawrence says in a letter, "that love is a secondary thing in life. The first thing is to be a free, proud, single being by oneself: to be oneself free, to let the other be free: to force nothing and not to be forced oneself into anything. . . . Love isn't all that important: one's own free soul is first."[41] In marriage a man has his consummation and his being: but the final consummation for him lies beyond marriage. Having deeply fulfilled himself in marriage, he should not come to rest, but must undertake the responsibility for the next step into the future by participating in some passionate, purposive activity. Acting in his role as a "creator, mover, maker" man acts in unison with other men in an "eternal" and "sacred relationship of comrades"—which is the final progression from marriage:

> Let there be again the old passion of deathless friendship between man and man. Humanity can never advance into the new regions of unexplored futurity otherwise. . . . Friendship should be a rare, choice, immortal thing, sacred and inviolable as marriage. Marriage and deathless friendship, both should be inviolable and sacred: two great creative passions, separate, apart, but complementary: the one pivotal, the other adventurous: the one, marriage, the centre of human life; and the other, the leap ahead.[42]

[40] *Fantasia*, p. 120.   [41] Nehls, I, p. 500.   [42] *Phoenix*, p. 665.

One requisite for the establishment of a new, spontaneous relationship between men, it would appear, is that they should have a new attitude towards one another—an attitude based on "a new reverence for their heroes" and "a new regard for their comrades".[43]   Lawrence's views about "heroes" among men were to undergo a change in the course of time, but when he wrote *Aaron's Rod* he was still playing with the idea—though, as we shall see, not without a certain amount of scepticism.

With these views of Lawrence in mind we can now turn to *Aaron's Rod* to consider the extent to which they can be said to be embodied in the novel itself.   There is, it would at once be apparent to any reader, only some general talk about "purposive activity" in the book, the action of the novel containing little to suggest this.   (The explanation for this, however, might be that Aaron has yet to attain "the stillness and sweet possession of [his] own soul"; and it is only towards the end of the novel that he begins to do so.)   Also, the novel ends on a very ambiguous note about what the nature of Aaron's relationship with Lilly is going to be.   But otherwise the development of the novel follows, I think, the general conception which I have tried to outline above.

Aaron Sisson, when the book opens just after the end of the war, is still living with his family.   He has been married twelve years, and his relations with his wife are now coming to a crisis, even though he is not consciously aware of it.   The "sickness of the unrecognised and incomprehensible strain" between him and his wife has not only set him apart from her, but also cut him off from his surroundings.   The "curious and deadly opposition" between their two wills causes in Aaron a "nauseating ache" and a hostile tension which extends to include his relation with the rest of his "circumambient universe".   He finds the "cosy brightness" of his home "unspeakably familiar" and unbearably monotonous: "The acute familiarity of this house, which had been built for his marriage twelve years ago, the changeless pleasantness of it all seemed unthinkable."[44]   For a time he has tried, and partially succeeded, in forgetting the deep feeling of antagonism towards his surroundings.   "A woman and whisky, these were usually a

---

[43] *Phoenix*, p. 665.   [44] *Aaron's Rod*, p. 8.

remedy—and music."[45] But now they have begun to fail him.
He still wants to let himself go, to "feel rosy and loving and all
that": but the hard opposing core in him—"this strained,
unacknowledged opposition to his surroundings"—sits deep
established in him like an obstinate black dog which growls
and shows its teeth at the very thought of any connexions. His
aloofness and "dead-level indifference" to his surroundings is
repeatedly stressed—until, about half-way through the novel,
his soul begins to open up to the magic of life again while he is
travelling in Italy. For the present he finds that his contact
even with the landlady of the Royal Oak—in the "great fierce
warmth" of whose presence he has so loved to luxuriate for
some time past—is distasteful to him. Her very lustfulness,
which had so pricked his senses once, now leaves him cold,
even deadly antagonistic to her. The thought of his wife leaves
him even whiter and colder, set in a more intense obstinacy.
He has turned away from the possessive love and good-will of
his wife, only to encounter "righteous bullying" in all those he
comes across. His unfaithfulness to his wife has only succeeded
in making her will, like his own, strong and unrelaxing, so that
there has come to exist a state of deadlock between them.
Then, suddenly, Aaron leaves his wife and children and goes
away. Why? Why does he go away like that? The question
is asked several times in the book itself, and many critics have
asked it since. It is, indeed, the crucial question in the novel,
and the reader has a legitimate right to ask for an explanation.
Does the book provide us with an answer?

Eliseo Vivas strongly condemns the book for its failure to
elucidate the grounds on which Aaron, without any explanation
or warning, decides to leave his family.[46] "What justifies the
action?" he asks, adding that he, as a critic, is asking for an
aesthetic justification, not demanding a moral justification for
"an unmitigatedly caddish act, a justification that will satisfy
my notions of the decent treatment a man owes his family and
himself".[47] The terms in which the case is put leads one to

[45] *Op. cit.*, p. 18.
[46] David Daiches has raised the same objection. Aaron, he says, leaves his
family "in a curiously fatalistic and irresponsible way that is never explored or
explained adequately". (Daiches, p. 174.)
[47] Vivas, p. 24.

doubt if Vivas was really looking for an "aesthetic" justification. It is probably true that neither Aaron nor Lawrence has any explanation to offer which would satisfy Mr Vivas's "notions of decent treatment": but if all he wanted was "a rendering, in whatever way the author chooses to give it, of that which gives Aaron's action its intelligibility in the story",[48] then it is difficult to understand why he should have failed to see that in one way the entire book is little more than an attempt to do just that.

Aaron's marriage to Lottie, we are told, turns almost at once into a relationship of conflict. It is not that they do not love each other. Aaron has loved his wife and has "never loved any other woman"; he has been a passionate lover, keeping back from her "nothing, no experience, no degree of intimacy". Lottie, too, has been passionately in love with him, has, indeed, "loved him to madness". But this love soon turns into "a kind of combat". Both of them have been brought up to consider themselves the first in whatever company or relationship they find themselves. Besides, Lottie has—not unexpectedly, though not quite consciously—imbibed the formulated and professed belief of the whole white world in "the life-centrality of woman". For this no blame is put on her, as "this great and ignominious dogma of the sacred priority of women" is shared not only by all other women but also by practically all men. The whole world around her thinks of Woman as the life-bearer, the life source, the centre of creation—whereas man is considered a mere adjunct. "She, as woman, and particularly as mother, was the first great source of life and being, and also of culture. The man was but the instrument and the finisher. She was the source and the substance."[49] Aaron himself, on one level, subscribes to this "*idée fixe* of today" that he should yield himself, give himself away to his woman in order to achieve the final consummation. In his "open mind" he has the ready-made and banal idea of himself as a "really quite nice individual", and from this comes his homage-rendering love and worship of his wife. For some time even Lottie is taken in by this manifest love. But "though you can deceive the conscious mind, you can never deceive the deep unconscious

<hr />

[48] Vivas, p. 24.   [49] *Aaron's Rod*, p. 154.

instinct".[50] So she finds herself despising him in "her terrible paroxysms of hatred for him". She cannot understand why she feels so dazed and maddened: for a long time she does not realise that in spite of all the wonder and miracle of their "heaven-rending passion" Aaron has been withholding the central core of himself, never giving himself to her. "He cheated and made play with her tremendous passional soul, her sacred sex passion, most sacred of all things for a woman. All the time, some central part of him stood apart from her, aside, looking on."[51] Aaron himself is not conscious of what is going on in his "passional soul" beneath his "conscious mask". But in him, we are informed by the narrator, is planted another seed. "Born in him was a spirit which could not worship woman: no, and would not. Could not and would not. It was not in him."[52] Lottie, however, feels instinctively sure that her man must yield to her "so that she could envelop him, yielding, in her all-benificent love. She was quite sure her love was all benificent. Of this no shadow of doubt." Her profound impulse and instinct, developed in her by the age she lives in, tell her that to be perfectly enveloped in her benificent love is the highest her man can ever know or reach. But as time goes by she comes to realise that she can never fully possess him, and then she is filled with hate for him:

> Cheated, foiled, betrayed, forced to love him or hate him: never able to be at peace near him nor away from him: poor Lottie, no wonder she was as a mad woman. She was strictly as a woman demented, after the birth of her second child. For all her instinct, all her impulse, all her desire, and above all, all her *will*, was to possess her man in very fulness once: just once: and once and for all. Once, just once: and it would be once and for all.
>
> But never! Never! Not once! Never! Not for one single solitary second! Was it not enough to send a woman mad. . . . She drove him mad too: mad, so that he beat her: mad so that he longed to kill her. But even in his greatest rages he was the same: he never finally lost himself: he remained, somewhere in the centre, in possession of himself.[53]

---

[50] *Op. cit.*, p. 155.   [51] *Op. cit.*, p. 156.
[52] *Op. cit.*, p. 155.   [53] *Op. cit.*, p. 157.

Lottie, we are told, remains a good wife and mother, fulfilling all her duties. But of one thing she is dead certain: that in the conflict with her husband she must never yield, must never capitulate, or abandon her divine responsibility as woman. "*He* must yield. That was written in eternal letters, on the iron tablet of her will. *He* must yield. She the woman, the mother of his children, how should she ever think to yield? It was unthinkable. He, the man, the weak, the false, the treacherous, the half-hearted, it was he who must yield."[54]

In order to escape his wife's terrible will—which, like a "flat cold snake coiled round his soul", is squeezing him to death—Aaron first takes to leaving her alone as much as possible, then is unfaithful to her. Lottie is "more than maddened": but he begins to be quite indifferent to her. Then she, too, learns to be indifferent to the fascination he exerts over her, and fights him with her powerful will "which presses and presses and cannot relax". Two wills are now wound tense and fixed. "She became the same as he. Even in her moments of most passionate desire for him, the cold and snake-like tension of her will never relaxed, and the cold, snake-like eye of her intention never closed."[55] The conflict, however, does not take place on a conscious level, and "neither of them understood what was happening".[56] There is, nevertheless, a deadlock between them, with neither of the two wills relaxing. At the point where the novel opens Aaron has just come to the realisation that at this "terrible passive game of fixed tension" Lottie would beat him.

> Her fixed female soul, her wound-up female will would solidify into stone—whereas his must break. In him something must break. It was a cold and fatal deadlock, profitless. A life-automatism of fixed tension that suddenly, in him, did break. His will flew loose in a recoil: a recoil away from her. He left her, as inevitably as a broken spring flies from its hold.[57]

Aaron is not yet fully conscious why he has left his wife. Lottie has no idea, either, why he has deserted her. She is aware that in his relationship with her he "kept himself back,

---

[54] *Ibid.*
[56] *Op. cit.*, p. 157.

[55] *Op. cit.*, p. 158.
[57] *Op. cit.*, p. 158.

always kept himself back, couldn't give himself":[58] but she does not connect this with Aaron's going away. She rather attributes his leaving her "with all the burden" to his being "selfish through and through"; later, she tells him that he ran away because he was "too weak", "unnatural and evil", "unmanly and cowardly".[59] Actually, she is completely puzzled by his conduct and can think of no convincing explanation for it. Aaron himself can only feel the unrelaxing tension within him, and goes away hating "the hard, inviolable heart that stuck unchanging in his own breast".[60] When he is asked by Josephine Ford why he had left his wife, he has "no particular reason" to offer.[61] On her insistence that he could not have left his wife and little girls for no reason at all, he still says

"Yes, I did. For no reason—except I wanted to have a bit of free room round me—to loose myself"

"You mean you wanted love?" flashed Josephine, thinking he said *lose*.

"No, I wanted fresh air. I don't know what I wanted. Why should I know?"

"But we must know: especially when other people are going to suffer so," said she.

"Ah well! A breath of fresh air, by myself. I felt forced to love. I feel if I go back home now, I shall be *forced*—forced to love—or care—or something."

"Perhaps you wanted more than your wife could give you," she said.

"Perhaps less. She's made up her mind she loves me, and she's not going to let me off."

"Did you never love her?" said Josephine.

"Oh yes. I shall never love anybody else. But I'm damned if I want to go on being a lover, to her or to anybody. That's the top and bottom of it. I don't want to *care*, when care isn't in me. And I'm not going to be forced to it."[62]

---

[58] *Op. cit.*, p. 39.   [59] *Op. cit.*, p. 120.   [60] *Op. cit.*, p. 40.

[61] In a later conversation with Sir William Frank at Novara, Aaron compares his abandoning his wife and children to a "natural event", as undeniable as birth or death. "It wasn't a question of reasons", he says, "It was a question of her and me and what must be" (p. 141). Aaron, though quite certain of the inevitability of his action, does not yet "know"—and therefore cannot explain—what he feels in his "passional soul".   [62] *Aaron's Rod*, p. 61.

P

Aaron's assertion that he is not going to care when care is not in him is—though he himself is not yet clear about its implications—an instinctive rejection on his part of "duty" and "responsibility" in terms of social morality,[63] and an acceptance of a deeper moral responsibility to himself. He is still—we are told—attached to his family, and has arranged for sufficient money to be paid over to his wife, having "reserved only a small amount for himself":[64] but he is not prepared to yield the mastery of his own soul and conscience and actions to anyone else. When, overcome by qualms concerning his abandoned family, he returns home after almost a year's absence, he is torn by conflicting emotions. "The place, the home, at once fascinated him and revolted him."[65] He foresees a "violent emotional reconciliation" with his wife, and is filled with a "violent conflict of tenderness": but when he actually meets her and hears her voice which is "full of hate", he is again overcome by the old "sickness of the unrecognised and incomprehensible strain between him and her".[66] She challenges him to tell her what he has against her: "Tell me! Tell me what I've done." But "telling isn't so easy—especially when the trouble goes too deep for conscious comprehension. He couldn't *tell* what he had against her. And he had not the slightest intention of doing what she would have liked him to do, starting to pile up detailed grievances. He knew the detailed grievances were nothing in themselves."[67] Even when Lottie is ready for a reconciliation and wistfully appeals to him to confess that he has been wrong to her, he cannot do it because beneath her pleading he can feel "the iron of her heart":

> The strange, liquid sound of her appeal seemed to him like the swaying of a serpent which mesmerises the fated, fluttering, helpless bird. She clasped her arms round him, she drew him to her, she half roused his passion. At the same time she coldly horrified and repelled him. He had not the faintest feeling,

---

[63] And society's opinion of him is given in Sir William Frank's genial words: "It is certainly a good thing for society that men like you . . . are not common" (p. 141). This is, of course, putting the case mildly. Much stronger language could be, and has been used in condemnation of an attitude like Aaron's.

[64] *Aaron's Rod*, p. 134.   [65] *Op. cit.*, p. 117.

[66] *Op. cit.*, p. 118.   [67] *Op. cit.*, p. 119.

at the moment, of his own wrong. But she wanted to win his own self-betrayal out of him. He could see himself as the fascinated victim, falling to this cajoling, artful woman, the wife of his bosom. But as well, he had a soul outside himself, which looked on the whole scene with cold revulsion, and which was as unchangeable as time.

"No," he said, "I don't feel wrong. . . ." She was defeated. But she too would never yield. . . . Come life, come death, she too would never yield. And she realised now that he would never yield. . . . He too would never yield. The illusion of love was gone for ever. Love was a battle in which each party strove for the mastery of the other's soul. So far, man had yielded the mastery to women. Now he was fighting for it back again. And too late, for the woman would never yield.[68]

Both Aaron and Lottie are too rigid in their attitudes for the conflict between them to find any resolution. Aaron, therefore, resolves on "life single, not life double". For the time being, he decides, his need is to be alone, to be himself: "Let there be clean and pure division first, perfected singleness. That is the only way to final, living unison: through sheer, finished singleness."[69]

Aaron returns to London; then finding that the town "got on his nerves", determines to clear out. Knowing that Lilly has gone to Italy, he decides to follow him there. It is in Italy, at Novara, that one Sunday evening Aaron, for the first time, becomes vaguely conscious of "the root cause of his strife with Lottie". He knows that in the kind of deadlock that exists between them neither of the two can be wholly at fault and that he himself is partly to blame. "Having a detached and logical soul, he never let himself forget this truth."[70] But whereas he was puzzled before, not knowing why there was so much conflict in his relations with his wife, now—even if he can see no solution—it is at least a defined situation:

He realised that he had never intended to yield himself fully to her or to anything: that he did not intend ever to yield himself up entirely to her or to anything: that his very being pivoted on the fact of his isolate self-responsibility, aloneness. His intrinsic and central aloneness was the very centre of his

[68] *Op. cit.*, pp. 122-3.   [69] *Op. cit.*, p. 123.   [70] *Op. cit.*, p. 154.

being. Break it, and he broke his being. Break this central
aloneness, and he broke everything. It was the great temptation, to yield himself: and it was the final sacrilege. Anyhow,
it was something which, from his profoundest soul, he did not
intend to do. By the innermost isolation and singleness of his
own soul he would abide though the skies fell on top of one
another, and seven heavens collapsed.[71]

This realisation comes to Aaron not as so many words or ideas;
with him it is more a case of silent, "wordless comprehension".
But in his own "powerful but subconscious" fashion Aaron
becomes aware that he had never wanted, and does not want,
to surrender himself utterly to either his wife or anybody else.

The last extreme of self-abandon in love was for him an act of
false behaviour. His own nature inside him fated him not to
take this last false step, over the edge of the abyss of selflessness.
Even if he wanted to, he could not. . . . For, according to all
the current prejudice and impulse in one direction, he too had
believed that the final achievement, the consummation of
human life, was this flinging oneself over the precipice, down
the bottomless pit of love. Now he realised that love, even in
its intensest, was only an attribute of the human soul: one of
its incomprehensible gestures. And to fling down the whole
soul in one gesture of finality in love was as much a criminal
suicide as to jump off a church-tower or a mountain-peak. Let
a man give himself as much as he liked in love, to seven thousand
extremities, he must never give himself *away*. The more
generous and the more passionate a soul, the more it *gives*
itself. But the more absolute remains the law, that it shall
never give itself away. Give thyself, but give thyself not
away.[72]

This "splendid love-way" requires that both man and woman
should maintain their separate identity in the relationship of
love. Aaron has at last come to accept the necessity of being
by himself—recognising that his state of loneliness is in itself a
fulfilment in so far as it marks the completion of a great stage
in the process of love. The attainment of singleness or aloneness, however, is only a preparation for fuller and more vital
relationships in the next stage. Aaron has so far been only

[71] *Op. cit.*, pp. 158-9.   [72] *Op. cit.*, pp. 161-3.

breaking loose from one connexion after another, snapping all old ties which had bound him to the people he has loved or liked. In a way he knows that he is thus "fulfilling his own inward destiny": but he also feels apprehensive at where it is leading him. "Why break every tie?" he asks himself, "In God's name, why? What was there instead?" And the answer he gets is: nothingness. "There was just himself and blank nothingness."[73] He realises that for the time being he is not moving *towards* anything, only moving away from everything. He is not seeking for love, or for any kind of unison or communion. "Only let him *not* run into any sort of embrace with anything or anybody—this was what he asked. Let no new connection be made between himself and anything on earth. Let all old connections break. This was his craving."[74] But sooner or later he must fall back into relationship—for cut off from all vital contacts he can only arrive at "blank nothingness". His very individuality, his "singleness" itself, is dependent on relationship. He, of course, cannot force himself into any living relationship, but must wait till some connexion naturally forms itself without any interference by him. Aaron's isolation from his wife and children had, in turn, led to his alienation from his surroundings. Now, in the reversal of the process, he succeeds first in establishing a rapport with the natural surroundings before he can enter into any meaningful human relationship.

Considerable prominence is given in the novel to the subject of Aaron's loss of contact with his "circumambient universe"; and it is, significantly, in Italy that he begins to get in touch with it again. The beautiful view he has on his very first morning in Novara—the winding river, the clear, clean air, the massive snow-streaked mountains—all this makes the universe live for him again for a time. The Alps seem to him like "tigers prowling between the north and the south"; the wind coming from the snow is like "the icy whiskers of a tiger": Aaron's "old sleepy English nature" is startled in its sleep. But he is not yet ready to come awake, not wanting to face the responsibility of the new life rising in him:

[73] *Op. cit.*, p. 174.   [74] *Op. cit.*, p. 175.

To open his darkest eyes and wake up to a new responsibility. Wake up and enter on the responsibility of a new self in
himself. Ach, the horror of responsibility! He had all his
life slept and shelved the burden. And he wanted to go on
sleeping. . . . He felt some finger prodding, prodding, prodding
him awake out of the sleep of pathos and tragedy and spasmodic
passion, and he wriggled unwilling, oh most unwilling to undertake the new business.[75]

Aaron can sense a new life-quality everywhere around him and
is aware of the dynamically different values of life in the country
he has come to. But his mind and soul are not fully opened up
to this new "spontaneous life-dynamic". Some days later,
travelling by rail from Milan to Florence on a "lovely, lovely
day of early autumn", he is again struck by the bigness and the
exposed beauty of the great plain of Lombardy. There seems
to him a kind of boldness and openness in the landscape which
impresses and fascinates him. Looking at his companions in
the third-class carriage, he finds the same quality of indifference
and exposed gesture in them, too.

It is, finally, in Florence—in the Piazza della Signoria with
its "clownish Bandinellis" and Michaelangelo's David—that
Aaron feels he has come to "one of the world's living centres",
and feels a new self, a new life-surge rising inside himself.
"Florence seemed to start a new man in him."[76]

As "a new man" Aaron not only feels free to get in touch
with other human beings, but also succeeds, with the help of
his flute, in performing the "little miracle" of awakening a new
woman in the Marchesa del Torre. For a long time he had
been gripped inside himself, hard and unyielding, his desire
for women fast withheld. "All his deep, desirous blood had
been locked, he had wanted nobody, and nothing. And it had
been hard to live, so. Without desire, without any movement
of passionate love, only gripped back in recoil! That was an
experience to endure."[77] Now his desire comes back, strong
and fierce. He feels his turn has at last come, that Aaron's rod
is going to blossom again: "The phoenix had risen in fire again,
out of the ashes."[78] The Marchesa, who had been for years

[75] *Op. cit.*, pp. 146-7.   [76] *Op. cit.*, p. 208.
[77] *Op. cit.*, p. 250.   [78] *Op. cit.*, p. 251.

shut in the "dank and beastly dungeon of feelings and moral necessity", also feels free to establish a connexion with Aaron "outside the horrible, stinking human castle of life". But for Aaron this relationship can be a success only if it proves to be radically different in nature from his earlier relations with women and leaves his intrinsic, inviolable self alone. It is not for nothing that he had left his wife, and had found that his experience with Josephine Ford nearly killed him, because he had been forced to "give in".[79] As it turns out, his relation with the Marchesa brings to him, at the very start, an awareness of the conflict within him. Realising that he is "sinking towards her", Aaron is terrified at the prospect of his being absorbed by her, and yet he also *wants* to sink towards her:

> The flesh and blood of him simply melted out, in desire towards her. Cost what may, he must come to her. And yet he knew at the same time that, cost what may, he must keep the power to recover himself from her. He must have his cake and eat it.[80]

But he cannot both eat his cake and have it. The Marchesa, we gather from her husband's reflexions on Eve, is the woman who merely takes a man to use him, to make of him that which will serve her desire. "She may love me," he says, "she may be soft and kind to me, she may give her life for me. But why? Only because I am *hers*. I am that thing which does her most intimate service."[81] It does not take Aaron long to discover that the Marchesa completely ignores him as an individual and uses him "as a mere magic implement";[82] that unless she herself wills it, his "male power"—of which he is so proud— can cast no spell on her. She rather seems, by withstanding him, to throw "cold water over his phoenix newly risen from the ashes of its nest in flames".[83] Yet his will is fixed on possessing her "whole soft white body . . . in its entirety, its fulness". That he finds this "soft white body" also "deadly in power" should come as no surprise. Like Skrebensky's desire for Ursula in *The Rainbow*, his passion for the Marchesa is "just unalloyed desire, and nothing else".[84] There is no personal intimacy or tenderness in the relationship: it is all sheer

---

[79] *Op. cit.*, p. 84.　　[80] *Op. cit.*, p. 244.　　[81] *Op. cit.*, p. 236.
[82] *Op. cit.*, p. 264.　　[83] *Op. cit.*, p. 252.　　[84] *Op. cit.*, p. 260.

destructive sensuality. No wonder then that "his desire and himself likewise [break] disastrously under the proving".[85] Seeing that Aaron had found his fuller relationship (of passion as well as tenderness) with Lottie unsatisfactory because it violated his "intrinsic and central aloneness", it was inevitable that his self-seeking relationship with the Marchesa should leave him with the feeling that "it simply blasted his own central life":

> His famous desire for her, what had it been but this same attempt to strike a magic fire out of her, for his own ecstasy. They were playing the same game of fire. In him, however, there was always something, all the time something hard and reckless and defiant, which stood apart. She was absolutely gone in her own incantations. She was absolutely gone, like a priestess utterly involved in her own terrible rites. And he was part of the ritual only, God and victim in one. God and victim. All the time, God and victim. When his aloof soul realised, amid the incantation, how he was being used—not as himself, but as something quite different: God and victim; then he dilated with intense surprise, and his remote soul stood up tall and knew itself alone. He did not want it—not at all. He knew he was apart. And he looked back over the whole mystery of their love contact. Only his soul was apart.[86]

Aaron's relation with the Marchesa both serves to clarify the nature of conflict in his relationship with Lottie and to bring to him a renewed and intensified awareness of his need to stand alone and possess his own soul. And this, it appears to me, is the significance of the episode in the novel.[87]

---

[85] *Op. cit.*, p. 261. [86] *Op. cit.*, pp. 264-5.

[87] It is interesting to note to what lengths critics sometimes go in their efforts to invent plausible explanations for an incident or episode in a Lawrence novel whose inclusion they cannot justify on artistic grounds but which is, nevertheless, too prominent and challenging to be simply ignored. F. R. Leavis, for instance, finds the Aaron-Marchesa episode "irritatingly unsatisfying" because it seems to him not completely significant. There is no inevitability, he says, about the episode as a part of Aaron's history. He, therefore, confidently concludes that it appears in the novel because "Lawrence himself had encountered the original of the Marchesa and been struck by her—been intrigued by her interest as a case". (Leavis, p. 49). J. I. M. Stewart, who also fails to see the significance of the episode for Aaron's story, dismisses it as "no more than one of those routine conquests of high-born ladies by proletarian lovers which it gave [Lawrence] pleasure to invent" (*Eight Modern Writers*, p. 537).

The theme of aloneness also serves to link Aaron with Rawdon Lilly. The close connexion between the conceptions of the characters of Aaron and Lilly has often been commented on. J. M. Murry, reviewing *Aaron's Rod*, remarked that "Aaron is the instinct to which Lilly supplies the consciousness".[88] Horace Gregory refers to Aaron and Lilly as two contradicting elements within Lawrence himself.[89] F. R. Leavis sees Aaron as "an *alter-ego*" and his questioning of Lilly as "something very like a *dialogue intérieur*".[90] There is no doubt a great deal of truth in these remarks,[91] though one must beware of taking them too literally. All that Lilly says in the novel about love, marriage, power, and possession of one's soul is, we might say, a total proposition which is put to the test in the novel. Parts of it find ready approval from other characters, and one gets the impression that the reader is also expected to concur; but certain other parts are looked at with suspicion by Aaron, and these he is unwilling to accept. The reader, I take it, is also meant to take them in this light and see these views of Lilly's for what they are. The novel, in any case, presents both a case and its criticism—though as I shall have occasion to say, the criticism is not strong enough for the book to be an artistically satisfying whole.

We find Lilly first of all enlarging on the theme of love in an argument with Jim Bricknell which, for the former, ends with "a punch in the wind". Jim complains that he is going to pieces, that life is leaving him because he has no one to love him. He believes that "Love is life", and that the highest a man is capable of is to sacrifice himself to love. To this Lilly replies by saying that what Jim calls love is actually a vice, "a sheer ignominy"; and that it is not the lack of love but the craving for love and self-sacrifice on Jim's part which makes him

---

[88] *Reminiscences*, p. 235. Lawrence sent a letter to Murry saying he understood *Aaron's Rod* "all right". (*Letters*, p. 574.)

[89] *D. H. Lawrence: Pilgrim of the Apocalypse*, New York (1957), p. 52.

[90] Leavis, p. 38. Graham Hough, too, interprets the exchanges between the two characters as "a dialogue of Lawrence with himself". (Hough, p. 99.) See also E. W. Tedlock, Jr., *D. H. Lawrence: Artist and Rebel*, Albuquerque (1963), p. 152.

[91] In the novel itself we are told that the two men have "an almost uncanny understanding of one another—like brothers", and also that "like brothers, there was a profound hostility between them". (p. 100.)

feel he is losing life. "You should stand by yourself and learn to be yourself", he tells him. These remarks by Lilly—which are elaborated in great detail in the course of the novel, especially in Lilly's conversations with Aaron—bear a direct relevance to Aaron's case. Aaron, too, like Jim, had at one time believed that the final consummation for him lay in sacrificing himself to love, forgetting that the self is greater than love. He, too, had mistaken the process of love for a goal.

> The aim of any process is not the perpetuation of that process, but the completion thereof. Love is a process of the incomprehensible human soul: love also incomprehensible, but still only a process. The process should work to a completion, not to some horror of intensification and extremity wherein the soul and body ultimately perish. The completion of the process of love is the arrival at a state of simple, pure self-possession, for man and woman. Only that. Which isn't exciting enough for us sensationalists. We prefer abysses and maudlin self-abandon and self-sacrifice, the degeneration into a sort of slime and merge.
>
> Perhaps, truly, the process of love is never accomplished. But it moves in great stages, and at the end of each stage a true goal, where the soul possesses itself in simple and generous singleness.[92]

Lilly firmly believes that before men and women can come together they must, in the first place, learn to stand by themselves, for "nothing is any good unless each stands alone, intrinsically".[93] He also holds that the relationship of marriage—which he calls *egoisme à deux*—should be extended, or re-adjusted, so that man can stand on his own legs and, uniting with other men, can bring back the spirit of adventure in life.[94] Graham Hough has expressed his doubts on the point, and his reading of what he calls "the queer semi-amorous wranglings between Aaron and Lilly" in Chapter x leads him to the conclusion that "they are looking for a substitute for marriage rather than a solution of its problems".[95] A similar point has also been made by H. M. Daleski in his recent book on Lawrence.[96] Such a view might be mistakenly seen to be

---

[92] *Aaron's Rod*, p. 162.
[93] *Op. cit.*, p. 85.
[94] *Op. cit.*, pp. 95-6.
[95] Hough, p. 98.
[96] *The Forked Flame: A Study of D. H. Lawrence*, London (1965), p. 190.

substantiated by the scene where Lilly brings the flu-stricken Aaron to his room and, finding that he is sulking himself out of life, massages his lower body with oil "as mothers do their babies whose bowels don't work":

> For a long time he rubbed finely and steadily, then went over the whole of the lower body, mindless, as if in a sort of incantation. He rubbed every speck of the man's lower body—the abdomen, the buttocks, the thighs and knees, down to his feet, rubbed it all warm and glowing with camphorated oil, every bit of it, chafing the toes swiftly, till he was almost exhausted. Then Aaron was covered up again, and Lilly sat down in fatigue to look at his patient.[97]

An attentive reading of the whole scene would, however, make it obvious that it is these personal contacts with other men based on love, sympathy, or sacrifice, that Lilly is moving away from. As he nurses Aaron, he is reminded of his wife Tanny's final remark after he had received a punch in the wind from Jim Bricknell: "You shouldn't try to make a little Jesus of yourself, coming so near to people, wanting to help them." Now he reflects that as soon as Aaron is better he, too, would probably give him a punch in the wind, metaphorically if not literally, for having interfered with him. A Jesus, he concludes, makes a Judas inevitable. Hence his decision: "All right, Aaron. Last time I break my bread for anybody, this is. So get better, my flautist, so that I can go away."[98] The conclusion that the impersonal, purposive relationship with other men that Lilly is seeking is presented "suspiciously like an alternative to marriage" is belied by the entire argument of the novel. Lilly makes it quite clear in the very first extended conversation he has with Aaron that when he speaks of man's learning to possess his own soul in patience and in peace, he does not have anything like a negative Nirvana in mind. It is a state in which one does not cease to love, or even to hate: in fact one can come to attain this state only "after a lot of fighting and a lot of sensual fulfilment. And it never does away with the fighting and with the sensual passion. It flowers on top of them, and it would never flower save on top of them."[99] It is thus obvious that the very basis of man's possessing his own soul

[97] *Aaron's Rod*, p. 91.   [98] *Op. cit.*, p. 92.   [99] *Op. cit.*, p. 99.

in fullness is assumed to be a satisfactory sensual fulfilment in
marriage. Moreover, a man can be best alone and at peace
only when his woman has also accomplished for herself the
possession of her own soul. This is, Lilly tells Aaron, what he is
hoping for[1] in his own relationship with his wife:

> ". . . And if Tanny possesses her own soul in patience and peace
> as well—and if in this we understand each other at last—then
> there we are, together and apart at the same time, and free of
> each other, and eternally inseparable." . . . "You learn to be
> quite alone and possess your own soul in isolation—and at the
> same time to be perfectly *with* someone else—That's all I ask."[2]

As Lilly explains in a subsequent conversation, in being "quite
alone" a man does not choose to be sentimental or lonely; he
merely learns, by choice, to be what by his own nature he
essentially is. In as much as he is a single individual soul he *is*,
ipso facto, alone. "In so far as I am I, and only I am I, and I
am only I, in so far, I am inevitably and eternally alone, and
it is my last blessedness to know it, and to accept it, and to live
with this as the core of my self-knowledge."[3]

Aaron can see that Lilly has, largely, learnt to be alone
with his own soul, and is even envious of him. He himself, he
feels, cannot yet stand by himself in the middle of the world
with nothing to hold on to. In one way the whole of Aaron's
story develops round his efforts to acquire the ability to stand
alone and be in possession of his own soul.[4] When he first hears

---

[1] This hope, however, we learn later on (p. 238), is not realised (within the
limits of the novel).   [2] *Aaron's Rod*, p. 99.   [3] *Op. cit.*, p. 239.
[4] Julian Moynahan, who thinks differently, takes the following entertainingly
"competent" view of Aaron's quest, adding some speculations on his future, to
boot: "On a hard view, and in the end the novel forces this view on all except
the most incompetent of Lawrence's readers, Aaron, like the majority of the
twenty thousand American men who take the option of a poor man's divorce each
year, deserts his family simply out of boredom. He becomes a plaything of the
idle rich, peddling his musical talent and sexual magnetism to neurotic upper-class
wives and mistresses in exchange for more or less luxurious lodgings, fees, and
sensations. He exploits the appetite of a jaded social set for queer birds and can
be expected to go on drifting until his luck runs out with the onset of age and the
decline of his novelty value. It is hard to imagine what he might be doing in
twenty-five years' time. Perhaps if Italy continued to suit his indolent disposition
he might be found improvising a musical background to speeches delivered over
the Italian radio by Ezra Pound". (Moynahan, pp. 100-1.) It would be interesting to learn which of the three "perennial tasks of criticism" (listed by him in the
Introduction to his book) Moynahan hopes to have accomplished here.

Lilly talk glibly—as it seems to him—of possessing one's soul in patience and in peace, he is provoked to retort back—and the retort is a comment on his own condition at the time—that in actual life one possesses one's soul neither in patience nor in peace, "but any devil that likes possesses you and does what it likes with you, while you fridge yourself and fray yourself out like a worn rag".[5] Lilly's words, however, remain with him and he is reminded of them a long time afterwards following the disillusion of his experience with the Marchesa. His instinctive reaction is one of deep hatred towards her, but he says to himself: "No, I won't hate her. I won't hate her."[6] Realising that he must learn to be in possession of himself, he refuses to follow the "reflex of his own passion" and decides that he is not going to feel bitter towards the Marchesa—seeing also that "she too was struggling with her fate" and had been nothing but generous towards him. This he does, we are told, "under the influence of Lilly".[7] With Lilly's help he also comes to understand, in part, his own position. Lilly explains to him in the last chapter of the book—entitled appropriately, and perhaps not without a touch of irony as well, "Words"—that his first and last responsibility is to his own self:

". . . You *are* yourself and so *be* yourself. Stick to it and abide by it. Passion or no passion, ecstasy or no ecstasy, urge or no urge, there's no goal outside you, where you can consum[m]ate like an eagle flying into the sun, or a moth into a candle. . . .

"There is only one thing, your own very self. So you'd better stick to it. . . . You've got one job, and no more. There inside you lies your own very self, like a germinating egg . . . and since it is the only thing you have got or ever will have, don't go trying to lose it. You've got to develop it, from the egg into the chicken, and from the chicken into the one-and-only phoenix, of which there can only be one at a time in the universe. . . . Your own single oneness is your destiny. Your destiny comes from within, from your own self-form. And you can't know it beforehand, neither your destiny nor your self-form. You can only develop it. You can only stick to your own very self, and *never* betray it. . . ."[8]

---

[5] *Aaron's Rod*, p. 99.   [6] *Op. cit.*, p. 225.
[7] *Op. cit.*, p. 256.   [8] *Op. cit.*, pp. 285-6.

Since the destiny one has to unfold comes from within, one must—Lilly's "flood of words" goes on—fulfil one's soul's impulse, whatever the impulse be. If the soul urges one to love, one must love. "If you've got to go in for love and passion, go in for them", he tells Aaron. But he also exhorts him to remember that love and passion are not the goal but only a means—the only goal being the fulfilment of one's own soul's active desire and suggestion. To all this Aaron does not object. He also agrees that to make love the supreme urge, or to assert that "love and love alone must rule" is "all a lie". But when Lilly goes on to expound his views on power, and to contend that in the mode of power woman must submit in a "deep, unfathomable free submission" to man, Aaron cannot acquiesce. He, to begin with, does not attach to power-urge the kind of significance given to it by Lilly. "I don't see power as so very important", he tells him. Moreover, despite Lilly's insistence, he cannot believe that woman will ever yield to what Lilly calls "the positive power-soul in man". Lilly goes on to suggest that Aaron himself has the need to yield sub-mission "to the heroic soul in a greater man". The novel ends rather inconclusively with Lilly's words to Aaron that his own soul will tell him to whom he should submit. The ending—which leaves the theme of power to be treated more adequately and comprehensively in the next two novels, *Kangaroo* and *The Plumed Serpent*—seems to me quite appropriate: but in handing over nearly all of the last "Words" chapter to Lilly, Lawrence, I think, failed to include in the book adequate criticism of Lilly's point of view. This is a serious flaw in *Aaron's Rod*, and in this respect it is probably the weakest of Lawrence's mature novels.

One artistic crime Lawrence is alleged to have committed in *Aaron's Rod* is to have addressed the reader directly.[9] H. T. Moore calls it an "awkward spot" in the novel;[10] A. Beal takes it to be "symptomatic of the artistic incoherence of the book's construction";[11] H. M. Daleski judges Lawrence's intrusions in the first person to be "a sign of weakness, not of strength".[12] Lawrence's address to the reader is neither a sign of his strength

[9] *Op. cit.*, p. 161.　　　　[10] *The Life and Works of D. H. Lawrence*, p. 154.
[11] *D. H. Lawrence*, p. 69.　　[12] *The Forked Flame*, p. 212.

nor of his weakness; it is only an instance of what Lawrence has called the "struggle for verbal consciousness" ("I do but make a translation of the man. He would speak in music. I speak with words"). It does imply a rejection of "neat works of art", finished and complete in all respects, which one could "walk round and admire".[13] And the rejection must be taken to be a deliberate one, as Lawrence did not *need* to make an address to the reader for the purposes of the narrative. Those critics who find this objectionable, approach the novel, it would appear, with some narrow, fixed, arbitrary concepts about the form of a novel; and their objections are essentially the same as those which Lawrence dealt with and answered so effectively in his letter to the Italian critic Carlo Linati.[14]

Middleton Murry, reviewing *Aaron's Rod* for the *Nation and Athenaeum* in 1922, hailed it as "the most important thing that has happened to English literature since the war"—adding that to his mind it was, in one respect, a work "much more important than *Ulysses*". As against this, Eliseo Vivas has in recent years been perhaps the strongest in his denunciation of the novel which seems to him to show "no trace of creative imagination whatever".[15] F. R. Leavis is, no doubt, right in saying that *Aaron's Rod* does not have "so complex and subtle an organisation"[16] as *Women in Love* has. It is also true that not everything in the novel can be said to be "fully significant": there are scenes and conversations which do not seem to me to be thematically integrated with the rest of the book. More important than all this, the novel is far more assertive and less self-critical than most other Lawrence novels are. But it is, nevertheless, a lively novel and an important one. The stress it lays on "aloneness" is very central to an understanding of Lawrence's treatment of man-woman relationship in all his work; and it also contains one of the clearest and most forceful statements of Lawrence's view that man's first responsibility is to himself, to his own soul within him.

[13] *Collected Letters*, ii, pp. 826-7. [14] *Ibid.*

[15] Vivas, pp. 21-2. David Daiches also damns *Aaron's Rod* in his own way by saying that it is "not a novel to be taken solemnly as it too often is". (Daiches, p. 176.) See also Leavis, p. 32; and Moynahan, pp. 111-3.

[16] Leavis, p. 181.

VII

The Dark God and The Morning Star

Aaron's question at the end of *Aaron's Rod*, "And whom shall I submit to?", elicits only an ambiguous answer from Lilly who merely says: "Your soul will tell you." Lawrence, it appears, is only vaguely aware yet of the nature and implications of man's submission to "the heroic soul in a greater man" that Lilly preaches to Aaron. In *Kangaroo* the unresolved questions of *Women in Love* and *Aaron's Rod*—man's relation to woman, to other men, and to his own soul—are taken up afresh and worked out in a new and notably different situation. At the end of the novel we are left with merely the negatives concerning the important question of man's participation in some impersonal male activity. Lawrence is still convinced that beyond having his roots in a satisfactory marriage relationship, man must also satisfy the imperative urge in him to "send out a new shoot in the life of mankind", by taking active part in "the effort man makes for ever, to grow into new forms": but he is unable to find out what shape this effort can take. This, however, does not limit or detract from the achievement of the novel which convincingly portrays the confrontation of a sensitive, alive individual possessing a soul of his own, with the option of taking a leading part either in a quasi-fascist or in a socialistic revolution—and his rejection of both alternatives, as they seem to him to deny the individual in man. Somers cannot finally accept either Kangaroo or Willie Struthers because both of them seem to him in the last analysis embodiments of the fearful and "criminal" mob-spirit. His experiences lead him to believe still more firmly in his "dark God"—in the unique individual soul, or the "profound unconscious" which he takes to be the source of all passions and of all new impulses in man.

Richard Lovat Somers, having made up his mind that in the post-war Europe "everything was done for, played out, finished", decides he must go to a new country—and he chooses to try "the newest country: young Australia". As soon as he gets there, however, he longs to go back: a long navel string, he feels, still fastens him to Europe:

> He felt he would have given anything on earth to be in England. It was May—end of May—almost bluebell time, and the green leaves coming out on the hedges. Or the tall corn under the olives in Sicily. Or London Bridge, with all the traffic on the river. Or Bavaria with gentian and yellow globe flowers, and the Alps still icy. Oh God, to be in Europe, lovely Europe that he had hated so thoroughly and abused so vehemently, saying it was moribund and stale and finished. The fool was himself. He had got out of temper and so had called Europe moribund: assuming that he himself, of course, was not moribund, but sprightly and chirpy and too vital, as the Americans would say, for Europe. Well, if a man wants to make a fool of himself, it is as well to let him.[1]

Now, in Australia, Somers is overpowered by a sense of the meaninglessness of everything. The sense of irresponsible freedom, of do-as-you-please liberty seems to him utterly uninteresting. "Great swarming, teeming Sydney flowing out into these myriads of bungalows, like shallow waters spreading, undyked. And what then? Nothing. No inner life, no high command, no interest in anything, finally."[2] The relatively well-to-do Australians, as he sees them, have no genuine culture: after all, even money is, ultimately, only a means to rising to a higher, subtler, fuller state of consciousness: but if "you flatly don't want a fuller consciousness, what good is your money to you?"[3] Somers, in struggling with the question of Australia, is actually trying to grapple with "the problem of himself". He is looking for some meaning in his new life. *Kangaroo* is a record of Somers-Lawrence's life-and-thought adventure, as well as of his attempts to understand his changing, developing self; and the novel can be best understood and appreciated only if the reader bears in mind what it was intended by its author to be. In the chapter "Bits" we have the following:

---

[1] *Kangaroo* (Phoenix Edition), pp. 14-15. [2] *Op. cit.*, p. 22.
[3] *Ibid.*

Q

Man is a thought-adventurer. Man is more, he is a life-adventurer. Which means he is a thought-adventurer, an emotion-adventurer, and a discoverer of himself and of the outer universe. A discoverer. . . .

Now a novel is supposed to be a mere record of emotion-adventures, floundering in feelings. We insist that a novel is, or should be, also a thought-adventure if it is to be anything at all complete.[4]

In *Kangaroo* the thought-adventure takes this form: the protagonist is confronted with the opportunity of becoming a "leader of men" in a more or less purely invented situation, set in Australia; he comes to realise what it would mean in practice; and he finally refuses to take his chance because it involves going against his deepest convictions.

When Somers comes to Australia he is "a black pessimist about the present human world", the war having burst his "bubble of humanity". He does not care about politics which he counts to be no more than a country's housekeeping. "If I had to swallow my whole life in housekeeping", he remarks in a conversation, "I wouldn't keep house at all; I'd sleep under a hedge. Same with a country and politics. I'd rather have no money than be gulfed in politics and social stuff."[5] He has always wanted to take part in some male, impersonal activity along with other men, but the idea of politics and political power is repugnant to him. He believes that a new inspiration must spring up and ripen before there can be any constructive change. And yet, realising that preaching or teaching would be of no use at the "world's present juncture", he is for a time tempted to believe that if there is "brave, faithful action", a new spirit might arise in the course of the action itself. "The men with soul and with passionate truth in them must control the world's material riches and supplies: absolutely put possessions out of the reach of the mass of mankind, and let life begin to live again, in place of this struggle for existence, or struggle for wealth."[6] Australia—the Australia of the novel—seems to him especially suited to such action; and when he is offered the chance to lead the Diggers' movement, he, at one point, is almost ready to join in and to give his hand to Jack

---

[4] *Op. cit.*, pp. 284-5.   [5] *Op. cit.*, p. 59.   [6] *Op. cit.*, p. 97.

Callcott as a pledge of everlasting friendship or comradeship: but at the last moment excuses himself—in more or less the same manner, ironically, in which Gerald Crich in *Women in Love* had excused himself from making a pledge of *Blutbrüderschaft* with Birkin.

> He [Somers] half wanted to commit himself to this whole affection with a friend, a comrade, a mate. And then, in the last issue, he didn't want it at all. The affection would be deep and genuine enough: that he knew. But—when it came to the point, he didn't want any more affection. All his life he had cherished a beloved ideal of friendship—David and Jonathan. And now, when true and good friends offered, he found he simply could not commit himself, even to simple friendship. The whole trend of this affection, this mingling, this intimacy, this truly beautiful love, he found his soul just sct against it. [7]

This, even though *Aaron's Rod* was a move in this direction, is a new and recent development in the consciousness of a Lawrence hero. Somers still wants some kind of living relationship with other men, but he now knows that it is not blood-brotherhood or love or affection that he wants. The development in the novel as a whole accounts for this change in Somers' attitude.

Soon after his first meeting with Kangaroo (as Ben Cooley, the Australian lawyer at the head of the Diggers' organisation, is popularly known), Somers finds himself involved in various conflicts. The encounter gives rise to conflict within Somers himself; it leads to a conflict with his wife; and it brings him into conflict with Kangaroo and what he stands for. All these conflicts are closely related, but it is the depiction of the last which takes up a relatively large portion of the novel.

Kangaroo's aim is to establish a kind of benevolent dictatorship in Australia. He believes that society should operate on one central principle, the principle of love, so that there is maximum of individual liberty and minimum of human distress. He asks for Somers' help in teaching men to love one another with a "pure and fearless love", "the perfect love men have for one another, passing the love for women." [8] The only way to save "the People", he says, is to lead them to a stage

---

[7] *Op. cit.*, p. 104. [8] *Op. cit.*, p. 331.

where man's love for wife and children, man's love for man, and man's love "for beauty, for truth, for the Right", are all made possible. Somers is convinced that the way Kangaroo puts it covers the "great wonderful range of love"; he is also certain that in order to be complete and whole, love must manifest itself in all these aspects. What he can no longer agree to is that love is or can be "the all in all". Much of what Kangaroo says is what Somers himself has at one time held. In fact some of Kangaroo's views are so remarkably similar to Lawrence's own as to be indistinguishable from some of his earlier writings. There is a strong suggestion that Kangaroo is in many respects a dramatisation of the self that Lawrence is growing out of.[9]

Somers shares these views of Kangaroo's without reservation: but he is at the same time conscious that there is also something more, something besides all this which he knows and which the other man does not. When Kangaroo says, "I believe in the one fire of love. I believe it is the one inspiration of all creative activity. I trust myself entirely to the fire of love", Somers cannot accept this belief in love being the exclusive force of living inspiration. What he says, in explanation of his dissent, about his awareness of "the great God" of the lower, dark self, appears to Kangaroo—as it does, at this stage, to the reader— to be incomprehensible "mysticism and metaphysics". This is because Somers is still in the process of defining to himself what this "dark God" of his actually means to him. He is, however, quite certain that it is not synonymous with Kangaroo's concept of love:

> "I know your love, Kangaroo. Working everything from the spirit, from the head. You work the lower self as an instrument of the spirit. Now it is time for the spirit to leave us again; it is time for the Son of Man to depart, and leave us dark, in front of the unspoken God: who is just beyond the dark threshold of the lower self, my lower self. . . ."[10]

To Kangaroo all this sounds to be the voice of some perverse demon inside Somers—the demon, however, with which the

[9] *Cf.* Kangaroo's views on the nature of evil, and of love, with Lawrence's own views quoted above in Ch. 1.

[10] *Kangaroo*, p. 134.

latter identifies himself.   What Kangaroo glorifies under the
name of "love" is seen by Somers to be merely the "sticky
stream of love, and the hateful will-to-love".[11]   That all
Kangaroo's ponderousness and insistence does amount to mere
vicious will-to-love is demonstrated by the manner in which he,
thwarted by Somers' refusal to yield to him, angrily and
haughtily brings their conversation to an abrupt and ominous
end:

> He had become again hideous, with a long yellowish face
> and black eyes close together, and a cold, mindless, dangerous
> hulk of his shoulders.   For a moment Somers was afraid of him,
> as of some great ugly idol that might strike.   He felt the intense
> hatred of the man coming at him in cold waves.   He stood up
> in a kind of horror in front of the great, close-eyed, horrible
> thing that was now Kangaroo.   Yes, a thing, not a whole man.
> A great Thing, a horror.[12]

The incident, with the feeling of deep fear it arouses in Somers,
leads directly to "The Nightmare", the long chapter recapitu-
lating the wartime experiences of the Somerses in Cornwall.
The presence of this seemingly irrelevant chapter has been
justified on the ground that it "explains the attitude and deepens
the characterization of the protagonist",[13] that it "illuminates
the background of Somers' thought",[14] and that it accounts for
what it was that drove Somers out of England and brought him
to Australia.[15]   It has also been pointed out that the chapter
should be seen as "an intensified literary creation", Lawrence's
actual letters of the war-time period being "far less hysterical,
far less full of egotistical self-pity, far more sane and balanced".[16]
But it must be said that no one who sets out to judge *Kangaroo*
on the basis of the conventional rules applied to the criticism
of fiction would find these arguments fully convincing: it has
to be admitted that the chapter is far too long for one to overlook

[11] *Op. cit.*, p. 213.   [12] *Op. cit.*, p. 214.

[13] H. T. Moore, *The Life and Works of D. H. Lawrence*, p. 170.

[14] Martin Jarrett-Kerr, *D. H. Lawrence and Human Existence*, London (1961),
p. 85.

[15] R. P. Draper, "Authority and the Individual: A Study of D. H. Lawrence's
'Kangaroo' ", *The Critical Quarterly*, i, iii (Autumn 1959), p. 208.

[16] Hough, p. 115.   It is, however, questionable if the chapter in the novel is
really as hysterical and full of egotistical self-pity as Graham Hough implies.

the definite break it causes in the continuity of the "story". If, however, we are prepared to accept the novel on its own terms, the thematic relation of the chapter to the "thought-adventure" in the book can be seen to be very close indeed.

The relevance of Somers' reflexions in The Nightmare chapter to the central theme of the novel is discussed, indirectly, by the author himself. The deep sense of fear that Somers experiences under the gaze of Kangaroo ("the great, close-eyed, horrible thing") gives rise to the acute remembrance of his wartime experience in England not only because one fear reminds him of another, but also because the two fears are essentially of the same kind, and of the same thing. "But first, why had it all come back on him? It had seemed so past, so gone. Why should it suddenly erupt like white-hot lava, to set in hot black rock round the wound of his soul?"[17] On reflexion, Somers comes to realise that he had been for some time experiencing spasms of "the same fear that he had known during the war: the fear of the base and malignant power of the mob-like authorities".[18] He has a dread of the democratic society which can so easily yield itself to be guided by "the vast mob-spirit". The very ultra-freedom in Australia frightens him as it seems to him "like a still pause before a thunder-storm".[19] He had seen men lose their "independent soul" and their "inward, individual integrity" during the war: even the best English consciousness, he remembers, had given way under stress and was swamped under the tide of events. "The English soul went under in the war, and, as a conscious, proud, adventurous, self-responsible soul, it was lost."[20] Somers, who had till then believed so much in everything—society and love and friendship—was driven to fall back on himself, and he learnt to stand alone as "his own judge of himself" absolutely:

> He took his stand absolutely on his own judgement of himself. Then, the mongrel-mouthed world would say and do what it liked. This is the greatest secret of behaviour: to stand alone, and judge oneself from the deeps of one's own soul. And then,

---

[17] *Kangaroo*, p. 265.

[18] Another parallel to the Cornwall experience is provided later when Somers is accused by Jack Callcott of being "a spy" (p. 297).

[19] *Kangaroo*, p. 265.   [20] *Op. cit.*, p. 226.

to know, to hear what the others say and think: to refer their judgement to the touchstone of one's own soul-judgement. To fear one's own inward soul, and never to fear the outside world, nay not even one single person, not even fifty million persons.[21]

Now in Australia his contact with Kangaroo and Willie Struthers, with "the accumulating forces of social violence", once again forces him to turn to his "own deepest soul". Kangaroo, with all his talk of love and the Power of Love, seems to him "the mob, really. See his face in a rage. He was the mob: *vengeful* mob. Oh, God, the most terrifying of all things."[22] It is the same with Willie Struthers. He is "the vengeful mob also. But if the old ideal had still a logical leaf to put forth, it was this last leaf of Communism—before the lily tree of humanity rooted in love . . . died its final death. Perhaps better Struthers than Kangaroo."[23] Somers finds there is very little to choose in Australian politics, and the choice means hardly anything to him. He can see that Struthers is quite right in maintaining that lords or doctors or financiers should not have more money than a simple working man just because they are lords and doctors and financiers: but he at the same time believes that "this theoretical socialism started by Jews like Marx", which appeals only to the will-to-power in the masses and makes money the whole crux, has "cruelly harmed" the working people:

> For the working people of Europe were generous by nature, and money was not their prime passion. All this political socialism—all politics, in fact—have conspired to make money the only god. It has been a great treacherous conspiracy against the generous heart of the people.[24]

Somers also accepts the validity of Struthers' views on the "trusting love of a man for his mate" which is to be the new tie between men in the building of a new society. This is, he thinks, what Whitman had in mind when he talked of the sacred and unselfish Love of Comrades. He recognises that "if our society is going to develop a new great phase, developing from where we stand now, it must accept this new relationship

[21] *Op. cit.*, p. 256.
[22] *Op. cit.*, p. 270.
[23] *Ibid.*
[24] *Op. cit.*, p. 204.

as the new sacred social bond, beyond the family. What he cannot believe in is the absoluteness of love—whether between man and woman or between man and man.

> Human love, human trust, are always perilous, because they break down. The greater the love, the greater the trust, and the greater the peril, the greater the disaster. . . . So it is when one individual seeks absolutely to love, or trust, another. Absolute lovers always smash one another, absolute trusters the same. . . .
>
> And yet, love is the greatest thing between human beings, men and women, men and men, women and women, when it is love, when it happens. But when human love starts out to lock individuals together, it is just courting disaster . . . because every individuality is bound to react at some time against every other individuality, without exception—or else lose its own integrity; because of the inevitable necessity of each individual to react away from any other individual, at certain times, human love is truly a relative thing, not an absolute. It *cannot* be absolute.[25]

Somers, then, does not question the place and importance of love—in any of its manifestations—in human life; his objection is to Kangaroo's as well as Struthers' insistence on the absoluteness of love. Love, he grants, is perhaps an eternal part of life: but it is only a part. And when it is treated as if it were everything, it becomes a disease, "a vast white strangling octopus". All things, he holds, are relative and "have their sacredness in true relation to all other things". Without "the God-passion", human love is, sooner or later, bound to kill the thing it loves; and he shudders to think of the time when, unsustained by "the great dark God", mates or comrades break down in their absolute love and trust. "With no deep God who is source of all passion and life to hold them separate and yet sustained in accord, the loving comrades would smash one another, and smash all love, all feeling as well. It would be a rare gruesome sight."[26]

In his attempt to express what he implies by the term "dark God"—which he is aware he at first merely repeats like a

[25] *Op. cit.*, p. 201.   [26] *Op. cit.*, p. 202.

phrase—Somers begins by differentiating it from Kangaroo's God of Love. From the great dark God emanates not only the spiritual love of Christ, but also the sensual passion of love; and it is time, he tells Kangaroo, for the spirit to leave us. The latter is, of course, not convinced; he does not even understand what Somers is talking about. The readers of *Kangaroo*, however, must attend to what Somers is trying to say, as otherwise they run the risk of either missing the main point of the novel, or altogether misreading it.

Who, or what, is Somers' "dark God"? Does Somers, or Lawrence himself, know clearly what he wishes the term to convey? Is it just "a piece of portentous flummery"? Graham Hough is of the opinion that we should accept the concept as something which Lawrence himself does not understand but which he is in the process of defining.[27] Anthony Beal, however, thinks that Lawrence "does little to define the dark gods".[28] J. I. M. Stewart suggests that the true face of the dark God is not revealed to us "because it is not revealed to Somers or to Lawrence".[29] R. P. Draper is uncertain whether the dark God should be understood as simply the antithesis of the God of Love, or should be taken as "a symbol for some pantheistic conception which gives the individual a profound sense of identification with 'great creative nature' and at the same time a sense of being commanded by a powerful authority within himself ".[30]

It must be clearly understood, to begin with, that neither Lawrence nor Somers is trying to define or give a fixed meaning to "the dark God"—simply because this God is "forever dark, forever unrealisable: for ever and for ever".[31] But if the unknown God is so plainly said to be "unutterable", "the forever unrevealed",[32] why expect Lawrence to define him, or why blame him for not doing so? The dark God, whom "you can never see or visualise"[33] must remain unknown because once you have defined him or described him, you make him "all-too-limitedly human", and turn him into an ideal God,

---

[27] Hough, p. 114.
[28] *D. H. Lawrence*, p. 75.
[29] *Eight Modern Writers*, p. 550.
[30] *The Critical Quarterly*, I, iii, p. 213.
[31] *Kangaroo*, p. 271.
[32] *Op. cit.*, p. 272.
[33] *Op. cit.*, p. 134.

"a proposition of the mental consciousness". All one can say is that he is "the great living darkness which we represent by the glyph, God".[34]

Having said that, one must add that short of giving a fixed definition of his dark god Lawrence does indicate sufficiently clearly what we are to understand by the references made to him in the book. He is, we arc told, not only the God of love, but also the God of fear, and of passion and of silence; he is the God that gives a man the deep blood tenderness that is deeper than love, the God that makes a man realise his own sacred aloneness. He is "the God who is many gods to many men: all things to all men. The source of passions and strange motives."[35] The great dark God is "the invisible stranger at the gate in the night, knocking. He is the mysterious life-suggestion, tapping for admission." He is not one god, but all the gods: he is Thor, Zeus, Bacchus, Venus—all of them. "When they come through the gate they are personified. But outside the gate it is one dark God, the Unknown."[36] All these statements do not, and are not intended to, add up to form a sharp or clear concept of what the dark God is. What he is, is left intentionally, and necessarily, vague and undefined. But what is of real importance to man is the relation he has with this God; and on this point the novel makes a straightforward and highly significant statement.

An individual has access to the dark god through his own "inward soul"; he gets into contact with him through "the profound unconscious". Every *living* human soul is a well-head to the "living darkness" which Lawrence refers to by the glyph, God. It is called "darkness" because it is unknown, and, in its entirety, unknowable. And it is "living" because it is all the time changing, developing, assuming new shapes, entering the human soul in the form of new impulses and life-suggestions.

> Into every living soul wells up the darkness, the unutterable. And then there is travail of the visible with the invisible. Man is in travail with his own soul, while ever his soul lives. Into his unconscious surges a new flood of the God-darkness, the living unutterable. And this unutterable is like a germ, a

---

[34] *Op. cit.*, p. 271.   [35] *Op. cit.*, p. 272.   [36] *Op. cit.*, p. 291.

foetus with which he must travail, bringing it at last into utterance, into action, into being. . . .

The long travail. The long gestation of the soul within a man, and the final parturition, the birth of a new way of knowing, a new God-influx.[37]

Somers, in the course of his experiences in Australia, comes more and more to put his trust in the God-influx. The only thing one can stick to, he decides, is one's own isolate being and the God in whom it is rooted. And the only thing one can look to is "the God who fulfils one from the dark".[38] Some men, some women must, of their own choice and will, abide by their own inmost being; and then in the stillness of their soul listen, listen to the voice of life within themselves, and try to know and speak and obey all they can. "Some men must live by this unremitting inwardness, no matter what the rest of the world does."[39] Somers' insistent use of "some" should not be overlooked, for he is unequivocal in his assertion that most people do not have a central self of their own. The man in the street is not a whole individual, but only "a bit"; he does not possess a soul he can call his own: he has only a minute share of the collective soul. These views lead Somers, on further reflexion, to a position which could well, on a superficial view, be regarded as radically anti-social and misanthropic:

Damn the man in the street, said Richard to himself. Damn the collective soul, it's a dead rat in a hole. Let humanity scratch its own lice.[40]

The logical next step is for him to isolate himself completely from the rest of mankind. But Somers is also acutely aware that one cannot lead a life of entire loneliness, "like a monkey on a stick, up and down one's own obstacle".[41] Man, at his highest, is an individual, isolate, alone, and in direct soul communion with the unknown God. But no man, not even the greatest, can live only by his spirit and his pure contact with the Godhead. He must live in vivid rapport with the mass of men, for if he denies this, he cuts his own roots.

[37] *Op. cit.*, pp. 271-2.   [38] *Op. cit.*, p. 335.   [39] *Op. cit.*, p. 155.
[40] *Op. cit.*, p. 287.   [41] *Op. cit.*, p. 289.

In his supreme being, man is alone, isolate, nakedly himself,
in contact only with the unknown God.

This is our way of expressing Nirvana.

But just as a tree is only perfect in blossom because it has
groping roots, so is man only perfected in his individual being
by his groping, pulsing union with mankind. The unknown
God is within, at the quick. But this quick must send down
roots into the great flesh of mankind.

In short, the "spirit" has got a lesson to learn: the lesson
of its own limitation. This is for the individual. And the
infinite, which is Man writ large, or Humanity, has a still
bitterer lesson to learn. It is the individual alone who can
save humanity alive. But the greatest of the great individuals
must have deep, throbbing roots down in the dark red soil of
the living flesh of humanity.[42]

The temptation to sever himself from the "flesh of humanity"
and lapse into a state of utter unconcern is particularly strong
for Somers in Australia—the raw, uncreated, strange continent. Lawrence has been highly praised for the "remarkable
precision" and "sustained brilliance" of his evocation of the
Australian environment in *Kangaroo*.[43] Richard Aldington, in
the introduction he has written to the novel, insists that the
supreme achievement of *Kangaroo* lies in its unforgettably vivid
and accurate pictures of Australia. What has not been
sufficiently recognised, however, is that these brilliantly drawn
pictures of Australia are there in the novel not just for their own
sake; they should be seen to be closely related to the development of the protagonist. In one of his letters Lawrence spoke
of Australia as "a most marvellous country" where one could
just "drift away, and live and forget and expire".[44] The fern-
dark aboriginal world of the Australian continent affects
Somers in exactly the same way. The utter unconcern of the
Pacific, for instance, has the effect of making him gradually
forget himself and the concern he feels for the world of men.
His only wish, then, is to be soul-less and alone.

To be alone, mindless and memoryless between the sea,
under the sombre wall-front of Australia. To be alone with a

---

[42] *Op. cit.*, p. 308.   [43] Daiches, p. 176.   [44] Nehls, II, p. 154.

long, wide shore and land, heartless, soulless. As alone and as absent and as present as an aboriginal dark on the sand in the sun. The strange falling-away of everything.[45]

Another time it is in the bush that he feels a torpor coming over him. His mind in a kind of twilight sleep, he seems to drift away into "the grey pre-world" where men did not have emotions or personal consciousness: he is gone into "the dark world before conscious responsibility was born".[46] In this state of "darkened wide-eyed torpor" he finds he just does not care for anybody or anything. "Worlds come, and worlds go: even worlds. And when the old, old influence of the fern-world comes over a man, how can he care? He breathes the fern seed and drifts back, becomes darkly half vegetable, devoid of pre-occupations."[47]

It is a very powerful influence of the spirit of place that Somers has to contend with in Australia. There are times when he is inclined to forget about his soul and its problems and to drift into "the torpid semi-consciousness of the world of the twilight". Once before, during his stay in Cornwall, he had felt he was drifting back into the "semi-dark, the half-conscious, the *clair-obscur*",[48] no longer wanting to struggle consciously along as a thought-adventurer. Now again Somers is tempted to give in to the place and to abandon the responsibilities of his consciousness: but as his words to Jaz (William James) at the end of the novel indicate he is able to resolve the conflict within him by firmly refusing to yield to the temptation:

"I won't give up the flag of our real civilized consciousness. I'll give up the ideals. But not the aware, self-responsible, deep consciousness that we've gained. I won't go back on that, Jaz, though Kangaroo did say I was the enemy of civilisation. . . . I am the enemy of this machine civilisation and this ideal civilisation. But I'm not the enemy of the deep, self-responsible consciousness in man, which is what I mean by civilisation. In that sense of civilisation, I'd fight for ever for the flag, and try to carry it on into deeper, darker places. It's an adventure, Jaz, like any other. And when you realise what you're doing, it's perhaps the best adventure."[49]

---

[45] *Kangaroo*, p. 339.   [46] *Op. cit.*, p. 180.   [47] *Ibid.*
[48] *Op. cit.*, p. 243.   [49] *Op. cit.*, p. 356.

The struggle for "deep, self-responsible consciousness" is the best adventure. But the specific form that Somers has visualised for this adventure, brings him into sharp conflict with his wife, Harriet. She cannot understand why, having come to a wonderful new country, they cannot be happy just the two of them living together.[50] "Why must you have more?" she asks him in exasperation. His answer that he must struggle with men and with the world of men for a time yet in order to make some kind of an opening, "some kind of a way for the afterwards", seems to her merely a sign of nervous obstinacy and self-importance in him. She has "no use at all for [Somers'] fiery courses and efforts with the world of men"[51] —especially as he has always to fall back, rather the worse for the attempt, on her. She finds it rather pathetic that he should choose to be so silly in refusing to be finally disappointed in his efforts with mankind. She also reminds him that he is already doing something impersonal and creative in his capacity as a writer. Somers recognises that there is a great deal of truth in what Harriet says, but in his stubbornness refuses to give way:

> "I want to do something with living people, somewhere, somehow, while I live on the earth. I write, but I write alone. And I live alone. Without any connection whatever with the rest of men."
> "Don't swank, you don't live alone. You've got *me* there safe enough, to support you. Don't swank to me about being alone, because it insults me, you see. I know how much alone you are, with me always there keeping you together."
> And again he sulked and swallowed it, and obstinately held out.
> "None the less," he retorted, "I do want to do something along with men. I *am* alone and cut off. As a man among men, I just have no place. I have my life with you, I know: *et praeterea nihil.*"
> "*Et praeterea nihil!* And what more do you want? Besides, you liar, haven't you your writing? Isn't that all you want, isn't that *doing* all there is to be done? Men! Much *men* there

---

[50] *Cf. Women in Love,* pp. 472-3. [51] *Kangaroo,* p. 65.

is about them! Bah, when it comes to that, I have to be even the only man as well as the only woman."

"That's the whole truth," said he bitingly.

"Bah, you creature, you ought to be grateful," cried Harriet.[52]

Harriet begins by opposing the very idea of Somers' doing some work with men alone, sharing some activity with them. She hates him for turning away from the personal life of intimacy to the impersonal business of male activity from which she is completely shut out. Later on, she comes to grant the necessity for impersonal activity but insists on being identified with it: she wants "to share, to join in, not to be left out lonely".[53] Somers, however, is equally insistent that the pure male activity should be womanless. "No man was beyond woman. But in his one quality of ultimate maker and breaker he was womanless."[54] Harriet denies this bitterly. She emphatically opposes "this principle of her externality". But Somers is determined that this is a matter outside the personal sphere of their two lives; and that once he has slowly and carefully weighed a course of action he would not hold it subject to Harriet's approval or disapproval. Harriet gradually comes to realise this, and is reconciled to the fact that if Somers must go on to other things outside of marriage, well, she would leave it alone as *his* affair. It only angers her that he should consider this activity even more important than their marriage. But she feels sure that

> he would come to himself and acknowledge that his marriage *was* the centre of his life, the core, the root, however he liked to put it: and this other business was the inevitable excursion into his future, into the unknown, onwards, which man by his nature was condemned to make, even if he lost his life a dozen times in it. Well, so be it. Let him make the excursion: even without her. But she was not, if she could help it, going to have him setting off on a trip that led nowhere. No, if he was to excurse ahead, it must be ahead, and her instinct must be convinced as the needle of a mariner's compass is convinced.

---

[52] *Op. cit.*, p. 66.   [53] *Op. cit.*, p. 94.   [54] *Ibid.*

And regarding this Australian business of Callcott's, she had
her doubts.[55]

Harriet, having once accepted Somers' status as the
onward-struggling male, is next asked to render the submission
due to him.   It perhaps needs to be said here that Somers is
not suggesting the general idea that "a healthy marital relation
depends on the acknowledgement of male dominance".[56]   It is
not at all a question of marriage relationship in the ordinary,
domestic sense of the term.   Somers claims no superiority over
Harriet on the basis of his sex as such. If he is to be "lord and
master", he is to be that only in his role as the forward-seeking
male exploring unknown worlds:

> She might remember that he *was* only human, that he had to
> change his socks if he got his feet wet, and that he would make a
> fool of himself nine times out of ten.   But—and the but was
> emphatic as a thunderbolt—there was in him also the mystery
> and the lordship of the forward-seeking male.   That she must
> emphatically realise and bow down to. . . .
> You can't have two masters to one ship.   And if it *is* a ship:
> that is, if it has a voyage to sail, a port to make, even a far
> direction to take, into the unknown, then a master it must have.
> Harriet said it wasn't a ship, it was a houseboat, and they could
> lie so perfectly here by the Pacific for the rest of time—or be
> towed away to some other lovely spot to house in.   She could
> imagine no fairer existence.   It was a houseboat.
> But he with his no, no, almost drove her mad.   The bark of
> their marriage was a ship that must sail into uncharted seas, and
> he must be the master, and she must be the crew, sworn on.
> She was to believe in his adventure and deliver herself over to
> it;   she was to believe in his mystic vision of a land beyond this
> charted world, where new life rose again.[57]

Harriet, however, cannot believe in this vision of the land where
men would be "more than they are now";   and so there is an
impasse.   Few readers would take exception to Somers'
attaching the importance he does to the effort man makes for
the creation of a better world.   At the same time few would be

[55] *Op. cit.*, pp. 98-9.   Somers himself has doubts about "this Australian
business".   He, too, is unsure of his "circumstantial standing", yet firmly sticks to
his essential position.
[56] Hough, p. 108.   [57] *Kangaroo*, pp. 176-7.

prepared to accept either the possibility or the desirability of restricting this activity to men alone, of making it an exclusively male prerogative. Somers, apparently, wants Harriet to form the centre of his life while he himself goes ahead making excursions into the future: but if she, too, chooses to take part in the building of this future, should he not, one asks, be glad to have her working side by side with him?

Most writers on *Kangaroo* have failed to appreciate its qualities, and have tended to underrate it as a novel. Vivas, for instance, having looked in vain for "the splendour and the ease of the still wings of the poet in the upper air" (!) concludes by calling it "this no-novel".[58] Moynahan also, carried away by the enthusiasm of his good-citizen criticism,[59] completely fails to see either the meaning or the form of the novel. "*Kangaroo*", he declares, "is the most padded and redundant of all Lawrence's novels".[60] In fact, however, the novel is a unified whole and everything in it is, and can be shown to be, connected with the central theme of Somers' relationships: his relation to Harriet, to the world of men engaged in some collective activity (be it a war or a revolution), and above all to "the dark God" (which in effect means his relation with his own soul). The novel, which is primarily an organised exploration of these relationships, also depicts Somers' efforts to understand what goes on inside himself, thereby revealing the inner conflicts which he must resolve in the process of re-estimating how much each of his various relationships means to him. Read as a "thought-adventure", as it should be if we are to understand and appreciate it, *Kangaroo* can be seen to have its own form and structure: the imagined circumstances in Australia and the seemingly unrelated wartime experiences of the Somerses combine to serve as a warning against putting too much trust in public values which get so easily corrupted in times of crises. The apparently anti-social and anti-democratic stand taken by Somers in the end is, paradoxically, the only truly and profoundly human attitude that an individual in his

[58] Vivas, p. 59.
[59] See Moynahan, pp. 104-7. Moynahan, it appears, cannot forgive Somers for not "running up the street after a policeman" after having witnessed the scene of violence at Canberra Hall.
[60] Moynahan, p. 101.

R

position can at certain times adopt. Human values must have
a deeper source than the social climate of the times; and the
only way to ensure that one does not go on worshipping ideas
and ideals long after they have gone dead is for one to refer
them from time to time to "the touchstone of one's own soul-
judgement". Somers clearly recognises man's need to be
livingly related to the rest of mankind, to have his roots deep
in "the dark red soil of the living flesh of humanity". He is also
certain that man must work together with other men for the
creation of a better world. But he can no longer accept either
"brotherly love" or "submission" as the basis of relationship
between men engaged in an impersonal, creative, "male"
activity. At the same time he begins to realise that he cannot
take part in mass activities or revolutions which kill the
independent, self-responsible soul in man. He is, therefore,
driven to a position of isolation from other men, in contact only
with the dark God. What, then, are the alternatives that we
are offered? What is to be the relation between man and man?
How is man going to work in conjunction with men in order
to make "some kind of a way for the afterwards"? The novel
gives no clear answers to these questions. But then, should one
demand these answers? *Kangaroo* explores artistically a
significant phase of our life in terms of man's complex relationships; it reveals to us certain conflicts we must face and resolve;
warns us against possible pitfalls; and makes us aware of some
of the questions we must ask ourselves, and answer for ourselves.
A novel need do no more.

The Plumed Serpent continues Lawrence's unremitting search
for "wholeness of being". In *Kangaroo* the direction taken in
this quest had involved a movement away from contact with
mankind. *The Plumed Serpent*, to restore the balance, makes a
move in the other direction by laying stress on man's need to be
livingly related not only to the dark God but also to humanity
and to the life of universe around him. Which of the two
directions are we to take as the right one? The answer is:
both, and neither. Neither the stress laid on individuality nor
the emphasis on relationships should be taken as a statement
of some absolute truth: the one must be seen in relation to the

other. There are times when the need is for greater communion, whereas at other times man has to learn to stand alone in possession of his own soul. The pattern given to *The Plumed Serpent* by Kate's alternate movements toward and away from contact is the pattern formed in the process of actual living by men and women striving to come to their "spontaneous-creative fulness of being". Kate herself does not clearly realise this, and wants to come to rest in her final acceptance of one position or the other: but we as readers are in a position to see that if she is to remain a living character she must neither totally reject nor altogether yield to what life in Mexico has to offer to her. If her last ambiguous words to Cipriano[61] are interpreted as indicative of her "final conviction"[62] and surrender, then surely Lawrence is neither consistent nor convincing. But there is no reason to believe that the conflict in her mind which has so far marked her response to Mexico, has suddenly been resolved at the end. On the contrary, there is every reason to suppose that she will continue to have revulsions against violence, crudity, and horror[63] of even the "new" life in Mexico. Doubts, reservations, partial recoils— all these go to make Kate what she is; and it is difficult to imagine her relinquishing these abruptly, without doing violence to her character.

Lawrence—for a time at least—regarded *The Plumed Serpent* as his most important novel ("I still say, this is the most important of all my novels."),[64] presumably because he had not only been able to invent a fable embodying his views but had also succeeded in creating a "myth" to suit his purpose. Or, to put it the other way round, as one critic does, in *The Plumed Serpent* he "not only created a religion on his own terms as a novelist may, but also a context in which to put it, his own aboriginal land, which he calls Mexico".[65] However, the

---

[61] "You won't let me go!" The short utterance has the peculiar quality of suggesting a somewhat different meaning after each fresh reading of the novel. For an account of several earlier, rejected endings of the novel, see L. D. Clark, *Dark Night of the Body: D. H. Lawrence's "The Plumed Serpent"*, Austin, Tex. (1964), pp. 46-7.

[62] Leavis, p. 68.

[63] *The Plumed Serpent* (Phoenix Edition), p. 419.

[64] *Collected Letters*, II, p. 859. See also pp. 844, 859, 860.

[65] Clark, p. 78.

Quetzalcoatl hymns, ritual dances or elaborate ceremonies should not be allowed to distract our attention from the underlying essential theme of the novel: the quest for wholeness of being. The "myth" itself might be of interest to scholars—and lengthy commentaries on its "sources and analogues" have already appeared[66]—but for an appreciation of the novel as such there is no need at all to look for anything beyond what is contained within the work itself. Lawrence, through Don Ramón, makes it quite plain that he does not intend the reader to attach more importance to the mythical structure he has created than is indicated in the book itself. As Ramón explains to Kate, Quetzalcoatl is to him "only the symbol of the best a man may be in the next days".[67] He says the same thing in different words to his wife Carlota. To her question what he thinks "this Quetzalcoatl nonsense" really amounts to, his answer is:

> "Quetzalcoatl is just a living word for these people, no more. All I want them to do is to find the beginnings of the way to their own manhood, their own womanhood. Men are not yet men in full, and women are not yet women. They are all half and half, incoherent, part horrible, part pathetic, part good creatures. Half arrived. . . . And so, having got hold of some kind of a clue to my own whole manhood, it is part of me now to try with them."[68]

The Morning Star, similarly, is for Ramón the unfathomable mystery at the centre of the universe, the "Quick of all beings and existence"; and if he calls it the Morning Star, it is, he says, simply because "men must give all things names".[69] Somers in *Kangaroo* had given it the name of "dark God"; Ramón, extending and elaborating the concept, calls it the Morning Star. Man, he believes, gets his manhood, his whole-

---

[66] L. D. Clark affirms that for the purposes of artistic appreciation *The Plumed Serpent* is a novel complete in itself: but his book, *Dark Night of the Body*, includes a discussion of the "historical and anthropological authenticity of its material". *Cf.* William York Tindall, *D. H. Lawrence and Susan His Cow*, New York (1939), pp. 113-56: also Harry T. Moore, *The Intelligent Heart* (1955), pp. 315ff. However, see Frieda Lawrence's rebuttal in *Frieda Lawrence: The Memoirs and Correspondence*, p. 322.

[67] *The Plumed Serpent*, p. 270. [68] *Op. cit.*, p. 207.

[69] *Op. cit.*, p. 249.

ness, from the God who is "inside the hearts of living men and women";[70] and there is nothing for a man to do except to be true to his own soul, and keep it in touch with "the heart of the cosmos".[71] The people, he thinks, have lost their connexion with God; and all his effort is directed towards the establishing of "a new connection between the people and God".[72] Ramón's quest is, thus, purely a "religious" one—not social or political. This fact is repeatedly emphasised in the novel; and neither references to "Don Ramón's Fuehrerprinzip"[73] nor questions about how the "rich thug" Ramón ("this idle, intensely vain hidalgo living on his wife's money") is going to provide the Mexican Indians with food, housing, and knowledge,[74] make much sense. "Only religion will serve", Ramón insists, "not socialism, nor education, nor anything."[75] He is determined to keep free from the taint of politics, because he thinks the surest way to kill any living inspiration or new spirit is to get it connected with a political party. "Above all things", he tells Cipriano, "I don't want to acquire a political smell. . . . Unless I can stand uncontaminated, I had better abandon everything."[76] Politics, he says, must go their own way: he has no intention of entering that world—which he leaves to people like Montes, the President of the Republic:

> ". . . Politics, and all this *social* religion that Montes has got is like washing the outside of the egg, to make it look clean. But I myself, I want to get inside the egg, right to the middle, to start it growing into a new bird. . . . Montes wants to clean the nest and wash the egg. But meanwhile, the egg will go cold and die. The more you save these people from poverty and ignorance, the quicker they will die: like a dirty egg that you take from under the hen eagle to wash it. While you wash the egg, it chills and dies. Poor old Montes, all his ideas are American and European. And the old dove of Europe will

---

[70] *Op. cit.*, p. 353. [71] *Op. cit.*, p. 191. [72] *Op. cit.*, p. 163.

[73] Allen Guttmann, "The Politics of Irrationality", *Wisconsin Studies in Contemporary Literature*, v (1964), p. 159. Guttmann's article is a good example of fairly clever but somewhat less than honest criticism, relying on quotations abstracted from their context and on deliberate suppression of facts not in consonance with the arguments advanced.

[74] Moynahan, pp. 90, 111.

[75] *The Plumed Serpent*, p. 261. [76] *Op. cit.*, p. 243.

never hatch the egg of dark-skinned America. The united [sic] States can't die because it isn't alive. It is a nestful of china eggs, made of pot. So they can be kept clean. But here Cipriano, here, let us hatch the chick before we start cleaning up the nest."[77]

It seems to him that if in trying to solve their social and economic problems men "deny the living life", they cause ten problems to spring up where there was one before; whereas if they were to seek life itself, life would resolve the problems in its own way —since problems only change with time and become different, but can never be finally solved:

". . . When men seek life first, they will not seek land nor gold. The lands will lie on the laps of the gods, where men lie. And if the old communal system comes back, and the village and the land are one, it will be very good. For truly, no man can possess lands. . . .

"Lay forcible hands on nothing, only be ready to resist, if forcible hands should be laid on you. For the new shoots of life are tender, and better ten deaths than that they should be torn or trampled down by the bullies of the world. When it comes to fighting for the tender shoots of life, fight as the jaguar fights for her young, as the she-bear for her cubs.

"That which is life is vulnerable, and only metal is invulnerable. Fight for the vulnerable unfolding of life. But for that, fight never to yield."[78]

All programmes based on so-called benevolence, but actually inspired by "hate"—"charity and socialism, and politics and reform"—will, Ramón fears, only succeed in finally destroying the "tender shoots of life" in the Mexican people. The world, he thinks, has gone as far as it could go in the good, gentle, and loving direction: the Church, at any rate, cannot help the Mexicans if only because it does not have "the key-word" to the Mexican soul. His own "clue-word" is Quetzalcoatl, "a new saviour with a new vision" who—he hopes—will connect the Mexicans with the universe. "The final mystery is one mystery. But the manifestations are many."[79] Quetzalcoatl, "the lord of both ways", is only one such manifestation, the

[77] *Op. cit.*, p. 188.　　　[78] *Op. cit.*, p. 359.　　　[79] *Op. cit.*, p. 358.

Mexican brand, signifying wholeness of being. What Ramón is trying to effect is "the fusion of the old blood-and-vertebrate consciousness with the white man's present mental-spiritual consciousness. The sinking of both beings into a new being."[80] Ramón himself, we are told at the end—though whether this is Kate's view or that of the author is not quite clear—has been able to bring together in himself the two great human impulses to a point of fusion: his "godliness" as "the living Quetzalcoatl" consists in his having succeeded in bringing the great opposites of blood and spirit into contact and into unison within him. "Not in the blood nor in the spirit lay his supremacy, his godhead. But in a star within him, in the mysterious star which unites the vast universal blood with the universal breath of the spirit, and shines between them both."[81] And his "great effort" is intended to help the Mexican people attain this fullness of being by becoming men of Quetzalcoatl. When Lawrence wrote in one of his letters, "I *do* mean what Ramón means—for all of us",[82] he should be understood to be pointing to Ramón's attempt to reconcile the two ways of consciousness—mental and physical. To say that Lawrence is "worse than silly" and displays a "failure of intelligence" in believing that "a contemporary society can be saved by instituting a synthetic savagery",[83] or to suppose that "in *The Plumed Serpent* Lawrence seems definitely to be recommending that we haul down the flag of our civilised consciousness"[84]—is to betray a well-nigh total lack of understanding of the novel. What "Ramón means" is not the institution of savagery or the abandonment of civilised consciousness, but the attainment of a balanced, integrated personality by bringing into unison the blood and the spirit, the dark and the light, the mind and the body, the eagle and the snake, Quetzal and Coatl: the aim is the enrichment, not the impoverishment of life. It is, however, true that the actual success of the Quetzalcoatl movement, as it is revealed in the novel, is only partial: what it succeeds in doing for the Mexican peon is to put him into

---

[80] *Op. cit.*, p. 413.   [81] *Op. cit.*, p. 416.
[82] *Collected Letters*, p. 859.   [83] Vivas, p. 29.
[84] Harry T. Moore, "The Plumed Serpent: Vision and Language", *D. H. Lawrence: A Collection of Critical Essays*, ed. Mark Spilka. Englewood Cliffs, N.J. (1963), p. 65.

touch with the life of the universe around him; but there is no
indication how he is going to add to his life the mental-spiritual
consciousness which Ramón and Kate already have and which,
therefore, gives them a crucial advantage over the common
Mexican people. But perhaps Ramón, as he puts it himself,
has done no more than make a beginning: "Possibly I am only
the first step round the corner of change."[85]

It should also be noted, as one critic has correctly pointed
out, that "doubt, hesitation and despair" form a significant
part of Ramón's quest, and that he himself recognises that his
role "includes the exploratory and the tentative".[86] In the
beginning he has only a vague idea of what he wants. "We
only half know ourselves", he confesses to Kate. "Perhaps not
so much as half."[87] He is not unaware that given the least
chance his people, even Cipriano, would not hesitate to betray
him; given one little vulnerable chink they would "leap at the
place out of nowhere, like a tarantula, and bite in the poison".[88]
At times he has doubts that he is making a fool of himself, and
wonders why he should care about other people. "I am a
prince of fools!" he says to Kate, "Why have I started this
Quetzalcoatl business? Why? Pray tell me why?"[89] There
are moments when he feels he is attempting the impossible,
and thinks he should either take his pleasure of life while it
lasts, or else "go into the desert and take my way all alone, to
the star where at last I have my wholeness . . .".[90] And yet he
realises that if he could also be with his woman, and with other
men, "in the Morning Star" which is the meeting-ground, his
joy and delight would be much greater. But the task Ramón
has undertaken—that of fighting "the dragon of Mexico"—is
an infinitely difficult one, and his success is a strictly limited one.
The Mexicans seem to "steam with invisible grudging hate, the
hate of demons foiled in their own souls, whose only motive is
to foil everything, everybody, in the everlasting hell of cramped
frustration."[91] Against this, he is afraid, he might not be able
to hold out for long. He knows quite well that "after all one

[85] *The Plumed Serpent*, p. 311.
[86] John B. Vickery, " 'The Plumed Serpent' and the Eternal Paradox",
Criticism, v (1963), pp. 121-4.
[87] *The Plumed Serpent*, p. 185. [88] *Op. cit.*, p. 189. [89] *Op. cit.*, p. 208.
[90] *Op. cit.*, p. 250. [91] *Op. cit.*, p. 402.

is always just a man", even while one acts "the living Quetzal-coatl": but since the change has to be made, somebody must make it. "One does what one must", he tells Kate. "And if one has wounds—à la guerre comme à la guerre!"[92]

Ramón, in making what he describes as "in truth my first great effort as a man", utilises to his own ends the mythical gods Quetzalcoatl and Huitzilopochtli, and the hymns and rituals he associates with them. To Kate's question, "Does one need gods?" his answer is: "Why, yes. One needs manifestations, it seems to me."[93] If God is to come to the Mexicans, he says, he must come to them "in a blanket and in huaraches"—in a manifestation, that is, which they can recognise. The hymns, in the same way, are used by Ramón as a means whereby he can communicate with the peons in metaphors that they can understand. The context of the religion that Lawrence creates in the pages of *The Plumed Serpent*, we must remember, is the novel itself, and not modern or ancient Mexico.[94] The hymns and rituals were designed to appeal not to the mental-spiritual consciousness of English and American critics, but to the old "blood-and-vertebrate consciousness" of the novel's Mexicans. Those who have failed to grasp this point have found it fit to criticise the hymns on the ground that they are "meaningless to the reader",[95] and that they are "formally abominable" and their "imagery is false".[96] The fact is that these hymns are, in their own way, admirable; their imagery is appropriate; and they have a clearly demonstrable meaning in the context of the novel. But this is beside the point. Their purpose in the book, as Lawrence has taken pains to indicate, is to enable Ramón "to speak to the Mexicans in their own language". The hymns are sung with— for the European ear of Kate—"no recognizable rhythm", but the singing "goes straight through to the soul";[97] the slow, regular thud of the drum acts "straight on the blood".[98] By

[92] *Op. cit.*, p. 405.   [93] *Op. cit.*, p. 288.
[94] A similar point is made by Clark (p. 76) though he draws different conclusions from this.
[95] Harry T. Moore in *D. H. Lawrence: A Collection of Critical Essays*, ed. Mark Spilka, p. 66.
[96] Hough, p. 137. See also West, p. 112.
[97] *The Plumed Serpent*, p. 122.   [98] *Op. cit.*, p. 116.

their slow monotony of repetition the songs of Quetzalcoatl are intended to "drift darkly into the consciousness of the listeners".[99] Abstract ideas are replaced by imagery: the dark unrevealed mystery at the centre of the universe (the dark God of *Kangaroo*) is referred to by such names as "the eye of the Father", "Dark Eye", "the dark sun", "the Master-sun, the dark one, of the unuttered name", "the Morning Star", "the Nameless", "the Unknown Mover". Quetzalcoatl is only its Mexican manifestation. He is "the Son of the Morning Star", but even he "know[s] Him not": "Beyond me is a Lord who is terrible, and wonderful, and dark to me for ever."[1] Quetzalcoatl himself is Lord of the Two Ways: "Out of the depths of the sky, I came like an eagle. Out of the bowels of the earth like a snake."[2] He is the man "who is whole", whose body and spirit and soul are at one. Ramón wants all men of Quetzalcoatl to be like this, to be men of the Morning Star: those who will be "lords of the day and night" but not lords and masters of men. "We will be masters among men, and lords among men", he says, "But lords of men, and masters of men we will not be."[3] His effort is to help men come to their manhood, women to their womanhood.

In an important way, however, *The Plumed Serpent* is not so much a novel about "Mexico" or about Ramón and his Quetzalcoatl movement, as about their relation to, and their impact on, a European consciousness such as Kate's. Her conflicting reactions to the "spirit of place" represent, to a considerable extent, Lawrence's own response to Mexico— attraction alternated by repulsion; and she is also given a large share of the author's critical intelligence. It is primarily this— the depiction of conflicting thoughts and emotions aroused in Kate—which makes the account of her experience in that "uncreated" country both interesting and valuable to the reader.

Kate arrives in Mexico a lonely, disillusioned, and embittered woman. She has no real contact with the world; says she hates "common people";[4] finds the human species loathsome;[5] and wishes to be "alone with the unfolding flower of

[99] *Op. cit.*, p. 258.   [1] *Op. cit.*, p. 342.   [2] *Ibid.*
[3] *Op. cit.*, p. 175.   [4] *Op. cit.*, p. 4.   [5] *Op. cit.*, p. 20.

her own soul".[6] But finding that her life is beginning to drift into "this sterility of nothingness which was the world",[7] she craves for "some human contact". She has made up her mind to cut herself off from all mechanical contacts, but she cannot bear to be cut off from everything: *Give me the mystery and let the world live again for me! Kate cried to her own soul. And deliver me from man's automation.*[8]

She decides that instead of going back to Europe, which is "all politics or jazzing or slushy mysticism or sordid spiritualism",[9] she must get the magic back into her life by letting "the sunwise sympathy of unknown people steal into her".[10] However, easier decided than accomplished. Mexico, she discovers, weighs down her soul with a "down-pressing weight upon the spirit". The spirit of the place is "cruel, down-dragging, destructive".[11] Some effluence, some vibration seems to come out of the earth to militate against "the very composition of the blood and nerves in human beings".[12] What the country wants to do all the time, Kate feels, is to prevent the spirit from soaring and to pull one down, pull one down with a slow, reptilian insistence: "She felt like a bird round whose body a snake has circled itself. Mexico was the snake."[13] She begins to wonder if America is really the great death-continent, "the great continent of undoing", which plucks at the created soul in man until it is finally destroyed.[14] She had come to America because the flow of her life had broken, and she had felt she would not be able to re-start it in Europe where men had lost their soul. But in Mexico it appears to her that people have never had a soul: their lives are not yet knit to a centre, "that centre which is the soul of a man in a man".[15] She is afraid of the natives, but the "dark-faced silent men" also touch "her bowels with a strange power of compassion".[16] The women, similarly, are "at once so fearsome and so appealing".[17] They fill her with "tenderness and revulsion".[18] These women, she decides, are "not quite created"; in their dark centreless eyes lurks something evil and snake-like. Kate is afraid of these men

---

[6] *Op. cit.*, p. 54.   [7] *Op. cit.*, p. 100.   [8] *Op. cit.*, p. 101.
[9] *Op. cit.*, p. 99.   [10] *Op. cit.*, p. 100.   [11] *Op. cit.*, p. 44.
[12] *Op. cit.*, p. 49.   [13] *Op. cit.*, p. 67.   [14] *Op. cit.*, p. 73.
[15] *Op. cit.*, p. 74.   [16] *Op. cit.*, p. 72.   [17] *Op. cit.*, p. 46.
[18] *Op. cit.*, p. 72.

and women because they seem to want to "pull her down, pull her down, to the dark depths of nothingness". This pulling down is, however, not altogether negative. She remembers what Don Ramón had told her about the "need to be drawn down, down, till you send roots into the deep places again".[19] Kate is "at once attracted and repelled" by the Mexican Indians. She is attracted because these people are still part of the Tree of Life and have roots which go down to the centre of the earth. But their strange, dark, reptilian heaviness, and their silent, dense opposition to the spiritual direction is repellent to her. They darkly and barbarically repudiate the spirit, "which is superior and is the quality of our civilization":

> Uncreated, half-created, such a people was at the mercy of old black influences that lay in a sediment at the bottom of them. While they were quiet, they were gentle and kindly, with a sort of limpid naïveté. But when anything shook them at the depths, the black clouds would arise, and they were gone again in the old grisly passions of death, blood-lust, incarnate hate. A people incomplete, and at the mercy of old, upstarting lusts.[20]

She detects in these men a demonish hatred of life itself. They are unable to extricate themselves from their past, and are subject to an ever-recurring deep lust of resentment. "Then, the in-striking thud of a heavy knife, stabbing into a living body, this is the best. No lust of women can equal that lust. The clutching throb of gratification as the knife strikes in and the blood spurts out!"[21] This helpless panic reversal, this lapsing back to old life-modes which brings lust and murder, is seen by Kate as unmitigatedly evil: but she is also convinced that mankind must go back in order to consciously and carefully pick up old threads: "We must take up the old, broken impulse that will connect us with the mystery of the cosmos again. . . ."[22]

Another thing Kate comes to realise for the first time during her stay in Mexico is that men and women are not created complete and ready-made. "Men today were half-made, and women were half-made."[23] She had believed that each individual had a complete soul and an accomplished self.

[19] *Op. cit.*, p. 76.   [20] *Op. cit.*, pp. 130-1.   [21] *Op. cit.*, p. 131.
[22] *Op. cit.*, p. 134.   [23] *Op. cit.*, p. 102.

Now she plainly realises that the world is full of half-made creatures who, nevertheless, try "with a collective insect-like will" to avoid the responsibility of achieving any more perfected being or identity. A single, separate soul is only half a soul. "It takes a man and a woman together to make a soul." Is she herself, she wonders, next to nothing when apart and alone:

> Was the individual an illusion? Man, any man, every man, by himself just a fragment, knowing no Morning Star? And every woman the same; by herself, starless and fragmentary. Even in the relation to the innermost God, still fragmentary and unblest.
>
> Was it true that the gate was the Morning Star, the only entrance to the Innermost? And the Morning Star rises between the two, and between the many, but never from one alone.[24]

Kate, in the course of time, is convinced of one thing, finally: that the clue to all new life, to all present living and future possibility, lies in the vivid blood relation between man and woman. She knows that if she merely goes on cultivating her ego and individuality, she would, like many other elderly women of her acquaintance, spend the rest of her life sitting in a London drawing-room, looking like one of those repellent "grey-ribbed grimalkins". She, therefore, decides that "rather than go like that", she would abandon some of her ego, and sink some of her individuality in her relationship with Cipriano. She, of course, does not give up her individuality altogether. "I must have both", she says to herself. "Ah yes! Rather than become elderly and a bit grisly, I will make my submission; as far as I need and no further."[25]

Kate's Quetzalcoatl marriage to Cipriano takes place appropriately outdoors in a downpour of "unceasing rain", signifying the union of earth and sky, above and below. For Kate, Cipriano, "the Pan male", has a fascination because through him she is put in touch with the "twilight of the ancient Pan world".[26] She is drawn to him at first unconsciously, then consciously, because her connexion with him means "the leap of the old, antediluvian blood-male into

[24] *Op. cit.*, p. 387.   [25] *Op. cit.*, p. 438.   [26] *Op. cit.*, p. 309.

unison with her". Kate's relationship with Cipriano remains
equivocal to the end, but it has a significance in that it
duplicates on a personal level—though in a crude manner, and
with even less success—Ramón's effort to effect the fusion of
the blood-and-vertebrate with the mental-spiritual consciousness.

Don Cipriano,[27] we are told, is "pure Indian".[28] There is
something undeveloped and intense in him, "the intensity and
the crudity of the semi-savage".[29] Kate cannot help feeling
that he wants her because of his own "incompleteness", that
she is just an object of his "intense, blind ambition".[30] As such
he seems "sinister to her, almost repellent".[31] His range is
strictly limited: a large part of his nature is just inert and
unresponsive, "limited as a snake or a lizard is limited".[32]
Though he himself professes to be "Ramón's man", Kate can
see that "in the long run he was nobody's man".[33] Ramón
himself is aware that given the chance Cipriano would not
hesitate to betray him and all his effort: "And Cipriano,
whenever he was away on his own for some time, slipped back
into the inevitable Mexican General, fascinated by the opportunity for furthering his own personal ambition and imposing
his own personal will."[34] He is all for "meeting metal with
metal"; enjoys chasing rebels; pursues the bandits with swift
movements, and punishes them ruthlessly—deriving, one cannot help remembering, the same "clutching throb of gratification as the knife strikes in and the blood spurts out", as the
"uncreated" Mexicans are said to obtain, when subject to the
"ever-recurring, fathomless lust" of resentment and hatred:

> He pursued the bandits with swift movements. He stripped
> his captives and tied them up. But if it seemed a brave man,
> he would swear him in. If it seemed to him a knave, a treacher-
> ous cur, he stabbed him to the heart, saying:
>   "I am the red Huitzilopochtli, of the knife."[35]

---

[27] Harry T. Moore's conjecture that Lawrence projects himself in *The Plume
Serpent* as Cipriano is a bit too fanciful.
[28] *The Plumed Serpent*, p. 59.
[29] *Op. cit.*, p. 62.   [30] *Op. cit.*, p. 231.   [31] *Op. cit.*, p. 233.
[32] *Op. cit.*, p. 307.   [33] *Op. cit.*, p. 311.   [34] *Op. cit.*, p. 250.
[35] *Op. cit.*, p. 364.

All this culminates in the chapter "Huitzilopochtli's Night" with the public executions at Sayula. What is deeply perturbing in the scene is not the fact itself of the executions—for these murderers "would suffer death by condemnation in most societies"[36]—but the manner in which it is presented, particularly the way Cipriano's actions are shown to have Kate's acquiescence and Ramón's open approval. Moreover, Ramón's and Kate's reactions are not at all consistent with what is revealed to us of their characters both before and after the event. Ramón, we are told, has all along tried "to avoid arousing resistance and hate". He insists that the Religion of Quetzalcoatl should be allowed to "spread by itself".[37] He particularly wants to avoid any violence or bloodshed.[38] When Holy Images are thrown out of one of the churches and replaced by papier-mâché Judases, leading to violence, he says the affairs of bloodshed are "far bitterer" to him than to the Bishop.[39] In a conversation with Kate, however, he says that it is very easy for him to make a mistake; and that he would rather err on the side of arrogance than make a sacrifice of himself.[40] But surely his sprinkling of the blood of Cipriano's victims on fire cannot be interpreted as just a ritualistic demonstration of this error. Kate's first reaction after witnessing the ceremony of executions is one of disgust. She is shocked and depressed. "It seemed to her all terrible *will*, the exertion of pure, awful will."[41] And against this manifestation of pure will she feels a deep revulsion rising in her soul. A little later, however, we are told—and this does not convince—that she refuses to judge Cipriano because she thinks he is "of the gods". "What do I care if he kills people?" she says to herself. "What do I care, what Cipriano Viedema does or doesn't do!"[42]

The fact, however, is that Kate Leslie does care, and continues to do so to the end of the book. There have been times when she has wanted to escape, to "flee away to a white man's country, where she could once more breath[e] freely".[43] She feels she is first and last a woman, and there is some part of her which thoroughly mistrusts "all that other stuff" of gods and goddesses in the Quetzalcoatl pantheon:

[36] Clark, p. 97. [37] *The Plumed Serpent*, p. 357. [38] *Op. cit.*, p. 259.

[39] *Op. cit.*, p. 262. [40] *Op. cit.*, p. 271. [41] *Op. cit.*, p. 385.

[42] *Op. cit.*, p. 392. [43] *Op. cit.*, p. 234.

"Oh!" she cried to herself, stifling. "For heaven's sake let me get out of this, and back to simple human people. I loathe the very sound of Quetzalcoatl and Huitzilopochtli. I would die rather than be mixed up in it any more. Horrible, really, both Ramón and Cipriano. And they want to put it over me, with their high-flown bunk, and their Malintzi: Malintzi! I am Kate Forrester, really. I am neither Kate Leslie nor Kate Tylor. I am sick of these men putting names over me. I was born Kate Forrester, and I shall die Kate Forrester. I want to go home. Loathesome, really, to be called Malintzi.—I've had it put over me."[44]

Kate is aware of the duality in herself. "There is a conflict in me," she admits to Ramón.[45] She cannot definitely commit herself either to the old way of life or the new. "She reacted from both." The old way, she knows, was a prison, and she loathes it. But the new way seems to deny her very individuality; and she also gets "a bit bored with living Quetzalcoatl—and the rest".[46] The novel ends with her decision to stay in Mexico, but she, nevertheless, continues to carry "conflicting feelings in her breast".[47]

William York Tindall, writing an introduction to the 1952 New York (Knopf) issue of the novel, defined *The Plumed Serpent* as "at once design and vision", comparable in splendour to "Kubla Khan" or to the paintings of Gauguin. Treating the novel as a myth of rebirth with a symbolic structure of its own, he judged it to be "a great metaphor for a feeling about reality". Most other comments on the novel, however, have been unfavourable: "a bad book and a regrettable performance" (F. R. Leavis); "the only cynical and heartless book Lawrence ever wrote" (Julian Moynahan); "is best regarded as an aberration" (H. M. Daleski); "a didactic treatise superficially novelised" (Eliseo Vivas); "that tremendous volcano of a failure", "the most ambitious failure among all Lawrence's novels" (Harry T. Moore). Don Ramón's experiment in *The Plumed Serpent* is, by and large, a failure: but this is not the same thing as saying that the novel is a failure. Ramón's effort to put the Mexican Indian in touch with the life of the

[44] *Op. cit.*, p. 369.   [45] *Op. cit.*, p. 427.
[46] *Op. cit.*, p. 425.   [47] *Op. cit.*, p. 441.

cosmos, and to help him attain an integrated, whole being by bringing the blood and the spirit into unison, does not meet with appreciable success. But what Ramón *means* is what the entire work of Lawrence (not only *The Plumed Serpent*) essentially means. Lawrence himself was confident that his "Quetzalcoatl novel will stand a lot of wear",[48] thinking that "the weary public" would in time "grow up" and come to understand it for what it is. Middleton Murry, who found *The Plumed Serpent* "a very remarkable novel", also expressed the same confident hope:

> It [*The Plumed Serpent*] is a very remarkable novel; but inevitably, not one that can be assimilated into 'the great tradition'. . . . It has its secure and significant place in the only tradition to which Lawrence belongs—namely the tradition of himself. That this will one day become a genuine tradition, I have little doubt. It will happen, as always, that his genius will gradually create the mode of perception by which it can be appreciated in its own revolutionary uniqueness.[49]

This extraordinary and important novel of Lawrence will, no doubt, come to be appreciated, and accepted, by more readers and critics in the course of time. It is, however, doubtful if it will be—at least for some time to come—numbered among his very best.

[48] *Collected Letters*, p. 860.   [49] *Love, Freedom and Society*, p. 59.

S

VIII

Tenderness

AN obvious and convenient link between *The Plumed Serpent* and the next novel, *Lady Chatterley's Lover*, is Lawrence's frequently quoted letter to Witter Bynner in which he calls the leader-cum-follower relationship a bore, and goes on to say that the new relationship "will be some sort of tenderness, sensitive, between men and men, and men and women, and not the one up one down, lead on I follow, *ich dien* sort of business".[1] For a better understanding of this statement one should also read Bynner's letter, published in his *Journey with Genius*,[2] to which Lawrence's is a reply. As a novelist, Lawrence felt he should be concerned not so much with depicting social change as with making conscious the changing thoughts and feelings within the individual. But this change in emphasis should not be taken to imply that he has gone back on his previous novel. He still believes in fighting for "whole consciousness", which was Ramón's aim; and if the stress in *Lady Chatterley's Lover* is on "phallic consciousness", which is "a vital part" of whole consciousness in man, this is because he found that the "irritable cerebral consciousness" had been exalted at the expense of "the real phallic insouciance and spontaneity".[3] The fight, therefore, has to be waged on behalf of "the phallic reality", though the aim is to attain a balance between the mind and the body, and to bring them into a harmonious relationship. *Lady Chatterley's Lover* was conceived by Lawrence as "a novel contrasting the mental consciousness

---

[1] *Collected Letters*, ii, p. 1045. See also Lawrence's earlier letter to Rolf Gardiner, where he says that "the whole business of leaders and followers is somehow wrong, now", and that even leadership should be based on "reciprocity of tenderness" rather than on "reciprocity of power". (*Letters*, pp. 704-5.)

[2] Bynner, p. 332.

[3] Letter to C. R. C. Conway (15 Mar. 1928) published in Harry T. Moore's *The Intelligent Heart*, p. 359.

with the phallic consciousness";[4] and it is the conflict between these two modes of consciousness which gives the novel its form and structure:

> As I say, it is a novel of the phallic Consciousness: or the phallic Consciousness versus the mental—spiritual Consciousness: and of course you know which side I take. The *versus* is not my fault; there should be no *versus*. The two things must be reconciled in us.[5]

Lawrence considered the phallus to be a great sacred image representing "a deep, deep life which has been denied in us";[6] and it was his sincere belief—he wrote to Harriet Monroe—that the phallic consciousness must be restored into our lives, because

> it is the source of all real beauty, and all real gentleness. And those are the two things, tenderness and beauty, which will save us from horrors. . . . And in my novel I work for them directly, and direct from the phallic consciousness, which, you understand, is not the cerebral sex-consciousness, but something really deeper, and the root of poetry, lived or sung.[7]

The distinction made here between the phallic consciousness and the cerebral sex-consciousness should in no case be lost sight of, for it is the "warm, blood-sex", which establishes the living and vitalising connexion between man and woman, that Lawrence believed in—not the modern sex which "is a pure matter of nerves, cold and bloodless".[8] Whereas the phallic reality is warm and spontaneous, "sex is a thing that exists in the head, its reactions are cerebral, and its processes mental".[9] This sex which is "a mental reaction nowadays, and a hopelessly cerebral affair",[10] Lawrence found ugly and repulsive. "And I, who loathe sexuality so deeply", he said in a letter in exasperation, "am considered a lurid sexuality specialist."[11] In *Lady Chatterley's Lover*, his "nice and tender phallic novel", Lawrence attempted to show how the sex relation can be

---

[4] *Collected Letters*, II, p. 1047.
[5] Lawrence's letter of March/April 1928, quoted in E. and A. Brewster, *D. H. Lawrence*, p. 166.
[6] *Collected Letters*, II, p. 967.   [7] *Op. cit.*, pp. 1046-7.
[8] *S.L.C.*, pp. 256-7.   [9] *Letters*, p. 710.
[10] *Collected Letters*, II, p. 954.   [11] *Ibid.*

"valid and precious" instead of being shameful. To the woman whom Lawrence had given the manuscript of his novel to type, and who had refused to go on typing after the first few pages because she found it too indecent, he wrote: "And remember, although you are on the side of the angels and the vast majority, mine is the truly moral and religious position."[12] Such was the misunderstanding of his intention—conscious intention, at any rate—in writing the book, that he had to reiterate time and again that he had not pandered to the pornographic taste, that he was not advocating "perpetual sex", that he was not suggesting that women should "go running after gamekeepers" or after anybody, that he more than anybody else deplored cheap, promiscuous, heartless sex. "Nothing nauseates me more than promiscuous sex in and out of season", he wrote Ottoline Morrell.[13] His purpose in writing *Lady Chatterley's Lover*, he continued, was "to make an *adjustment in consciousness* to the basic physical realities". For the modern man and woman, he believed, the full, conscious realisation of sex (*i.e.* "warm blood desire") was of the utmost importance. "And this is the real point of this book", he wrote in "A Propos of *Lady Chatterley's Lover*", "I want men and women to be able to think sex, fully, completely, honestly, and cleanly."[14] (Sex, that is, which is a delicate flow of blood-sympathy—not the "nervous, personal, disintegrative sort". Care must be taken to distinguish between the two different senses in which Lawrence uses the word "sex"—the way he himself understands it, and the way he thinks the "moderns" do. As he puts it himself: "It is a mistake I have made, talking of sex I have always inferred that sex meant blood-sympathy and blood-contact. Technically this is so. But as a matter of fact, nearly all modern sex is a pure matter of nerves, cold and bloodless.") There should be a balance and harmony between the consciousness of body's sensations and experiences and these bodily sensations and experiences themselves:

> And if I write a book about the sex relations of a man and a woman, it is not because I want all men and women to begin having indiscriminate lovers and love affairs, off the reel. . . .

---

[12] *Op. cit.*, p. 1032.   [13] *Op. cit.*, p. 1111.   [14] *S.L.C.*, p. 227.

What you have to do is to get out of the state of funk, sex funk. And to do so, you've got to be perfectly decent, and you have to accept sex fully in the consciousness. Accept sex in the consciousness, and let the normal physical awareness come back, between you and other people. . . . It is the most important thing just now, this gentle physical awareness. It keeps us tender and alive at a moment when the great danger is to go brittle, ˈhard, and in some way dead.[15]

Some of the subsidiary, though not unimportant, points in *Lady Chatterley's Lover* (such as: what happened on the "night of sensual passion"? How successful or justified is Lawrence's use of "four-letter words"?) have been the subject of so much controversy and critical attention in recent years that it needs to be emphasised that the theme of the novel is tenderness in human relationships (Lawrence at one time wanted to change the title of his novel to *Tenderness*).[16] The sexual scenes between Connie and Mellors in the later part of the novel have the kind of significance they have in the story only in the context of what we are told in the earlier part of the book.

The novel begins with the words: "Ours is essentially a tragic age, . . ." In what sense is our age essentially tragic? The tragic conception of life, in Lawrence's view, arose when "the grand idealists"—Buddha, Plato, Jesus—destroyed for man his "great relationships" with the circumambient universe by their teaching that "the only happiness lay in abstracting oneself from life".[17] Men and women today are almost totally abstracted from the world they live in and are reduced to mere separate personalities. We no longer know the world in togetherness with ourselves; our knowledge is almost exclusively mental, rational, scientific—knowledge in apartness. The great saviours and teachers only cut us off from "the rhythmic life of the seasons, birth and death and fruition", and turned us into "separate little entities". When we first meet the three principal characters in the novel—Connie, Clifford, and Mellors—each of them is a separate, isolated individual, having no living relationship with anything or anybody. Clifford remains to the end isolated and apart, enclosed within his life of cerebral consciousness and its dead relationships;

[15] *Op. cit.*, pp. 141-2.   [16] *Collected Letters*, ii, p. 1030.   [17] *S.L.C.*, p. 262.

whereas for the other two there is the possibility that they might find some "religious and poetic" meaning in their life of togetherness, with its changing, developing relationships. In *Lady Chatterley's Lover* Lawrence has dramatised the conflict between two modes of consciousness—cerebral and phallic; and between two kinds of relationships—dead and living.

Sir Clifford is presented in the novel as a character who has lost all connexion with his fellow men and women. He is kind and polite, but the warmth of his heart is entirely gone. Whatever relationships he has are mechanical and dead. He is alone and isolated, incapable of any "togetherness". He has over-developed his mental consciousness at the expense of his "emotional and human life". In all this he can be said to be "a pure product of our civilization".[18] To some extent we are all part of this civilisation, and to that extent we are all Cliffords and hence targets of the novel's attack. In criticising Clifford and what he stands for, Lawrence—contrary to the popular belief—was criticising not just an individual or a social class, nor even a "type", but an attitude, and an aspect of the civilisation of which he himself was so much a part. If he shows no "pity" for Clifford and is unsparing in his condemnation of him, this is because he is castigating a part of himself. Diana Trilling—though the expression "extreme cruelty" used by her seems to me a bit too strong—is undoubtedly right when she says:

> Everybody knows Lawrence was representing an image of himself in the gamekeeper Mellors in *Lady Chatterley's Lover*. But Lawrence was not only Mellors in that novel, he was Clifford Chatterley as well. . . . This is what licenses his quite extreme cruelty to Clifford Chatterley. Chatterley is himself.[19]

This has the support of Frieda Lawrence also who has remarked that "the terrible thing about Lady C. is that Lawrence identified himself with both Clifford and Mellors".[20] Lawrence is not "kind" to Clifford, whose own "kindness" is, underneath, mere coldness of heart: but his attitude is not

---

[18] *Op. cit.*, p. 266.
[19] "A Letter of Introduction to Lawrence", *Partisan Review*, xxv, i (Winter 1958), pp. 39-40.
[20] *Memoirs and Correspondence*, p. 352.

without real, discriminating sympathy. "For even satire is a form of sympathy."[21] It was Lawrence's passionate concern for the future of mankind which made him show up Clifford for what he is—for Clifford, after all, only forms a part of the "new race of mankind, over-conscious in the money and social and political side, on the spontaneous, intuitive side dead, but dead. Half-corpses, all of them: but with a terrible insistent consciousness in the other half."[22]

Clifford marries Connie during the war when he is home for a month on leave. Then he goes back to Flanders, only to be shipped back home again six months later "more or less in bits". He gradually recovers and is able to return to life again, but "with the lower half of his body, from the hips down, paralysed for ever". Why did Lawrence make Clifford paralysed? In "A Propos of *Lady Chatterley's Lover*" he says:

> I have been asked many times if I intentionally made Clifford paralysed, if it is symbolic. And literary friends say, it would have been better to have left him whole and potent, and to have made the woman leave him nevertheless.
>
> As to whether the "symbolism" is intentional—I don't know. Certainly not in the beginning, when Clifford was created. When I created Clifford and Connie, I had no idea what they were or why they were. They just came, pretty much as they are. But the novel was written, from start to finish, three times. And when I read the first version, I recognised that the lameness of Clifford was symbolic of the paralysis, of most men of his sort and class today. I realised that it was perhaps taking an unfair advantage of Connie, to paralyse him technically. It made it so much more vulgar of her to leave him. Yet the story came as it did, by itself, so I left it alone. Whether we call it symbolism or not, it is, in the sense of its happening, inevitable.[23]

The paralysis of Clifford, as Lawrence explains in a letter also, is symbolic in the sense in which "all art is *au fond* symbolic, conscious or unconscious".[24] He had not deliberately worked symbolically, but the character of Clifford as it took shape in his imagination turned out to be an apt symbol of the

[21] *Lady Chatterley's Lover* (Phoenix Edition), p. 92.
[22] *Op. cit.*, p. 140.   [23] *S.L.C.*, pp. 266-7.   [24] *Collected Letters*, ii, p. 1194.

over-intellectualised and emotionally paralysed humanity of the
day, and Lawrence recognised the unconscious symbolism later
on.   Those who have pointed out that "the physical crippling
of Clifford greatly weakens the story"[25] are only saying what
Lawrence's "literary friends" had suggested and which
Lawrence's "daemon" could not accept.   And Lawrence's
"daemon" was probably quite right.   Lawrence could have
left Clifford "whole and potent" and yet made Connie's leaving
him plausible by turning him into a contemptible character.
But he was not writing an allegorical fable in terms of wholly
"good" or wholly "bad" characters; and he was not interested
in presenting Clifford as "an odious character".[26]   In any case,
in so far as Clifford's physical disability is concerned he himself
is obviously in no way to blame.   Graham Hough is, generally
speaking, right when he says that Lawrence's position is made
"all the stronger" by the facts that Clifford cannot help himself,
and that Connie is a loyal and kind woman and there is "every
moral and humane reason" against her doing as she does:

> Lawrence has often been criticised for the implied cruelty
> of the attitude to Clifford, ... I formerly shared this view, but
> have now come to believe, within the given context, that it is
> wrong.   Connie's actions towards him are not excused, for
> they are never discussed, in the ordinary moral terms. . . .
> The cruelty in the book is the cruelty of life rather than that of
> the author or even of his characters.   Lawrence has weighted
> the scales against himself by making Clifford an object of pity
> as well as of legitimate dislike;   but no one could maintain that
> the development from the given circumstances is not probable
> in itself or not consistent with the nature of things.[27]

The criticism the novel makes of Clifford is also the substance
of Lawrence's attack on modern civilisation with its preponderance of "cerebral consciousness".   Most modern men
and women, as Lawrence saw with dismay, had been turned
into half-corpses: they were most of them, notwithstanding all

---

[25] Harry T. Moore, *The Life and Works of D. H. Lawrence*, p. 208. See also his
views in *The Intelligent Heart* (1955), pp. 359-60; and in *Miscellany*, p. 264. Moore,
it appears, would have been satisfied if Lawrence had made Clifford into another
Michaelis.

[26] Vivas, p. 123.   [27] Hough, p. 165.

the "machine fucking" (as Mellors puts it) that goes on, paralysed in "the emotional and humanly-individual part". It was Lawrence's concern for his fellow men and women who had—so he believed—gone nearly dead in so far as their affective life was concerned, which made Lawrence intensify his attack on over-intellectualisation in modern life.[28]

When Clifford and Connie are married, the sex part does not mean much to either of them—though apart from this they are very close together in an intimacy which is deep and "beyond sex". Sex seems to them merely an accident, an adjunct—"one of the curious obsolete, organic processes which persisted in its own clumsiness, but was not really necessary".[29] Then with the injury received in the war Clifford is so much hurt that "something inside him was perished, some of his feelings had gone. There was a blank of insentience."[30] Whatever warmth of heart was there in him, is killed by the war.[31] When he comes to live in Wragby Hall, he has very little connexion with other people; he is not really in touch with anyone. Connie feels even she cannot really touch him, since in the last issue he is "just a negation of human contact".[32] In this state he takes to writing stories—stories that are cleverly written but are "in some mysterious way, meaningless". Even in the stories there is "no touch, no actual contact".[33] These smart stories are something new and "entirely personal", and have "no organic connection with the thought and expression that had gone before".[34] But his writing brings him fame and success; and success—the bitch-goddess Success, as Tommy Dukes calls it, after Henry James—restores to him his confidence and his equanimity. He is surrounded at Wragby Hall by his old Cambridge friends, young intellectuals who all "believed

[28] For an account of some of the differences between the three versions of *Lady Chatterley's Lover*, see E. W. Tedlock, in *The Frieda Lawrence Collection of D. H. Lawrence Manuscripts*, Albuquerque, N.M. (1948), pp. 279-316.

[29] *Lady Chatterley's Lover*, p. 12.   [30] *Op. cit.*, p. 6.

[31] That Clifford is also *physically* disabled, does not, in so far as the development of the story in Lawrence's novel is concerned, materially affect his relationship with Connie—except that it makes it much more difficult for her to leave him. The crippling of Clifford, however, serves the important function of keeping the readers in touch with his fate, even while they come to recognise his emotional attitudes as wrong and distasteful.

[32] *Lady Chatterley's Lover*, p. 15.   [33] *Ibid.*   [34] *Ibid.*

in the life of the mind".[35] Connie has to listen to these "highly-mental gentlemen"[36] making their "immensely important" speculations and using "millions of words, in the parade of the life of the mind". She finds it fun, to a certain extent. "But what cold minds!" Even Tommy Dukes, who expresses some of Lawrence's own views, is a mere windbag. "Talk, talk, talk! What hell it was, the continual rattle of it!"[37] All that can be said in Dukes's favour is that he is at least honest in his thinking. As far as words go, his utterances are not unlike those of his creator. "Real knowledge," he says, "comes out of the whole corpus of the consciousness; out of your belly and your penis as much as out of your brain and mind. The mind can only analyse and rationalise."[38] But as he says himself he is "only a 'mental-lifer' ".[39] His intellectual beliefs are all right, but when it comes to deeds, he feels he cannot really want a woman: "I just simply can't vibrate in unison with a woman." Julian Moynahan finds the presence of Clifford's cronies in the novel superfluous. Even Dukes, he says, only anticipates the views of Mellors who needs no "press agentry" as he can very well "speak for himself".[40] It is odd that Moynahan should have failed to see what has been made so obvious: that these "highly-mental gentlemen", including Tommy Dukes, have only learnt the Word, but are incapable of deeds in accordance with their words. As Lawrence puts it in "A Propos", "It is the Deed of life we have now to learn: we are supposed to have learnt the Word, but, alas, look at us. Word-perfect we may be, but Deed-demented."[41] The title of Moynahan's book, *The Deed of Life*, is, ironically, taken from this quotation.

As years go by Connie feels the bruise of fear and horror coming up and spreading in Clifford. "The bruise was deep, deep . . . the bruise of the false inhuman war."[42] Clifford is still quite alert, mentally: but the paralysis, the bruise of the great shock was gradually spreading in his affective self". Seeing the "background of his mind" fill up with nothingness, Connie dimly realises "one of the great laws of the human soul":

---

[35] *Op. cit.*, p. 29. [36] *Op. cit.*, p. 33. [37] *Op. cit.*, p. 69.
[38] *Op. cit.*, p. 35. [39] *Op. cit.*, p. 37. [40] Moynahan, p. 156.
[41] *S.L.C.*, p. 260. [42] *Lady Chatterley's Lover*, p. 46

that when the emotional soul receives a wounding shock, which does not kill the body, the soul seems to recover as the body recovers. But this is only appearance. It is really only the mechanism of the re-assumed habit. Slowly, slowly the wound to the soul begins to make itself felt, like a bruise, which only slowly deepens its terrible ache, till it fills all the psyche. And when we think we have recovered and forgotten, it is then that the terrible after-effects have to be encountered at their worst.[43]

Clifford tends to fall into fits of depression and to go vague and absent. Connie realises that it is "the wound to his psyche coming out":[44] but there is nothing she can do about it. It is only later when Clifford begins to take an active interest in the mines that he feels a new sense of power coming into him:

It gave him a sense of power, of power. He was doing something: and he was *going* to do something. He was going to win, to win: not as he had won with his stories, mere publicity, amid a whole sapping of energy and malice. But a man's victory.[45]

Clifford's success in the field of industrial activity is undoubted. As a practical man and a master, he proves to be amazingly astute and powerful. This, in itself, goes to his credit: but—and this is the substance of Lawrence's criticism—this success is attained at the expense of his emotional and human life. While he is mastering the technicalities of modern coal-mining, he lets his humanly-individual part go pulpy, and becomes "almost a *creature*, with a hard, efficient shell of an exterior and a pulpy interior, one of the amazing crabs and lobsters of modern industrial and financial world, invertebrates of the crustacean order, with shells of steel, like machines, and inner bodies of soft pulp."[46] No wonder, then, that he comes to believe that "the industry comes before the individual".[47]

Connie, when she marries Clifford, has had her tentative love affairs based on "all the passion of mental attraction",[48] and has learnt to take the "sex-thrill" as a sensation without in the least yielding her "pure and noble freedom", which, to her, is "infinitely more wonderful than any sexual love".[49] Her

[43] *Op. cit.*, p. 46.   [44] *Op. cit.*, p. 58.   [45] *Op. cit.*, p. 99.
[46] *Op. cit.*, p. 100.   [47] *Op. cit.*, p. 165.   [48] *Op. cit.*, p. 8.
[49] *Op. cit.*, p. 7.

relationship with Clifford develops into a deep personal intimacy because unlike other young men "who insisted on the sex thing like dogs", he is not just keen on his "satisfaction". When he returns home crippled, she sticks to him passionately because he has been hurt so much.[50] Their intimacy, however, is an affair of the mind only; they cannot even bring themselves to talk to each other on matters concerning their bodily existence. "They were so intimate, and utterly out of touch."[51] Connie has no contact with other people at Wragby, either; has no "real connection" with them. Her existence seems to her "all a dream", or a "simulacrum of reality".[52]

> Time went on. Whatever happened, nothing happened, because she was so beautifully out of contact. She and Clifford lived in their ideas and his books. . . . Time went on as the clock does, half-past eight instead of half-past seven.[53]

To escape the restlessness arising out of her "disconnection", she starts going to the wood: but even the wood is no real refuge or sanctuary for her as she has no connexion with it: she never really touches the "spirit of the wood" itself. She becomes vaguely aware that she has lost all touch with "the substantial and vital world".[54] Knowing what torture Clifford would feel at the slightest sign of flirtation on her part, she gives no encouragement to the men who are nice and attentive to her, and remains "quiet and vague". Then comes Michaelis, "the outsider",[55] himself a lonely figure, out of "contact with his surroundings";[56] and she gives herself to him out of sheer compassion and sympathy for him. "To her it meant nothing except that she gave herself to him."[57] He also rouses in her "a wild, craving physical desire", which, however, he cannot satisfy: "he was always come and finished so quickly, then shrinking down on her breast, and recovering somewhat his effrontery while she lay dazed, disappointed, lost".[58] But she knows how to get her sexual thrill out of him; she has not forgotten what she had learnt as a young girl at Dresden—that "she only had to hold herself back in sexual intercourse, and

[50] *Op. cit.*, p. 15.   [51] *Op. cit.*, p. 17.   [52] *Op. cit.*, p. 18.
[53] *Op. cit.*, pp. 18-19.   [54] *Op. cit.*, p. 19.   [55] *Op. cit.*, p. 22.
[56] *Op. cit.*, p. 23.   [57] *Op. cit.*, p. 24.   [58] *Op. cit.*, p. 27.

let him finish and expend himself without herself coming to the crisis: and then she could prolong the connection and achieve her orgasm and her crisis while he was merely her tool."[59]

When Michaelis points out to her that Clifford is "entirely wrapped up in himself", and has really no use for her, she can see the truth in this. Her marriage with Clifford is now little more than "the long slow habit of intimacy, formed through years of suffering and patience".[60] Clifford's ideas about marriage, even his desire for a son, seem to her curiously impersonal: all his talk about "integrated life" and about arranging "this sex thing as we arrange going to the dentist"[61] seems to her mere words, meaning really nothing. "The only reality was nothingness, and over it a hypocrisy of words."[62] She feels an inward dread and emptiness gradually spreading in her. Yet when Michaelis suggests her leaving Clifford, she cannot agree. "It may seem to you Clifford doesn't count", she tells him, "but he does. When you think how disabled he is. . . ."[63] Moreover, a relationship based on mere sex-thrill and sensual satisfaction is not enough to lure her away from her life with Clifford; and if later on she decides to abandon him, it is in exchange for a whole new life of emotions, warmth, and tenderness that her relationship with Mellors brings to her. The short-lived affair with Michaelis comes to an end when on one occasion, after they have made love, he tells her in a bitter and sneering voice, "You couldn't go off at the same time as a man, could you? You'd have to bring yourself off! You'd have to run the show!" Connie is stunned by this unexpected piece of brutality:

> This speech was one of the crucial blows of Connie's life.
> It killed something in her. She had not been so very keen on
> Michaelis; till he started it, she did not want him. It was as
> if she never positively wanted him. But once he had started
> her, it seemed only natural for her to come to her own crisis
> with him. . . . Her whole sexual feeling for him, or for any
> man, collapsed that night. Her life fell apart from his as
> completely as if he had never existed.
> And she went through the days drearily. There was

---

[59] *Op. cit.*, p. 7.   [60] *Op. cit.*, p. 41.   [61] *Ibid.*
[62] *Op. cit.*, p. 47.   [63] *Op. cit.*, p. 49.

nothing now but this empty treadmill of what Clifford called the integrated life, the long living together of two people, who are in the habit of being in the same house with one another. Nothingness![64]

Into this life of "nothingness" comes the gamekeeper "like a sudden rush of a threat out of nowhere".[65] Like other characters in the novel he is, as Connie observes, a "separate fellow",[66] "aloof, apart",[67] "a man very much alone and on his own",[68] "a creature purely alone".[69] Yet there is also a certain warmth about him, and it is this which starts in Connie a weary yearning and a sense of dissatisfaction with her life. As she looks one day at her reflexion in the mirror, the sight of her naked body turning "greyish and sapless" arouses in her a deep sense of injustice and a cold indignation against Clifford and "all the men of his sort who defrauded a woman even of her own body". In a way, she knows poor Clifford is not to blame. "His was the greater misfortune." It is, she recognises, all part of a general catastrophe:[70]

> And yet was he not in a way to blame? This lack of warmth, this lack of the simple, warm, physical contact, was he not to blame for that? He was never really warm, not even kind, only thoughtful, considerate, in a well-bred, cold sort of way! But never warm as a man can be warm to a woman, . . .[71]

In devoting her life to Clifford, Connie begins to wonder, is she not sacrificing herself to "a cold spirit of vanity, that had no warm human contacts"? But even now when Michaelis proposes that she should marry him and get divorced from Clifford, she cannot do it: her "heart simply stood still at the thought of abandoning Clifford there and then. She couldn't do it. No . . . no! She just couldn't."[72]

---

[64] *Op. cit.*, pp. 50-1. [65] *Op. cit.*, p. 42. [66] *Op. cit.*, p. 43.

[67] *Op. cit.*, p. 44. [68] *Op. cit.*, p. 55. [69] *Op. cit.*, p. 61.

[70] *Cf.* Lawrence's letter to Brewster: "One resents bitterly a certain swindle about modern life, and especially a sex swindle. One is swindled out of one's proper sex life, a great deal. But it is nobody's individual fault: fault of our age: our own fault as well". (*Collected Letters*, II, p. 967.)

[71] *Lady Chatterley's Lover*, p. 65. [72] *Op. cit.*, p. 72.

However, finding that she is "so utterly out of touch"[73] with Clifford ("He never took her hand and held it kindly."), and that Wragby and all the people in it only give her a feeling of "unspeakable depression", she again starts going to the wood as often as possible—often towards the little clearing with the hut where the pheasants are reared. The keeper who cherishes his solitude, resents the intrusion—especially as he does not want to come into contact with a woman again. He has reached the point where all he wants is to be left alone. "His recoil from the outer world was complete; his last refuge was the wood; to hide himself there!"[74] He wishes above all things that Connie would leave him to his own privacy: he dreads, "with a repulsion almost of death, any further close human contact".[75] Connie, too, becomes aware that he avoids her on purpose.[76] It is at this stage—when Mellors' isolation from the world is more or less complete, and when Connie is more acutely aware of "the agony of her own female forlornness"[77] than she has ever been before—that the first significant contact between them takes place. They are both sitting in front of a coop, Connie holding a little chick in her hands:

> The keeper, squatting beside her, was also watching with an amused face the bold little bird in her hands. Suddenly he saw a tear fall on to her wrist.
> And he stood up, and stood away, moving to the other coop. For suddenly he was aware of the old flame shooting and leaping up in his loins, that he had hoped was quiescent for ever. He fought against it, turning his back to her. But it leapt downwards, circling in his knees.
> He turned again to look at her. She was kneeling and holding her two hands slowly forward, blindly, so that the chicken should run in to the mother-hen again. And there was something so mute and forlorn in her, compassion flamed in his bowels for her.
> Without knowing, he came quickly towards her and crouched beside her again, taking the chick from her hands, because she was afraid of the hen, and putting it back in the coop. At the back of his loins the fire suddenly darted stronger.

[73] *Op. cit.*, p. 102.   [74] *Op. cit.*, p. 80.   [75] *Op. cit.*, p. 81.
[76] *Op. cit.*, p. 103.   [77] *Op. cit.*, p. 104.

He glanced apprehensively at her. Her face was averted, and she was crying blindly, in all the anguish of her generation's forlornness.[78]

The keeper takes her to the hut, and though the sexual intercourse that follows marks the beginning of their relationship, it is not a very satisfactory beginning. To Connie it means "nothing"—which is not unlike her first experience with Michaelis. Only, since Michaelis has killed something in her, even her desire for her own "satisfaction" is no longer there: "She lay still, in a kind of sleep, always in a kind of sleep. The activity, the orgasm was his, all his: she could strive for herself no more."[79] Mellors does experience "pure peace", and feels connected with life again: but he also thinks he has brought "a new cycle of pain and doom" on himself. He is sorry for the sake of Connie because he is afraid the "insentient iron world", the malevolent society "ready to destroy whatever did not conform", would like to "do her in" because she is tender, "tender with a tenderness of the growing hyacinths".[80] He decides he must "protect her with his heart" as long as he can, but knows that he alone cannot change the world:

> Oh, if only there were other men to be with, to fight that sparkling electric Thing outside there, to preserve the tenderness of life, the tenderness of women, and the natural riches of desire. If only there were men to fight side by side with! But the men were all outside there, glorying in the Thing, triumphing or being trodden down in the rush of mechanized greed or of greedy mechanism.[81]

Connie's relationship with Mellors brings to her a sense of human warmth and tenderness she has not known before, and also wakens her to the beauty of life around her. But the development of this relationship, as even the descriptions of repeated but meaningfully different sexual scenes between them would indicate, is a slow and complex process. At first Connie remains "apart in all the business", and feels "left out, distant", alone in her "separateness".[82] It is not until the time when Mellors says they "came off together"[83] that she really begins

[78] *Op. cit.*, p. 105. [79] *Op. cit.*, p. 106. [80] *Op. cit.*, p. 109.
[81] *Op. cit.*, p. 110. [82] *Op. cit.*, p. 115. [83] *Op. cit.*, p. 123.

to get in touch with him ("Sex is only touch, the closest of all touch", Mellors remarks later on). Connie feels another self born in her and with this self she adores him. But she also fights against this "full soft heaving adoration of her womb", because it means "the loss of herself to herself". She is afraid that "if she adored him too much, then she would lose herself, become effaced, and she did not want to be effaced, a slave, like a savage woman. She must not become a slave."[84] For a time her self-will asserts itself and she thinks of taking up her passion "with her own will": the man dwindles into a contemptible object, the mere phallus-bearer, an Iacchos to her Bacchante, "to be torn to pieces when his service was performed".[85] But she also knows how "barren" and wearisome this destructive passion is; so she resolves that she would rather give up "her hard bright female power". Despite her decision, however, she carries mixed emotions to her next meeting with the gamekeeper. She is "divided between two feelings";

[84] There are passages in *Lady Chatterley's Lover* and *The Plumed Serpent* which have presented some difficulty to a few critics who, misreading these, have come to the mistaken conclusion that Lawrence advocates complete passivity and voluntary foregoing of the orgasm for the woman. Lawrence's attack was directed against the insistence today, even in the sex act, on conscious, mental "satisfaction". In *Lady Chatterley's Lover* there is strong implicit disapproval of the sex relations Connie has with Michaelis, and before that with "the German boy" in Dresden, because she makes use of the man as "merely her tool", and uses "this sex thing to have power over him". Connie herself is not blamed for this as she is forced to be active because Michaelis, "like so many modern men, . . . was finished almost before he had begun". The fault, we are to understand, lies with modern sex which is only "intellectual reactions reflected down onto physical process". (*Collected Letters*, II, p. 1048.) The same criticism is made of Mellors' sexual relations with his wife Bertha Coutts who, after the man had really finished, would "start on her own account" and bring herself off "tearing and shouting . . . tear, tear, tear as if she had no sensation in her except in the top of her beak, the very outside top tip, that rubbed and tore". Those who regard *this* as "the natural female orgasm" have cause enough to protest. As to Lawrence's views on feminine passivity, we have the following in an early letter to Blanche Jennings: "By the way, in love, or at least in love-making, do you think the woman is always passive . . . enjoying the man's demonstration, a wee bit frit—not active? I prefer a little devil—a Carmen—I like nothing passive". (*Collected Letters*, I, p. 45.) And if what Mellors says in the novel is any indication of Lawrence's own views, there should be no doubt that his opinion in this matter remained practically unchanged. Mellors makes so much of his and Connie's having "come off together"; tells her he hates it when the woman passively "lies there like nothing" as if she found "the actual thing . . . a bit distasteful"; and states quite explicitly that he could never get his pleasure and satisfaction of a woman unless she got hers of him at the same time.

[85] *Lady Chatterley's Lover*, p. 124.

T

"something in her quivered, and something in her spirit stiffened in resistance". A careful reading of the three successive descriptions of sexual intercourse that Lawrence introduces at this point reveals how this resistance is gradually overcome and she can wholly give herself to the experience which fills all her consciousness and brings her deep fulfilment.

To begin with, Connie's spirit seems to "look on from the top of her head" and she cannot help viewing the performance as ridiculous and contemptible:

> Cold and derisive her queer female mind stood apart, and though she lay perfectly still, her impulse was to heave her loins, and throw the man out, escape his ugly grip, and the butting over-riding of his absurd haunches. His body was a foolish, impudent, imperfect thing, a little disgusting in its unfinished clumsiness. For surely a complete evolution would eliminate this performance, this "function".[86]

And yet it is not that she wishes to be left out: she really wants to love the man, but is prevented by the powerful inward resistance that has taken possession of her. Touched by her own "double consciousness and reaction", she begins to weep. A little later when Mellors takes her in his arms, she begins to "melt in a marvellous peace" and the resistance is gone:

> She yielded with a quiver that was like death, she went all open to him. And oh, if he were not tender to her now, how cruel, for she was all open to him and helpless!
> She quivered again at the potent inexorable entry inside her, so strange and terrible. It might come with the thrust of a sword in her softly-opened body, and that would be death. She clung in a sudden anguish of terror. But it came with a strange slow thrust of peace, the dark thrust of peace and a ponderous, primordial tenderness, such as made the world in the beginning. And her terror subsided in her breast, her breast dared to be gone in peace, she held nothing. She dared to let go everything, all herself, and be gone in the flood. . . . Oh, and far down inside her the deeps parted and rolled asunder, in long, far-travelling billows, and ever, at the quick of her, the depths parted and rolled asunder from the centre of soft

---

[86] *Op. cit.*, p. 158.

plunging, as the plunger went deeper and deeper, touching lower, and she was deeper and deeper and deeper disclosed, and heavier the billows of her rolled away to some shore, uncovering her, and closer and closer plunged the palpable unknown, and further and further rolled the waves of herself away from herself, leaving her, till suddenly, in a soft, shuddering convulsion, the quick of all her spasm was touched, the consummation was upon her, and she was gone. She was gone, she was not, and she was born: a woman.[87]

For Connie the experience this time is both a sacrifice of her self and a new birth. And now when she touches the body of Mellors it is "the sons of god with the daughters of men". But it is still an experience which she is conscious of, and can afterwards speak of, as having been "so lovely!". The third time all consciousness is gone:

And this time his being within her was all soft and iridescent, purely soft and iridescent, such as no consciousness could seize. Her whole self quivered unconscious and alive, like plasm. She could not know what it was. She could not remember what it had been. Only that it had been more lovely than anything ever could be. Only that. And afterwards she was utterly still, utterly unknowing, she was not aware for how long. And he was still with her, in an unfathomable silence along with her. And of this, they would never speak.[88]

The passage, however, which has received a great deal— indeed far too much—of critical attention in recent years, is the one describing the "night of sensual passion" spent by Mellors and Connie just before the latter's departure for Italy. Since so much has already been written about the episode, one would very much like to leave it alone, but for the fact that sometimes even little misinterpretations, if they remain unrefuted, come to be regarded as the final word on the subject. This has the effect—in some cases, at any rate—of distorting the reader's view of the work as a whole, or at least of diverting the reader's attention from the main theme to relatively minor points in the work in question. H. M. Daleski, for instance, after referring to the opinions of Eliseo Vivas, Andrew Shonfield, G. Wilson

[87] *Op. cit.*, pp. 159-60. [88] *Op. cit.*, p. 161.

Knight, and John Sparrow,[89] so easily and confidently concludes that "we can now take it as established beyond doubt that the 'night of sensual passion' is a night on which Mellors had anal intercourse with Connie", and then goes on to investigate the "significance of the experience".[90] Since he takes it for granted that what he imagines as established is a fact rather than an opinion, it is no wonder that he does not even make a reference to the correspondence which appeared following the publication of the articles he mentions.[91] A brief discussion of the issues involved is given in an Appendix at the end of this book. An attentive reading of the novel itself should, however, convince any reader that most comments on the passage in question are better read as interesting revelations of the working of the critics' fanciful minds, than as critical remarks on Lawrence's novel. The account of sensual passion ("this piercing, consuming, rather awful sensuality") should, moreover, be understood to have its crucial importance[92] only as part of a larger, total relationship growing between Connie and Mellors; for "sheer fiery sensuality",[93] in itself, as Connie later observes, is destructive, and becomes mechanical, "weary, tired, worn-out sensuality"[94] when it is not accompanied by tenderness. "I loved last night", she says to Mellors, "But you'll keep the tenderness for me, won't you?"[95] A little later she tells her sister Hilda that it makes a great difference if one knows both "real tenderness" and "real sensuality" with the same person.[96] That Mellors is going to keep the tenderness for her, or at least intends to do so, is revealed by his desire to be in "tender

[89] See, respectively, Vivas, pp. 133-5; "Lawrence's Other Censor", *Encounter*, xvii (Sep. 1961), pp. 63-4; "Lawrence, Joyce and Powys", *Essays in Criticism*, xi (Oct. 1961), pp. 403-17; and "Regina *v.* Penguin Books Ltd.", *Encounter*, xviii (Feb. 1962), pp. 35-43.

[90] *The Forked Flame*, pp. 304 ff.

[91] See *Encounter* (March, April, May, and June 1962); *The Spectator* (2, 9, and 16 Mar. 1962); and *Essays in Criticism*, xii (1962), pp. 226-7, pp. 445-7; and xiii (1963), pp. 101-4, 202-5, 301-3. See also the earlier article by Colin Welch, "Black Magic, White Lies", *Encounter* (Feb. 1961), pp. 75-9; and the correspondence appearing in the two subsequent issues (March and April) of that magazine.

[92] That it has this kind of importance for Connie also, is made clear when she says to Mellors the next morning, "Don't you think one lives for times like last night?".

[93] *Lady Chatterley's Lover*, p. 234.

[94] *Ibid.*

[95] *Op. cit.*, p. 232.

[96] *Op. cit.*, p. 233.

touch" with her (" 'I stand for the touch of bodily awareness between human beings,' he said to himself, 'and the touch of tenderness.' "); and when Connie tells him he has "the courage of [his] own tenderness", he, on reflexion, agrees, and goes on to say that the crying need of the day is that people should get into delicate and tender touch with one another: "And it is touch we're afraid of. We're only half-conscious, and half-alive. We've got to come alive and aware." [97] In spite of his fear of the "bad time coming", he is—as his letter to Connie which concludes the novel shows—hopeful that they will be able to keep alive "the little forked flame" that has come to exist between the two of them:

> All the bad times that ever have been, haven't been able to blow the crocus out: not even the love of women. So they won't be able to blow out my wanting you, nor the little glow there is between you and me. . . . I believe in the little flame between us. . . . We fucked a flame into being. [98] Even the flowers are fucked into being between the sun and the earth.

---

[97] *Op. cit.*, p. 256.

[98] Something needs to be said about Lawrence's use of "four-letter words", since there is still considerable misunderstanding about it. Lawrence's purpose in using these words was, in the first instance, to make a move towards freeing the language of "various artificial taboos on words and expressions". (*Collected Letters*, II, p. 1158.) That, notwithstanding the attempt he made in the novel, the connotations, generally speaking, of the "obscene, physical" words remain "either facetious or vulgar", and that "no writer can alter the connotations of a whole section of the vocabulary by mere fiat" (Hough, p. 161), is, I think, quite true. And Lawrence himself cannot have expected a sudden miraculous change to take place in people's habits of thought and speech. But he wanted to and did make a beginning; and a beginning, he believed, had to be made because he saw a close connexion between people's attitude to the taboo words and their attitude to the physical reality to which these words referred, and was convinced that "the phallic reality" should be given "its own phallic language" to save it from "the 'uplift' taint" (*S.L.C.*, p. 267). Lawrence was trying neither to "hallow" or "purify" the "obscene" words (see Katherine Anne Porter's article in *Encounter*, Feb. 1960), nor to lift the phallic reality "to a higher plane" (*S.L.C.*, p. 267). On the contrary, he described this as "the greatest blasphemy of all". He simply wanted people to openly and consciously *accept* the phallic reality and the phallic language. He was in fact not considering the matter on the level of linguistic convenience: even his insistence on the use of phallic language had a clearly defined purpose. He was simply trying, in his small way, to help restore to mankind a whole range of emotional and passional life which it had lost because of the excessively "mental-spiritual" attitudes and artificial taboos that exist in the present civilisation.

But it's a delicate thing, and takes patience and the long pause.[99]

Lady Chatterley's Lover cannot be said to mark an advance over the previous novel, *The Plumed Serpent*. In it Lawrence returns to a theme already treated in detail in the earlier novels. In a way the theme is basic to all Lawrence's work: but until we come to the last novel we are struck, as we move from one novel to the next, by the continual extension of the areas of human experience imaginatively explored. In *Lady Chatterley's Lover* many of the larger themes of Lawrence's mature work are touched on,[1] but the brief references to them are nearly lost in the over-all impression the book leaves on the reader—which is one of more or less exclusive preoccupation with the emotional and sexual relations of man and woman. To some, who share the view of F. R. Leavis and object to the book's "offences against taste", this emphasis is far too deliberate to allow the book to be a "wholly satisfactory work of art";[2] to others like Katherine Anne Porter, *Lady Chatterley's Lover* is "not . . . a work of good art"—indeed a "tiresome" and "laboriously bad" book—because Lawrence was a "badly flawed" artist, and was "as wrong as can be on the whole subject of sex".[3] It is no part

---

[99] *Lady Chatterley's Lover*, pp. 278-9.

[1] For instance, the theme of man's "aloneness" (pp. 132-4); his relation to other men, and to society and the means of production (pp. 98-100, 140, 146, 199-203, 277-8); the need for purposive activity (p. 255), etc.

[2] Leavis, pp. 70, 294.

[3] "A Wreath for the Gamekeeper", *Encounter*, xvi (Feb. 1960). Miss Porter, who describes the novel as "the fevered day-dream of a dying man . . . indulging his sexual fantasies", says she cannot see in the "sad history" of Connie and Mellors anything but "a long, dull, grey, monotonous chain of days, lightened now and then by a sexual bout". Well, people have been known to suffer from curious disabilities. But when Miss Porter goes on to tell us that "there is no wine, no food, no sleep, no refreshment, no laughter, no rest nor quiet—no love" in this "sad history", one feels reasonably sure that instead of reading the novel before writing her article, she only went back to "some passages of unintentional hilarious low comedy" which she remembered from her "first" reading of the novel "thirty years ago"; or how could she have missed the mention of milk, tea, coffee, cocoa, beer, bread, butter, cheese, ham, bacon, potatoes, mutton chops, pressed-tongue, pickled walnuts (pp. 152, 153, 181, 184, 224-5, 229, 230) in the book? If Miss Porter's opinion of the novel is what she says it is, one really ought not to blame her for not wanting to read it again. But in that case, one cannot help wondering, what obliged her to rush into print! See also: Richard Aldington, "A Wreath for Lawrence?", *Encounter*, xvi (April 1960); together with the correspondence on the subject in that periodical in the issues of April and May 1960.

of literary criticism to dispute people's opinions of other people's opinions on sex: but considering what Lawrence had set out to do in his novel, it is a remarkably mature,[4] well-written and eminently successful work. And if it cannot be ranked with *The Rainbow* or *Women in Love*, it is not because it is not an artistic success, but because it is strictly limited in its range, and is not exploratory in nature in the sense in which Lawrence's best novels are.

[4] A comparison with Lawrence's second novel, *The Trespasser*, is instructive. Both novels, in the main, treat of a similarly limited theme; yet anyone who reads them both cannot fail to see how much more mature, meaningful, and better in every respect the later novel is.

IX

Conclusion

To be alive, to be man alive, to be whole man alive: that is the point. And at its best, the novel, and the novel supremely, can help you.[1]

THE exploratory nature of Lawrence's novels makes them the central and most significant part of his achievement as a writer. Taken together they can be said to constitute an "unpremeditated spiritual autobiography". Each of the novels is a complete and coherent work of art in itself; yet also gains in significance when seen as part of a larger pattern. However, Lawrence's vision of life, as embodied in his fiction, does not have a fixed, static, rounded-off form; it is a developing vision, livingly and changingly revealed in the novels as it took shape in his creative imagination. It is in this sense that Lawrence's novels are a record of his "life-and-thought adventure". They tell the story of the development of his soul; of his "profoundest experiences in the self" brought to the level of consciousness and expressed in artistic terms, so that what is revealed to us is far more valuable and meaningful than a mere direct account of a writer's "personal" life. The "desires, aspirations and struggles" dramatised in the novels are not just Lawrence's own; they reflect the desires, aspirations, and struggles of a large section of humanity.

Lawrence held the view that the soul comes into being not at birth, but in the midst of life; that it is "something which must be developed and fulfilled throughout a life-time, sustained and nourished, developed and further fulfilled, to the very end".[2] This development is possible only through a vivid relatedness between the individual and the circumambient universe, because no individual being can be fully itself until "opened in the bloom of pure relationship . . . to the entire

[1] "Why the Novel Matters", *Phoenix*, pp. 537-8.   [2] *S.L.C.*, p. 249.

living cosmos".[3] The story of the soul's development is, therefore, told in terms of relationships; and all Lawrence's novels
are, basically, artistically organised revelations of "the changing
rainbow of our living relationships". It is the exploration, and
depiction, of these relationships and the conflicts in them, which
gives the novels the supreme value they have for us: they reveal
to us what we in our living, developing selves are; and by
doing that help, or can help us live fully and livingly. ("To be
alive, to be man alive, to be whole man alive", as Lawrence
puts it in the essay "Why the Novel Matters".)

The first two novels make the initial general statement that
the flesh and the spirit, the mind and the body, need to be
brought into a harmonious balance in us. *Sons and Lovers*,
which develops this theme specifically, gives an account of the
first important stage in man's struggle to attain "wholeness of
being": the novel ends with Paul's determined move towards
independent manhood. At the end of the next novel, *The
Rainbow*, we see Ursula awaiting her fulfilment in the "new
world" which she hopes will soon come into being. The new
world, however, never comes as Lawrence's vision of it as an
immediate practical possibility is destroyed by the war. In
Women in Love, therefore, the fulfilment attained is only partial:
as far as man-woman relationship is concerned, Birkin's
relation to Ursula is shown to be more or less complete and
satisfactory: but having made his marriage the centre of his
life he also wants an additional relationship of friendship with
another man. Exploration of the nature and purpose of man-
to-man relationship forms the main theme of the three important
novels that follow—*Aaron's Rod*, *Kangaroo*, and *The Plumed
Serpent*.

The essentially religious or creative motive, Lawrence
believed, is the first motive of all human activity. Man lives
"from an inherent sense of purpose": the desire for collective
purposive activity, the desire to make, with other men, "a little
new way into the future", is man's ultimate and greatest desire.
"Primarily and supremely man is *always* the pioneer of life,
adventuring onward into the unknown . . .".[4] Therefore,
having deeply fulfilled himself in marriage, a man must take the

---

[3] *R.D.P.*, p. 211.   [4] *Fantasia*, p. 106.

next step of participating in some "purposive activity" with the
aim of "making a new world". Fulfilment in marriage is only
a preparation for new responsibilities ahead, though a necessary
preparation; for no purposive passion can endure for any
length of time unless it is based upon the sexual fulfilment of
the vast majority of individuals concerned. At the same time
there can be no successful sex union unless the greater hope of
passionate purposive activity "fires the soul of man all the
time":

> It cuts both ways. Assert sex as the predominant fulfilment,
> and you get the collapse of living purpose in man. You get
> anarchy. Assert *purposiveness* as the one supreme and pure
> activity of life, and you drift into barren sterility.... You have
> got to base your great purposive activity upon the intense
> sexual fulfilment of all your individuals.[5]

The relationship between men engaged in impersonal,
purposive activity (and the nature of this activity itself) is the
subject of experiment in the novels which follow *Women in Love*.
In that novel the relationship proposed was some kind of
Blutbrüderschaft. Lilly, in *Aaron's Rod*, suggests that man-to-man
relationship might be the submission of one man to the "heroic
soul in a greater man". *Kangaroo* rejects both these bases of
male companionship, just as it also rejects collective activity
for the possession of political power as a desirable form of
passionate purposive activity, on the ground that such political
activity disregards the individual soul in man. In *The Plumed
Serpent* Lawrence makes a more ambitious attempt to test
through his imaginative work the acceptability of collective
"religious" action, but even this is not a success. All experi-
ments in these novels obviously end in failures. Lawrence is
plainly unable to visualise any collective activity for men which
should at the same time safeguard the individual soul in each
man. The suggestion put forward in *Lady Chatterley's Lover* that
the basis of relationship between men would be "reciprocity of
tenderness" remains a vaguely realised concept, for neither
Mellors nor Lawrence is in a position to say how the fight
against "Mammon" and "mechanised greed" is to be waged.
Lawrence remains to the end convinced of man's inherent need

[5] *Op. cit.*, p. 108.

to make a collective effort for the creation of a new and better world, but apparently cannot find any positive answer to the question what form this purposive activity is to take. The question is still with us, and will continue to be the passionate concern of all those who care for the future of mankind but are not totally and uncritically committed to any of the current political philosophies. We have yet to devise a form of social organisation where men can act collectively for the creation of a better future for mankind, and yet remain individuals with souls of their own. Even Lawrence's "negative and despairing social vision", as Middleton Murry has remarked, "was essentially more honest and, in truth, more inspiring than that of those, whether capitalists, or socialists, or communists, who believe, or act as though they believed, that the machine will itself produce the millennium. They utterly ignore the prodigious difficulty of bringing into being a society of men who can use the machine without being dehumanised by it."[6]

Linked with Lawrence's recognition of man's need for collective activity is his realisation that there must also be separate individuality: "Man must act in concert with man, creatively and happily. This is greatest happiness. But man must also act separately and distinctly, apart from every other man, single and self-responsible. . . . These two movements are opposite, yet they do not negate each other."[7] Lawrence himself, as Aldous Huxley has also pointed out, alternated between these two movements: as he travelled round the world after the war he felt "drawn towards his fellows and then repelled again";[8] he would make up his mind to force himself into some relation with society, and would then withdraw into himself again. These two opposite movements—his desire to be associated with other men in some meaningful activity, some form of struggle to change the world, and his inability to do so on his own terms—are clearly reflected in the following excerpts from his letters:

> More and more I feel that meditation and the inner life are not my aim, but some sort of action and strenuousness and pain and frustration and struggling through. (2 Jan. 1922.)

---

[6] *Love, Freedom and Society*, pp. 115-6.   [7] *Phoenix*, p. 156.
[8] *Collected Letters*, II, p. 1267.

Perhaps it is necessary for me to try these places, perhaps it is my destiny to know the world. . . . It is all a form of running away from oneself and the great problems: all this wild west and the strange Australia. But I try to keep quite clear. (29 Sept. 1922.)

I also fight to put something through. But it is a long, slow, dark, almost invisible fight. (8 Nov. 1923.)

I should love to be connected with something, with some few people, in something. As far as anything *matters*, I have always been very much alone, and regretted it. But I can't belong to clubs, or societies, or Freemasons, or any other damn thing. So if there is, with you, an activity I *can* belong to, I shall thank my stars. But, of course, I shall be wary beyond words of committing myself. (?22 Jul. 1926.)

What ails me is the absolute frustration of my primeval societal instinct. . . . I think societal instinct much deeper than sex instinct—and societal repression much more devastating. There is no repression of the sexual individual comparable to the repression of the societal man in me, by the individual ego, my own and everybody else's. I am weary even of my own individuality, and simply nauseated by other people's. (13 Jul. 1927.)

At times, one is *forced* to be essentially a hermit. I don't want to be. But anything else is either a personal tussle, or a money tussle: sickening: except, of course, just for ordinary acquaintance, which remains acquaintance. One has no real human relations—that is so devastating. (3 Aug. 1927.)

The whole scheme of things is unjust and rotten, and money is just a disease upon humanity. It is time there was an *enormous* revolution—not to install Soviets, but to give life itself a chance. What's the good of an industrial system piling up rubbish, while nobody lives. We want a revolution not in the name of money or work or any of that, but of life—and let money and work be as casual in human life as they are in a bird's life, damn it all. Oh it's time the whole thing was changed, absolutely. And the men will have to do it—you've got to smash money and this beastly *possessive* spirit. I get more revolutionary every minute, but for *life's* sake. (28 Dec. 1928.)

If one is a man, one must fight, and slap back at one's enemies, because they are the enemies of life. And if one can't slap the

life-enemies in the eye, one must try to kick their behinds—a
sacred duty. (7 Feb. 1929.)

You will see, the future will bring big changes—and I hope one
day we may all live in touch with one another, away from
business and all that sort of world, and really have a *new* sort of
happiness together. (22 Feb. 1929.)

By this time Lawrence was convinced that there must come a
change in the social system, sooner or later, not merely because
conditions change, but because people themselves change. As
new feelings arise in men, new values also emerge. He hoped
that the whole industrial system, with its "money arrangement"
and "the awful fight for money", would change for the better
and give way to a society where life, work, property, human
relations—all would be different. He was, however, sceptical
of revolutionary changes in the social structure which leave
men inside themselves the same as before. Also, he believed,
"it is change in feelings which makes changes in the world".[9]
As a writer, he realised, his primary interest lay in revealing
through his novels what people are "inside themselves":

> As a novelist, I feel it is the change inside the individual
> which is my real concern. The great social change interests me
> and troubles me, but it is not my field. I know a change is
> coming—and I know we must have a more generous, more
> human system based on the life values and not on money
> values. That I know. But what steps to take I don't know.
> Other men know better.
>
> My field is to know the feelings inside a man, and to make
> new feelings conscious.[10]

It needed all the gifts of a Lawrence to make these new feelings
articulate and to give them an artistic expression in the novels.
It is a distinctive sign of his greatness that he proved equal to
the demands this extremely difficult task makes on the linguistic, intellectual and imaginative resources of a writer.
Tributes to Lawrence's "extremely acute intelligence" (A.
Huxley) have been paid by many; but we should not overlook
the fact that his "supreme intelligence" (F. R. Leavis) was
developed to this high degree not in the abstract or, as it were,

---

[9] *Assorted Articles.* London (1930), p. 55.   [10] *S.L.C.*, p. 137.

for its own sake. He also knew how to make the best use of this intelligence. Lawrence's own comment on this subject, made while answering some of his "Accumulated Mail", is worth quoting:

> Another friend and critic: "Lawrence is an artist, but his intellect is not up to his art."
> You might as well say: Mr Lawrence rides a horse but he doesn't wear his stirrups round his neck. And the accusation is just. Because he hopes to heaven he is riding a horse that is alive of itself, not a wooden hobbyhorse suitable for the nursery.
> —And he does his best to keep his feet in the stirrups, and to leave his intellect under his hat, when he is riding his naughty steed. No, my dears! I guess, as an instrument, my intellect is as good as yours. But instead of sitting in my own wheelbarrow (the intellect is a sort of wheelbarrow about the place) and whipping it ecstatically over the head, I just wheel out what dump I've got, and forget the old barrow again, till next time.[11]

Lawrence attempted to present in his novels the totality of human experience in all its complexity and depth. The novels tell the story of "whole man alive" in terms of his living relationships; and the form and style employed are governed by the novelist's purpose of revealing his vision of life conceived as a series of relationships, with all the conflicts involved. Lawrence did not suffer from any obsession for "form". Each work of art, he believed, has its own form which is unrelated to any other form. He, therefore, refused to imitate earlier writers, the "damned old stagers": "They want me to have form: that means, they want me to have *their* pernicious ossiferous skin-and-grief form, and I won't."[12] Lawrence's novels have a definite organic form, but it is a form of their own. Lawrence, as Richard Aldington has noted, "at the very beginning of his career . . . had scrapped all the heavy pedantry about the art and craft of fiction, form in the novel and so forth, which were then—and for all I know still are—fashionable among self-appointed critics."[13] The plots of his novels are not made up of external events; it is the inner experience and

---

[11] *Phoenix*, p. 805.   [12] *Collected Letters*, i, p. 172.
[13] *Portrait of a Genius, But . . .*, London (1950), p. 95.

conflicts in relationships portrayed which give them their unity and organisation. Similarly, his interest was in the *relationships* of his characters, not in their personalities—whatever the number of dimensions critics might look for, or find, in them. He uses a repetitious style because, he says, it comes naturally to him. It is not difficult to see the appropriateness of this style to the kind of experiences he wanted to communicate through his prose.

> It is a psychological fact, that when we are thinking emotionally or passionately, thinking and feeling at the same time, we do not think rationally: and therefore, and therefore, and therefore. Instead, the mind makes curious swoops and circles. It touches the point of pain or interest, then sweeps away again in a cycle, coils round and approaches again the point of interest. There is a curious spiral rhythm, and the mind approaches again the point of concern, repeats itself, goes back, . . . yet again turns, bends, circles slowly, swoops and stoops again, until at last there is the closing-in, and the clutch of a decision or a resolve.[14]

Lawrence's "incantatory prose" might be said to have the quality of reaching the whole of our consciousness: its appeal is to our emotions as well as to our intellect. The continual, slightly modified repetition[15] used in the novels has an important function which should not be lost sight of. Those who object to Lawrence's use of incremental repetition need only try and re-write a typical Lawrentian passage in plain, concise prose to realise how much the language loses in the process.

To appreciate any of the mature novels of Lawrence one must begin by recognising that his main theme was not life as it is lived on the surface, but life in its undercurrents. If we sometimes get the impression that his characters occasionally act or feel in a way we have not normally known ourselves or others to act or feel in life, this might be because not all of us can ordinarily know what goes on in the "deep passional soul" —which is what Lawrence sought to make conscious and

---

[14] *Phoenix*, pp. 249-50.
[15] The influence of the English Bible on Lawrence's prose style is much too obvious and well known to need mention here.

articulate in his writings. His art "discovers" for us "a new world within the known world". It gives a new meaning to our life and our experience. Lawrence's achievement as a writer has, in the last fifty years, been highly acclaimed, among many others, by Katherine Mansfield ("the only writer living whom I profoundly care for"), E. M. Forster ("the greatest imaginative novelist of our generation"), J. M. Murry ("the most significant writer of his time"), Harry T. Moore ("one of the richest reading experiences of our time"), and F. R. Leavis ("one of the greatest novelists" "a creative writer of the greatest kind"). To say now that in the present writer's opinion Lawrence is among the greatest of all novelists, and the most important English writer of this century, would be merely adding one more view to the long list referred to above. Perhaps a judgement of that sort is best left to each individual reader; what one can do, in conclusion, is to point again to the evidence on which all claims are based—to the novels themselves. They are by no means "perfect". Let us hope no one is going to tell us they are. Their imperfections are a part of their strength; their unfinished nature itself contributes to their greatness. Lawrence, as he put it himself in one of his letters (quoted above, on p. 7), did not "care a button" for neat works of art, finished and complete in all respects. He averred:

> A book should be either a bandit or a rebel or a man in a crowd. People should either run for their lives, or come under the colours, or say *how do you do*? . . . An author should be in among the crowd, kicking their shins or cheering on to some mischief or merriment. . . . And art, especially novels, are not like theatres where the reader sits aloft and watches—like a god with a twenty-lira ticket—and sighs, commiserates, condones and smiles.—That's what you want a book to be: because it leaves you so safe and so superior, with your two-dollar ticket to the show. And that's what my books are not and never will be. You need not complain that I don't subject the intensity of my vision—or whatever it is—to some vast and imposing rhythm—by which you mean, isolate it on a stage, so that you can look down on it like a god who has got a ticket to the show. I never will: and you will never have that satisfaction from me. . . . whoever reads me will be in the thick of

the scrimmage, and if he doesn't like it—if he wants a safe seat in the audience—let him read somebody else.[16]

It is not as rounded-off, static, "immortal" works of art, but only in as much as they are living, moving "bright book[s] of life" which are going to "help us to live, as nothing else can" that Lawrence's novels can have the supreme importance they have for us.

[16] *Collected Letters*, II, pp. 826-7.

"The Night of Sensual Passion" in *Lady Chatterley's Lover*

The most painstakingly and cogently argued case for the *penetratio per anum* reading[1] has been presented by John Sparrow.[2] Mr Sparrow puts together Connie's reaction on receiving Clifford's letter in Venice, Duncan Forbes' comment, and Clifford's later remarks on Bertha Coutts' accusations against Mellors, and gives the verdict that what had seemed "a reasonable guess" to Andrew Shonfield[3]— that Connie was made a victim of anal perversion on the night of sensual passion—can be "shown conclusively" to be "an absolute certainty"; and that Lawrence "himself approved of the practice in question". Colin McInnes's retort in his Reply to Sparrow (even if all available evidence points out[4] that Lawrence himself most probably would not have shared this view) seems an eminently apt one. He says:

> The human bodies of both sexes being constructed, by nature's wisdom, as they are, it seems likely, to say the least, that all sexual possibilities and permutations among men and women are practised, always have been, and always will be. Even a superficial knowledge of sexual customs in the past, and of those today in the most diverse lands, suggests this is a basic fact of nature which no opinion (still less any law) will alter much.[5]

But when he goes on to say that "the Warden's [Mr Sparrow's]

[1] See above, pp. 283-4.

[2] *Encounter*, Feb. 1962, pp. 35-43. Mr. Sparrow avers it is not his purpose to criticise *Lady Chatterley's Lover*, yet cannot refrain from twice making the pronouncement that it is a failure as a work of art (pp. 36, 43).

[3] *Encounter*, Sep. 1961, p. 64.

[4] See Lawrence's condemnation of "dirt lust"; and the sharp distinction that the "really healthy human being", he points out, instinctively makes between "the sex functions and the excrementory functions" (*S.L.C.*, p. 205). *Cf.* Mellors' low opinion of women who "make you go off when you're *not* in the only place you should be, when you go off". (p. 187.)

[5] "Experts on Trial: A Comment on Mr Sparrow", *Encounter*, xviii (March 1962), p. 63.

judgement is impeccable", he is almost certainly mistaken. Andrew Shonfield had partly based his argument on the following passage:

> She [Connie] had often wondered what Abélard meant, when he said that in their year of love he and Heloïse had passed through all the stages and refinements of passion. The same thing, a thousand years ago: ten thousand years ago! The same on the Greek vases, everywhere! The refinements of passion, the extravagances of sensuality! And necessary, forever necessary, to burn out false shames and smelt out the heaviest ore of the body into purity. With the fire of sheer sensuality.[6]

When some correspondents, replying to Sparrow, doubted if references to Abélard and to Greek vases could possibly bear a construction agreeing with his interpretation of the episode, John Sparrow replied:

> Several critics have (no doubt innocently) mis-represented my argument by suggesting that I relied on references in Lawrence's text to "Greek vases" and to the works of Abélard. These ambiguous references prove nothing, and they formed no link in my chain of reasoning. (I may add that the reference to Cellini, though unequivocal, does not, as some have supposed, of itself prove the case; what is decisive is that reference taken in conjunction with Lady Chatterley's reception of the letter that contained it.)[7]

Mr Sparrow had no doubt forged a "chain of proof" which, at least to his own thinking, was "complete and irrefragable". And he was, not unexpectedly, reassured when he discovered that no one had "even attempted to pick a hole in the *nexus* of reasoning" by which he had reached his conclusion. But was there any need really for anyone else to pick a hole, when Mr Sparrow had done it himself, and done it so well! What is decisive, he says, is the reference to Cellini "taken in conjunction with Lady Chatterley's reception of the letter that contained it". And what *is* Lady Chatterley's reaction to the letter that contains this reference? If one might trust the text of the novel itself, Connie's reception of the letter is

---

[6] Though only God knows what Mr Shonfield had seen on the Greek vases. We, at any rate, are not told. Perhaps his own "other censor" prevented him from making public his valuable discoveries. As to Abélard and Heloïse, it should be amusing to hear someone argue that their "refinements of passion" are to be construed to refer to "the practice . . . known in English law as buggery".

[7] *Encounter*, xviii (June 1962), p. 84.

described in these words: "The irritation, and the lack of any sympathy in any direction, of Clifford's letter, had a bad effect on Connie."[8] What exactly, one wonders, does Mr Sparrow want to prove by this! And if he has in mind Connie's reaction to an earlier letter from Clifford,[9] he forgets that while we as readers can relate one part of the novel to another, Connie, living in Venice, had no other source of information, and cannot be expected to have fore-knowledge of the reference to Benvenuto Cellini in Clifford's subsequent letter. Also, we are told that Connie reacts to the earlier letter in that manner because she has fallen into "a state of funk",[10] from which she soon recovers, and thinks thus of Mellors: "What had he done, after all? what had he done to herself, Connie, but give her an exquisite pleasure and a sense of freedom and life? He had released her warm, natural sexual flow."[11] Moreover, is the reference to Cellini and "the Italian way" as "unequivocal" as has been claimed? Mr Sparrow quotes from the original Italian, but the excerpts he gives can have a quite different meaning when read in their context. One cannot ignore the fact that it is a false charge brought against Cellini by his mistress, on the advice of a lawyer; and that when he is accused of having used Caterina "in the Italian manner", his reply is: "If I have done so, it was only because I wished to have a son like the rest of you."[12] When it is explained by the judge that "the accusation was quite other", his retort is that in that case, since Caterina "knew more about it than I", they must be talking of some French custom rather than an Italian one. It is obvious that what "Benvenuto Cellini says", and what he understands by "the Italian way" (". . . I wished to have a son like the rest of you.") is not quite what we have been led to suppose that he does: it might very well be, as Clifford says, just a question of "unusual sexual postures". (Though Mr Sparrow imagines he has "conclusively disproved" this!) Duncan Forbes's statement about Mellors' having made love to his wife "all ends on", in the same manner, cannot be said to be unequivocal. All this, it

---

[8] *Lady Chatterley's Lover*, p. 249.

[9] "Connie remembered the last night she had spent with him, and shivered. He had known all that sensuality, even with a Bertha Coutts! It was really rather disgusting. It would be well to be rid of him, clear of him altogether. He was perhaps really common, really low". (p. 247.)

[10] *Op. cit.*, p. 244.   [11] *Ibid.*

[12] *The Life of Benvenuto Cellini*, tr. Anne Macdonell (London, 1903), II, p. 57. J. A. Symonds' translation, to which Mr Sparrow at this point refers, is not helpful. In *La Vita di Benvenuto Cellini*, per cura de B. Bianchi (Firenze, 1852), the words are: "Allora io dissi: se io avessi usato seco al modo Italiano, l'arei [l'avrei?] fatto solo per d'avere un figliuolo, si come fate voi altri" (p. 343).

might be added, is not intended to "prove" anything. The point, in itself, notwithstanding the space that has been given to it here for the reasons stated on pp. 283-4, does not deserve all the importance that has been attached to it. (Besides, we must not forget that what we are actually dealing with is Connie's understanding of Clifford's version of a third person's report of Bertha Coutts's alleged accusation against Mellors.) But since so much has been made of "a complete exposition of truth" in this matter, it is as well that "the full truth" be "made clear and brought home" to all concerned.

Select Bibliography

I. WORKS BY D. H. LAWRENCE

(A) LETTERS AND ESSAYS

Assorted Articles. London (Martin Secker) 1930.

The Collected Letters of D. H. Lawrence, ed. Harry T. Moore (2 vols). London (Heinemann) 1962.

Fantasia of the Unconscious and Psychoanalysis and the Unconscious, Phoenix Edition. London (Heinemann) 1961.

The Letters of D. H. Lawrence, ed. Aldous Huxley. London (Heinemann) 1956.

Phoenix: The Posthumous Papers of D. H. Lawrence, ed. Edward D. McDonald. London (Heinemann) 1961.

"Prologue to *Women in Love* (unpublished)", in *Texas Quarterly,* VI (1963), i, pp. 98-111.

Reflections on the Death of a Porcupine and Other Essays. Philadelphia (Centaur Press) 1925. Lonnon (Martin Secker) 1934.

Selected Literary Criticism, ed. Anthony Beal. London (Heinemann) 1956.

Sex, Literature and Censorship, ed. Harry T. Moore. London (Heinemann) 1955.

Studies in Classic American Literature, Phoenix Edition. London (Heinemann) 1964.

The Symbolic Meaning: The Uncollected Versions of "Studies in Classic American Literature", ed. Armin Arnold. London (Centaur Press) 1962.

(B) NOVELS AND SHORT STORIES

Unless otherwise noted, all works listed are in the Phoenix Edition (Heinemann).

Aaron's Rod. London 1954.

Apocalypse. Florence (G. Orioli) 1931. London (Martin Secker) 1932.

The Complete Short Stories (3 vols). London 1956.

Kangaroo. London 1955.

Lady Chatterley's Lover. London 1963.

The Lost Girl. London 1955.

Mornings in Mexico and Etruscan Places. London 1956.

The Plumed Serpent. London 1955.

The Rainbow. London 1955.

The Short Novels (2 vols.). London 1956.

Sons and Lovers. London 1956.

The Trespasser. London 1955.
Twilight in Italy, Pocket Edition. London (Heinemann) 1954.
The White Peacock. London 1955.
Women in Love. New York (Modern Library) n.d. London 1960.

(c) POEMS

The Complete Poems (3 vols.), Phoenix Edition. London (Heinemann) 1957.

II. BIOGRAPHICAL AND CRITICAL STUDIES

The Achievement of D. H. Lawrence, eds. Frederick J. Hoffman and Harry T. Moore. Norman (University of Oklahoma Press) 1953.
ALDINGTON, RICHARD. "A Wreath for Lawrence", in *Encounter*, XVI, iv (April 1960) pp. 51-4.
——. *Portrait of a Genius, But.* . . . London (Heinemann) 1950.
BEAL, ANTHONY. *D. H. Lawrence*, Writers and Critics Series. Edinburgh (Oliver & Boyd) 1961.
BEEBE, MAURICE. "Lawrence's Sacred Fount: The Artist Theme of *Sons and Lovers*", in *Texas Studies in Literature and Language*, IV, pp. 539-52.
BEEBE, MAURICE and TOMMASI, ANTHONY. "Criticism of D. H. Lawrence: A Selected Checklist with an Index to Studies of Separate Works", in *Modern Fiction Studies*, V, i (Spring 1959), pp. 83-98.
BRANDA, ELDONS. "Textual Changes in *Women in Love*", in *Texas Studies in Literature and Language*, VI (1964) pp. 306-21.
BREWSTER, EARL and ACHSAH. *D. H. Lawrence: Reminiscences and Correspondence.* London (Martin Secker) 1934.
BYNNER, WITTER. *Journey with Genius: Recollections and Reflections Concerning the D. H. Lawrences.* London (Peter Nevill) 1953.
CHAMBERLAIN, ROBERT L. "Pussum, Minette, and the Africo-Nordic Symbol in Lawrence's Women in Love", in *PMLA*, LXXVIII (1963) pp. 407-16.
CLARK, L. D. *Dark Night of the Body: D. H. Lawrence's "The Plumed Serpent".* Austin (University of Texas Press) 1964.
CLEMENTS, A. L. "The Quest for the Self: D. H. Lawrence's *The Rainbow*", in *Thoth* (University of Syracuse) III (1962) pp. 90-100.
DAICHES, DAVID. *The Novel and the Modern World.* Chicago (University Press) 1960.
DALESKI, H. M. *The Forked Flame: A Study of D. H. Lawrence.* London (Faber) 1965.
DAVIS, HERBERT. "*Women in Love*: a Corrected Typescript", in *University of Toronto Quartery*, XXVII (October 1957) pp. 34-53.
DRAPER, R. P. "Authority and the Individual: A Study of D. H. Lawrence's *Kangaroo*", in *The Critical Quarterly*, I, iii, pp. 208-15.
EMPSON, WILLIAM. "Lady Chatterley Again", in *Essays in Criticism*, XII (1963) pp. 101-4.

E. T. [JESSIE (CHAMBERS) WOOD]. *D. H. Lawrence: A Personal Record.* London (Cape) 1935.

FAHEY, WILLIAM A. "Lawrence's *The White Peacock*", in *The Explicator*, XVII, iii (1958) Item 17.

FORD, GEORGE H. "An Introductory Note to D. H. Lawrence's Prologue to *Women in Love*", in *Texas Quarterly*, VI, i (1963) pp. 92-7.

——. " 'The Wedding' Chapter of D. H. Lawrence's *Women in Love*", in *Texas Studies in Literature and Language*, VI, ii, (1964) pp. 134-47.

FREEMAN, MARY. *D. H. Lawrence: A Basic Study of His Ideas.* New York (Grosset & Dunlap) 1955.

GOLDBERG, S. L. "The Rainbow: Fiddle-Bow and Sand", in *Essays in Criticism*, XI (1961) pp. 418-34.

GOODHEART, EUGENE. *The Utopian Vision of D. H. Lawrence.* Chicago (University Press) 1963.

GREGORY, HORACE. *D. H. Lawrence: Pilgrim of the Apocalypse: A Critical Study of D. H. Lawrence.* London (Martin Secker) 1934. New York (Grove Press) 1957.

GURKO, LEO. "*The Trespasser*, D. H. Lawrence's Neglected Novel", in *College English*, XXIV, i (1962) pp. 29-35.

GUTTMANN, ALLEN. "D. H. Lawrence: The Politics of Irrationality", in *Wisconsin Studies in Contemporary Literature*, V (1964) pp. 151-63.

HOUGH, GRAHAM. *The Dark Sun: A Study of D. H. Lawrence.* London (Gerald Duckworth) 1956.

IDEMA, JAMES M. "The Hawk and the Plover: 'The Polarity of Life' in the 'Jungle Aviary' of D. H. Lawrence's Mind in *Sons and Lovers* and *The Rainbow*", in *Forum* (Houston, Texas) III, vii (1961) pp. 11-14.

JARRETT-KERR, MARTIN [TIVERTON, FATHER WILLIAM]. *D. H. Lawrence and Human Existence.* London (SCM Press) 1951.

KETTLE, ARNOLD. *An Introduction to the English Novel*, Vol. II. London (Arrow Books) 1962.

KAZIN, ALFRED. "Sons, Lovers and Mothers", in *Partisan Review*, XXIX, iii (1962) pp. 373-85.

KNIGHT, G. WILSON. "Lawrence, Joyce and Powys", in *Essays in Criticism*, XI, iv (1961) pp. 403-17.

LAINOFF, SEYMOUR. "The Rainbow: the Shaping of Modern Man", in *Modern Fiction Studies*, I, iv (1955) pp. 23-7.

A D. H. Lawrence Miscellany, ed. Harry T. Moore. Carbondale (Southern Illinois University Press) 1959.

D. H. Lawrence: A Collection of Critical Essays, ed. Mark Spilka. Englewood Cliffs, N.J. (Prentice-Hall) 1963.

LAWRENCE, FRIEDA. *The Memoirs and Correspondence*, ed. E. W. Tedlock. London (Heinemann) 1961.

LEAVIS, F. R. *D. H. Lawrence: Novelist.* London (Chatto & Windus) 1955.

——. " 'Lawrence Scholarship' and Lawrence", in the *Sewanee Review*, LXXI, i (1963) pp. 25-35.

——. In the *Times Literary Supplement*, 19 April 1957, p. 241.

McInnes, Colin. "Experts on Trial: A Comment on Mr. Sparrow", in *Encounter*, xviii (March 1962) pp. 63-5.

Moore, Harry T. *The Intelligent Heart*. London (Heinemann) 1955.

———. *The Life and Works of D. H. Lawrence*. London (Unwin Books) 1963.

Moynahan, Julian. *The Deed of Life: The Novels and Tales of D. H. Lawrence*. London (Oxford University Press) 1963.

Murry, J. Middleton. *Between Two Worlds*. London (Cape) 1935.

———. *Love, Freedom and Society*. London (Cape) 1957.

———. *Reminiscences of D. H. Lawrence*. London (Cape) 1933.

———. *Son of Woman*. London (Cape) 1931.

Nehls, Edward. *D. H. Lawrence: A Composite Biography* (3 vols.) Madison (University of Wisconsin) 1957-59.

Newman, Paul B. "D. H. Lawrence and the Golden Bough", in *Kansas Magazine* (1962) pp. 79-86.

Nicholes, E. L. "The 'Simile of the Sparrow' in *The Rainbow* by D. H. Lawrence." *Modern Language Notes*, lxiv (1949) pp. 171-4.

Nin, Anaïs. *D. H. Lawrence: An Unprofessional Study*. London (Spearman) 1961.

Panichas, George A. *Adventures in Consciousness: The Meaning of D. H. Lawrence's Religious Quest*. The Hague (Mouton) 1964.

Peter, John. "The Bottom of the Well", in *Essays in Criticism*, xii (1962) pp. 226-7; xiii (1963) pp. 301-2.

Porter, Katherine Anne. "A Wreath for the Gamekeeper", in *Encounter*, xvi, ii (February 1960) pp. 69-77.

Potter, Stephen. *D. H. Lawrence: A First Study*. London (Cape) 1930.

Read, Herbert. "On D. H. Lawrence", in *The Twentieth Century*, clxv (June 1959) pp. 556-66.

Robson, W. W. "D. H. Lawrence and *Women in Love*", in *The Modern Age*. Harmondsworth (Penguin Books) 1961.

Schorer, Mark. "Fiction with a Great Burden", in *The Kenyon Review*, xiv (Winter 1952) pp. 162-8.

Scott, Nathan A., Jr. *Rehearsals of Discomposure*. London (John Lehmann) 1952.

Sharpe, Michael C. "The Genesis of D. H. Lawrence's *The Trespasser*", in *Essays in Criticism*, xi (1961) pp. 34-9.

Shonfield, Andrew. "Lawrence's Other Censor", in *Encounter*, xvii (September 1961) pp. 63-4.

Sparrow, John. "Regina v. Penguin Books Ltd", in *Encounter*, xviii, ii (February 1962) pp. 35-43; xviii (June 1962) pp. 83-8.

———. in *Essays in Criticism*, xiii (1963) pp. 202-5, 303.

Spender, Stephen. *The Creative Element: A Study of Vision, Despair and Orthodoxy among some Modern Writers*. London (Peter Nevill) 1953.

———. *The Destructive Element: A Study of Modern Writers and Beliefs*. London (Cape) 1935.

Spilka, Mark. *The Love Ethic of D. H. Lawrence*. Bloomington (Indiana University Press) 1955.

SPILKA, MARK. "Was D. H. Lawrence a Symbolist?", in *Accent* (Winter 1955) pp. 49-60.

STEWART, J. I. M. *Eight Modern Writers*. Oxford (Clarendon Press) 1963.

TEDLOCK, E. W., Jr. *D. H. Lawrence: Artist and Rebel*. Albuquerque (University of New Mexico Press) 1963.

——. *The Frieda Lawrence Collection of D. H. Lawrence Manuscripts*. Albuquerque (University of New Mexico Press) 1948.

TINDALL, WILLIAM YORK. *D. H. Lawrence and Susan His Cow*. New York (Columbia University Press) 1939.

TIVERTON, FATHER WILLIAM. See under Jarrett-Kerr.

TRILLING, DIANA. "A letter of Introduction to Lawrence", in *Partisan Review*, xxv, i (Winter 1958) pp. 32-48.

VAN GHENT, DOROTHY. *The English Novel: Form and Function*. New York (Rinehart) 1953.

VICKERY, JOHN B. "*The Plumed Serpent* and the Eternal Paradox", in *Criticism*, v (1963) pp. 119-34.

VIVAS, ELISEO. *D. H. Lawrence: The Failure and the Triumph of Art*. London (Allen and Unwin) 1961.

WEISS, DANIEL A. *Oedipus in Nottingham: D. H. Lawrence*. Seattle (University of Washington Press) 1962.

WELCH, COLIN. "Black Magic, White Lies", in *Encounter* (February 1961) pp. 75-9.

WEST, ANTHONY. *D. H. Lawrence*, The Novelists Series. London (Arthur Barker) 1957.

WIDMER, KINGSLEY. *The Art of Perversity: D. H. Lawrence's Shorter Fictions*. Seattle (University of Washington Press) 1962.

Index

UNDONE BY THE
BILLIONAIRE
DUKE

UNDONE BY THE BILLIONAIRE DUKE

BY

CAITLIN CREWS

MILLS & BOON

First published in Great Britain 2017
by Mills & Boon, an imprint of HarperCollins*Publishers*
1 London Bridge Street, London, SE1 9GF

Large Print edition 2018

© 2017 Caitlin Crews

ISBN: 978-0-263-07335-5

This book is produced from independently certified FSC™
paper to ensure responsible forest management. For more
information visit www.harpercollins.co.uk/green.

Printed and bound in Great Britain
by CPI Group (UK) Ltd, Croydon, CR0 4YY

To Maisey Yates and Nicole Helm
for encouraging my flights of fancy—like
rearing horses and billowing cloaks...oh, my!

CHAPTER ONE

ELEANOR ANDREWS WAS certain that she could handle the likes of Hugo Grovesmoor, and no matter that no one had ever quite managed to do so before in living memory. As the papers shrieked daily, the Twelfth Duke of Grovesmoor was not only known to be a terrible villain in every salacious way imaginable, he was *impossible*. Too wealthy. Too full of himself. And worse still, so appallingly and egregiously handsome that he'd essentially been born spoilt through, and had only descended further from there.

Into pure, hedonistic, and ruinous devilry. Usually with pictures.

And Eleanor was delivering herself directly into his clutches.

"Don't be so dramatic," her younger sister Vivi said with a sigh, sending her long and lively brunette curls slithering this way and that every time she exhaled. When all Eleanor had done was express the tiniest hint of concern about her brand-new role as governess to the poor seven-year-old in notorious Hugo's care.

As occasionally trying as Vivi was—and if Eleanor was honest with herself, it was more *often* than *occasionally*—Eleanor couldn't help but love her. Desperately. Vivi was all she had left after their parents had been killed years ago in the tragic car accident that had nearly claimed young Vivi's life, as well. Eleanor never forgot how close she'd come to losing Vivi, too.

"I don't think I was being dramatic at all," Eleanor replied. She chose not to point out that the opera heroine histrionics were usually Vivi's department. Surely that went without saying.

Vivi was addressing Eleanor through the mirror in the bedroom of the tiny, crowded, so-called "one-bedroom" flat they shared in one of London's less fashionable neighborhoods. The "one bedroom" in question being the space on the far side of a bookcase in the long room with a cramped kitchenette slung beneath the eaves on the other end. Vivi was applying a third, slick layer of mascara to her lashes, the better to emphasize the eyes one of her many boyfriends had once called *as warm and bright as new gold.* Eleanor had heard him—as had half the street in the village where they'd grown up as their distant cousin's charity cases after their parents had been killed and Vivi had finally gotten out of the hospital—given that the poor sod had been shouting it toward Vivi's window long after the pubs had closed, as pissed as he was poetic.

Vivi lowered the mascara wand and rolled said *new gold eyes.* "You won't actually *see* Hugo. You're going to be the governess of his ward who, let's face it, he can't possibly like that much. Given all that messy history. Why would he give either one of you the time of day?"

A dismissive wave of her hand encompassed all the salacious details everyone knew about Hugo Grovesmoor, thanks to the fascination the tabloids had always had with him.

Eleanor knew the three main points as well as anyone. The dramatic on-and-off relationship with beloved society darling Isobel Vanderhaven, whom everyone had been certain Hugo would ruin with his shocking brand of commit-

ted wickedness that even Isobel's innate goodness couldn't cure. The way Isobel had left him
for good when pregnant with his best friend's
Torquil's child, because, everyone agreed, love
had finally triumphed over wickedness and Isobel deserved better. And Isobel's celebrated marriage to and subsequent tragic boating accident
with said former best friend, which had resulted
in famously reluctant Hugo being named the legal
guardian of the child whose very existence had
wrecked his chances with the lovely Isobel forever.

All this while the nation jeered, applauded, and
mourned in turn, as if they knew all of these people and their pain personally.

"A man as rich as Hugo is dripping in properties and can't be expected to visit even half of
them in the course of a year. Or even five years,"
Vivi said with the same nonchalance, and Eleanor reminded herself that her sister would know.

After all, Vivi was the one who'd spent time
with Hugo Grovesmoor's sort of people. She
was the one who'd attended the posh schools
and while she hadn't exactly distinguished her-

self academically, she'd certainly had a sparkling social calendar that had carried over to her life in London. It was all in service to the glittering marriage they were both certain Vivi would manage to score any day now.

Vivi was eighteen months younger than Eleanor and the beauty of the pair of them. She had the sort of slim-hipped, smoky-eyed, lush-mouthed prettiness that left men struck dumb when they beheld her. Literally. Her wild curls gave the impression she'd just rolled out of someone's bed. Her just-wicked-enough smile hinted that she was up for any and all adventures and suggested that if a man played his cards right, that bed could be his.

And to think that after the accident, the doctors had doubted she'd ever walk again!

Vivi had proven herself to be more or less catnip for a certain sort of man. Usually one endowed with a great many estates and a bank account to match, even if, so far, she hadn't quite managed to break out of the "potential mistress" box.

Eleanor, on the other hand, went to very few

parties while working at least one job and sometimes more, when things got rough. Because
while Vivi was the pretty one, Eleanor had always been the sensible one. And while she'd had
her moments of wishing she, too, could have been
as effortlessly charming and undeniably pretty
as her sister, Eleanor was twenty-seven now and
had come to a place of peace with her role in life.
They'd lost their parents and Eleanor couldn't
bring them back. She couldn't change the many
years of hospitals and surgeries that Vivi had survived. But she could take on a bit of a parental
role with Vivi. She could hold down decent jobs
and pay their bills.

Well. Vivi's bills. There was no point gussy-
ing up Eleanor in the sort of slinky, breathtak-
ingly expensive clothes Vivi had to have to blend
in with her highbrow friends—and *that sort of
thing* required money. Money Eleanor had always
made, one way or another.

This latest job—as governess to the most hated
man in England—would be the most lucrative
yet. It was why Eleanor had resigned from her
current position as a front desk receptionist at

a bustling architecture firm. Vivi had been the one to hear of the governess position through her high-flying set of friends, since men like the Duke did not exactly pin up adverts in the local pub. More important, she'd heard what the Duke intended to pay his governess. It was so much more than all the other jobs Eleanor had taken—combined—that she hardly dared do the math, lest it make her dizzy.

"The rumor is the Duke has dismissed all the governesses he's been sent. Being a distraction is apparently the top reason for getting sacked and, well..."

Vivi had shrugged with a regret that had not struck Eleanor as being entirely sincere. Her small, perfect, perky breasts had moved enticingly behind the filmy little silk dress she'd worn to some or other desperately fashionable soirée that evening, as if in an approving chorus.

"But you *might just be perfect!"*

The sleek agency that had handled the interview had agreed, and here Eleanor was, packing up her case for the trip into the wilds of the Yorkshire moors to what had to be the most overwrought of all the ducal properties in England. Groves House, as the sprawling dark mansion was quaintly called as if it wasn't large enough to merit its own postal code, had been looming over its vast swathe of the brooding moors for centuries.

"A governess is a lowly member of his household staff, Eleanor," Vivi was saying now, with another eye roll. "Not a guest. It's highly unlikely you'll encounter Hugo Grovesmoor at all."

That was more than fine with Eleanor. She was immune to star power and the sense of self-importance that went along with it. She told herself so all the way up on the train the next morning as it hurtled at high speeds toward deepest Yorkshire.

She hadn't gone to the north of England since she was a child and their parents had still been alive. Eleanor had vague memories of traipsing about the walls that surrounded the ancient city of York in a chilly summer fog, with no idea, then, how quickly everything would change.

But there was no point heading down that sort of sentimental road now, she told herself sternly as she waited in the brisk October cold at the York rail station for one of the slower, more infrequent local trains out into the far reaches of the countryside. Life went on. That was just what it did, wholly heedless and uncaring.

No matter what anyone might have lost along the way.

When Eleanor arrived at the tiny little train station in remote Grovesmoor Village, she expected to be met as planned. But the train platform in the middle of nowhere was empty. There was nothing but Eleanor, the blustering October wind, and the remains of the morning's fog. Not exactly an encouraging beginning.

Eleanor cast a bit of a grim eye at the case she'd packed with what she'd thought she'd need for the first six weeks she'd agreed to spend at Groves House without any break. It was only the one case. Vivi needed to travel with bags upon bags, but then again, she had a *wardrobe*. Eleanor had no such problems. And no excuses. It took a second or two to pull up a map on her mobile and find it was a twenty-to-thirty-minute walk to the only stately manor in the area. Groves House.

"Best set off, then," she muttered to herself.

She heaved her heavy shoulder bag higher up on her shoulder, grabbed the handle of her roller bag and tugged on it, and strode off with every confidence in the world. Or every appearance of confidence, anyway, she amended when she walked for five minutes down the road only to realize she should have headed in the opposite direction, away from the quaint little town arranged on either side of a slow river.

Once headed in the right direction, Eleanor tried to channel Maria Von Trapp as she trudged along the lonely country road that wound further and further into the fog and the gloom. She marched on, aware of her breathing in the otherwise still afternoon and very little else. She'd lived so long in the hectic rush of London now that she'd almost forgotten the particular quiet of country lane, particularly one that seemed to be swallowed up by moors in all directions and peaks here and there that she expected would have names. If only she'd researched them.

She found the turnoff for Groves House between two stone pillars and started up the drive.

It wound about just as much as the road had, and was only differentiated from the lane she'd left behind by its absence of hedges and proper stone walls. And its slight incline straddled by lines of stout and watchful trees. She'd lost track of how many turns she'd taken and how far she'd gone from the road when she looked out in front of her and saw the house at last.

Nothing could have prepared her.

The house loomed there on the far ridge. It was rambling, yes, a jumble of stone and self-importance, but none of the pictures she'd seen had done it justice. There was something about it that made a raw sort of lump catch there in her throat. There was something about the way its interior lights scraped at the gloomy afternoon that seemed to speak to her, though she couldn't think why.

She found she couldn't look away.

It was not a welcoming house. It was not a *house* at all, for that matter. It was much too large and starkly forbidding. And yet somehow, as it gleamed there against the fall night as if daring the dark to do its worst, the only word that echoed inside Eleanor's head was *perfect*.

Something rang in her then, low and long, like a bell.

She didn't know why she couldn't seem to catch her breath when she started walking again, her case seeming heavier in her grip as she headed further up the hill.

And that was when she heard the thunder of hoof beats, bearing down on her.

Like fate.

His Grace the Duke of Grovesmoor, known to what few friends he had left and the overly familiar press as Hugo, found fewer and fewer things cleared his head these days. Drink made his skull hurt. Extreme sports had lost their thrill now that his death would mean the end of the Grovesmoor line of succession after untold centuries, tossing the whole dukedom into the hands of grasping, far-removed cousins who'd been salivating over the ducal properties and attendant income for perhaps the entire sweep of its history.

Even indiscriminate sex, once his favorite

go-to for obliteration on a grand scale, had lost its charm now that his every so-called "indiscretion" went rabbiting off to the papers before the sheets had gone cold to tell further tales in the nation's favorite narrative. Evil, soulless Hugo, despoiler of saints and heroes, etc. He was either glutting himself in excess to hide from his dark regrets or he was so extraordinarily shallow that a shag or two was all he was capable of. The stories were all the same and always so damned boring.

It galled him to admit it, but the tabloids might actually have won.

The particular horse he rode today—the pride of his stables, he'd been informed, as if he gave a toss—liked him as little as he liked it, which meant he found himself rampaging across the moors very much as if he'd sprung forth from a bloody eighteenth century novel.

All he needed was a billowing cloak.

But no matter how far he rode, there was no escaping himself. Or his head and all his attendant regrets.

The vicious creature he rode clearly knew it. They'd been playing a little domination game for weeks now, raging across the whole of Hugo's Yorkshire estate.

So when Hugo saw the figure slinking along in the shadows up the drive to Groves House, all he could think was that it was something *different* in the middle of an otherwise indistinguishably gray afternoon.

God knew Hugo was desperate for anything different.

A different past. A different reputation—because who could have foreseen what his shrugging off all those early tabloid stories would lead to?

He wanted a different *him*, really, but that had never been on offer.

Hugo was the Twelfth Duke of Grovesmoor whether he liked it or did not, and the title was the important thing about him. The only important thing, his father had been at pains to impress upon him all his life. Unless he bankrupted his estates and rid himself of the title altogether, or died while engaged in some or other irresponsible pursuit, Hugo would simply be another notation in the endless long line of dukes bearing the same title and a healthy dollop of the same blood. His father had always claimed that knowledge had brought him solace. Peace.

Hugo was unfamiliar with either.

"If you're a poacher, you're doing a remarkably sad job of it," he said when he drew close to the stranger on his property. "You really should at least *try* to sneak about, surely. Instead of marching up the front drive without the slightest attempt at subterfuge."

He reined in the stroppy horse and enjoyed the dramatic way he then reared a bit right in front of the person creeping up his drive.

It was then that he realized his intruder was a woman.

And not just any woman.

Hugo was renowned for his women. Bloody Isobel, of course, like a stain across his life—but all the other ones, too. Before Isobel and after. But they all had the same things in common: they were considered beautiful by all and sundry and wanted, usually quite badly, to be photographed next to him. That meant fake breasts, whitened teeth, extensions to thicken their silky hair, varnished nails and careful lipstick and fake lashes and all the rest of it. So years had passed since he'd seen a real woman at all, unless she worked for him. His crotchety old housekeeper, for example, who he kept on because Mrs. Redding was always as deeply disappointed when he appeared in the tabloids as his father had been. It felt so comfortable, Hugo often thought. Like a lovely, well-worn hair shirt tucked up next to his skin.

The woman who stared up at him now, looking nowhere near as shocked or outright terrified as Hugo imagined he would be if he'd found himself on the underside of a rearing horse, was not in the least bit beautiful.

Or if she was, she'd gone to significant lengths to disguise it. Her hair was scraped back into a tight brown bun that made his own head ache just looking at it, without a single flyaway to suggest she was actually human. Even her fringe was ruthlessly cut across her forehead to military precision. She wore a bulky, puffy sort of jacket that covered her from chin to calf and made her look roughly the size of one of the grand, gnarled old oaks dotting the property. She clutched a large black bag over her shoulder and tugged a rolling case along behind her, and she had death grips on both. Her cheeks looked flushed with the cold and there was no denying she had a delicate nose a great many of his own ancestors would have envied, given the curse of what was known as The Grovesmoor Beak that seemed to afflict the females in the line unfairly.

But most of what struck him was the expression on her face.

Because it looked a great deal like a scowl.

Which was, of course, impossible, because he was Hugo Grovesmoor and the women who usually crept onto his various properties without invitation found the very idea of him—or to be more precise, of his net worth—so marvelously attractive that they never stopped smiling. Ever.

This woman looked as if she'd crack in half if she attempted the smallest grin.

"I'm not poaching, I'm a governess." Her voice was cool, and something else that Hugo couldn't identify. "My ride from the train station didn't materialize or I assure you, I wouldn't be marching anywhere, much less up this very long drive. Uphill."

It dawned on him then. That "something else" in her voice he hadn't been able to place. It was *annoyance.*

Hugo found it delightful. No one was *annoyed* with him. They might hate him and call him Satan and other such tedious things, but they were never *annoyed.*

"I should have introduced myself, I think," he said merrily, as the bastard horse danced murderously beneath him. The woman did not appear to know her own danger, so close to sharp hooves and the thoroughbred's temper tantrums. Or, more likely, she didn't care, as she was too busy trying to win a staring contest with Hugo. "Since you're lurking about the property."

"It is not lurking to walk up the front drive," she replied crisply. "By definition."

"I am Hugo Grovesmoor," he told her. "No need to curtsey. After all, I'm, widely held to be a great and terrible villain."

"I had no intention of curtseying."

"I prefer to think of myself as an antihero, of

course. Surely that merits a bow. Or perhaps a small nod?"

"My name is Eleanor Andrews and I'm the latest in what I've been told is a long line of governesses," the woman told him from the depths of that quilted monstrosity she wore. "I intend to be the last, and if I'm not very much mistaken, the way to ensure that happens is to keep my distance."

Hugo was used to women making similar announcements. *You're terrible,* they'd coo, lashes batting furiously. *I'm keeping my distance from you.* This usually led directly to the sort of indiscriminate evenings from which he was now abstaining.

He had the lowering realization that this woman—wrapped up in a hideous puffy coat with her chin jutting forth and a scowl across her face—might actually mean it.

"Your Grace," he murmured.

"I beg your pardon?"

"You should address me as Your Grace, particularly when you imagine you are taking me to task. It adds that extra little touch of pointed disrespect which I find I cannot live without."

If Eleanor Andrews was appropriately mortified by the fact she'd addressed a peer of the realm—who happened to also be her new boss—so inappropriately, she gave no sign. If anything she seemed to pull herself up straighter in her vast, quilted shroud, and made no attempt to wipe off that scowl.

"A thousand apologies, Your Grace," she said crisply, as if she wasn't in the least bit intimidated by him. It made something in Hugo…shift. "I was expecting a ride from the train station. Not a walk in the chilly countryside."

"Exercise improves the mind as well as the body, I'm told," he replied, merrily enough. "I myself was blessed with a high metabolism and a keen intelligence, so I've never had to put such things to the test. But we can't all be so lucky."

There was enough light that he could tell that there was a remarkable sort of honey in the brown of this woman's eyes as they glittered furiously at him. He couldn't imagine why that shocked him, but it did. That there should be anything soft about such a bristling, black-clad, evidently humorless female.

That he should notice it.

"Are you suggesting that I am not as lucky as you?" she asked, with exactly the sort of repressed fury Hugo would expect to hear from a woman he'd just obliquely called fat.

"That depends on whether or not you imagine that the storied life of a pampered duke is a matter of luck and circumstance. Rather than fate."

"Which do you think it is?"

Hugo nearly smiled at that. He couldn't have said why. It was something to do with the way her eyes gleamed and her surprisingly intriguing mouth was set, flashing more of that annoyance straight at him.

"I appreciate you thinking of my well-being," she said with what he was forced to concede was admirable calm, all that flashing annoyance notwithstanding. "Your Grace."

Hugo grinned down at her, hoping she found having to look so far up at him as irritating as he would have.

"I wasn't aware that the last governess left,

though I can't say I'm surprised. She was a frag-ile little thing. All anime eyes and protracted spells of weeping in the east wing, or so I'm told. I'm allergic to female tears, you understand. I've developed a sixth sense. When a woman cries in my vicinity, I am instantly and automatically transported to the other side of the planet."

Eleanor only gazed back at him. "I'm not much of a crier."

Hugo waited.

"Your Grace," he prodded her again when it was clear she had no intention of saying it. "I wouldn't insist upon such formality but it does seem to chafe, doesn't it? How republican of you. And really, Eleanor, you can't expect to mold a young mind to your will and provide fodder for the therapy bills I'll be expected to pay out from her trust if you can't remember the courtesy of a simple form of address. It's as if you've never met a duke before."

She blinked. "I haven't."

"I'm not a particularly good representative. I'm far too scandalous, as mentioned. Perhaps you've heard." He laughed when she did a terrible job of keeping her face blank. "I see you have. No doubt you're an avid fan of the tabloids and their daily regurgitations of my many sins. I can only hope to be even half as colorful in person."

"And it's Miss Andrews."

It was Hugo's turn to blink. "Sorry?"

"I would prefer it if you call me Miss Andrews." She nodded then, a faint inclination of her head, which he supposed was as close to any kind of recognition as he'd get. *"Your Grace."*

Something moved in him then, far worse than a mere shift. It felt raw. Dangerous.

Impossible.

"Let me clear something up from the start, Miss Andrews," he said, while his terrible horse tried to trick him into easing his hold on the reins. "I'm exactly as bad as they say. Worse. I ruin lives with a mere crook of my finger. Yours. The child's. Random pedestrians minding their own business in the village square. I have so many victims it's a bit of luck, really, that the country still stands. I'm my own blitzkrieg. If you have a problem with that, Mrs. Redding will be happy to replace you. You need only say the word."

If that affected this maddening woman in any way, she hid it behind her mountainous coat and that equally dour gray scarf.

"I told you, I have no intention of being replaced." He couldn't say he liked the exaggerated note of patience in her voice then. "Certainly not of my own volition. Whether you wish to replace me or not is, of course, entirely up to you."

"I might." He arched a brow. "I do detest poachers."

She eyed him as if he was her charge, not his ward. *His ward.* He hated even thinking those words. He hated even more the fact that Isobel had done exactly what she'd spitefully promised she'd do, time and again: kept her hooks in him even from beyond the grave.

"You should do as you please, Your Grace, and something tells me you will—"

"It is my gift. My expression of my best self."

"—but I might suggest you see how I handle the child before you send me packing."

The child. His ward.

Hugo hated that he was required to think about anyone's welfare at all when he cared so little for his own. He had extensive staff in place, paid handsomely to think about the health and happiness of all his many tenants and other staff members and various employees, leaving him free to lounge about being as useless as he liked.

Which—he'd read in the papers and heard from a chorus of people who would know, like his own dearly departed father—was all he was good for.

The girl, however, was a different sort of responsibility than real estate in Central London or a selection of islands in the Pacific or a coffee plantation in Africa or whatever else was in his holdings.

To say Hugo bitterly resented this was putting it mildly.

"What an excellent idea," he murmured. "I'll see she's waiting for you in the great hall when you finally make it to the house. It shouldn't be long. Five minutes' walk if you keep a good pace."

"You must be joking."

"Fair enough. Ten minutes' walk if your legs are shorter than mine, I suppose. I'm afraid I can't tell, as you appear to be wearing enough goosedown to leave the entire goose population of the United Kingdom shivering and bare. Assuming that's what's making you so…" He nodded at her voluminous black tent. "Puffy."

"Your hospitality is truly inspiring, Your Grace," she said after a moment, and the fact she managed to keep her face and voice smooth… poked at him.

He didn't like it.

Just as he really, *really* didn't like the fact that he couldn't remember the last time anyone or anything had managed to get beneath his skin.

"That is, as ever, my only goal," he replied.

And then, because he could—because he'd dedicated himself to being every bit as awful as he was expected to be, if not worse—Hugo spun the horse around, galloped off, and left the problematic Miss Eleanor Andrews there to find her own damned way to his house.

And his ward.

And this life of his that he'd never wanted, but had inherited anyway. Some would claim he'd earned it. That he deserved it and more.

That it really was fate, not luck, after all.

Hugo knew it didn't matter. He was trapped in it all the same.

CHAPTER TWO

FIFTEEN MINUTES LATER, Eleanor trudged up to the front of the house at last.

The front door itself rose forbiddingly up over a circular area directly in front of it that was paved with smooth stones and accented by the remnants of a garden turning brown as winter approached.

It seemed like an omen. Though Eleanor did not permit herself to believe in such things, of course.

The closer she'd got to the house, the more she'd wondered exactly why she'd agreed to any of this in the first place. Was it truly necessary that she isolate herself in this creepy old manor house? Was all that lovely money really worth marooning herself in Yorkshire with a man she'd never imagined she'd meet face to face—and didn't want to meet again, thank you?

And why couldn't Vivi do something for herself for a change?

But such thoughts made her feel disloyal. A little bit sick to her stomach. It felt like an act of betrayal when Vivi had come so close to losing her own life in that terrible accident. And had fought so hard to stay here. And walk again. Eleanor had been the only one left unscathed.

Sometimes she felt the guilt of that as if it was her own scar, slashed bright and hot across her whole body.

"Stop feeling sorry for yourself," she told herself briskly, pulling herself together as best she could. "You already took the position."

She rang the great and imposing bell that hung beside the door before she could think better of it, tugging on the slick old pull once. Then again.

It sounded long and low and deep, like some throwback to medieval times. She half expected knights in shining armor to come cantering up, wittering on about old King Arthur and ladies in lakes.

She was coming over all fanciful. That was what that man had done to her with his smirk and his amusement and his *mouth* when he was nothing but the same unsavory character she'd read about in the papers all these years. Only worse.

The fact that he was infinitely better-looking than any picture she'd ever seen of him didn't help. Worse, he was not nearly as fatuous as she'd imagined and he'd been entirely too sardonic besides. Her knees hadn't felt right since.

But as the door swung inward, she found herself staring not at a disgraceful duke in all his questionable glory, but down into the bright blue eyes and suspicious face of a little girl.

A little girl with silky red-gold hair plaited on either side of her head and a brace of adorable freckles across her nose. A little girl who made Eleanor's breath catch, because it was impossible to look at her and not see her very famous, very dead mother. Isobel Vanderhaven of the sunny smile and titian hair, who'd looked like everybody's best friend and the girl next door—if, that was, you happened to live next to one of her parents' rolling vineyards in South Africa.

"I don't need a governess," the child announced at once. In a tone that could only be called challenging.

"Of course you don't," Eleanor agreed, and the girl blinked. "Who *needs* a governess? But you are lucky enough to have one anyway."

The little girl considered her for a moment, as the October wind blustered and moaned, rushing in from the moors smelling of rain and winter.

"I'm Geraldine." Her lower lip protruded just slightly, and made her look her age, suddenly. "But you probably know that. They always know that."

"Of course I know your name," Eleanor said briskly. "I couldn't very well take a job if I didn't know the name of my charge, could I?"

It was clear to Eleanor that this child would keep her standing on the doorstep until the end of time if she didn't do something about it herself. So she pushed open the door with her free hand, and brushed straight past Geraldine, who watched her with a mixture of surprise and interest.

"They usually just stand in the drive, texting and whingeing," she piped up.

"Who is 'they'?" Eleanor reached past Geraldine once she'd stepped inside and shut the door, firmly, which took some doing because it outweighed her by approximately seven tons. And when she turned around to face the hall that had been waiting there behind her, she was glad the little girl didn't appear to be paying strict attention to her.

Because she was standing in a bloody castle.

Or close enough, anyway. Groves House had looked so grim and brooding from the outside, but here in the spacious foyer, it gleamed. Eleanor couldn't tell how it was doing that, precisely. Was there gold in the walls themselves? Was it the way the chandeliers hit all the paintings and the elegant furnishings and the rest of the things that seemed to clutter up rich people's foyers, that she'd only ever seen before on episodes of *Downton Abbey*?

"Everyone knows my name," Geraldine was saying with all the self-possession of the very young. "Sometimes they yell it at me in the village. You're the fifteenth governess so far, did you know that?"

"I did not."

"Mrs. Redding says I'm disobedient."

"What do you think?" Eleanor asked. "Are you?"

Geraldine looked a bit thrown by the question. "Maybe."

"Then you can stop, if you like." Eleanor eyed the mutinous little face before her and didn't see any disobedience. She saw a lonely little girl who'd lost her parents and had been sent off to live with a stranger. Eleanor could certainly relate. She ducked her chin so her face was closer to Geraldine's and whispered the thing that no one had ever bothered to say to her when she'd been heartsick and orphaned, waiting to find out if Vivi would make it through her latest surgery. "It won't matter either way, you know. Whether you're good or bad. I can already tell we'll be great friends and that means we always will. Friends don't change their minds about each other when things get tough, after all."

All Geraldine did was blink. Once, then again. But that was enough. Eleanor started unzipping her big coat.

"She's not any more disobedient than any other small human creature," came a male voice Eleanor wished she didn't recognize, wafting down the length of the hall as if it, too, was made of gold. And was set to shine. "She's seven. Let's not put the child in a cage so quickly, shall we?"

It took her a moment to find Hugo in all the dizzy brilliance of the bright foyer. But then there he was, sauntering out of one of the connected rooms toward the front door as if he hadn't a care in the world.

Because of course, he didn't.

He looked nothing like a duke should, Eleanor thought darkly. No Hooray Henry red trousers or Barbour slung just so for the most hated man in all of England. Not for Hugo. He came towards her in an old, battered pair of jeans. He had his hands thrust into the pockets like some kind of slumming American celebrity. He wore a T-shirt, cleverly ripped here and there, like those Eleanor had seen in the posh shops that Vivi preferred. It was the sort of T-shirt that would've looked like a soiled tissue on a lesser man. But Hugo hadn't been lying about his metabolism. Or anyway, that was how Eleanor tried to view the magnificent specimen of male beauty walking toward her then: in terms of his metabolism.

Because everything on Hugo Grovesmoor's body was cut to perfection as if he was another piece of statuary in his own hall. His chest was ridiculous, broad at the top and narrow near his hips and stunningly ridged in between. He looked as if he should be racing about in a loincloth, banging on about Sparta. Instead, his dark eyes were the precise shade of a lazy glass of whiskey, his dark hair looked very much as if he'd been galloping around in a bedchamber instead of on horseback, and that little curl in the corner of his mouth was nothing short of disastrous.

Because Eleanor could feel it everywhere. Lighting her up in places she'd long since forgotten about.

She didn't know what that dark, edgy thing was that wound around inside of her then. What she did know was that it was Hugo's fault.

"The child is already in a cage," Eleanor retorted before she could think better of it. She flicked a glance around the vast hall, which was even bigger and more magnificent at a second glance, and just as dizzying, from the plump chandeliers to the acrobatic sconces on the walls. "A large one, I grant you."

Hugo kept moving toward her, eventually coming to a stop a few feet away. And then they were all three standing there in various degrees of awkwardness, right in front of the big front door.

It was worse when he was close, Eleanor was forced to admit. It made her feel raw and unsteady inside. It had been bad enough when he was up on the back of that giant horse, hooves flailing every which way and that mocking voice of his like a weapon, but Hugo even closer was confusing. Eleanor eyed him balefully, as if that might do something about that bright nonsense sloshing around inside of her and making her feel...things.

Way too many *things*.

In entirely too many places.

She told herself that it was only that she still had her big, heavy coat on. The coat was the reason she was flushed. Too warm. Almost itchy, somehow. It had nothing at all to do with him.

Next to her, Hugo did nothing to change the

impression she'd had of him from across the hall. Or up on that horse, for that matter. And once the shock of his astonishing male beauty wore off— or, if she was more precise, dimmed a slight bit when she managed to breathe—she found that what really exuded from him like his own, very rich and unmistakable scent was all that arrogance.

That smile of his only deepened then. It was as if he could read her mind.

But he directed his attention to Geraldine. "Well?"

The little girl only shrugged, a sullen look on her cute little face.

"No point letting this one settle in like the others, if you're only going to complain about it later." Hugo's voice was…different, Eleanor thought. Not exactly softer, but more careful.

She was so busy trying to figure out what the difference was that she almost missed what he'd said.

"I beg your pardon. Are we discussing my employment?"

Hugo slid that gaze of his back to her. Too lazy.

Too hot. She could feel it in too many places. More than before, and hotter.

"*We* are." He raised a dark brow. "It appears you're doing nothing but eavesdropping."

Eleanor's teeth hurt, and she unclenched them. "It would be eavesdropping if I was hid behind one of the flower arrangements, blending into all this feverish decor." She forced herself to smile, and the fact that it was difficult made her uneasy. More than uneasy, but she did it anyway. "*I* am not eavesdropping. But *you* are being remarkably inappropriate."

"It's a bit of bad form to hurl accusations like that at an innocent child, don't you think?" Hugo asked lazily, and Eleanor had the strangest thought that he was teasing her.

But why would the Duke of Grovesmoor tease anyone, much less someone as insignificant as Eleanor, a governess he apparently no longer wished to hire? She thrust that aside and concentrated on the only part of this bizarre interaction that she could control. Or try to control, anyway.

"I think all three of us are perfectly aware who I'm speaking to." Eleanor gazed down at Geraldine then, and this time her smile was genuine. "It won't hurt my feelings if you'd like me to leave, Geraldine. And I don't mind it if you say so to my face. But the Duke is very deliberately putting you in a position where you can act out his bad impulses, and that isn't fair."

"Life isn't fair," Hugo murmured, a bit too dark and smooth for Eleanor's peace of mind.

Eleanor ignored that, wishing it was as easy to ignore him. "It's also perfectly okay not to know," she told the little girl. "We met all of five minutes ago. If you'd like to take a little bit longer to make up your mind, that's fine."

"You say that with such authority," Hugo said. "Almost as if we stand in your house instead of mine."

Then he looked around as if he'd never laid eyes on the hall before in his life, when Eleanor knew full well that he'd been born here. Apparently, the Duke liked a bit of theater. She filed that away.

"But no," he continued, as if anyone had argued with him. "It's the same hall I remember from the whole of my benighted childhood, when governesses far stricter than you failed entirely to make me into a decent man. Portraits of my dreary ancestors lining the walls. Pedigrees as far as the eye can see. Grovesmoors in every direction and back again. Which would suggest that the authority lies with me and not you, would it not?"

"Funny," Eleanor said coolly, keeping her gaze fixed to his as if she wasn't the least bit intimidated. Because she certainly shouldn't have been, and why should it matter to her that his gaze felt as intoxicating as it looked? "The agency is under the impression that in this situation, Geraldine has the authority."

"Do you think so?" Hugo asked with a dangerous sort of laziness in his voice, then.

She didn't know what he might have said then. Something like temper stormed about in that gaze of his, making her breath feel heavy and tight in her chest.

But she knew, somehow, that it wasn't temper. Not quite.

"I like her," Geraldine chimed in then. "I want her to stay."

The Duke didn't shift his eyes from Eleanor's.

"Your wish is my command, my favorite ward,"

he said in that same careful tone, and maybe Eleanor was the only one who could hear all those undercurrents. Or feel them, anyway. Swishing around inside of her as if she'd had entirely too much to drink.

As if he was a new brand of spirit served in far more than the usual measures.

Everything felt hot. Entirely too sharp, as if there were some unseen hand clenched around them, gripping them tight. This close, Eleanor was sure that she could feel the heat of the Duke's body, making that T-shirt of his seem sensible. Making her feel that much warmer and uncomfortable in her own skin.

It's only the coat, she told herself desperately, but he was still so close. And much too tall. He towered over her the same way he had on that damned horse, and she assured herself there was no particular reason she should have the image of its flailing hooves, rearing up over her, when it was only a man standing in front of her in an entryway. Just a man. No dangerous animal in sight.

She was sure he almost said something, but he

didn't. Instead, he shifted. He pulled one hand out of his jeans pocket, and lifted it. That was all. If she'd seen a stranger do it on the street, she wouldn't have thought of it as any kind of gesture. It seemed accidental.

But it wasn't, she realized the next moment, because suddenly the hall was filled with people.

Geraldine was swept away in the care of two clucking nannies. Someone took Eleanor's bags, another person took her coat, and then suddenly there was a very neatly dressed, efficient-looking older woman bearing down on her with a tight smile on her mouth and her steel gray hair tucked back in a bun that looked a great deal like Eleanor's own.

"Mrs. Redding, I presume," Eleanor said as the woman drew close.

"Miss Andrews." The woman greeted her in the same briskly matter-of-fact tone Eleanor recognized from the telephone calls they'd had. "If you'll come with me."

As Eleanor followed her deeper into the depths of the great house, she realized that the Duke was nowhere to be seen. Then he'd disappeared in all the commotion.

She told herself she was relieved.

"I do apologize that there was no one waiting to collect you from the station," the housekeeper said as she strode through the maze of halls, not pausing for an instant to give Eleanor a glimpse of the splendor closing in on all sides. Eleanor found she was grateful. She was afraid that if she stopped or stared for too long at any one thing, in any of the many beautiful rooms they hurried past, she'd be mesmerized for days. "It was an oversight."

Eleanor doubted that, for some reason. Or she doubted that this woman made any oversights, perhaps. But this was her first day, and she had the distinct impression she'd already irritated her employer, so there was no reason to dig that ditch any deeper.

"I had a lovely walk," she said instead. "It was a nice chance to take in the area. And quite atmospheric."

"The moors are nothing if not filled with atmosphere," the housekeeper said, an undercurrent in her voice that made Eleanor's ears prick up. "You'll want to be careful of the winds, however. They crop up out of nowhere and howl terribly wherever they go. They have a way of getting under your skin, you'll find. Whether you're aware of it or not."

Eleanor didn't think Mrs. Redding was talking about the Yorkshire wind. Or not only about the Yorkshire wind.

"I'll be certain to dress appropriately for the elements, then," Eleanor said after a moment, her tone even.

The woman led her down an endless hallway, then stopped at the far end.

"These are your rooms," Mrs. Redding said, waving Eleanor into the waiting suite. "I hope it will be sufficient. I'm afraid it's a bit less spacious than some of the previous governesses were hoping for."

Eleanor wanted to tell the woman she had been expecting a closet, or perhaps a cot down in a basement. Wherever the servants were kept in a place like this.

But she couldn't get the words out of her

mouth, because she was too busy being overwhelmed. Again.

Mrs. Redding had said *rooms* not *room*, and she hadn't misspoken.

The flat she shared with Vivi could easily have fit into one part of the large room she walked into first, and it took her long, stunned moments to realize that it was, in fact, her own sitting room. And Mrs. Redding was still going, straight into the next room, which it took Eleanor another long beat to realize was a great closet. For the grand wardrobe she didn't possess.

The bedroom itself was on the far side of a huge bathroom that looked like a spa to Eleanor's untutored eyes, and as she walked into it, trailing behind Mrs. Redding, Eleanor was certain that this was the biggest dwelling space she'd ever been in.

One side of the room was dominated by a massive four-poster bed with carved wood posts and more carved wood as a canopy over top, like some kind of queen's bower. There was another fireplace, and more places to sit around it, as if the whole sitting room wasn't enough.

Eleanor's breathing had gone a bit shallow. But she pulled it together, and smiled serenely at Mrs. Redding.

"It will do," she murmured, trying her best to sound dry and sophisticated and professional. Instead of like an overexcited child in a candy store.

After the older woman left her, with instructions about where and when Eleanor was to present herself later for a tour and a breakdown of her duties, Eleanor found herself standing in the middle of this bedroom she couldn't imagine ever calling her own. If possible, she felt more out of place than she had downstairs, where somehow the Duke's arrogance had made her forget herself and Geraldine's fierce, obvious loneliness had caught at her.

But here in these sumptuous rooms, she had nothing to fight. No one to defend. Only elegant emptiness all around.

Nothing but herself.

Whoever the hell that was.

CHAPTER THREE

HUGO HAD NO idea what had gotten into him.

He didn't know what it was about starchy, overly puffy-coated Eleanor Andrews that scraped beneath his skin. But there was no denying the fact that he, Hugo Grovesmoor, who had never chased a woman in his entire life, had been *lying in wait* for this one.

It was extraordinary.

Hugo told himself he needed to see what on earth was hidden beneath that enormous coat of hers, that was all. That not knowing might keep him up at night. Was she a marshmallow creature like the monster in that old movie? Or had she hid her true, svelte form away in a billowy suit of armor?

And he knew when she didn't back down in the foyer or unzip that great horror of a coat more than an inch or two that he needed to retreat back to his part of the house, carry on living the life of ease and leisure and loathing the whole of the world begrudged him these days, and forget all about his ward and the governess she'd decided to favor on sight. He knew it.

So he had no explanation for why he found himself lurking about in the wing he'd given over to Geraldine because he knew Mrs. Redding was giving Eleanor a tour and showing her where and how she'd be expected to do her work. The governess's quarters were in this same wing, one floor above, right up the nearby stairs—a fact that there was absolutely no reason at all for Hugo to keep reciting to himself.

"I didn't expect to see you, Your Grace," Mrs. Redding said when she swept out of the nursery that was now a playroom and found Hugo inspecting the rather horrifying paintings hanging on the walls in the hall that he remembered from his own childhood.

"I can't imagine why not, Mrs. Redding." Hugo kept studying the garish painting in front of him as he spoke. "I do own the house and am known to be in residence. Surely I could be expected to turn up sooner or later."

"In the child's wing? Unlikely." The older woman could still manage to infuse every syllable with genteel condemnation. A true skill, he'd always thought. "And yet here you are."

Hugo turned then, smiling faintly at Mrs. Redding as he looked behind her to where Eleanor stood.

And he understood in an instant that he'd made a terrible mistake.

Because Eleanor was not as puffy and large as her coat had suggested. Nor was she as whipcord-skinny as a gazelle's thigh, as many of her predecessors had been, eyes gleaming with avarice and ambition.

Quite the opposite, god help him.

The damned woman had the body of a goddess. A naughty fertility goddess. Eleanor had lush hips and generous breasts, sweetly separated by a tiny waist that made him hunger to test the span of it with his own hands. She was dressed in a perfectly conservative and appropriately opaque blouse over sensible trousers with a cardigan tossed on besides, and she still looked like an old pinup model. Her body was so markedly opulent that it made her harshly scraped back hair all the more intriguing—in that Hugo wanted to get his hands in it. Or feel it all over his naked body while she was engaged in other things, none of them involving any sort of harsh scraping at all.

Hugo knew he needed to stop. Now.

He needed to turn around this minute and get himself away from her, especially when she frowned at him from behind Mrs. Redding, and from beneath that fringe of hers. The legions of other women who had come this house and tried it on with him had pouted at him. They'd simpered and giggled. They'd made eyes at him over his ward's head and had dressed in preposterously inappropriate clothing while supposedly out taking walks on the grounds in the middle of rainstorms in the hope of attracting his notice.

Eleanor Andrews, on the other hand, barreled about in the ugliest coat he'd ever beheld in his life as if she didn't care whether or not she was found attractive, made no secret of the fact she held Hugo in rather low regard, and aimed disapproving frowns at him while she stood on his property as if she didn't expect to receive her salary from his accounts.

It was almost as if she didn't want anything from him.

That notion was so revolutionary it shook him a little. He found himself very nearly frowning himself, but caught it just in time. Hugo Grovesmoor did not *frown*. That might indicate he had thoughts, and that would never do. He was considered nothing more than a vessel of pointless and predatory evil, sent to earth to ruin every good thing in it at will.

He'd learned his place a long time ago.

And yet, "I'll finish giving Miss Andrews her tour of the premises," he heard himself say.

And then wondered if the rest of his admittedly impure thoughts were being broadcast on his face when both women stood there staring back at him. Then again, that was the benefit of owning half of England, wasn't it? He could bloody well do as he liked.

"Was I unclear?" he asked softly.

Mrs. Redding huffed slightly at that, but excused herself in the next moment because bristle as she might, the woman knew her place. And that left Hugo exactly where he shouldn't be, under any circumstances. Alone with Eleanor.

His ward's latest governess who happened to have the kind of body that made him feel like an adolescent boy all over again, all cock and delicious promise.

"How remarkably kind of you to take time out of your busy schedule to welcome a lowly member of your staff, Your Grace," Eleanor said as Mrs. Redding's steps faded away, down the stairs and off into the busier parts of the house. Leaving them alone with nothing but the wind outside and the far-off sounds of Geraldine at her dinner on the other end of this hall, chattering away with her usual brace of nannies. "When I assume you must have any number of urgent ducal matters that require your attention."

"Dozens at every moment," Hugo agreed cheerfully, when what he actually had was the good sense to hire excellent people to handle such things. "And yet here I am, ready to wait on you hand and foot like a good host."

She smiled. It was a frozen sort of smile that

shouldn't have hit him like that. Like a lick of heat in the place he was entirely too hard already.

"But I am not a guest, Your Grace," Eleanor said stiffly, as if he'd insulted her by suggesting otherwise.

"I'm certain I heard explicit criticism regarding my hospitality, did I not? Outside, when there was some question as to whether or not you were poaching from the estate?"

"There was never any real question about whether or not I was poaching, surely."

"And yet I felt as if I had many questions, none of which were answered. And many more of which were complicated by your performance in my foyer."

She made no apparent attempt to keep herself from frowning at him all the more furiously. "My 'performance'?"

Hugo waited, brows raised expectantly, and her frown deepened.

"Your Grace," she managed to get out, sounding even stiffer than before.

Hugo tried as hard as he could to keep his mind free of any thoughts about Geraldine. Lest they stray from the girl he'd been called upon to care for, and end up on her mother instead.

And the less he thought about Isobel, the better.

The less anyone thought about Isobel, the better, in his opinion. Not that anyone had asked Hugo's opinion on Isobel in quite some time.

But as was to be expected, thoughts of Isobel and the damage she'd done—and still did despite the fact she was dead and buried—only made him angrier.

Not that he was angry, of course.

Hugo Grovesmoor was never *angry.* Angry was for people who had emotions, and it had been established long ago that he lacked that particular human frailty. In every paper possible. Over and over again.

"I don't know what else to call it but a performance." He felt his gaze go narrow. "Perhaps you can explain to me why you gave a little girl such false hope. Is that your angle?"

"Geraldine is a lovely young girl," Eleanor said in her prim way that made Hugo feel more of the sorts of things he was famous for never, ever feeling. In a great mad rush that made his fingers itch to touch her. "She does seem lonely and a bit lost, if I'm honest." Eleanor's startling gaze, frank and sturdy on his, made an interesting sort of heat pool inside of him. Hugo didn't like it. But not liking it, it turned out, didn't make it go away. "I look forward to being able to help her in some way. Assuming, of course, I'm allowed to do that."

"Do you imagine I would prevent you from doing the job for which I hired you in the first place? You have the most curious notions, Miss Andrews. Quite a fanciful imagination, it appears. Are you entirely certain that you are the best choice for a little girl you consider lost and lonely?"

The unfathomable woman shrugged as if it was no matter. "Whether I'm a good choice or bad choice, it appears I'm the only governess here."

"A circumstance that could change in an instant. On a whim. My whim."

Another shrug. "There's nothing I can do to control your whims, Your Grace. Is there? Best to muddle along and hope for the best, I think."

"The best being today's display? Telling a vulnerable child you'll always be her friend before you've taken off your coat or unpacked? Without knowing if she even likes you?" He shook his head. "Most women in your position play their games with me, Miss Andrews. They tend to leave the girl alone."

She stood there in her frumpy little outfit that should have made her look dumpy and instead made him think that he'd never seen a woman more magnetic. Especially since she didn't seem to be the least bit aware of it.

"All the more reason that someone ought to pay attention to the poor thing," she said briskly. "She's thirsty for a little companionship, clearly."

Eleanor was still eyeing him as if he was something distinctly unsavory as she spoke. And there was absolutely nothing new about that look. Hugo had seen that particular expression on more faces than he could begin to count. Friends, family members—or what few of each remained, anyway—and strangers on the street alike. He wasn't usually a receptacle for friendly glances, a fact of his existence he'd become inured to long since.

But for some reason, seeing that same old look

on this woman's face dug into him. As if that *you are judged and found wanting* gaze she kept trained on him was attached to a sharp implement and she was raking it over his skin, if not jabbing it straight into his gut.

"Why do you want this job?" He didn't know why he bothered asking when he already knew. There were two reasons women applied for this position and Eleanor clearly wasn't thinking she'd angle her way into bed, which was a crying shame any way he looked at it. That left the money.

"Why wouldn't I want this job?" she asked, very coolly, in reply. "Fourteen other women had this job before me. It's obviously very popular."

"That's not an answer. And I can actually tell the difference between an answer and a nonanswer, which I accept may come as something of a surprise to you." He smiled at her, and made sure to show all his teeth. "I'm not just a pretty face, Miss Andrews."

If possible, her frown darkened even further. "I'm not following this conversation at all. Have you decided, now that I've actually moved into this house and have already met your ward, that it might be a good time to conduct a personal interview?"

"And if I am?"

"I think it's a little late. Don't you?"

"And I think, unless I'm very much mistaken or have succumbed to death without my knowledge—which should make this conversation significantly more upsetting than you seem to find it at present—that I am your employer. Or am I lost in some kind of dread fever dream, imagining myself the Duke of Grovesmoor?"

Hugo didn't know exactly when he realized he'd moved a little too close to her. Or perhaps she'd moved to close to him, he couldn't tell. All he knew was that they were no longer standing across from each other on different sides of the wide hallway. Instead they'd somehow closed the distance, and had met in the middle now.

Entirely too close to each other for Hugo's peace of mind, or whatever passed for that state. Because when he was closer to her, he was even more fascinated by her. He'd entertained the notion that it was the novelty of that hideous coat she'd worn earlier that had intrigued him, but no. He was still intrigued now.

More so.

The goddess curves didn't exactly help the situation, especially when she put her hands on her hips, which only made her lush figure that much more impossible to ignore.

"I don't know if you're imagining it or not," Eleanor said in a tone that only just managed to qualify as polite, "but if you're not the Duke of Grovesmoor, you've certainly managed to take on an identity with a remarkable amount of baggage."

Even that little swipe at his history intrigued him, because it was so direct. She was unlike any woman he'd ever encountered, even without that eyesore of a coat. It was something about the way she stood, wholly unimpressed and unintimidated by him, hands on her hips and her brown gaze utterly clear of any attempt at feminine wiles. It was the belligerent tilt of her jaw and the way she was clearly endeavoring to look down her nose at him from beneath her razor-sharp fringe. He imagined she did the same with her charges when they got uppity, and it didn't seem to matter to her that she was much shorter than he was.

And Hugo realized in that moment that he was perfectly content with being hated. He was used to being the focus of any number of dark feelings, vicious rumors, and random character assassinations. But he wasn't used to outright defiance. And certainly not to his face. For a man who had always considered himself entirely too modern for his circumstances, Hugo found that there was more than a little Ancient Duke in him than he'd ever imagined before. Because he wanted to pull rank. Badly.

Except it was more than that. He didn't want to crush *her*. The truth was, this woman made him *hungry*.

Hugo wanted a taste of her so badly that he could feel the need of it marching inside of him, as if his body was staging a full-scale mutiny. He didn't think he'd ever felt anything like it in his life. Hell. He knew he hadn't.

He was ravenous.

"I would suggest, Miss Andrews," he said, very carefully and very deliberately, and he kept his damned hands to himself despite the fact it took a Herculean application of self-will, "that you endeavor to recall which one of us is the Duke and which one the governess."

If Hugo expected her to be cowed by that, he was in for a surprise.

"I am not likely to forget that anytime soon," Eleanor replied without appearing to take even a moment to pause or rethink a thing. Not her belligerence or the way she stood there and took him on, exactly as she had outside. And certainly not her position—here in this house, much less here, in his grasp. "I was promised very little interaction with the owner of the house, Your Grace. That you were not available, ever, was made abundantly clear in all of the interviews."

"Most of the enterprising women who apply for the position want to see me, Miss Andrews. You must realize that it's the primary reason they condescend to grace these halls with their presence. And the primary reason they are sacked shortly thereafter."

She tilted her head slightly to one side. "And what did they do to get sacked?"

"I will leave that to your imagination."

"Did you chase all of them down on the grounds of the estate, charging about on a great big horse?"

He almost laughed at that. And it might have been that which floored him the most.

"And I ask again, why do you want this job? Because you don't seem to understand the usual boundaries that govern a woman in your position. Or have the faintest sense of self-preservation."

"I beg your pardon, Your Grace," she said in that same brisk tone, as if she thought she was managing him. As if both he and Geraldine were under her care, and he was the more difficult one by far. "All I'd like to do is start working. There's a little girl having her tea at the other end of this hall and it would be nice to get to know her a bit before our lessons start. If there isn't anything else…?"

"I am the boss, Miss Andrews," he reminded her. From between his teeth. "You are the employee. Everything about the way you are speaking to me is disrespectful, not to mention foolish. Why would you try to antagonize the person who pays your spectacularly generous salary?"

Her frown smoothed out a bit, though she didn't precisely soften. And still, Hugo wanted to taste that faint crease between her brows, where the edge of her fringe kissed her skin the way he wanted to do.

"In point of fact, I won't be paid for two weeks," she said after a moment, as if she couldn't help herself. Maybe she really couldn't.

He couldn't have said why that notion washed through him like a new sort of heat.

"A notable distinction," Hugo murmured.

And then, because he loved nothing more than complicating any given situation beyond repair, the better to make it worse, he kissed her.

They were standing so close that it seemed almost impossible to avoid for another second. Maybe that was his excuse. He slid his palm over her cheek, marveling at the sensation of such sweet, silken skin beneath his hand despite how severely she'd been regarding him all this time, and then it was the easiest thing in the world to hold her fast and claim her mouth with his.

And then they were in real trouble, because she tasted like magic.

CHAPTER FOUR

ELEANOR HAD NO idea what was happening.

He was kissing her.

Hugo was *kissing* her. The hated Duke of Grovesmoor himself had his *mouth* on hers.

And nothing about that was all right. It was dangerous and it was terrible and it was shocking—

But even worse, she liked it.

She more than liked it.

There were no words—and least none she knew—that could begin to describe how much she liked it.

It was like fire. It was an explosion, and only the fact that he was holding her against him kept her from shattering into a million pieces, she was sure of it.

What Eleanor knew about kissing could be summed up in two very short words: not much. But the single adolescent fumbling she'd subjected herself to at a mortifying school disco years and years ago bore no resemblance to this.

Hugo's mouth on hers was untroubled, somehow. Unhurried. He sampled her lips as if he planned to keep on doing so for hours. Days, perhaps. He seemed entirely and wholly unrushed, teasing her and tasting her, then licking his way inside to do it all over again.

With a devastating thoroughness that made her tremble. Everywhere.

And she didn't know what was worse, that mouth of his licking fire into her in ways she could hardly begin to process, or the heat of his hand as he held her face to his. Her cheek felt as if it had been branded, as if he was still pressing a red-hot iron to her skin, but for some reason she had no desire whatsoever to step away.

And still he kissed her.

As if a kiss was not a finite thing, a buss on the cheek or halfhearted peck, easily given and more easily forgotten. A real kiss—because Eleanor had no doubt that what Hugo was doing to her was the real thing, something she'd had no idea even existed all this time—was more of a slow burn.

It was longing made physical, then slowly kindled into an ache.

And oh, how Eleanor ached.

She didn't know how she'd ended up standing so close to him in the first place. She'd told herself repeatedly to keep her distance from the man, because no good could possibly come of their proximity when she was so *aware* of him, and then there she was. Stood in the center of the hallway with her hands on her hips as if she'd half a mind to scold the man, or as if she'd forgotten herself completely and was dressing down *the Duke*. Eleanor had no idea what had come over her. It was like an out-of-body experience. As if she was being haunted by some stroppy, mouthy ghost that was taking her over and making her act as if she very much wanted to be fired on her very first day...

She hadn't the slightest idea what she thought she was doing.

And now this.

Whatever *this* was, that was setting her on fire and tearing her apart at once.

But then it hit her, as his impossibly addictive

mouth moved on hers, making her feel as if a lightning flash had been trapped between them. This was Hugo Grovesmoor. *This was what he did.* She hadn't expected him to be as articulate as he was, it was true. She'd expected his dark good looks to seem seedy and tatty in person—and she'd imagined she'd barely see him. But it occurred to her that she should have expected this kind of thing from him.

Hugo was a man who was willing to use his body to get what he wanted. Anything he wanted. Particularly if it was harmful to others. How could Eleanor have let herself forget? The fact that his kiss felt like a revelation was something that should have filled her with shame.

It would, she was certain, just as soon as she had time to collect herself.

Somewhere that lightning wasn't burning her alive.

Eleanor pushed at his chest, and that was problematic too, because he appeared to be made of more of that iron. Worse, he was much too hot beneath that soft T-shirt, and she had no desire whatsoever to let go.

No matter how she knew she should.

Lazily, taking his time, Hugo raised his head. His whiskey-colored eyes gleamed as he gazed down at her and Eleanor could feel that, too. She could feel so many things she thought she might collapse. Part of her wanted nothing more than to let all that emotion take her straight down to the floor, but she was made of sterner stuff. She'd had to be. She had Vivi to think about.

"Is this why all fourteen previous governesses left?" Eleanor demanded, and she was horrified to hear her voice shake. "Is this a test?" She swallowed, hard. "Geraldine is only just down the hall."

Something flashed in those dark eyes of his, but he dropped his hand. And Eleanor told herself that what rushed in her then was relief. Triumph. Not something a great deal more like loss.

She could feel the way he kissed her everywhere, in ways that made no sense. There was a twisting, melting ball of sensation deep in her belly. There was a rawness in her chest. Her breasts felt weighted, heavy. And there was a dampness behind her eyes that she knew perfectly well was too complicated to be simple tears.

"I enjoy nothing more than living down to each and every one of a person's low expectations of me, of course," Hugo said in that mocking, cut-glass way of his. "Do you not find me entertaining, Miss Andrews? Could there be anything more delightful than to discover I am exactly as you imagined I'd be? Depraved and indifferent and thoroughly spoiled, inside and out?"

Eleanor had been thinking along those lines herself, but somehow, hearing him say it all out loud like that—with such bitterness, and something she could have sworn bordered despair—made something inside of her turn over.

But she shoved it aside, because none of this should have happened. Not with her. She wasn't the sort of woman men grabbed and kissed in spontaneous bursts of passion. That was Vivi's life. Her sister was forever fending off male attention wherever she went. That was how Eleanor knew that there was no reason for a man like Hugo to put his hands on her unless that was just something he did as a matter of course, the way the tabloids had always claimed—or if he was making fun of her, somehow.

She'd never heard of mockery by kiss, but what did she know? She'd spent her life working rather than socializing, and she'd never bloomed into a needy curiosity of the opposite sex the way everyone had claimed she would. Something that made her profoundly grateful, as what she didn't need or even wonder about, she couldn't miss.

"I think it's best if we pretend this never happened," she said, as evenly as she could, pleased to find she'd managed to strip the tremor from her voice.

Hugo regarded her from the near foot of height he had on her, and the fact he was dressed so casually, she realized, did nothing to take away from that matter-of-fact power he seemed to exude even so. How had she not noticed that before?

Because he hides it, a voice from deep inside of her replied with far too much authority. *In the same way you lie to yourself about the things you need.*

Eleanor didn't like that at all. She ignored it.

"That will make it difficult, you understand, to sell your salacious story to the tabloids," Hugo was saying in a cold sort of tone, as if he was discussing something that wouldn't affect him one way or the other.

"I couldn't do that if I wanted to, which I don't." Eleanor thought her voice softened at the end there, so she tried to even it out again. She put her spine into it. "I signed an extremely comprehensive nondisclosure agreement, Your Grace. Surely you must be aware of it."

"What I am aware of is that the penalty for breaking that nondisclosure agreement is a certain amount of pounds sterling. Should the tabloids offer, say, twice that amount, it might well be worth it to break the agreement. To a certain type of person, of course."

"I..." Eleanor very rarely found herself a loss for words. She didn't understand the sensation warring inside of her. That strange longing, or the fact she had to curl her hands into fists at her side to keep them to herself. She, who was not the sort of person who liked to touch others or even to be touched herself. She, who had never had to fight *not* to touch someone in her life. She was baffled. "I would never do that."

"Because you are such a good person, naturally. My mistake."

His sardonic tone could have stripped the paint from the walls and Eleanor nearly checked to see if it had. But didn't, because she could feel her reaction in the flush that heated her cheeks, and she thought that was more than enough of a response.

"Because who would do that?" she asked, almost helplessly.

The expression on the Duke's face was all razor-sharp amusement, but all Eleanor could feel in the space between them was more of that same bitterness that cut a little too close to despair. Dark and thick and everywhere.

Hopeless, she thought, and didn't know why that made her ache again, the way she had when he'd kissed her. Only sharper.

"Everyone has their price, I assure you," Hugo said quietly.

As if he was making a prediction. A terrible one.

"Do you?" Eleanor dared to ask.

The expression on his face then made her heart kick at her, then sink into that same sharp ache. But his laugh was worse, dark enough to fill the hall, if not the grand house arrayed all around them, too.

"Especially me, Miss Andrews," he told her, almost gently. Though his dark eyes blazed, and were anything but gentle. Anything but soft. "Me most of all."

Eleanor woke in a room fit for a princess and told herself that the unsettling scene in the hallway that had kept her awake and that kiss that had invaded her dreams hadn't happened.

Because surely she could not possibly have been so stupid as to go full *Jane Eyre* on the very first day of her new job, within hours of meeting the Duke and his ward. Before she'd even unpacked her case or figured out what her new job actually entailed. Eleanor had never been that kind of silly. She'd never had the time or, if she was honest, the inclination to fling herself headlong into the sort of mad passions and silly entanglements the bright young things all around her seemed to flock to so mindlessly, like moths to a wholly avoidable flame.

Until last night, Eleanor would have confidently asserted that she simply didn't have those sorts of feelings or bodily reactions. That she wasn't wired that way.

She decided she would treat that kiss as if it hadn't happened, because it shouldn't have. And because she had no idea how to handle all the things she *felt*. As if she was a moth battering itself against a light after all.

But she soon found that it didn't matter how she handled what should never have happened, because the Duke was nowhere to be found over the next few weeks.

Eleanor told herself that was a good thing.

Geraldine was a bright, often funny kid, and even on her less than stellar days, it was far more interesting to work with her than it was to answer ringing phones and take the odd bit of abuse from walk-ins and disgruntled clients and snarky deliverymen. Far better Geraldine than her last immediate supervisor, Eleanor thought more than once.

"I feel terrible that I pushed you into taking this strange job," Vivi told her a few days into her time at Groves House.

"It's actually a good fit, believe it or not. I like it."

Vivi plowed right on, her voice merry and sharp. "I bullied you into it and now you're trapped in the bowels of Yorkshire in some moldering old stack of stones."

Eleanor was sunk deep into her luxurious bathtub, bubbles high and the hot water silky against her skin. She had a book on her little bath tray, a glass of wine and some fine cheese she'd never tasted before, and a fire crackling in the other room. She and Geraldine had spent the day investigating the sciences and giggling uproariously for no particular reason, until Eleanor had delivered her to the nannies who supervised the little girl's tea and bedtime.

"The poor tyke can't go to a proper school, can she?" the slightly friendlier of the two notably unfriendly nannies had said out in the hall after Geraldine had run into her rooms, as if Eleanor had argued otherwise. "Those worthless journos won't leave her alone for a minute. If I knew who sold them stories about the Duke I'd give them a piece of my mind, believe me."

As if Hugo was a good man who merited that kind of defense.

The other woman had huffed off after Geraldine. Leaving Eleanor finished with lessons—and thus finished with her work for the day—at four-thirty. Which was late, as they were usually finished hours sooner unless they'd taken a little trip further afield.

Eleanor had never had such easy, comfortable hours.

But for some reason, she didn't tell Vivi any of that, and not only because that sharp merriment in her voice suggested her sister had been tossing back spirits.

"I'm fine, really," Eleanor said instead, like a proper martyr.

And felt terrible about herself as Vivi mouthed a few more drunken apologies, then rang off.

But not terrible enough to correct her sister's impression that she was muddling through dire circumstances in their next conversation. Or the next. Or, for that matter, let Vivi know that she had in fact met the disgraced Duke himself. More than "met" him.

She told herself that because that kiss had been such an egregious misstep, and because the Duke had disappeared thereafter, it hadn't happened. So there was no need to tell Vivi about it, as her sister would only leap to the wrong conclusions.

But something deep inside her whispered a different, darker reason.

Eleanor ignored that, too.

The truth was that Eleanor had wanted to become a teacher years ago, but hadn't thought she could make enough money at it to serve Vivi's purposes and hers—and certainly not without heading back to school to get the proper certification. There had obviously been no time for that. *I can only be dazzling for a few years, after all,* Vivi would say. Working with Geraldine was a lot like fulfilling an old dream. It was like a little glance down the road not taken, which, Eleanor found, she liked as much—if not more—than the one she'd been on all this time.

And with her focus on Geraldine and the new

lessons she plotted out every night on her laptop, she hardly noticed the absence of the Duke.

Until she fell asleep, that was, when that kiss haunted her dreams.

And Eleanor woke each morning flustered and red-faced, and entirely too warm. Because in her dreams, vivid and wild, they didn't stop at a single kiss.

CHAPTER FIVE

"HIS GRACE WILL not be returning from Spain today as planned," Mrs. Redding announced one morning, when Eleanor had dropped by the housekeeper's office off the kitchens to go over Geraldine's schedule of excursions so the cook and staff could be kept informed.

Eleanor blinked. "Oh?"

Later, Eleanor thought immediately, she'd be furious with herself for sounding something other than blandly disinterested. But all she could do now was gaze back at the disapproving older woman and pretend she hadn't sounded a little too intrigued.

Maybe more than a little. She hated herself for that, too.

"We expected him in residence today," Mrs. Redding said matter-of-factly, very much as if she hadn't heard anything in Eleanor's voice. Eleanor told herself that *of course* she hadn't. It was all in her head, because Eleanor was the one wandering around with the guilty conscience—and the memory of that kiss. Not Mrs. Redding. She hoped. "But his plans have changed, and he will be making a brief trip to Dublin before returning."

"I didn't realize he wasn't in residence now," Eleanor lied, her voice as bland as she could make it. She punctuated it by taking a calm sip of her tea.

Mrs. Redding eyed her as if she knew the tea was a prop. "When the Duke is in residence, he likes to have Geraldine presented to him at least every other week at dinner. By the child's current governess, so he can assess both Geraldine's and the governess's progress."

"Well, I suppose that explains why the Duke has appeared so hands-off since I arrived." Eleanor managed a laugh. "I thought perhaps he didn't have much interest in his ward."

The temperature in the room seemed to plummet at that. Eleanor watched Mrs. Redding's gaze frost over right there before her.

"It would be wiser to put a little less stock in

what people say about His Grace from afar," the housekeeper said, as if each syllable cut the roof of her mouth on the way out. "That tabloid creation bears no resemblance to the man I've known since he was a child. A man who took in an orphaned child out of the goodness of his heart and is still painted a villain for it."

Eleanor took her time placing her cup of tea back in its saucer, surprised at the vehemence in the older woman's voice.

"Having a ward thrust upon one and being expected to raise them must be something of an adjustment," she said after a moment.

Mrs. Redding shifted behind her desk, and gazed at Eleanor for a moment over the top of her eyeglasses.

"We are a mite protective of the Duke here," she said with the same quiet intensity, and Eleanor couldn't tell if that was a warning or an explanation. "It's a rare stranger indeed who has his best interests at heart. He has been so long in that spotlight that the spotlight is all anyone sees, but we see the boy who grew up here." Her gaze edged back into chilly territory. "The whole of England might be dedicated to telling nasty stories about His Grace, but they are never told here. Ever."

Eleanor couldn't help feeling as if she'd been slapped again. And harder, this time. As if the fact no one had met her at the train station when she'd arrived had been a test, not an oversight. She wanted to ask Mrs. Redding directly but didn't quite dare.

It was the same with all the staff in Groves House, she found as the days passed and the weather grew more blustery and grim. Each day was bleaker than the one before. The trees grew ever more stark and the rain fell colder. Icier. And the other members of the household were as uninterested in Eleanor's presence weeks into her residence as they'd been at the start. She ended up eating her meals alone in her own rooms because when she entered the common staff areas, all conversation stopped, which did not exactly aid the digestion.

"What do you mean they're all offish?" Vivi asked in one of their phone calls. She sounded distant and preoccupied, the way she often did when Eleanor called her instead of the other way around. As if she had her mobile clamped to her shoulder while she bustled about doing other things. Much more important things, her distracted tone suggested.

Eleanor told herself, brusquely, that it wasn't entirely fair to attach meaning to Vivi's *tone*. They each played their parts, after all. If she had a problem with that, she'd had years to say so. She could have objected years ago when their reluctant, distantly related cousin had eyed the pair of them as adolescents and set the course of their lives.

"Might as well marry a rich man as a poor man," she'd tutted at them one afternoon. *"You two have nothing in this world but Vivi's pretty face. I'd use it to better yourselves, if I were you."*

"I mean exactly that." Eleanor said now, scowling at the memory. As if Vivi hadn't already been a miracle, walking the way she had when the doctors thought she never would. And it wasn't entirely true that all they had was Vivi's face, was it? Because what was Vivi's face without

Eleanor's financial wizardry and prowess with a sewing needle? "They're a closed group. No newcomers."

Eleanor had taken to walking in the evenings and tonight she'd taken the back stairs that led from the kitchen into a wing she never been in before. She'd climbed up to the second floor and found herself in a long hallway that doubled as an art gallery. Obvious, recognizable masterpieces worth billions were flung on walls next to what looked like very dour and period-appropriate versions of Hugo. But she concentrated on her phone call, not the wigs and funny hats and companion animals in the portraits before her.

Vivi sighed, which definitely put Eleanor's back up, and no matter that she tried to pretend otherwise. "Are you there to make friends, Eleanor?"

"Of course not." She could hear the tension in her voice, and forced herself to take a breath. "I know why I'm here, Vivi. All I'm saying is that it wouldn't be the worst thing to have a friendly face about the place. That's all."

Vivi, clearly no longer feeling guilty or bullying or drunk, sighed again.

"Don't go moping about the place. No one likes an Eeyore."

Eleanor found she was scowling at the painting in front of her, biting her tongue. As in, literally pressing it against her teeth to keep from saying something back in the same dismissive tone.

"I should think you ought to feel grateful that you're not required to work so hard for the friendship of people you won't know in a year's time," Vivi said dismissively.

It hadn't really occurred to Eleanor to think about the people here—or her position here or whole solitary little life here, really—as temporary. But of course it was. Even if all went well, a girl only needed a governess for so long.

"I think I have a few years before I can happily drift off into the sunset," she pointed out, and she was proud of herself for sounding as if she was smiling, not scowling. "Geraldine is seven, not seventeen."

Vivi laughed. "You're not disappearing into the north forever, Eleanor. You're supposed to make us enough to cover our bills and then come back."

"I didn't realize that was the plan. Especially when the longer I stay, the more I'll make."

"Eleanor, please," Vivi said, her tone light. But there was something beneath it that wedged its way into Eleanor's stomach and sat there. Heavily. "I can't possibly do all this without you. You're on holiday, nothing more."

Eleanor finished off the call, and found herself staring blankly out one of the windows in this strange art gallery hall, her stomach still not quite right. Because it was tempting to pretend that Vivi couldn't do without her emotionally, that she missed Eleanor herself, but deep down, Eleanor suspected that wasn't true. Just yesterday Vivi had been in a panic about how to pay all the bills and get the rent in, and she'd moaned something about what a tip the flat was since there was no one to tidy it up.

Because, of course, the person who usually handled all those things was Eleanor.

It was a good thing Vivi thought Eleanor was suffering in a pile of debris in the middle of a moor. Because if her sister had any idea how luxurious Eleanor's lifestyle was at present, Eleanor had no doubt Vivi would contrive a way to get herself up to Groves House so she could enjoy it herself.

And Eleanor was obviously far more deeply selfish than she'd ever imagined, because for once in her life, she didn't want to share something with the sister she'd always loved to the point of distraction.

She stuck her mobile in the pocket of the black trousers she wore and moved over to the windows. The gallery was set up over the back of the house and looked out over the tangle of the back gardens that led straight into the brooding moors. There was a full moon tonight, tossing a spooky sort of silvery light here and there, silently moving in and out of the clouds, and making the whole of Yorkshire seem to gleam.

If gloomily.

Maybe it was because she was tucked away in this desolate old house. Maybe it was because the halls were always empty, the locals were unfriendly, and the nights were already starting to seem as if they lasted three times as long as the day. Maybe it was because she felt a bit too much like a gothic waiting to happen, locked away in here.

But when had she decided that she was so all right with being alone? Her goal had always been Vivi's great marriage. She'd never thought about what *she* would do once that happened.

She shivered as she thought about the Duke's mouth on hers, firm and commanding. And if the highlights of her circumscribed life were the potent, powerful dreams that shook through her every night, all featuring Hugo in searing detail, well. That was more than some people ever had. Maybe it was enough.

Eleanor took a deep breath and vowed it would be. It would have to be.

"Dare I hope that your unexpected appearance outside my private rooms is an invitation, Miss Andrews?"

Eleanor told herself she was hallucinating. Auditory hallucinations, which were really just another part of a regular old haunting, according to all the scary films she'd seen in her time.

She took her time turning to check. And it was worse than any run-of-the-mill haunting.

Hugo stood there at the other end of the long gallery. And this time, he looked exactly like a duke. Exactly like every fantasy Eleanor had ever had of a man that powerful, for that matter. He was dressed all in black and looked vaguely historical. It took her a shattering beat of her heart or two to realize it was because he wore a top hat that should have looked absurd over a long black cloak that did. Or anyway, should have. *Would have*, even, had another man worn it.

But Eleanor was very much afraid, as her throat went dry and her stomach twisted into something that wasn't quite anxiety, that there was nothing Hugo could do that was truly absurd. Now when he looked the way he did.

And certainly not when he was looking at her.

"You appear to be dressed as if you've been off visiting Regency England," she said dryly. And only she had to know that the dryness in her mouth was more physical response to him than any attempt on her part to sound indifferent.

"Naturally," Hugo said, as if an agreement. "I've been out terrifying the tenants and topping barmaids in my stagecoach." He raised a brow.

"Or possibly I was attending a Halloween party, complete with fancy dress. You must be aware that it's the end of October."

She was aware of almost nothing but him. That was the terrifying truth that seared its way through her then, making her entire body feel... different. As if there was a fire in her bones, and it was changing her. Or had already done so, dream by dream, without her realizing it.

Hugo moved toward her in that graceful way of his, as if he was half liquid. When he drew too close, Eleanor desperately wanted to think of something appropriately boring and dampening to say—but instead found that she still couldn't seem to think of anything at all but the sensation of his mouth on hers.

His gaze darkened, as if her thoughts were written all over her face, but if they were he didn't say a word. He only kept moving, brushing past her and indicating that she should follow him with nothing more than a supremely arrogant tilt of his chin. And yet Eleanor found herself obeying.

As if this was as close to happy as she was likely to get.

Hugo stopped at the door at the far end of the gallery and looked back over his shoulder.

"Come," he said, and Eleanor didn't know if she was tempted or terrified. Or some far more potent combination of both.

All she knew was that she picked up her pace, on command.

And Hugo's dangerous mouth curved. "Perhaps it's time I conducted that interview, after all."

Hugo felt like the big, bad wolf.

It was not exactly unpleasant. God knew he'd had nothing to do these past years save sharpen his fangs.

And the distance he'd put between him and this governess who shouldn't have tempted him hadn't dulled a thing. Not the impossible lushness of her curves or that tiny waist that mesmerized him. Not her apparent inability to cower before him like almost every other person he encountered in this house.

Above all, it had failed to dull his reaction to her.

He was hard and needy in an instant, and inviting her into his private library was only going to make it worse. He knew he shouldn't do it. He knew better than to tempt himself—because when had he ever resisted temptation?

But when his hand was on the door, she stopped, and she looked at him as if she was fighting her way out of a magic spell.

"I can't… Is that your bedroom?"

Hugo was merely a man. And not a good one. It took everything he had not to throw her over his shoulder and carry her off to his actual bedroom.

"That tone of voice would be so much more effective if you were clutching a strand of pearls, I think," he said instead, like a bloody saint. Maybe that was why he sounded so gruff. "As it is, the offended virgin act needs a little bit of work."

Eleanor blinked, and straightened. "So I should take that as a yes, this is in fact your bedchamber."

There was no earthly reason why Hugo should be baring his teeth in a poor semblance of a smile, far too much wolf and very, very little of him—even that less than stellar man he usually was.

"If you are so eager to take to my bed, you need

only ask. These games are so unbecoming, Miss Andrews. Do you not think?"

"Your Grace..."

But she didn't turn tail and run.

Hugo smirked at her, because it was that or touch her, and once he started he doubted he'd stop for at least a week. Maybe three. She'd haunted him across the planet, with her defiant gaze and her unimpressed mouth and all of her mouthwatering curves. He'd decided that if she was going to torture him, she might as well do it in person.

"Relax. This is my library. Not a den of iniquity." His lips twitched. "Depending, I suppose, on what books you choose to read."

He threw the door open and strode through. He did not look behind him to see if she followed because that, too, was tempting fate.

If she was walking away from him, he didn't know what he'd do.

The very thought appalled him. Who *hadn't* walked away from England's most reviled man? He welcomed it. He thrived on it. He certainly shouldn't care in the least what this governess did.

But once again, she followed him, and he was forced to admit he liked it. And that there was something else simmering in him when she shut the door behind her. It felt a bit too much like relief, though Hugo knew that couldn't be it. True villains felt nothing, through and through. They were made of stone and had no regrets.

Everybody said so.

He waved his hand at the comfortable leather chair before the crackling fire, and allowed himself a small, triumphant smile when she sat. Obediently. Despite that look in her dark eyes that suggested that at any moment, she might break for it.

Hugo told himself he wouldn't chase her if she did. Of course he wouldn't. But as he rid himself of the top hat and his great cloak, he wasn't entirely sure.

"I've been in the grand library downstairs," Eleanor said after the silence drew out. "This is built on a smaller scale, but is no less impressive."

"I'm delighted you think so. I did wonder."

She was looking at his books, not him, but he

was sure he saw her lips move as if she was biting back a smile.

"Fat mysteries next to battered paperbacks," she murmured, gazing around the room. "Ruminations on astral physics and—is that philosophy?—next to the entire series of Harry Potter books."

"Signed first editions, obviously."

"Careful," Eleanor said softly, still not looking at him. "Books tell a whole lot more about a person than the things they say. Or the things others say. Well-worn books tell all manner of inconvenient truths about their owners."

Something rushed through Hugo then, almost as if he was lightheaded. Or drunk.

Foreboding, he thought grimly.

As if, were she to look too closely at the truths his books told about him, she'd know what was real and what wasn't. And everything would change. *He* would change.

And Hugo was perfectly content to stay exactly as he was. Hated and all the more powerful for it. The more they made him into the bogeyman, the happier he was.

Because all those people who had bought Isobel's act deserved to imagine that the love child she'd made with that idiot Torquil was forced to pay for her parents' sins in the grip of a monster like him. They deserved to worry themselves sick about it, torturing themselves as they imagined scenes of neglect and abuse, because that was the least that could be expected from the villain Isobel had created.

"Every good story needs a villain, darling," she'd told him archly that first time.

That being the first time Hugo had woken to find a version of himself he didn't recognize in the papers. The first time he'd had the sickening realization that the fake version was more believable. That even when he tried to clear his name or at least tell a different side to the story, no one wanted to hear it. Terrible Hugo was far more compelling than the real one ever could have been.

He remembered the time he'd tracked her down across the planet in Santa Barbara, California, to demand that she stop the insanity, years into her game. That she stop telling those lies. That she leave him out of the sick games she liked to play with people's lives—and not because it bothered him. He'd long passed the point where anything she did could bother him. But his father had still been alive then, and it had wrecked the old man.

"Hurting your lovely old father isn't my goal, of course," Isobel had murmured, out by one of those impossibly still and blue California pools, all hipbones and malice in a tiny bikini. She'd smiled at him over her oversized sunglasses. *"It's a happy bonus, that's all."*

"There is nothing you can do to me, Isobel," he'd told her fiercely then. *"You cannot take my heritage from me. You cannot siphon off a single penny of my fortune. Whether I am liked or I am hated, I will still become the Duke in due course. Grovesmoor will carry on. Don't you understand? I'm bulletproof."*

But she'd only laughed at him.

"And I'm a better storyteller," she'd said.

Hugo had borne the brunt of that damned story of hers for years. He still did. But now he had his own weapon in the form of a child everyone assumed he hated and the world's endless censure.

And he had no intention of giving it up.

Certainly not to a governess with the body of a screen idol and too much uncertain temper in her dark eyes. A woman who looked for truth in his books and didn't know when to back down from a fight she couldn't win.

No matter how much he wanted her.

CHAPTER SIX

ELEANOR COULD ONLY stare at the Duke's book collection for so long before it became awkward. Or rather, a little too obvious that she was going out of her way to avoid looking at him directly.

She told herself she was simply appreciating the amount of literature he kept on his shelves and at hand at all times, that was all. The truth was she'd never lived in a place where she could keep more than her absolute most favorite books on what little shelf space she could spare. She wouldn't have minded spending a few hours getting lost in this place.

But, of course, her employer had not called her into his library to offer her the chance to browse.

Pull yourself together, Eleanor, she chided herself.

She sat on the edge of a buttery soft leather chair, afraid to let herself sink back into it. Afraid she'd never pull herself out again. But when she was finally sure that her expression was nothing but serene and dared to look at him again, everything had gotten much worse.

Much, much worse.

Because while Hugo had removed that top hat and cloak that made him look like something out of the sort of fantasies Eleanor had never had before coming to Groves House, Hugo in nothing but exquisitely fitted dark trousers and a white shirt that opened at the neck was infinitely more dangerous.

And tempting in all kinds of ways she'd never experienced before in her life.

She could feel each and every temptation as if it was a separate strand of heat, swirling around inside of her and making her feel like a stranger to herself.

Hugo moved from the great desk where he'd carelessly tossed his coat and hat, and stalked across the room toward her. Of course he wasn't *stalking*, Eleanor told herself sharply. The man was simply walking from one end of the library to the other. The way people did when they wished to cross a space.

There was no reason at all that she should find herself holding her breath the way she was. Or clenching tight every single muscle in her body as she perched on the edge of that heavy chair, until she thought she might snap in half.

Hugo dropped himself down into the leather chair across from hers. He did not exactly sit nicely. Instead, of course, he sprawled. He was bigger every time she looked at him, it seemed, and his solidly built body covered more than simply the chair. His legs were long and he thrust them out before him, eating up the thick rug that was all that sat between their chairs.

He wasn't simply *sitting there*, Eleanor thought, with a mounting sense of unease. He seemed to claim the entire room with that offhanded masculine grace of his. As if he was the hazard, not the fire, which crackled away beside them and yet seemed to dim everything that wasn't Hugo.

It would be a lot easier, Eleanor reflected with no little hysteria, if the man was as seedy and dissolute as he'd always seemed in the tabloids. Instead of finely chiseled everywhere and exuding entirely too much sheer, powerful certainty the way other men reeked of cologne.

"How fares my ward?" Hugo asked.

So politely, so mildly, that Eleanor thought she must have been imagining the strange currents that seemed to fill the room—and her—with such an odd, electric sensation. It was clearly her, she told herself sternly. She was the one who was having some kind of allergic reaction to being in this man's presence. Or perhaps it was all those centuries of Grovesmoor influence and authority that he wore so easily when he was meant to be nothing but a layabout. Eleanor supposed it could even be the broad span of his shoulders, entirely too sculpted and athletic for a man so famously devoted to his own leisure.

But when she met his gaze, she understood that she wasn't suffering from some allergy to the aristocracy. Or if she was, he was too. Because his dark eyes burned with a bright, intent fire Eleanor didn't recognize, but could feel. Everywhere.

"Geraldine is very well," she said before she forgot to respond. Which wouldn't do at all.

Thinking about the little girl was the way to survive this, clearly. Eleanor made her spine as much of a straight line she could bear without actually hurting herself, and folded her hands neatly in her lap. She found that if she gazed at Hugo's chin instead of directly into his overwhelming, challenging gaze, she could pretend to be looking at him without actually risking too much direct eye contact.

And that little disconnection made it possible for her to catch her breath. To keep her heart from beating entirely too fast. Or anyway, pretend that she had herself under control, which would have to be enough.

"She's quite intelligent. And funny, it turns out. Not all little girls are funny, of course." Eleanor felt herself flush slightly, because she sounded a great deal as if she was babbling. And she never babbled. "Not that I have vast experience with seven-year-old girls, but I was one."

Hugo looked boneless and hungry, and the combination made Eleanor's pulse dance.

"Some time ago, if I'm not mistaken," he said.

"A lady does not discuss her age, Your Grace."

"You're a governess, are you not? Not a lady in the classic sense, if you will excuse the pedantry. But more to the point, you're entirely too young to become missish and coy about your age. Surely that is the province of women significantly longer in the tooth than you."

Eleanor found she was meeting his gaze, and had no idea when she'd given up the chin offensive. It was a mistake. She felt as if she'd sat out in the sun too long and was now a miserable prickle everywhere she had skin.

"I'm twenty-seven, if that's what you're asking. And I hope that you're not asking that. Because that would be unpardonably rude."

Hugo's lips twitched. "The horror."

"And I'm surprised that a duke of England should bother himself to pull rank. Surely in the absence of a Windsor lurking about, that's a bit redundant."

"You cannot be surprised, Miss Andrews." The corner of Hugo's mouth tipped up, but if that was a smile, it was entirely too dark. "I have yet to encounter a single story ever told about me that did not make it clear I am the worst kind of person. A stain upon the nation."

"Are you suggesting that I believe everything I've read about you? My understanding—" culled entirely from books and television and supermarket checkout queues, which she did not plan to share with him "—was that most celebrities claim that the things that are written about them in places like the tabloids are lies."

Something in his expression shifted. Eleanor couldn't put her finger on it. It was as if he turned quietly to stone, everywhere, even as his gaze changed. Melted, she would have said, if she were the fanciful sort. Into a far more powerful spirit, more intense than his usual whiskey.

"And if I were to tell you that, indeed, nearly everything that has ever been written about me in the press is a lie, you would believe that?"

Hugo wasn't exactly smirking, but there was no mistaking the challenge he'd thrown at her or the way he lounged there in the chair opposite her while he did it. His oddly intent gaze was taut on hers while one long finger tapped the side of his jaw, rough now instead of clean-shaven.

He looked decadent. Sinful.

Eleanor had absolutely no trouble believing every wicked thing she'd ever heard about him. Ever.

And it did absolutely nothing to diminish his appeal.

"Your reputation precedes you, of course, Your Grace," she said briskly, fighting to keep her wits about her when she couldn't seem to pull in a full breath. "But it is not your reputation that concerns me. It is your ward's education."

"A clever dodge, Miss Andrews, but I'd prefer it if you answered the question."

Eleanor reminded herself that this was not a situation that required her honesty. This man was not interested in her frank opinion of him. How could he be? Hugo was the Duke of Grovesmoor. And her employer. If he wanted to pretend that the stories about him were lies, it was only in Eleanor's best interest to agree.

Because, as her sister reminded her almost every night, this was about the money. It was most certainly not about that odd weight in her chest that urged her to do the exact opposite of what she knew to be necessary. And smart.

She ignored that weight. She shoved it aside and pretended she couldn't feel it. She made herself smile. Politely.

"Everyone knows the tabloids are filled with lies," she murmured, hoping that placated him. "All smoke, no fire."

Hugo shook his head as if he were disappointed in her. "I believe you are lying, Miss Andrews, and I am shocked onto my soul." That curve in the corner of his mouth deepened. "And yes, I do have one. Clouded and murky though it may be."

It was entirely too easy to drift off, staring at this man in all his dark, threatening beauty, as if he was an approaching storm and the worst that could happen to her was that she'd get a bit wet. But she had to stop thinking of him that way. She had to do something about the strange signals her body sent off that made her entirely too nervous. That tightness in her breasts. The knotted thing in her belly. And that odd, melting sensation lower still.

She had to remember what she was doing here.

It was about the money and it was about Geraldine, and all these strange electrical moments were distractions, nothing more.

Because of course they couldn't be anything more.

"I've given Geraldine a series of tests and have found she's well above her year in most areas. Whatever the previous fourteen governesses might have lacked, they were clearly decent tutors. She's very bright and quite advanced."

"I'm delighted to hear it." He did not sound delighted.

"I believe she will make you proud," Eleanor said, and realized almost instantly that it was the wrong thing to say. Of course it was the wrong thing to say. The child was not his. Geraldine was his ward, not his daughter. It was entirely possible that the only proud day of his life would be the day she reached her majority and was no longer his responsibility.

And none of that was her business, as Mrs. Redding had suggested.

"I'm sorry," she said quickly, before he could respond. Then, as if the apology needed explanation, she pushed on. "I always wanted to be a teacher when I was younger, but then I took a little bit of a detour."

"Into a number of office positions in London," he said, without consulting any notes. Meaning he just knew that. Eleanor told herself that wasn't strange at all, and there was absolutely no reason that prickling feeling should intensify until she felt goose bumps on her arms.

"Yes," she confirmed. "This governess position is new to me. Perhaps in my enthusiasm, I've overstepped."

For a long moment, Hugo said nothing. But it wasn't as if his silences were empty. On the contrary, everything felt thick. The air. That raw thing that kept expanding inside her chest, until once again, she didn't think she could pull in a full breath. But the longer she stared at his mesmerizing face, and those unholy eyes of his, the less she cared.

"You do not treat me like a monster, Miss Andrews." Hugo's voice was a smooth lick against the quiet that surrounded them. "I find it disconcerting that you do not, when everyone else does. Why don't you?"

Eleanor felt her lips part at that, and quickly snapped her mouth shut. "I don't know what you mean."

"I think you do. Women normally approach me in one of two ways. They either fling themselves at me, desperate for my touch and my attention. Or they cower, certain that a stray graze of my finger will ruin their reputations forever, and more importantly, leave them mere, shivering wrecks of their former selves thanks to my supposed evil powers—but not in any fun way. Yet you do neither."

There was a note in his voice that she didn't understand, but it seemed to wind its way through her like honey. Or something far more intoxicating.

"I apologize, Your Grace," she managed to say. "I was unaware that a certain reaction was called for the part of the job. To you, I mean. Perhaps it's silly of me, but I thought my relationship with Geraldine was the point."

"No one takes this job for the child. One way

or another, they always take it for me. The fact that you do not wish to admit this only makes you more curious. And I should not have to tell you that making yourself the focus of my attention...has consequences."

Eleanor was clenching her hands together entirely too tightly, something she only noticed when they went numb. She forced herself to unlace her fingers and sensation came back in a rush. She ignored it when they began to sting.

"I would prefer not to be crass, Your Grace, but you give me no choice."

"I am all ears, of course. I enjoy crassness very much. You must realize this."

"I'm sure you're a very nice man. Deep down," she added at his snort. "But of course you must realize that the position's salary is what's attractive. While you have a certain charm, I suppose, that really isn't why I came. I told you before. I was assured—repeatedly—that I would never see you."

"I have a very large and extraordinarily healthy ego, Miss Andrews, and yet it withers before you. Most women would scramble up the Cliffs of Dover if they imagined they might catch a glimpse of me."

"I suspect your ego is quite robust and will survive handily. And I am not most women."

"You most certainly are not."

Eleanor caught herself before she flung something back at him. There was no call to come over all caustic and acerbic, which seemed to be her happy place where the Duke was concerned. It wouldn't help her in any way to actively antagonize him. Hugo might have been eyeing her in very much the same way a large, indolent house cat might an extremely foolish mouse. But that didn't mean she should scamper out there of her own volition and show him her belly.

Think of the money, she told herself sternly. *Think of Vivi.*

She surged up and onto her feet at that. "It's late, Your Grace."

"It is not yet midnight." He didn't bother to glance at the watch on his wrist, which Eleanor could tell must have cost a fortune or two, since it looked like it belonged on the side of an old town hall in Prague. "It is scarcely ten."

"Which is late for those of us who rise with small children in the morning."

"There it is," he said softly and, if she was not mistaken, with some satisfaction. "There is that fear of me I recognize."

"It's not fear, it's anxiety," she corrected him. "It makes me anxious to have these confusing conversations. Surely you can understand that. I work for you."

"Of course I can't understand any such thing. I've never worked for anyone in all my days."

Eleanor waved a hand at the stuffed shelves on all sides. "Thank goodness you have all these books, then, to allow you a different perspective than your own."

"I think you're lying again, Miss Andrews," Hugo said, and his voice had gone silky. Dark. Something much worse than simply decadent.

And it shuddered through Eleanor. It made her ache. Everywhere.

Her pulse fluttered about weakly and she thought perhaps she shouldn't have had those prawns for her tea. Then she wondered what had become of her that she was standing here, actively wishing she was ill. Instead of the alternative.

"You've lost me once again," she told him. Faintly.

"What you're feeling right now is not fear," Hugo told her, and there was that certainty again. Pouring out of him as if he'd never suffered a moment's doubt about anything in his charmed life. "Or anxiety about speaking to your employer. You can feel how quickly your heart beats, can you not? And that hot and restless yearning in the pit of your stomach?"

She flushed hot and, she feared, red. "No."

"The funny thing about a man like me is that I cannot abide lies to my face. There are too many in print." He smiled. "Try again."

"I'm a bit overtired, actually. I'd like to be excused so I can take to my bed, please."

"Bed is the cure, Miss Andrews, but I'm not talking about sleeping. And I think you know it."

Eleanor found she was gaping at him. Again. And this time, she didn't have it in her to do anything about it.

"Are you... You can't..."

And Hugo laughed, stealing the heat from the fire and the air from the room.

Then, worse, he unfolded himself from his chair and rose to his feet. And suddenly, the library seemed like a closed fist—a vicious and unbreakable grip all around her. Forget breathing—Eleanor wasn't sure she could stand. But she also couldn't seem to move away the way everything in her screamed she should. It was as if she was frozen in place, though there wasn't a single part of her that was cold.

Not one.

"You look very much like a woman who can think of nothing at all but the way I might kiss you," Hugo said softly.

"That can't happen," Eleanor breathed.

"It already has. It will again. I'm afraid it is inevitable."

He reached over and fit his hands to her cheeks. And as if that was not bad enough, he used one thumb to trace slowly, lazily over her mouth, as if he was learning the contours of her lips.

If he'd doused her in gasoline and lit a match,

she could not have burned hotter. Or brighter. And god help her, it was all so *wrong*.

"See?" His voice was so low, so sure, it seemed to interfere with her ribs. "Not fear at all."

He shifted, lifting her chin and her face toward his, and Eleanor panicked. Or anyway, that was what she thought that was, that blinding rush of sensation that was too electric and too impossible to be borne.

"I'm asexual," she blurted out.

She expected that announcement to stop him. To stop everything. To make all of this stop pulsing and whirling and make a little sense again.

But Hugo made a noise, deep in his throat, that sounded like a cross between a laugh and a sort of growl. He didn't let her go. If anything, his hands held her faster. And she felt them in even more places.

"Are you?" He didn't sound particularly fussed.

"Well, yes." This close, it was almost impossible to remember what she meant to say—it was those eyes of his. And worse, his mouth. His lush, wicked mouth, that hovered far too close to hers and made everything in her a molten sort of heat. "I always have been, I suppose."

"Have you?"

"Yes," she said, with a bit more asperity. She would have kicked herself if she could. And if she could remember how to operate her legs. "I don't feel things, you see. I'm sorry if that makes things awkward."

"It would," Hugo agreed. He moved closer to her, making his impossibly well-formed chest part of the whole…problem. "But I think you feel quite a lot."

"I most certainly do not," Eleanor retorted, despite the fact that she did indeed feel entirely too much. Everywhere. And constantly. And she couldn't tell if she was sick or panicked or something in between. But she was certain there was some other explanation than the heat she could see in his whiskey-colored eyes.

"I suspect that what you've been, little one," Hugo murmured, his voice a low rumble that she could feel inside of her like a kind of earthquake, "is bored."

And then he set his mouth to hers, and proved it.

CHAPTER SEVEN

THIS KISS WAS different from the last.

Eleanor would not have imagined in a million years that she would ever be in a position where she was noting the difference between kisses, having never expected to spend much time kissing anyone, but here she was. This one was different than the lazy way he'd taken her mouth in the hall outside the nursery.

Much different. Much…hotter.

There was urgency this time. Bright fire and driving need.

Or maybe, she thought with no little wonder, that was her.

Hugo dropped his hands from her face and slid them down her back. He pulled her up against him, and it was as if everything inside her head simply went white. Blank. She disappeared into the sound of her heart, clattering wildly against her ribs, and the impossible, wild beauty of his mouth on hers.

Over and over again.

In some distant part of her mind, Eleanor knew this was a mistake. *She knew it.* But she couldn't seem to stop herself. She didn't *want* to stop herself. He angled his head and took the kiss deeper. Hotter. Wetter and wilder.

And she was content to let him guide her. Teach her. Take her over and burn her alive.

He kissed her again and again, bending her backward as he did. One of his hands found the small of her back and held her fast against him as he continued to use that mouth of his like some kind of slick weapon. Eleanor found her arms around his neck, but had no memory of putting them there. Maybe there was something inside of her that knew she needed to hold on. Or be lost forever in this storm she should have had the good sense to avoid.

But she didn't want to avoid it. She wanted to dance in it. She wanted to shout down the thunder and let the rain wash her clean.

She didn't even know what that meant, but she

wanted it, and every time he dragged his lips across hers, she thrilled to it.

And then there was what he did with his hands. She couldn't work out which was worse, that he seemed to know her so much better than she knew herself, or that she was afraid she might explode with every sizzling new touch.

He slid his free hand down her side as if he was testing her shape, spilling heat wherever he went, then sliding around to grip her bottom and pull her even closer.

"Perfect," he muttered against her mouth, and a sheer, shivery sort of reaction burst inside of her at that.

Pleasure, she thought. *Pure pleasure.*

She had never allowed herself that sort of thing before. She hadn't known it existed, if she was honest. But Hugo's hands on her body opened up a new window into near-unimaginable delights and Eleanor couldn't seem to keep herself from tossing herself headfirst into them. Whatever they were. Whatever the price.

"More," Hugo said in a low, dangerously gruff voice, moving his mouth down the line of her neck.

And when the world seemed to shift, the floor moving beneath them and the fire spinning in a giddy loop, it took Eleanor a moment to realize that it was because Hugo was doing it. She didn't think her feet hit the ground as he picked her up and swung her around until her back was to the bookshelf.

Then he pressed himself against her as if he couldn't bear another inch of separation between them.

Eleanor supposed she should have objected to that—to all of it—but she was entirely too busy being overwhelmed by him. All of him. Her mind could hardly keep up with what was happening to her body. What he was *doing* to her body.

And what her body was doing to her, every time she shivered. Every time she surrendered. Every time she let out sounds she didn't recognize.

Hugo's mouth was a torment. A reward. Both at once.

He stroked his hands down the length of her arms and threaded his fingers with hers. Then, never breaking contact with her lips, he lifted her arms up above her and pinned her wrists to the bookshelves at her back.

"Stay still," he ordered her.

And it didn't occur to Eleanor to do anything but obey him. She was quivering too much. She was too undone. She was lost in this, whatever it was, and she wasn't sure she could make her way out of it.

Scarier still, she wasn't sure she wanted out in the first place.

Hugo muttered something that she couldn't quite make sense of, and then he shifted back slightly so he could look down at her, moving his hands so that one rested on each side of her face. In some far-off corner of her mind it occurred to Eleanor to worry that he might find her lacking. That looking at her the way he was might break this spell, whatever it was. Because this was a man who could sleep with any of the great beauties of their age at will. And had.

But when he finally dragged his gaze back to hers, all thoughts and insecurities vanished. Because Eleanor might not have done this before. She might have no idea how this had happened or what she was meant to do next. But she'd never seen anything so hot or so needy in all her life as that look on Hugo's face.

It was so intense it felt like a kind of devastation, rolling over her and flattening her and changing her, but she was still standing.

Somehow, she was still standing, and she couldn't seem to step away from him. She couldn't even bring herself to try.

Hugo moved then. He traced his way down her neck, then moved his hands to cup her breasts, making her breath desert her in an audible rush that embarrassed her, it was obvious. But there was something reverent in the way his hands curved around her, testing her through the layers she wore and dragging those expert thumbs of his over her nipples—and the crazy part was that she could still feel the heat of his palms. Flooding into her. Making her feel even more needy and wild.

He made another one of those distinctly male noises deep in his throat, low and somehow untamed, that made everything inside Eleanor bristle into a kind of liquid awareness. Shocking and bright, even as it pooled low in her belly.

"Later," he said, and it sounded like a promise.

Eleanor had no idea what he was talking about. And she didn't care, because he kept going. He bent closer to her as he traced his way down the length of her body, finding the indentation of her waist and then the swell of her hips and taking his time learning both.

And then he found his way to the fastening of her trousers, and it was as if everything inside of her toppled over and crumbled into dust. Just like that.

"I told you not to move your hands." Hugo's voice was dark, demanding.

And it wasn't until he spoke that Eleanor realized she'd brought her hands down toward his shoulders. To push him away? To draw him closer? She had no idea. But she did as he asked, because she couldn't think of what else to do, and she raised her arms back up over her head again.

And Hugo simply pulled the fastening of her trousers open, then dipped his hand inside, as if it was inevitable.

It felt as if it was.

There was no sound in the library. There was the snap and rustle of the fire, and then a harsh sort of noise that it took Eleanor long moments to realize was her own breathing. Panting, more like, that she could barely hear over the noise in her head that she thought was her heart. Beating madly.

But if Hugo heard any of it, he liked it. That was what that hard smile on his beautiful face told her. She could feel it wash over her like its own sort of glare, making her feel exposed. As if he could see things she wasn't even aware she was showing.

"I'm pleased that you're allowing this experiment, little one," he said, a certain satisfaction in his voice that should have alarmed her. She knew it should have, but she couldn't quite bring herself to react to it. "Given how well you know your own desires."

"I don't know what you…"

"Hush."

Once again, Eleanor obeyed him. Because he was sliding his fingers down, down, all the way into her panties, and that made everything in her...constrict. Shudder.

And then he curved his fingers around to cup her where no one else had ever touched her.

Eleanor realized as her legs went to jelly that she lacked the ability to stand.

But Hugo was holding her up with that big body of his and one hard hand at her hip. Even when he let out the sort of laugh that should have been outlawed as a public safety hazard, he kept her upright.

"I must tell you, Miss Andrews, you are remarkably wet for one who claims she is asexual."

"Wet?" she asked. On a choppy little breath.

"Very, very wet," Hugo amended, his voice little more than a dark growl.

And then he began to stroke her.

Sensation buffeted her from all sides. He was all around her. He loomed above her, and his shoulders blocked out the rest of the house, and more, the world she could hardly recall outside it. She could smell him, an intriguing male scent that put her in mind of the fire behind them and soft, buttery leather, only much warmer. She could taste him in her mouth, like the kind of spirits she only dared sip at Christmastime, and then only in minuscule quantities.

And she could feel him. Good god, could she feel him.

He moved the hand at her hip back to her jaw, smoothing his palm around to hold her where he wanted her. And there was a smile on his face when he lowered his head to take her mouth once more.

Eleanor could taste that, too. And god help her, he was like a bottle of the good stuff, with every demanding slide of his tongue against hers.

And all the while, he stroked her. He slipped in and around her folds, slippery and hot when she'd never felt anything like it before. When surely it should mean something was wrong, but nothing *felt* wrong.

Eleanor couldn't think. She couldn't control herself. She was lost between his mouth and his hand, and she simply followed the rhythm he set as he built that storm in her.

Higher and higher. Darker and wilder.

And she didn't know when it dawned on her

that it was going to break. That the tightness in her belly and the need and the hunger could only go one way, and it was going to happen whether she wanted it or not. That the wall that seemed to bear down on her was entirely unavoidable, and coming much too fast—

"Don't fight it, little one," Hugo murmured. He lifted his mouth from hers the slightest little bit, so Eleanor could taste his words on her lips.

"I'm not fighting anything," Eleanor gasped out. Crossly.

But then it was happening.

It was like a golden sort of crash, fast and slow at once. A shower of fire and sparks, magic and longing, as debilitating as it was delicious. It roared through her, from the top of her head straight down to the tips of her toes that she dug into the floor beneath her feet as if that could keep her holding on.

She bumped against his marvelous, wicked hand and she threw her head back, and still his mouth was there against her neck, urging her on. Taking her wherever he wanted to take her, and all she could do was let him.

He was even laughing slightly, she noticed with something like panic, as she fell and fell and fell.

And hoped like hell that Hugo would catch her on the other side.

Making his starchy little governess come apart beneath his hands was the hottest thing Hugo could remember doing.

Ever.

The little sounds she made. The dazed wonder in her wide eyes. Even that frown at the end, and her sharp little voice before she broke to pieces.

He didn't understand how it was possible when he should have no further to sink, but Eleanor Andrews was ruining him.

But Hugo shoved that aside. For any number of reasons, not least of which was the fact that he had already been ruined. A long, long time ago. There was no lower place for Hugo Grovesmoor to go. He should know. He'd tried to find it over and over again.

And no innocent woman deserved a man that self-destructive. Especially not a woman like this one, who had confused her own inexperience for disinterest. That was how little she knew of men.

He would eat her alive.

And it said something about him, didn't it, that he rather liked that idea.

She was limp and dazed and breathing heavily, so he shifted her off the bookcase and swept her up into his arms, entirely too aware of the way she melted against him. He carried her over to the wide sofa and settled her on it, more than a little concerned about how uncharacteristically gentle he was with this woman. Automatically. When he was not exactly known for his sweet bedside manner. He did not lounge around, shyly reading verses of poetry from slim volumes and softly asking permission to touch a lover's ankle.

Please.

Hugo had always assumed that what poetry was in him was rough and raw and best expressed with his hands. And his body.

And the dark things he could do with both. And did, again and again.

He'd never had any complaints. In person, that was. The tabloids were a different story, but even those fabricated fantasies never claimed he was a bad lover. Simply that he was a very, very bad man.

But still. Untried innocence was not his thing. No matter how sweet the taste, still there on his tongue. Driving him that much closer to madness.

He made himself stand, something furious in his chest and all that leftover heat and hardness making his trousers feel too tight, and waited for her to come back to him.

It took her a long time. And it occurred to him that a woman who fancied herself asexual and was so obviously a stranger to her own body was perhaps significantly less experienced than he'd been thinking. Almost as if she was something more than "inexperienced." Almost as if...

But that was impossible, of course. This wasn't the dark ages.

"Are you a virgin?" he asked, perhaps a bit too abruptly.

On the deep leather couch, Eleanor stirred. She looked around as if she didn't know where she was, and didn't recognize the library either way. Or him. She sat a little bit straighter as she took him in. Her hands went first to her head and she smoothed back the one or two strands that had dared to come loose from that ruthless bun she always wore. Only then, when she'd secured her dark hair in its cage, did she shift against the seat, look down, and note that her trousers were still wide open.

And Hugo found he was captivated by the red flush that took her over, staining her cheeks and making her brown eyes gleam from beneath her fringe with that hint of honey that he thought might be his undoing.

Eleanor swallowed, hard, and he saw a frown etch itself between her eyes again. But she didn't say anything. She only fastened her trousers and sat a bit straighter. Only then did she look up at him, and something about the steady way she did it made him feel like the monster he knew he was. More so than usual, that was.

She looked breakable.

It should have made him hate himself all the more, that he should so effortlessly stain whatever he touched. But that was not his primary reaction to the mounting evidence that no one had touched Eleanor but him.

Indeed, what he was feeling—in every part of him, like a thread of wild heat—was significantly more primitive.

"Whether I am or am not a virgin, I can't imagine how that's any of your business at all," she said coolly. Her brows rose slightly. Arrogantly, he would have said, had anyone ever managed to outdo him in that arena. "Your Grace."

And Hugo stopped feeling badly about the whole thing.

"That is not a very nice tone to take with a man who just made you come," he pointed out, all silk and threat. "So hard you nearly broke off the shelf of an ancient bookcase."

"The bookcase appears to be holding up just fine."

"Given that you had your back arched and your eyes closed while you rode my hand, I rather doubt you have the slightest idea how close you came to bringing down the whole of my collection on your head."

"I wish it had," she said, and while her gaze grew darker, her tone only chilled further. "Everything that's happened here is almost too inappropriate to bear. I will tender my resignation in the morning, of course."

Hugo lifted one shoulder, then dropped it. "If you wish. But it will be a wasted effort. I won't accept it."

She scowled at him. "Of course you will."

He didn't know why she amused him. She shouldn't have. He'd fired many of her predecessors for far less than this. The one who'd tracked him down in the gardens to let him know she was without her undergarments. The one who'd pouted prettily at him over Geraldine's head when the child had needed a doctor. The alarming one who'd left lavender-scented unmentionables all over the house, for servants and Hugo alike to find in the most curious of places. He hadn't thought twice about sacking any of them.

He should have welcomed Eleanor's resignation. Hell, he should have demanded it himself the moment he'd seen her outside the nursery, divested of that awful coat and obviously a problem. With killer curves.

Hugo had no idea what the hell was wrong with him.

"I fear I must remind you—and not for the first time—that I am the Duke of Grovesmoor."

"I know who you are. Everybody knows who you are."

"Then you should know how pointless it is to argue with me." He watched as she rose to her feet, and didn't bother to hide his satisfaction when she had to reach out a hand to steady herself. "Instead of discussing resignations that will never come to pass, why don't you tell me why you insist on scraping your hair back into that painful-looking bun?"

"Because it's professional," she snapped. "And also none of your business."

Hugo kept his gaze trained on hers. Very slowly, very deliberately, he lifted his hand and put the fingers he'd sunk deep inside of her softness into his own mouth. Then licked them clean.

Her mouth fell open. Her pretty face went pale, then red.

"I can still taste you, Eleanor," he said, a bit more roughly than planned, because she affected him too damned much. "It's a bit too late for boundaries, don't you think?"

Eleanor flinched. And he wasn't at all surprised

when she turned around, then fled the library and his presence, coming as close to running from the room as a person could without actually breaking into a sprint.

Hugo didn't blame her at all.

He blamed himself. And the fact he really could taste her, sweet and sharp and intoxicating, was his own cross to bear as the night wore on. As he sat in his library and brooded into his fire and contemplated just how destroyed he was. How much of a monster was he, really, if he'd become the disreputable, distasteful Old Duke locked away in his ancient house, terrifying virgins? Why not simply start belching out flames and singeing the livestock, while he was at it?

But when the next day came and went with no resignation letter on his desk and Eleanor still in residence, his commitment to his self-flagellation…shifted.

Because it was one thing to lure an unwilling virgin into his dragon's lair.

It was something else again when she knew who he was, and what he might do…and stayed anyway.

CHAPTER EIGHT

"You have a visitor."

Eleanor looked up from the textbook she and Geraldine were poring over in the grand library to see Mrs. Redding standing over them, looking more crisp and disapproving than usual. Which was quite a feat.

"A visitor?" she echoed, trying to work out from the other woman's expression what that could possibly mean. Eleanor didn't know anyone in the area. Aside from a few rambles about the village with Geraldine, she hadn't spent much time off Hugo's estate in the five and a half weeks she'd been here.

"It is not encouraged for staff to invite friends and family to the estate," the housekeeper said coldly, as if she'd caught Eleanor throwing a party like an errant teen. "We are not guests of His Grace. We are members of his staff. I'm certain this was covered extensively in the interview with the placement agency."

"I haven't invited anyone," Eleanor protested, but it was no use. Having rendered her judgment, Mrs. Redding had already turned and was making her brisk way to the door, every line of her body showing her offense at Eleanor's transgression.

Eleanor gave Geraldine a reading assignment to keep her occupied, then followed Mrs. Redding's crisp footsteps toward the front of the house.

There was only one person who knew where she was, but there was no way Vivi would be here, surely. Vivi preferred to stay in the bright lights of London, or in the posh homes of friends abroad. She certainly didn't venture into the north of England. Under any circumstances.

That's a bit harsh, isn't it? she chastised herself as she walked.

Something was the matter with her. It had been growing inside of her since that terrible night in the Duke's private library a week ago. As if he'd infected her with his touch. With the things he'd made her feel. She found herself tense and strange. Snappish with Vivi on the phone and even less able to sleep than she had been before.

It was her horror with her own behavior, she told herself stoutly as she made her way toward the great foyer. She'd allowed herself to be compromised and worse, she kept letting it happen.

The Duke hadn't touched her again, which meant it was all she thought about.

But what he was doing was worse. Dropping by Geraldine's lessons as the mood took him, for example, when Eleanor had assumed he was off somewhere else being Hugo on his usual international stage.

"This does not sound like the Latin I was forced to learn," Hugo had said from behind her, out in the back gardens one unexpectedly fine morning, making Eleanor jump as she walked and then instantly try to conceal her reaction from Geraldine.

"It's French," Eleanor had said sternly.

"I am aware of that, thank you," Hugo had replied as he'd moved to walk beside her. In French, which had made Geraldine giggle.

And Eleanor had wanted nothing more than to

ask him to leave them to their walk and French conversation, but, of course, she couldn't. It was his property. And his ward, for that matter. But she'd been psyching herself up to demand he re-spect Geraldine's lesson time when he started talking to the little girl directly.

In perfect French, unlike Eleanor's, which had been cobbled together from her time in school and the job she'd had for a year when she was barely twenty at a French company based in Eng-land.

And he kept it up for the better part of the next twenty minutes, as if Eleanor wasn't there.

It had made her heart beat a little too fast in her chest. And it had made Geraldine glow, which was worse—because Eleanor had no defense against her scrappy charge.

And when he took his leave he bowed to Ger-aldine and only pinned Eleanor briefly with an unreadable look in his dark whiskey eyes. That had haunted her long after.

"Come have dinner with me," he'd said another afternoon, appearing in the library when Eleanor had thought she and Geraldine were on their own.

Eleanor had instantly checked to see where the little girl was, but she was still at one of the tables in the center of the huge library, poring over a dictionary as she picked ten vocabulary words to use in the new story she was writing in the journal Eleanor had her keep.

"I appreciate the offer, Your Grace," she'd said as frostily as possible. *"But I'm afraid that's impossible."*

"For all you know I intended to whisk you off to Rome for the evening."

Eleanor scowled at the book in front of her, though she'd stopped seeing the words on the page in front of her the moment he'd materialized at her side. *"That would be almost incomprehensibly inappropriate."*

"I would hate to be incomprehensible," Hugo had murmured in that sardonic tone of his that made her think of his body pressed against hers and his clever hands between her legs. *"My private dining room will have to do."*

"That is equally inappropriate," she'd said sharply.

"But more comprehensible."

"Your Grace—"

"It's a bit late for that, Eleanor," he'd said quietly. *"Don't you think?"*

"I do not think," she'd retorted, struggling to keep her voice in a whisper. She'd glanced at Geraldine, then back at Hugo again. *"This is a game to you. But it's a job to me. And more people than just me depend on it."*

Hugo's impossible mouth had shifted into one of those half smiles that haunted Eleanor when she slept. And when she wasn't sleeping, too.

"If I hadn't tasted your innocence myself I'd assume that meant you had a child of your own hidden away somewhere."

"I don't have a child, I have a sister," Eleanor had said in an undertone.

"A younger sister?"

"Vivi is twenty-five."

"And she is unwell?"

Eleanor had frowned at him. *"No, she isn't unwell. But I'm the one who pays the bills."*

One of Hugo's brows rose. *"You pay for your twenty-five-year-old sister?"*

And it had occurred to Eleanor that she'd never

had to explain her situation to anyone before. Most people didn't ask such impertinent questions and if they had, she wouldn't have felt compelled to answer them.

"It's complicated," she'd said after a moment. *"Vivi is very talented, but it's not always easy to find the right place for her to shine. Once she does, everything will seem a good deal more... balanced."*

There had been something entirely too perceptive in Hugo's gaze, then.

"Are you trying to convince me?" he'd asked. *"Or yourself?"*

When Geraldine had called out that she was finished, breaking the tight little knot that had seemed to hold them both where they stood, Eleanor had been unreasonably grateful.

Hugo made her feel like she no longer fit in her own body.

Not that she felt much like herself now, she was forced to admit as she hurried along the main floor toward the foyer.

Who exactly are you? a little voice asked from deep inside her, and to her shame it sounded a little too much like Hugo's. *Who exactly are you so desperate to hold on to?*

She shook her head to get that voice to shut up, for a change. And then she turned the final corner that delivered her into the great foyer and stopped.

Because Vivi was standing there.

For a moment, Eleanor couldn't make any sense of it.

There was no reason on earth for Vivi to be in Yorkshire, much less in the grand foyer of Groves House. Back in London, when Eleanor had asked if her sister planned to come up and visit her when she finally got a break after her first six weeks, Vivi had been noncommittal.

I can't possibly know what I'll be doing so far in the future, she'd said. Dismissively, Eleanor thought now. But at the time she hadn't thought much of it. That was Vivi's style, after all. So effervescent and carefree that she never knew what she was going to be doing from one moment to the next, much less six weeks out. *But I doubt very much that I'll have any business in Yorkshire.*

But she'd said *Yorkshire* the way some people might say *nuclear waste facility.*

Eleanor told herself she had to be mistaken, but the woman who stood at the other end of the foyer was indisputably Vivi. She was microscopically thin, the better to show off the excruciatingly expensive designer jeans she wore thrust down low on her jutting hipbones. The denim licked down her minuscule thighs before disappearing into a pair of recognizably chic boots. She wore the sort of coat and scarf that would not look out of place in Sloane Square, and she wore her hair in the usual temperamental way. It was wild and wavy, pouring down her back and over her shoulders in an artful sort of tangle that was meant to look as if it never saw a brush or a styling tool, when the fact was, it took hours for Vivi to make it look just so. As she moved closer, Eleanor could see that her sister's lips were pursed slightly as she took in the wealth on display across every inch of the deliberately jaw-dropping entryway. More, she had a particular gleam in her eyes that Eleanor recognized all too well.

Avaricious, that voice inside her whispered.

Eleanor told herself to stop. She was being severe and unfair. She should have been delighted to see her little sister. She was. Of course she was.

"Vivi? What are you doing here? Is everything all right?"

Vivi took her time meeting Eleanor's gaze. Her own lingered on the walls, on all that gold and gilt, stretching out in all directions. Statues and flowers and paintings that went all the way up to heaven and back. And that was just the foyer.

"Aren't you the dark horse," Vivi murmured.

"You don't look as if anything terrible has happened," Eleanor continued, telling herself that there was no need to read into her sister's dark tone.

Vivi eyed her, her hands stuck into the back pockets of her jeans and her hips thrust out in what could only be called an aggressive posture. Eleanor ignored that, too.

"You told me this place was a tired old mausoleum. A crumbling pile of rocks, plunked down in the middle of a moor with heather growing all over it like a weed." Vivi sniffed and jutted her chin at all the lavish displays before her. "Apparently not."

"You were the one who called it a pile of rocks," Eleanor pointed out, still keeping her voice calm and even and something like soothing. "I just didn't argue."

"I had no idea you were so secretive, Eleanor. Is that a new personality trait?"

"Surely you didn't really think that the Duke of Grovesmoor lived in a crumbling pile of stones." Eleanor made herself smile. "Given that he owns the better part of England."

"It's quite intriguing that you've decided you need to keep secrets from me now that you work in such a posh old house, isn't it?"

There was no denying the fact that there was more than little attitude in her sister's voice. But Eleanor ordered herself to remain calm, and not only because she never called her miracle of a sister out on anything, much less *tone*. But because she couldn't trust the things that were happening inside of her.

The truth was that she hadn't felt much like herself since Hugo had kissed her that first time.

Maybe Vivi was right and Eleanor had gone squirrely and secretive. She'd never done anything like that before.

And when, exactly, were you permitted to have any kind of a life before? that voice inside demanded. *Or have you forgotten that your whole existence is catering to Vivi's life, not yours? She just doesn't like imagining that anything might have shifted.*

It was possible that Eleanor didn't really like it all that much, either.

"If I failed to tell you something it wasn't for any nefarious reason," she said, still keeping her voice even. "I thought you knew everything there was to know about this position. You're the one who recommended I interview for it in the first place."

Vivi shook her hair back from her face, though none had fallen forward. "I assumed he'd thrown the kid in some second-rate cottage somewhere rustic. Not *this.*"

Eleanor did not rise to the defense of *the kid.* She did not dig into Vivi's assumptions about rustic cottages. And she did not ask herself why it was apparently perfectly all right for her to live somewhere not quite as nice as Groves House. Because Vivi didn't mean it. Vivi came across as thoughtless, but only because every thought that moved through her head came out of her mouth, not because she harbored any ill will. It was part of the larger-than-life charm that Eleanor had been grateful for every single moment since Vivi hadn't died in the car accident that had claimed their parents.

She reached out a hand to place it on her sister's arm and build a bridge, but Vivi pulled away.

"Vivi, whatever is the matter?" she asked.

And she wasn't surprised when her sister's expressive eyes filled with emotion. Not quite tears, but their glassy precursor. This felt like normal, suddenly. Like common ground again. Vivi had problems and Eleanor fixed them. That was the way the world turned.

"Everything." Vivi's voice was ever so slightly husky, as if from the force of her feelings. "The rent wasn't paid. The credit card is full. The flat is a *complete* tip. I can't find anything and what

I can find is filthy and I don't know what to do about any of it."

"You didn't pay the rent? And you went over the maximum on the credit card?" Eleanor shook her head, feeling dazed. "But I left you the money—"

"And that's not the worst of it. Peter's asked Sabrina to marry him." Vivi stared at Eleanor as if she should have an explosive response to that bit of news. Eleanor only blinked and Vivi made a frustrated, impatient sort of noise. "*Lord* Peter, Eleanor. Hello. Only the man who's been crucial to my happiness for as long as I can remember."

"As long as you can remember," Eleanor repeated dryly.

Vivi waved a hand. "This past month, anyway. We've been *quite* close."

"And by this past month," Eleanor said, trying her best not to panic at what Vivi must have done to their finances in so short a time, "do you mean the month that I've been here, in this house that you might have noticed is miles and miles away from anything, teaching lessons to a seven-year-old child?"

"The point is that everyone thought that I

was in with a chance," Vivi complained. "But he chose *Sabrina*, of all people. The cow. She's no better than she has to be and who cares if her father has all that money? But everything's gone pear-shaped." Vivi held Eleanor's gaze for a moment, then shifted to look around the foyer again, almost as if she was calculating something as she did. "It was time to make myself scarce, that's all. I thought I'd hole up with you for a little while."

"Vivi," Eleanor said softly. "What did you do?"

Her sister shrugged, though it was more of a defensive gesture than anything else. "Some people need to learn how to have a bit of a laugh, that's all."

Eleanor suddenly became very aware of where they were standing. The foyer appeared empty, but Eleanor had been in Groves House too long now. She knew that the Duke's staff were everywhere. That every word was being watched, recorded, judged. That whatever Vivi might have done, the whole house didn't need to know about it.

Though it was entirely possible that all of England would, if she'd got up to her usual tricks. And found her way into the tabloids again. Of course, Vivi would likely view that sort of exposure as a great success.

"Come on," Eleanor said, reaching out once more and this time, actually taking hold of her sister's arm. "This is not the place to talk about this. We'll go somewhere a bit more private."

Vivi certainly didn't evidence any sense of urgency as she sauntered along, letting Eleanor keep hold of her as they walked. Eleanor didn't know why it made her teeth clench, hard. This was nothing new. This was who Vivi was. She never thought things through. The rent, the credit card, whatever idiotic thing she'd done to Lord Whoever and his new fiancée. She expected the whole world to revolve all around her, and because of that, it usually did.

Or Eleanor's did, anyway. It always had.

But Groves House wasn't the place for Vivi, something deep and dark in Eleanor's gut insisted. She couldn't let her sister take—

Eleanor was ashamed of herself. There was nothing here that was hers. There was nothing anyone could take from her, especially not the sister she loved. The sister she would give anything to if she had the chance. The sister who had somehow survived that accident, and kept Eleanor for being all on her own.

That was what she was telling herself, fiercely and on repeat, when she turned the corner that led toward the nursery wing where her rooms were and nearly ran straight into Hugo.

And she knew who she was then, in an instant. She knew too much about the feelings she'd been telling herself were uncertain for so long now. Particularly after what happened in his library a week ago. Oh, the lies she'd told herself to explain it all away...

But there was nothing but truth here, pouring into the hallway like the diffident light of the afternoon outside.

Eleanor did not want Vivi to meet Hugo.

There was something inside of her, hunched and ugly, all claws and spite. And it was dragging all of its sharp edges around and around in the pit of Eleanor's stomach, because it wanted to avoid this. It would have done anything to avoid exactly this.

She did not want Hugo to behold her vibrant, charming sister who wrapped men like him around her fingers.

Or tries, anyway, that ugly little voice hissed.

But it was too late.

Because Vivi recognized Hugo instantly. Of course she did. Eleanor knew her sister, but even if she hadn't she'd have understood the change in her sister's body language. Suddenly everything was languid, easy. Suddenly Vivi's eyes seemed smoky, and the little giggle she let out was the same.

Eleanor had never wanted to slap her hand over her sister's mouth before. Or at least, she'd never wanted it this badly.

"I had no idea, Miss Andrews," Hugo drawled, coming to a stop a few feet away, his dark gaze unreadable, "that governesses could multiply in the space of an afternoon. Like geese. How extraordinary."

Eleanor watched that gleaming gaze of his flick over her sister, and was more than a little surprised when it returned to her. But perhaps he was outraged. Perhaps he was looking for an explanation as to why he'd been kissing the likes of Eleanor when all the while he could have had Vivi.

And that ugly thing inside of her grew thicker. Burrowed deeper. But there was no stopping a speeding train, and Vivi had always been far more dangerous than any high-speed rail.

"Your Grace," Eleanor said stiffly, especially when Vivi seemed to melt into her side, holding on tight to Eleanor as if she was her very own plush toy. "May I present my sister, Vivi."

"You may," Hugo said in that same sardonic drawl that made heat bolt through Eleanor, but didn't seem to have the same effect on Vivi. "If you feel you must."

Eleanor frowned at that, but her attention was drawn by her sister, who couldn't seem to stop that damned giggle.

Be kind, Eleanor told herself sternly. Hugo was an overwhelming man. Anyone would be expected to overreact to the sight of him.

"I am honored, Your Grace," Vivi simpered.

Then she batted her eyelashes at Hugo. "And here I thought every duke in the land was over the age of fifty."

"It only feels that way," Hugo replied with that liquid ease of his that made the bottom of Eleanor's stomach disappear. "It is the obsequiousness that ages a man, not the title."

Eleanor flushed on her sister's behalf, but it was a wasted effort as Vivi hardly seem to notice that the Duke had just taken her down a peg or two. Or perhaps she did notice. Perhaps that was her sister's true secret weapon, all this time. Maybe Vivi got her mileage out of pretending not to notice the very clear signals sent all around her.

But in either case, Eleanor frowned at Hugo, because she wasn't pretending anything.

"If you'll excuse us," she said, perhaps too severely, "I must show my sister to my rooms and then return to my duties."

"I'm sure Geraldine can manage," Hugo said offhandedly.

"Have you been supervising her reading, Your Grace? I had no idea you had taken such an active interest."

"I have been supervising my accounts," Hugo said in a faintly chiding tone that made Eleanor flush slightly. Again. "Which is how I know that I employ a veritable fleet of overpriced nannies. The child is more than fine. Always."

Vivi laughed again then, though there was nothing to laugh about in Eleanor's opinion. Then she let herself flop a bit toward Eleanor, as if she was giving her a hug from the side.

"You must forgive my sister, Your Grace," she said merrily. "She's ever so serious. She always has been. It won't surprise you to learn her favorite color is gray."

Eleanor told herself there was no reason for it, but that didn't stop the feeling of betrayal that swept over her. And the injustice of it, to have Vivi cut her down like that and call her *gray*, of all things, when it wasn't even true.

But there was nothing to be gained by arguing the point. There was no arguing with Vivi.

"My favorite color is not gray," Eleanor heard herself say, to her own astonishment. And once she'd started it seemed silly not to carry on. "On the contrary, I prefer a bright and cheerful red. It just so happens, however, that one cannot march about life forever dressed like a cardinal."

Next to her, Vivi slid Eleanor a cool look. She pretended not to see it.

But she was certain Hugo did. Just as she was certain that Vivi was about three seconds away from hurling herself across the space that separated them to make a complete fool of herself. All over him.

And the truth was, Eleanor could hardly blame her. She'd made a fool of herself over him herself, hadn't she? Such a fool of herself, in fact, that she hadn't even realized she was doing it until now.

When it was much too late.

Hugo was devastating. Full stop. Today he was affecting his international rock star look again. His dark hair looked messy, the intriguing kind of messy that made Eleanor want to test it with her fingers. His dark eyes were lit with that suppressed humor of his, dark and sardonic. He wore another one of his battered T-shirts that left nothing of his perfect chest to the imagination and another pair of jeans that hugged him in all the wrong places, as if he aspired to give the two-fingered salute to the fusty dukedom with every breath and outfit. And as if there were no autumn drafts snaking along the halls and no wind rattling the windows, come to that.

Or as if he was immune to all of it, because he was that darkly beautiful.

But Eleanor was quite certain that all Vivi saw when she looked at him were pound notes.

"If you wish to wear red, I would not object," Hugo said, a current of dark laughter in his voice. "There is no required uniform, Miss Andrews. I hope Mrs. Redding didn't mislead you on that score."

"Oh, you silly old thing," Vivi cut in then, with a little trill in her voice, and though her eyes were on Hugo she was clearly speaking to Eleanor. Or pretending to, anyway. "You know that red doesn't suit you."

Hugo's attention swung back to her sister, and Eleanor was glad, because she felt stricken straight through. Ashamed, if she was honest with herself at last.

Had she really imagined that she was anything

to a man like this but a diversion while he was bored? Even for a moment?

She knew the way of the world. There was a reason Vivi was the one who flitted about with people of Hugo's ilk, and it wasn't only because she was thinner and prettier. It was because she bloomed in such circumstances. She came alive. She stole all the light from the room.

Men like Hugo were destined for women like Vivi. Women like Eleanor were destined to be exactly what she was here in Groves House: staff. And that was all right, she told herself fiercely as she watched her sister show her dimples to Hugo. Some people were meant for the shadows and Eleanor had long since accepted that she was one of them. She didn't know what had happened to her over the past nearly six weeks, stuck away in this rambling old house with only a seven-year-old to talk to. She'd started believing in the sort of fairy tales she read to Geraldine. Or she'd been tempted to, anyway.

She'd even let Hugo touch her.

When she knew—when everyone knew—that he was a man who toyed with others. And so what if he'd claimed the tabloids had lied about him? That was what he would say.

She didn't understand how she'd allowed herself to feel so many impossible things inside and then lie to herself about it. Because if she'd been as unaffected by Hugo as she'd claimed she was—as she'd been so sure she was—nothing Vivi was saying or doing could possibly have bothered her.

And that was the trouble. It bothered her a lot.

"You must bring your sister to dinner, Miss Andrews," Hugo said, snapping Eleanor back to the issue at hand, and she tried to stop noticing that his eyes looked like overpriced whiskey. Especially when she couldn't read the expression in them, as he looked from Eleanor to Vivi and then back again. "In my private room. Tonight."

"I would love to, Your Grace," Vivi trilled— but Hugo was already walking away.

Eleanor pulled her arm away from Vivi's then, and hated herself for it.

"There's no need to respond," she said matter-of-factly. "He is the Duke and this is his house.

That was not a request or an invitation, it was an order."

Eleanor set off again then, aware that her sister was following behind her. And that Vivi was laughing softly under her breath, which the tight, thickening thing inside of her knew could only bode ill. But she refused to look over her shoulder to see. She refused to give in to the dark things sloshing around in her gut.

She refused to be the person she'd apparently become.

Eleanor finally reached her rooms, and threw her door open, beckoning for Vivi to come inside.

And then had to ask herself why she was surprised that her sister entered the room very much the way she had, back when she'd arrived. Staring all around at the sheer luxury. Eleanor found herself standing there in the sitting room, rooted to the floor as Vivi gave herself a tour, feeling awkward and angry and deeply disappointed in herself.

"My, my, my. This just gets better and better."

Vivi's faintly accusing voice floating in from one of the other rooms struck Eleanor in the heart. Because the truth was, she felt guilty. Horribly guilty.

And she knew why.

Her sister would have been here like a shot if she'd had any idea the sort of opulence that was on display at every turn in Groves House. That alone would have encouraged her. But Hugo's presence? Her sister would have done anything to meet the Duke of Grovesmoor. And Eleanor still couldn't explain to herself, not reasonably anyway, why she hadn't let Vivi know from the start that Hugo was in residence.

"You fancy him."

Eleanor's head shot up at that. She found Vivi leaning in the door that led from the sitting room to the bathroom, a considering look on her pretty face.

"Don't be absurd," she said. "He's my employer."

Vivi shook her head, and there was a sharp light in her eyes that Eleanor couldn't say she cared for at all. "Why else would you have lied to me?"

"I've never lied to you, Vivi. And you still

haven't told me why you're here. Not the real reason."

"I missed you."

Something pointed seem to lodge in Eleanor's side, because she wanted that to be true. And she also knew it wasn't.

"I don't think so," she said quietly. "You've had scandals and overdrawn bank accounts before without getting on a train. What makes this different?"

"I don't want to talk about London. It's so boring. What's not boring is you holed up in this gorgeous house with Hugo Grovesmoor. Something you failed to mention to me, night after night after night. If that's not a lie, Eleanor, I don't believe I know what one is."

"You were certain I would never encounter him," Eleanor replied, and she was aware of the fact that she was trying much too hard to keep her voice even. Though she allowed the slightest hint of impatience, as if this was one of Vivi's flights of fancy that she was called upon to temper. Because it should have been. "And I saw no reason to tell you of his comings and goings, because I hardly know when or if I'll lay eyes on him."

"You met him before today."

"Yes, I met him. If you consider being presented to him like any other member of staff 'meeting' him." She made quote marks in the air with her index fingers, and shook her head at her sister. "I think when you meet men it's a little more momentous than when I do."

She expected Vivi to argue. But instead, her sister only smiled. Which did not make Eleanor easy in any way, because she knew Vivi. There was always a scheme. There was always the next plan. The smile was never acquiescence.

Or worse, that little voice chimed in, *she agrees.*

When had she become so awful about her own sister?

And anyway, Vivi was changing the subject. "Why have I been shuffling about London, forced to spend my nights in a grotty bedsit, when you've been living it up like the landed gentry?"

"These are the governess's quarters," Eleanor said. She made herself smile. "This is what passes for a grotty flat to a duke."

"You are in terrible, terrible trouble, big sister," Vivi said, but if there was a storm, it had passed.

Once again, Eleanor saw before her the sister she knew. With a mischievous look in her golden eyes and an infectious grin. She blinked, doubting herself. It was as if she'd made her sister into some kind of enemy the moment she'd dared walk into the house—which said nothing nice about Eleanor. It said a whole lot, however, about jealousy and envy and a whole host of other, vile things that Eleanor didn't want to admit were sloshing around inside of her.

Congratulations, she thought. *You're a terrible person.*

"I know you have to work," Vivi continued merrily. "I'll take you to task later. In the meantime, I think I'll help myself to that glorious bath."

Eleanor stood there for a long while after her sister disappeared. After she heard the water turn on in the bathroom, splashing into the huge tub. She stood there and she tried to collect herself.

She tried to remember the person she'd been before she'd come to this far-off place, and more, before she'd let Hugo touch her. Change her.

Make her into that jealous, dark-minded creature who was selfish beyond measure.

She told herself that it was over. That whatever the spell was that had held her in its grip these last weeks, Vivi's appearance had broken it. It was time to wake up and remember what she was doing here.

She made the money. Vivi was the one who reeled in men like Hugo. And for good reason. She was the sort of girl who caused scandals that ended up in tabloid newspapers. She was *someone*.

Eleanor had never been anybody.

She forced herself to leave, then. She closed the door to her own rooms quietly behind her and headed into the hall. She had to find Geraldine and get back to her job, which was the only reason she was here. The fact of the matter was that Vivi should never have come here, but she had. And worse, she'd run straight into the Duke within moments of her arrival, when he could have thrown them both out.

But he hadn't done that. And Eleanor knew why.

And if something lodged in her heart, making it feel cracked straight through, she told herself it was nothing.

Nothing at all. Nothing new.

Nothing that mattered.

CHAPTER NINE

HUGO COULDN'T SLEEP.

As he was not a man unduly plagued with the demands of conscience, this was not an issue he generally struggled with. But it wasn't some new-found and unruly set of principles that kept him up tonight, roaming his own halls like his very own ghost story.

It was Eleanor.

Eleanor, who he'd come to depend upon over these last weeks. For her starchiness. Her prim disapproval. Every spicy, challenging word that fell from her notably disrespectful mouth—the very same mouth that Hugo had tasted and which haunted him more than he cared to admit to himself, even now.

He had the terrible suspicion she would haunt him forever, not that he allowed himself to think such things. Not when he refused to think about next week, much less the rest of his life. Or anything approaching *forever*.

But the Eleanor he rather thought he'd come to know had disappeared tonight.

She'd been noticeably absent when he'd run into her and her sister in the hall outside the summer salons, en route to the nursery wing. Gone was the fiercely capable Eleanor who'd been giving him hell and in her place was a far more quiet and distant version, as if she'd been trying to disappear where she stood.

Hugo hated it.

He'd never met Vivi Andrews before. But he knew her at a glance, because he knew her type intimately. It took him all of two seconds on his laptop to find entirely too much about the actual Vivi Andrews, and the sorts of shenanigans she got herself into with high-profile members of the aristocracy. The more he read about her, in fact, the less he understood about Eleanor. How was she so forthright and dependable when Vivi was anything but?

The truth was, the younger Andrews sister— who Eleanor was supporting, if he'd understood that right, which made no sense while Vivi pranced about decked out in the sorts of labels the heiresses of his acquaintance wore because their fortunes were so vast that a six-thousand-pound T-shirt was a "little treat"—was the sort of creature Hugo usually slummed around with. Vivi had showed him her true colors in their first meeting, all batting eyelashes and come-hither smiles as if they'd been in a club instead of a hallway in his ancestral home. And she'd kept it up throughout dinner while Eleanor sat beside her, subdued. Vivi had distinguished herself by being endlessly pouty, unkind at the slightest provocation, and obviously convinced that she was a great, rare beauty when the truth was, thousands of equally ambitious girls looked just like her. Her sister was the rare beauty, but he had no doubt Vivi wouldn't see it that way.

She looked nothing like Isobel, and yet the resemblance was impossible to miss. Hugo felt Vivi's attention the way he'd always felt anything that reeked a bit too much of Isobel's sort—like an oily sort of shame inside him, as if the fact a person like her was so obviously interested in him made him somehow like them.

Because, after all, it had. Given enough time, he'd become exactly who Isobel had made him, hadn't he?

He hadn't cared much for that thought, either.

"It astonishes me that you are sisters," he'd said during their excruciating dinner.

Eleanor appeared to have taken it upon herself to embody the very soul of the starchiest possible governess, with Victorian overtones. Her hair was more severe than he had ever seen it before, wrenched back from her poor face as if she was trying to pull it out, so that only her fringe offered any kind of relief. And he doubted it was a coincidence that she'd chosen to wear black. All black, save for a hint of gray in the shirt she wore beneath her cardigan, as if she was in mourning.

Or as if she was reacting to her sister's earlier claim that it was her favorite color. A poke at Vivi, he wondered? Or a twisted sort of penance?

"Don't be silly, Your Grace," Vivi had simpered at him. She'd been in a slinky sort of red dress Hugo thought would have been more appropriate for a club in Central London than a country duke's dining room. But the point was likely to draw his attention to all the skin the tiny dress left bare. "Everyone swears we are practically twins."

He was apparently not supposed to realize that she was being cruel.

But before he could express his feelings on that—which, it turned out, were extensive and a bit overprotective—Eleanor had sighed. Mightily.

"No one has ever said that. Not one person, Vivi. Anywhere." She'd aimed one of her chillier smiles at Hugo. "My sister and I are quite aware of our differences, Your Grace. We choose to revel in them."

Vivi laughed then, long and loud. The way Hugo had then realized, belatedly, she would continue to do all night. Because she clearly imagined she was being lively and full of fun, or whatever it was women like her told themselves to justify their behavior. He should be better versed in it, he knew. He'd heard it all before.

Sometimes from his own mouth.

He'd settled himself in for an endurance event.

But it had turned out that he was more than capable of blocking out the likes of Vivi Andrews. She'd brayed on about the guest suite she'd been given while she remained in Groves House and something about her feelings regarding the Amalfi Coast, and Hugo had watched Eleanor disappear. Right there in front of him. She'd simply…gone away.

It had made Hugo edgy. And something far darker and more dangerous than that.

And now he was wandering his own damned halls, scowling at the portraits of men who looked like him, wondering why the plight of a governess and her family were getting to him like this.

Well. He wasn't wondering. He knew.

Watching Vivi create an entire character she called Eleanor—stiff and humorless and faintly doltish and unattractive—while Eleanor sat right there and was not only none of those things, but offered no defense against the brush that was being used to paint her, was maddening. But it was also familiar.

It was what Isobel had done to him.

He was in the grand ballroom, glaring out at

the rain that lashed at what was left of the garden this far into fall, when he heard a faint noise from behind him. Hugo turned, and for a moment he couldn't tell if he'd conjured up the sight before him or if she was real.

But god, how he wanted her to be real.

Eleanor moved across the floor, light on her bare feet. She wore some sort of soft wrapper that showed him the better part of her legs and made Hugo wonder what was beneath it. But the thing that made his chest hurt was that finally, her hair was down. It wasn't ruthlessly scraped back and forced to lie flat and obedient against her skull. It was glossy and dark and swirled around her shoulders, making her look softer. Sweeter. Even that razor-sharp fringe seemed blurred.

Mine, he thought instantly.

And he wanted her so badly that he assumed this was a dream.

Until she stopped walking, jerked a little bit, and stared directly at him as if she hadn't seen him until that very moment.

"Are you hiding in the shadows deliberately?" she asked him, and even her voice was different this long after midnight. Softer. Less like a challenge and more like a caress.

"My ballroom, my shadows," Hugo said, and he hardly recognized his own voice, come to that. He sounded tight. Greedy. As if the need that pounded in him was taking over the whole of him, and the truth was, he wasn't sure he had it in him to care. "By definition, I think, I cannot be hiding. You should expect to see me anywhere you go in these halls."

Eleanor didn't respond to that. Her lovely face seemed to tense, as if it was on the verge of crumpling, and he couldn't bear that. He couldn't stand the idea of it. He'd told her that tears were anathema to him. He'd told her he put distance between himself and the faintest hint of them.

And yet he found himself moving toward her, his gaze trained on her as if he expected her to be the one who turned and ran.

"Why are you looking at me like that?" she asked, her voice a small little rasp against the thick, soft air in the old ballroom. The chandeliers were dim high above and it made the room feel close. Somehow intimate.

"You should not allow your sister to treat you like that," he told her, his voice much darker than it should have been. Much more severe. But he couldn't seem to do anything about that when it was taking everything he had to keep his hands to himself.

But Eleanor only shrugged. "You don't know Vivi. She doesn't mean anything by the things she says. Some people don't think before they open their mouths."

"You are mistaken," Hugo said, stopping when he was only a foot or so away from her, and still managing not to touch her. He expected her to move away from him. To bolt. Or square off her shoulders and face him with that defiance of hers that he'd come to look forward to in ways he couldn't explain to himself. Not to his own satisfaction. And not tonight, when neither one of them should have been here in this room where no one ventured by day. "Poison drips from every word she hurls at you. And you believe it. Sooner or later, you believe all of it."

Eleanor shook her head, though her gaze was troubled. "Vivi's young. She'll grow out of it."

"She's what? A year or so younger than you?"

"You don't understand the sorts of people she knows. Viciousness is a sport. When she's not trying to imitate them, she's really quite sweet."

But Eleanor's voice sounded so tired then.

"I know exactly how this story goes," Hugo told her quietly. "I've heard all these excuses before. I used to believe them all myself."

"You don't have a sister. And you don't understand. I almost lost her when we lost our parents. Who cares about a few thoughtless words?"

But Hugo cared. And the undercurrent in Eleanor's voice suggested she might, too, whether she wanted to admit it or not.

"I had a best friend," Hugo said softly. "And despite the fact we knew each other in the cradle, I eventually lost Torquil to the same poison that made me a villain in the eyes of the world. That's the trouble with the sort of hatefulness your sister seems so comfortable with. It doesn't go away. It doesn't fade. It corrodes."

"Isobel," Eleanor whispered.

Hugo didn't like her name in Eleanor's mouth. As if that alone could poison the woman who stood before him against him. Just the mention of her.

"Isobel and I dated, if that is what it can be called, for two weeks." He couldn't keep the bitterness from his tone. The truth was, he didn't really try. Because what was there now besides that bitterness? What was left? Only the stories Isobel had told about him, his inability to refute any of them, and the long game of revenge he was playing against all those who'd chosen to believe it. "Two weeks, that is all. There was no on-and-off nonsense, stretching on for years. There was barely any affair to speak of. There were two entirely physical weeks when I was too young to know better, and then I cut it off."

Eleanor's gaze searched his. "I don't understand."

"Of course you don't understand. I assure you, I do not understand it myself. Isobel didn't like the fact that while she wanted our relationship to be something more than it was, I did not." He felt his mouth flatten. "And she didn't see why she should have to accept any reality that she didn't like. So she made her own."

"You can't mean…" Eleanor took a deep breath that made her hair move about on her shoulders. And Hugo couldn't keep himself from reaching out then. If he was honest, he didn't try too hard.

He reached over and ran his fingers through the fall of her hair, dark and enticing. It felt warm against his fingers, as if she was giving off heat like some kind of sun, and as soft as he'd imagined. And when he was finished running his fingers through it—at least for now—he didn't let go. He held on to a hank of her hair, as if he needed it. As if it was some kind of talisman.

Or she was.

"At first it was just sad." He didn't like talking about any of this. It only occurred to him then that he never had before. Because who could he have told? Everyone had already come to their own conclusions. "She would contrive to be somewhere I was and the next thing I knew there was a photograph in a tabloid, and breathless speculation about whether or not we were back on. At first I didn't even realize that she was the one calling the paparazzi herself. But as time went on, of course, the coverage took a distinctly darker turn."

He didn't know what he expected from Eleanor. An instant refusal, perhaps. After all, Isobel had been a sunny ambassador of goodwill. Everyone said so. She had been all that was light and good and the only strange thing she ever done in her life, according to the coverage of her that she'd manipulated constantly, was try to date a monster like Hugo. It wouldn't have surprised him if Eleanor had argued with him. If she'd tried to deny the story that he was telling.

But she didn't say a word. Her solemn gaze was fixed to his, and she seemed ready enough to hear him out.

No one else had ever given him that courtesy. Hugo felt something sharp, wedged there in the vicinity of his heart, but he had no name for it.

"As time went on Isobel became more and more unhinged. She got together with Torquil, of course, but that wasn't enough for her. Because the truth was, she knew that wouldn't hurt me. If he wanted to be with her that meant nothing to me either way, and that was what she couldn't stand. It was right about the time she convinced my friend, who'd known me all his life, that I'd treated her abusively in private that it occurred to me her only real goal was to hurt me. However possible."

"If you didn't care for her at all," Eleanor said softly, "and you weren't even involved with her in the ways she claimed, how could she ever have hurt you?" She seemed to think better of that as she said it. "Your friend's betrayal must have hurt, of course."

Hugo shrugged. "Sometimes a woman comes between friends. To be honest, I wasn't worried. I thought that he'd come out of it with continued exposure to her."

"I can't pretend to know how it feels to have lies about myself splashed all over the paper," Eleanor began.

"It was my father."

It sat there so starkly. That ugly little truth that Hugo had never dared utter out loud before to anyone but Isobel, and only that once. And not only because there was no one else to hear it. But because naming it gave it power and he had never wanted to do that. He had never wanted to give Isobel the satisfaction—not even in death.

"I was all the old man had," Hugo managed to say, aware there was a kind of earthquake in him, tearing through him and reducing him to rubble. And yet he stood. "And I was a terrible disappointment to him."

"I'm sure you're mistaken," Eleanor breathed, that honey in her dark eyes gleaming with sympathy. "Maybe you only thought he felt that way."

"I know he felt that way, little one." Hugo's voice was soft. "He told me so."

And he stopped trying to fight that feeling inside of him then. That sharp thing in his chest only seemed to bleed out more at that stricken look on Eleanor's lovely face. As if she couldn't imagine such a thing, that an old man could think so little of his only son.

But Hugo knew he had.

"My father was prepared to put up with a certain amount of foolishness, because he was old-school and he'd had what he called his 'day in the sun.' He very much believed that boys were indeed boys." Hugo felt his mouth curve, though it was no smile. "But his expectation was that such conduct unbecoming in a Duke of Grovesmoor would end. If not during my university years, then shortly thereafter. Except I met Isobel two years after I left Cambridge, when I was still committed to every wild oat a man could sow. And that was when she started her campaign."

"Surely your father didn't believe the tabloids."

"Of course not. My father would never sully his eyes with such trash. The trouble wasn't the tabloids themselves. It was that everyone who did read the tabloids accepted everything they read in them as fact. And it wasn't only the scandal rags. There were cleverly disguised hit pieces in more reputable magazines that made me seem seedy and vaguely disgusting. And soon enough, that was how I was discussed. Not just in salacious news programs, but right here, in my father's own home. To his face."

"Who would do something like that?" Eleanor asked, and if he hadn't been looking right at her, with her eyes wide and filled with distress, he might have imagined she was faking. "And why would your father believe the kind of person who would slander his own son directly to him?"

It was an excellent question, and one Hugo wished he could ask the old man.

"Sometimes a rumor is far worse than a fact," he said instead. "Facts can be proven or disproven, most of the time. But rumor can live on forever. It commands a life of its own and dignified silence doesn't refute it. And sooner or later, whether you mean to or not, you find that you're living in it. Against your will."

"There was nothing you could do?" She shook her head as if to clear it. "No way you could tell the truth?"

"That's the thing about rumors like that, little one," Hugo murmured. "They're *more* believable than the truth. My father was a man of the world. He'd flirted with his own share of potential scandals in his day. It made no sense to him that a pretty girl like Isobel, who could have anyone, would waste her time pretending to have a relationship with the one man who didn't want her. And I think you'll find that it didn't make sense to anyone else, either."

"But surely you could prove it."

"How?" Hugo wasn't surprised when Eleanor didn't have an answer. "Where there's smoke, people always look for a fire. And the more that fire burns, the more everyone believes that you must have had a hand in setting it, or you'd put it out. But Isobel had no intention of ever letting it die down."

He thought of that endless blue afternoon in all that Santa Barbara sunshine. The way Isobel had smiled at him.

You'll always be mine, Hugo. Always. No matter where you go or what you do, no one will ever see you without thinking of me.

"I'm surprised you didn't date her just to keep her quiet," Eleanor said then, scowling furiously—but not, for once, at him. "Just to make her stop."

Hugo let out a low noise. "I thought about it, of course. But I didn't want to be anywhere near her. And then, of course, came Geraldine."

"None of this is her fault," Eleanor said at once. Fiercely.

"Of course not," Hugo said shortly. "I don't bear the child any ill will."

"But—"

"But I don't mind if the world thinks I do," he finished for her. He shook his head. "Before there was Geraldine, there was Isobel and her pregnancy. And believe me, she used it like a hammer." He dropped that piece of Eleanor's hair then, because his hands were curling into fists and he thought he'd better keep them to himself. "She told my father the child was mine."

"She left you. She married your friend. How could it be yours?"

"She didn't leave me." Hugo realized he'd growled that out like a savage, and fought for calm. "We were never together. But she told my father that we had been. And then she told him that I refused to do my duty. That I told her to get rid of it. That I was, in short, every bit the callous and unfeeling character she'd painted me in the tabloids. And in those rumors."

"You must have insisted on a blood test to prove that you're not the father."

"I did," Hugo bit out. "But he died before I

could show him that proof. He had heart failure and never recovered, and doctors can use any terms they wish to explain what happened. But I think the shock killed him."

He'd forgotten that they were standing in the middle of the ballroom. Because all he could see was Eleanor, and that terrible look on her face. As if there was nothing in the world but the two of them and the way they stood so close together, as if what he was telling her here was far more important than a mere story. As if it was something infinitely more critical than the past he was still paying for.

It was, he understood. He was telling her the truth about the most hated man in England, and she believed him.

She believed him.

Eleanor moved then, tipping herself up on her toes and fitting her palms to his chest. One of them right there where his heart still hurt.

As if she knew.

"I'm so sorry, Hugo," she whispered, her voice intense and low. "I'm ashamed to say I believed the stories, too."

Hugo felt a kind of bitterness twist through him then, though there was a warmth in it this time, as if it was something a little more complicated. He reached up and covered the hand over his heart with his.

"Do you know," he said quietly, "that you are the only person I have ever met who's apologized? When you are the one who's done the least damage."

She bit her lip, and electricity pounded through him, reminding him of all the ways this woman got to him. All the ways she was clearly the death of him.

"I've spoken to you as if I knew you. As if the stories I read were the truth, when of course they couldn't be. The truth is never so black and white, is it? No heroes, no villains, just people."

"Perhaps. But there are also Isobels in this world. They prey on others because they can. It gives them pleasure. And Eleanor, your sister is one of them."

She tried to pull her hand away, but Hugo held her fast.

"You don't understand," she said, her voice fierce again.

"But I do." Hugo moved closer then, until there was only the scantest bit of air between the two of them. "Tonight you're barefoot, your hair is down, every inch of you is feminine and soft."

"I didn't expect to run into anyone in what I wear to bed."

He took his free hand and placed it over her lips. He smiled down into the crease between her eyes. He felt things he'd never thought were real, before tonight.

"Eleanor. Who told you feminine and soft is bad?"

"Not bad," Eleanor said against his finger, sending delicious little licks of heat spiraling through him. "But not me." Her frown intensified. "It's cruel of you to pretend that you can't see it, now that you've met Vivi. I'm not the pretty one. I never was."

"Your sister is pretty, yes," Hugo said, dismissively. "In a very particular way that would, I imagine, appeal to a very particular man. But you?" He shifted his hands, smoothing them over her cheeks and then down to curl into the nape of her neck. "Little one. How can you not realize that you are beautiful? Stunning? There is no comparison."

Her marvelous eyes filled with emotion. Her perfect mouth trembled.

"You don't have to lie to me, Your Grace," she whispered.

And Hugo didn't know what to do with a woman who'd believed that he was a better man than anyone had believed him to be in years—making everything inside him shift and change—but not that she was the most beautiful creature he thought he'd ever beheld.

So he did the only thing he could. He kissed her.

CHAPTER TEN

IT WAS LIKE DANCING.

Eleanor wasn't sure she should let herself fall into something that felt a little too much like a fairy tale here in the middle of a ballroom, but his mouth was on hers again and she couldn't seem to think of anything else. Or she didn't want to think about anything else.

She didn't want to think about how little she'd cared for her sister tonight, which made her feel small. Petty. Selfish beyond measure.

But not enough to stop.

She didn't want to think about the fact that she'd left her room after tossing and turning for hours, and despite what she might have let Hugo think, she knew that she hadn't been dressed like a governess should have been. Or even as a guest should have been when she'd eased her door open and crept down the hall. She been filled with a kind of despairing recklessness, a restless need that had urged her to *do something* with all the pent-up hurt and betrayal she'd felt after dinner. She'd convinced herself that it was an excellent idea to wander the halls of Groves House half-dressed. Hair down. Bare feet.

Had she wanted this all along?

But she didn't really care if she had, because it felt like dancing.

Hugo kissed her and he kissed her. His hands moved from the nape of her neck, smoothing their way down the line of her back, and fastened thrillingly at her hips, drawing her against him.

He kissed her as if there was nothing else but that. Nothing in all the world but the slide of his mouth on hers.

"I can't get enough of you," Hugo muttered against her lips, as if it hurt him to say that. "I can't get enough."

And when he bent, then lifted her into his arms, Eleanor knew she should have protested. Nothing had made this any less wrong than it had been yesterday. Or a week ago. Or ever. She was still his employee.

But he was Hugo Grovesmoor. And Vivi was right here, in this house, but he hadn't chosen her.

He'd chosen Eleanor. He'd called her beautiful and he'd kissed her, *after* meeting Vivi. After Vivi had launched a full-scale offensive, in fact, and gotten nowhere.

For the first time in her life, someone had chosen Eleanor.

She didn't have it in her to pull away.

Hugo carried her through the house. Eleanor had no concept of what time it was, only that the last time she'd heard the clocks chime, it had been after midnight. But as far she was concerned, the night could last forever. She hoped it would.

She rested her head against Hugo's wide shoulder, and let the house drift past her as he carried her. Through the halls and up the stairs that led to his private wing. And this time, he did not take her to his library, or to that dining room of his where she'd spent all evening feeling as if she didn't exist, but further on. Down to the end of that same hall, and into the rooms that waited there.

She had a dreamy sort of impression of magnificence. Bold, masculine furnishings, dark woods and impressively large paintings and rugs so lavish it seemed a shame to walk on them. A massive stone fireplace that made her think of medieval castles, and that was only the living room.

But Hugo kept going. And with every step he took toward what had to be his bedroom, Eleanor's heart kicked at her. Harder and harder.

And then they were there, standing by the side of a massive bed that would have dwarfed a room any smaller than this one, and Hugo was shifting her. Placing her down on the edge of his mattress as if she was infinitely precious to him.

And Eleanor felt shivery. Fragile all the way through.

Because she couldn't think of another time in her life that anyone had treated her like that, as if she mattered. Oh, she assumed her parents had. But the truth was that she couldn't remember any longer. What she remembered was taking care of others.

She tilted her face up, so she could study Hugo's gorgeously male expression—hungry and intense—as he gazed back at her. He made her feel like she was dancing even when she was still. He made her feel small in all the best ways.

The truth was that he made her feel like the kind of girl she'd never been. Light, airy. Charming beyond measure.

He made her feel the way she'd always imagined it felt to be Vivi.

Eleanor still couldn't believe that she was the one sitting here, on the edge of the Duke's bed. That he hadn't picked Vivi when he'd had the chance.

But she had no intention of throwing this away. This was her chance at last. To experience everything she never had before. To be that girl some part of her had always dreamed she could have been, maybe, if things had been different.

"I would tell you I don't bite, little one," Hugo said in that smokily amused way of his. It reverberated up and down her spine, then pooled somewhere low in her belly, where it began to pulse. "But that would be a lie."

"I'm not afraid of you," she managed to say.

Hugo looked amused. Something like delighted.

"No, you are not. And it is one among many reasons you are under my skin." He studied her. "But still, you're still looking at me as if you expect me to eat you alive."

"Oh," Eleanor said softly. "I thought that was exactly what you intended to do."

Hugo let out a breath. Or perhaps it was a laugh. Either way, it shimmered in Eleanor like light.

"You'll be the death of me," Hugo muttered.

And then he was moving. He hooked an arm around Eleanor's waist and hauled her along with him as he crawled toward the center of the bed. And then, marvelously, he stretched out on top of her and settled the whole of his lean, hard body between her legs.

"Breathe," he told her, and she knew she wasn't mistaking that unholy amusement in his dark gaze. His eyes looked even more like whiskey tonight, or perhaps it was just that this close, she couldn't pretend that she was anything but drunk.

On him.

"I'm breathing," she whispered.

"See that you continue," Hugo ordered her in

his lazy, aristocratic way. "I haven't killed a virgin yet."

And Eleanor loved the fact that he knew. That she didn't have to make any long, drawn-out confession. When she'd thought about this moment—in those few and far between moments when she still imagined that this was any kind of possibility, that she might give herself to a man—she'd always assumed that she would have to offer extensive explanations. She would have to tell a reasonable story about why a woman her age had never quite managed to get here before, horizontal on a bed. She would have to talk about how distant she'd always felt from others her age, in part because she'd felt so responsible for Vivi, and how that had always seemed to leave her on her own. And she'd never been able to conjure up a way to tell someone that story without coming across as some kind of freak. Better to lock all that away. Better to convince herself that not only didn't she care, but she didn't feel the same things others did.

But Hugo didn't seem to care about any of that. Not why she was a virgin at twenty-seven. Not how. The only thing he seemed to care about was that he was the one braced over her, gazing down at her as if she was a treat. As if he wanted nothing more than to bury himself in her.

As if it was only a matter of time before he did.

It took Eleanor long moments to realize what that sensation was that snaked his way through her. A blistering sort of relief.

Because she felt safe. Somehow, someway, Hugo Grovesmoor made her feel safe, here in his bed where that should have been the very last thing she felt.

She hadn't known that was possible.

"Stop thinking so hard, little one," he said then.

"That's easy for you to say," she retorted. And his mouth was at her neck, so she felt it when he smiled.

"This is very simple," he told her, and there was a serious note beneath all that lazy heat. "If I want you to do something, I'll tell you what and how to do it. Otherwise, all you need to do is enjoy yourself."

Eleanor frowned at him, and he must have

sensed it, because as he looked up that smile of his widened.

"That sounds very selfish."

"Eleanor, please." Hugo shook his head. "You cannot possibly be more selfish than I am. I promise you."

And then he put his mouth against her skin again, and Eleanor stopped thinking about anything.

Hugo took his time.

He tasted her everywhere. First he ran his hand over every part of her he could touch. He traced her collarbones. He tested her figure, spending a lot of time on her waist and the generous curves above and below. He made her writhe side to side beneath him, and when he had enough of that, he stripped her of her wrapper and her silky little nightie, and he did it all over again.

But this time, he used his mouth too.

He took her nipples in his mouth and sucked on them until she sobbed. He played with her. He made her arch up against him and cry out, over and over, and only when she felt limp and outside herself did he shift down the length of her body.

And then put his mouth between her legs.

Shattering the world into a white hot panic.

He licked into her. What he'd done with his fingers in the library had been astonishing enough, but this was worse. Better.

This was unlike anything Eleanor could possibly have imagined.

And when that wall came at her this time, she wasn't afraid of it. She let him throw her over the edge once, then again, and she shook and shimmered all the way down.

When she opened her eyes again, Hugo was naked too. And he was crawling his way over her again, his eyes locked to hers.

"You're holding up beautifully," he said, that curve in his lips. "I haven't even had to tell you to lie back and think of England."

"I always thought that would be unsanitary," she blurted out. That curve in his mouth bloomed into a real smile.

"You may well be the death of me, Eleanor. Here. Tonight."

"It always sounded so…" She trailed off, aftershocks still shuddering through her.

"It is *so*," Hugo told her. "That's what makes it so much fun."

And then Eleanor's attention was stolen away by the way Hugo settled himself against her once more.

And this time, she could feel everything.

That beautiful chest of his, chiseled and perfect and hot to the touch. But more than that, there was that heavy, foreign part of him that she could feel nudging up against the place where she was soft and melting. It made her shudder.

She reached down between them and wrapped her hand around him. His breath hissed out of him, hard. And there was that strange glitter in his eyes.

Eleanor pulled her hand away. Guiltily. "I'm sorry," she said hesitantly. "I didn't mean to hurt you."

"You didn't hurt me." Hugo's voice was strangled. "I promise you, there's no possible way you could hurt me. But hold off on that for now."

Eleanor realized in the next instant what she'd done. She did read, after all. And she had certainly watched enough television in her time. But nothing had prepared her for how different it was in real life. Hugo was big and sculpted and stunning, and still he shuddered when she touched him. How could she have known? A thousand Hollywood movies were nothing next to the feel of his body above hers, and the way that silken length of his had burned itself into her palm.

Hugo shifted. She felt the tip of him nudge its way between the folds he'd licked, and then begin to move. Up and around. Nudging against the place that made her shiver the most, wilder and wilder each time.

"Will it hurt?" she asked.

Hugo's dark gaze glittered. "Hideously."

"Is that meant to be reassuring?" she asked him, and it was hard to catch her breath. But not because she was afraid of the potential pain.

"You strike me as a woman who appreciates the truth, Eleanor. Are you not?"

"Surely it can't be that bad or people wouldn't do it all the time."

"If you already know," Hugo drawled, "then why did you ask?"

Eleanor scowled at him. She opened up her

mouth to snap something at him, and that was when he slid himself inside of her.

All the way inside of her.

Eleanor choked back whatever she might have been about to say. Pain lanced through her—

But it wasn't pain. In the next instant, she realized that it was sensation, certainly, and almost too much of it. Still, it wasn't *pain.*

It was somehow sharp and full at once. She felt exposed, even though Hugo covered the whole of her body with his. She felt shaky and taken, and still, somehow, fragile and precious at once.

"Did it hurt?" Hugo asked, his voice little more than a growl.

Eleanor tested it. She shifted her hips a little bit this way, then that. Then again.

And each time she moved, the sensation changed. The fullness remained, but the sharpness eased. Until she started to suspect that the fullness was warmth. She tried it again, and again, and sure enough the more she moved, the warmer it got.

And it spiraled out from that place inside her, and set the rest of her on fire.

"Hideously," she whispered up at him.

Hugo grinned. And then he began to move.

And Eleanor understood that she'd only known sparks.

This was the fire.

Hugo was thorough. He set a slow, easy pace, and Eleanor met it as she wrapped herself around him. And then she mirrored him. She did what he did.

He put his mouth on her skin and she returned the favor. When he thrust deep into her, she lifted her hips to meet each stroke. And the more she did it, the less smooth and studied he became.

Until he seemed as out of breath and outside himself as she was.

Something cracked wide open inside of her. She felt it happen as he slammed into her, sending that impossible joy dancing all through her veins.

"What the hell you doing to me?" Hugo whispered fiercely, his face in the crook of her neck.

And that crack only widened further, and filled with light.

He'd chosen her. And here, beneath him, with him deep inside of her and everything fire and need and all that beautiful hunger, she couldn't help but believe that maybe he needed her, too.

Not because she was a woman to scratch some itch. He was Hugo Grovesmoor. He could have any woman he liked for that kind of thing, she knew that. But because she was her, specifically.

Because together, they were *them*.

And that was more precious than anything, even all the priceless things cluttering up this rambling old house.

With every deep stroke, every life-altering thrust, she believed it more.

And when she found herself falling this time, cracked wide open and full of him, it felt like love.

Especially when Hugo followed her over, shouting out her name.

CHAPTER ELEVEN

IT WAS VERY early the next morning when Eleanor finally slipped from Hugo's bed, placing her unsteady feet on the floor beside the massive bed where she'd slept in snatches and learned a whole lot of things about pleasure.

Dark, delirious, wondrous things that still moved in her, making her flush hot and red all over again, just remembering.

She ached everywhere, she realized as she stood. Places she'd had no idea *could* ache were half on fire, making her feel as if she'd woken up in someone else's body. There were tugs here and vague abrasions there, and she could remember something wild and carnal and inexpressibly beautiful to explain each one.

Eleanor thought she ought to be ashamed. Maybe she would be, later. When the reality of last night had time to settle. But right here, right now, she didn't regret a thing.

She found the nightclothes she'd worn last night and pulled them back on, trying hard not to remember exactly how Hugo had pulled each of them off her. Trying hard not to slip off into that same red haze again, all flushed and needy.

She peeked over her shoulder at the bed again, some part of her still unable to believe that any of this had happened. One red-hot image after the next chased itself through her head, in case her body couldn't tell her what had happened, inside and out. But if she'd had any lingering doubt, the sight of Hugo sprawled out there across the better part of his bed got rid of it.

She had tasted every inch of him. She'd taken that enormous length of his deep into her mouth, and had learned how to taste him and tease him the way he'd done to her. He'd taught her how to kneel up over him, and had taken her that way. He'd taught her all the wicked things he could do with his hands, and she'd tried to do the same to him. Over and over again.

She had no idea there were so many different ways—an infinite number of ways, apparently— to do the same thing. Crack apart like that and fall together, sleep entangled, then wake to do it again.

And the greedy part of her wanted to experience all of them. Every last possible way to explode like that. Here and now, though she was a little bit stiff and still achey. Eleanor didn't care, as long she got to experience it all with Hugo.

Hugo, who lay on his back with his arms splayed wide, as commanding in his bed as he was out of it. Hugo, who looked more approachable when she slept. No smirking. No mocking tone of voice. No reminders that he considered himself the biggest monster in England, because everyone else did.

Everyone except Eleanor, that was.

She tucked her hair behind her ears and forced herself to turn around. To walk toward the bedroom door, and then, harder still, to walk out and leave Hugo there behind her when that was the last thing she wanted to do.

Because whatever else happened, she had a job to do. A little girl who had enough of people in her life abandoning her in one way or another, and didn't need more of that from Eleanor.

And if there was a part of her that didn't want to be there when Hugo woke, well. She told herself that was nothing but her inbred practicality. The man might not have had the relationship everyone thought he'd had with Isobel Vanderhaven, but that didn't mean he been a saint.

Eleanor refused to be that silly virgin she'd certainly read enough about and seen too many times on-screen. The one who fell head over heels at the first hint of a man's interest and made a complete fool of herself.

There wasn't much she could do about the first part of that, but she'd be damned if she'd make a fool of herself. Not if she could avoid it.

Once outside of Hugo's rooms, she ducked her head down and moved as quickly as she could through the house without actually breaking into a run. It was still early, so she thought it was likely that no one would be up and around yet. Even so, she took the back stairs whenever possible, the better to be sure no one saw her wandering around, so far from her own rooms, in her revealing sleepwear.

"Better safe than sorry," she muttered to herself.

And then she let out a huge sigh of relief when she made it to her door. All she could think about, then, was that enormous tub in her bathroom and slipping her whole, sweetly aching body into the deep embrace of it. She pushed her way through the door, already piling her hair on the top of her head in anticipation.

"Where have you been?"

Eleanor flinched at the sound of that voice. It startled her so badly that it took her longer than it should have to realize that it was Vivi, of course. Because who else could it be?

She dropped her arms, the hair she hadn't quite managed to put into a knot tumbling down around her shoulders, and she told herself she had no reason whatsoever to feel guilty. About anything.

And yet that was exactly what she felt as she found her sister standing there in the doorway to the bedroom, her arms crossed and a flat sort of look on her face.

For a moment, they stared at each other across the stillness of the early morning.

"Sometimes when I can't sleep," Eleanor said

with as much quiet dignity as she could manage, "I walk in the halls. It gets the blood moving, at the very least."

Vivi let out a small sort of laugh that suggested she didn't find anything funny at all.

"You can't possibly expect me to believe that, can you? I'm your sister, not your seven-year-old student."

"What are you doing here, Vivi?" Eleanor asked softly. "The guest suites are clear across the house."

Vivi's mouth was a taut line, and that flat look was still making her new gold eyes look a bit more tarnished than usual. "I went looking for you. I was after a little bit of sister time. And guess what? You haven't been here for hours."

"You wanted sister time in the middle of the night?" Eleanor asked, and she didn't try too hard to keep the skepticism out of her voice. "Did you imagine that I would be awake? Or did you think you would wake me up, even though I have to get up and work in the morning?"

Neither one, she was well aware, said great things about how her sister saw her. Hugo's words swirled around in her head, and it seemed she couldn't banish them the way she wished she could. And something sour was sloshing around in her belly, making it worse.

Because Eleanor didn't know that it would really be all that out of line if Vivi *had* assumed that Eleanor would be perfectly all right with being woken up at all hours. Wasn't that what her role had always been? And there was only one person who had demanded Eleanor stay in that role. Eleanor herself.

She had always been so desperate to be needed, because love was tricky and people died and took their love with them. Need was better. Need made her indispensable.

But it had never made her feel as alive as Hugo had. As if she'd been sleepwalking for years.

"Do you think I can't tell what you've been up to?" Vivi asked. Her voice was strange. As flat as her gaze, and yet there was that sharp undercurrent. "How could you do this?"

"I don't know what you think I've done." Eleanor squared her shoulders and forced herself to ignore the part of her that had always been afraid to square off with Vivi. Because if she lost Vivi on top of everything else she'd lost, what would she have? She clarified. "To you."

Vivi shook her head. "All the things I've done, all the trouble I've gone to for *us*, Eleanor. And you can't even tell me the truth."

"I think that's unfair."

"If you had something going on with the Duke, you should have told me, so I wouldn't have bothered making a fool of myself at that dinner last night." Vivi shook her head. "Am I just a party trick you like to trot out to amuse yourself and your aristocratic friend?"

The sweeping injustice of that was almost enough to knock Eleanor back a step or two.

"I don't have any 'aristocratic friends,' Vivi," Eleanor managed to say, her voice on the verge of trembling. It felt a lot like anger, something she'd always swallowed down before. Something she'd always pretended she didn't feel, no matter what. "I think we both know that's you, not me. I work at Groves House. You're on holiday. It's been years since we decided it would make sense for you to make like a socialite and land a rich husband, and all you've done since is go to parties and spend the money I make. Which one of us is the party trick?"

She heard her own words hanging there in the quiet of the room, and could feel them shaking around inside of her, like a new kind of shivering. And she didn't know if she needed to lie down. Or possibly get sick. Or apologize, instantly.

But she didn't do any of those things. She should have said something years ago. She'd bitten her tongue and she'd bitten her tongue—and it was funny, wasn't it, that it took Hugo teaching her all the other, more fun things she could do with it to loosen it at last.

Eleanor waited to feel shamed by that, but it didn't come.

"This is why they call him a monster," Vivi said softly. "You know that, right? He ruins everything he touches. Even us."

Abruptly, Eleanor was finished with this conversation. She'd had enough. She straightened herself up and reminded herself that she was a grown woman. Not a teen who'd been caught sneaking about after curfew. She didn't have to stand here and offer explanations.

And she certainly didn't need to listen to her sister's malicious and uninformed thoughts about Hugo.

"I don't need an interrogation, Vivi," she said then. Not unkindly. Just matter-of-factly. "I really do have to work in a couple of hours."

"You can't possibly think—" Vivi began, a scornful sort of note in her voice that Eleanor didn't like at all.

"I don't ask you to account for yourself, do I?" she retorted, cutting Vivi off as she moved across the floor toward the doorway her sister stood in. "I choose to believe that everything you do, you do with both our best interests at heart. I don't understand why you can't extend me the same courtesy."

She brushed past Vivi then, half expecting her sister to grab her arm and escalate things the way she'd been known to do in the past, but Vivi only watched her—closely—as she made her way into the bathroom. Eleanor turned on the taps, ran her fingers through the water as she fiddled with the temperature, and pretended everything was normal. That she was still a virgin. That she was still the same person she'd been yesterday.

That she hadn't spent her night so full of Hugo in every possible way that she could barely breathe now.

The truth was, she didn't want to breathe.

And love her sister as she might, she didn't want to share what had happened with her. Eleanor wanted to keep it to herself. She wanted to hold it tight.

She wanted to hoard it, a bright, gleaming evening set against the rest of her practical life.

"He will chew you up and spit you out," Vivi said darkly from the door. "That's what he does, like it's his job. Because he doesn't have a real job."

Eleanor shook the water off her hand as she straightened. There were so many things she could say to that. For example, she could point out that Vivi had dressed for dinner last night as if she was perfectly willing to risk a few tooth marks. But she didn't. She only walked to the bathroom door and she smiled at her sister.

"Are you concerned for me?" she asked quietly. "Or is this something else?"

Vivi flushed at that. Her eyes narrowed. "Of course I'm concerned for you. What else would it be?"

"I can't imagine."

"I'm not jealous of you, Eleanor, if that's what you mean."

"Perish the thought," Eleanor said dryly.

"The truth is, I know what men like Hugo Grovesmoor are like. You don't. I've spent years around his type while you've…"

"Yes." Eleanor nodded. "While I've scuttled about in the shadows like the help."

Vivi let out a breath, and if Eleanor wasn't mistaken, the look in her new gold eyes then was pity.

Something in her froze solid.

"If you don't like your life, you should change it," Vivi said quietly. "I'll help. But Hugo Grovesmoor isn't a change, Eleanor. He's an atom bomb. And I understand that you're hopped up on hormones right now and feeling lavish, but I don't think you're prepared for the damage a man like him will do."

"I love you, Vivi," Eleanor managed to say past the sudden, sinking feeling inside of her, because who was she kidding? She knew nothing about men, much less men like Hugo. Why was she so certain she was right and Vivi was wrong? "You know I do. But I have to get ready for my day."

"I love you, too," Vivi retorted. "And don't worry. I'm going to prove it. I'll take care of you. I always said I would."

Eleanor didn't know what that meant and more, she was certain she didn't want to know, especially once Vivi left.

She ran her bath and she sat in it for a long time, until the water grew cold and the clock in her living room told her it was time to move. Then she climbed out, toweled off, and got dressed for her usual day with Geraldine as if she was still the same old Eleanor in the same old body she'd had before.

Because she was, damn it. No atom bombs. No damage.

She was exactly who she'd always been, despite

her ill-considered words to Vivi. She castigated herself for each and every one of them as she took Geraldine through her lessons, the last she'd have for a few days now that Eleanor's initial six weeks were up and Eleanor was due a brief holiday. They talked about what Geraldine would do over her break. They talked about the books Geraldine was reading and Geraldine's many adventures with Pono, the rooster plush toy she liked best.

They did not see the Duke. Eleanor told herself she was grateful. Because she didn't want to be that silly virgin—the one even her own sister seemed certain she already was—and that meant she'd needed the day to regain her equanimity.

"You're fine now," she told herself stoutly as she climbed the stairs from the nursery that led to her rooms. "Perfectly fine, as ever."

But when she let herself into her rooms, Vivi was waiting. Again.

"You should have just had a cot brought in," Eleanor said mildly.

"I think you'd better pack, love," Vivi replied. "We'll need to leave tonight."

"No need for that, surely," Eleanor said. She

sank down on the nearest upright, Elizabethan chair. "We can leave in the morning. More chance of a train, I'd think."

"You don't understand," Vivi said, and while her voice was patient, her gaze was not. Her eyes fairly danced, too bright and a bit too sharp, as if she'd been at the spirits again. "You're not going to want to be here in the morning."

Eleanor discovered that she was tired. Very, very tired. That was what happened when a person got all of about twelve minutes of sleep all night long. She couldn't say she regretted it. But it had obviously dulled her brain, because she wasn't following Vivi at all.

"Vivi," she began, "I really don't…"

"I told you I would take care of you and I meant it," her sister said stoutly. "There are certain tabloids that are so desperate for a story about Hugo that they'd pay anything for a fake one. Which means they'd pay twice that for a real one."

Eleanor was glad she was sitting down, because she thought that if she hadn't been, she might have fallen.

"No," she managed to say from a far distance,

while her ears buzzed at her and her lunch threatened the back of her throat. "I signed a nondisclosure agreement. I can't sell anything."

"You can't," Vivi said with a hard sort of shrug.
"But I can. There's been nothing new on Hugo in
ages. Everyone's tired of speculating what hor-
rors he's visiting on that poor kid. A sex romp
with the governess is exactly what they'd expect,
isn't it?"

"I forbid it," Eleanor snapped, and she hardly
recognized her own voice. Or the fact she'd
surged to her feet and had balled her hands up
into fists.

Vivi only eyed her from across the room, that
pitying look on her face again.

"I thought you'd say something like that."

"You thought correctly."

"Which is why I didn't consult you." Vivi shook
her head. "It's done, Eleanor. We have five hun-
dred thousand pounds in our account and you
don't have to say a word. Or do another thing.
Our troubles are over. But the story is running to-
morrow." Vivi tilted her head, taking in the house
all around them. This life Eleanor had known

better than to get too attached to—hadn't she? And Hugo, whose name seemed to detonate inside of her, shaking through her. Shaking her. "And if I were you, I wouldn't be here when he reads it."

CHAPTER TWELVE

ELEANOR HAD BETRAYED HIM.

What bothered Hugo most was that somehow, this entirely predictable turn of events surprised him.

"Off to catch the last train," Mrs. Redding had said yesterday afternoon when Hugo had actually lowered himself to ask where Eleanor was, with her usual disapproving sniff. "A bit keen to celebrate her time off, if you ask me."

"No one did," Hugo had replied, with a smile. A cheeky one. Which had done absolutely nothing but make the old woman roll her eyes. Their love language, he'd told himself.

But that had been before the tabloids published their usual filth and innuendo in the morning. That had been when he was still looking forward to seeing her. Craving it, if he was honest. He'd woken yesterday morning to find her missing from his bed and it was as if he was missing a limb. As if they'd spent every night of a good five years sleeping wrapped around each other in the same bed, and her sudden absence hurt.

Hurt.

He didn't understand it. Or perhaps he didn't want to understand it. Yesterday, all he'd wanted was to lose himself in her innocence. Her sweetness. And all that intoxicating heat.

Somehow he'd forgotten to be cynical where Eleanor was concerned.

An unforgivable oversight.

Because sometime yesterday, when he'd still been lying in his bed surrounded by her scent and marveling at the notion that innocence could be so addictive—transformative, even, which should have appalled someone as calcified in his own bitterness as Hugo had been for years—Eleanor had not been doing the same. Instead, she had been sharing what had happened between them with her sister. Reporting back, perhaps, that their plan had worked? And sometimes after that, Vivi had sold an extraordinarily salacious and sordid tale to the most shrill and suggestive of the tabloids about *Horrible Hugo*, the *Most Hated*

Duke in England, and his *Sexcapades with his Governesses.*

Really, Hugo could have written it himself.

What astonished him was that he hadn't. He'd let his guard down for the first time since Isobel had gotten her hooks in him—hell, he'd even told Eleanor the truth. As if she was someone he could trust. As if, when she'd sounded so appalled at the very notion that anyone could sell him out to the tabloids, she'd meant it.

Hugo couldn't trust anyone. Ever. How many times did he need to learn it?

The truth was, he'd handed Eleanor and her sister all the ammunition they'd need. Fourteen previous governesses, all unceremoniously sacked. When the suspiciously unknown sister of a periodic tabloid bit of arm candy, the overly ambitious Vivi—whose desperation repeatedly led her to all sorts of entanglements that found their way into tawdry little tell-alls—had turned up, Hugo should have seen this coming.

Why hadn't he seen this coming?

Hugo treats his governesses like his own private harem!

That was what the paper screeched, in that awful tone they used when they were putting words into people's mouths. Then again, he imagined a woman who could giggle aggressively the way Vivi Andrews had could turn a pointed phrase or two when she had a mind to.

He doesn't give a toss about poor Isobel's baby, preferring depraved sex romps in his country estate to changing nappies.

It was nothing he hadn't read before a thousand times. It wasn't even particularly well done, in his opinion, given he was now a kind of connoisseur of tabloid hit pieces. A giant spread with vague accusations about unsavory sexual practices, a glamour shot of Vivi as if she was the governess in question next to a picture of what might have been Eleanor in a hooded something or other, and an excuse to fling pictures of lost, sainted Isobel and Torquil all over the place. Along with everyone's favorite picture of toddler Geraldine—all gap teeth and copper curls, looking lost and in need of nappy-changing—as if she'd been preserved forever at an age when Hugo's neglect could have resulted in her toddling about in her own filth.

He was tempted to ring up Vivi Andrews himself and demand a cut of what must have been a very tidy profit. But he couldn't do that, could he, because that would mean very coldly and calculatedly discussing when and how Vivi and her sister had decided to set him up so beautifully.

And then asking the question he wanted to know the answer to but was afraid to ask: How had they known that Eleanor's brand of stroppy innocence would send him crashing to his knees? He'd had women throwing themselves at him his entire life. Some were desperate for the title. Others only wanted a little turn in the tabloids. He'd have said that there was no possible approach he hadn't grown tired of years ago.

But somehow they'd picked the one that worked.

He had a lot of questions for Eleanor. He was even tempted to question whether her virginity had been real—but no. He knew better. He'd been there. The betrayal was real, but so was that night. So was what had passed between them.

Hugo might not know much, but he knew that.

Not that it helped. He still found himself stalking around his damned house in the gloomy twilight, like a sepulchral poet or something equally tragic.

Hugo couldn't remember the last time he'd surrendered so completely to self-pity. He made his lonely, nauseatingly melancholic way into his library, broodingly eyeing the shelves he'd once told Eleanor she'd nearly knocked down. Tonight he was tempted to knock them down himself. With a bottle of whiskey and his own hard head.

Because he never learned.

He was the monster of all of England's most fervent fantasies, paying out his penance in his rambling out house, alone. Forever.

Nothing could change that. Not his own disinterest in the narrative. Not the fact his ward was, despite all wailing to the contrary, a healthy and relatively happy child. Not a scowling, insufficiently respectful governess who'd treated him as an irritant to be borne, much like the sulky moors all around.

He might have imagined that things had changed that night and that wildly optimistic morning after, but that was only more proof that he was an idiot of epic proportions.

"Nothing new in that," he muttered to himself, not even bothering to scowl at the fire. "It's the bloody story of my life."

As was the certainty that somehow, he would pay for this, too.

The door to the library opened then. Hugo watched, bemused, as it scraped its way inward across the thick rug on the floor. Almost as if the person entering the room wasn't strong enough to move it.

He blinked when he saw the figure standing in the door then. It was Geraldine, who never sought him out of her own accord, and never here. She usually suffered warily through her dinners with him, eyeing him suspiciously from her place down the table. Tonight she looked less like the celebrated daughter of a world-renowned beauty and more...like a kid. Her copper-colored plaits stood out at odd angles from her head, she was dressed in a jumper and jeans like any random child might have been, and her little face was drawn into a frown.

She looked sturdy. And surly, Hugo couldn't help but notice.

"Yes, my ward?" he drawled. He lounged back in his chair before the fire and raised his brows at her, doing his best, as ever, to sound like a proper guardian instead of the world's favorite scandal.

The little girl screwed up her nose while the corners of her pudgy mouth turned down, but she kept her scowl aimed right at him.

Evidence of Eleanor's teaching, clearly, he thought, and hated the lancing sensation of something that couldn't be pain—because he refused to accept pain—straight through him.

"Nanny Marie says Miss Andrews is never coming back."

Hugo waited for her to continue, but Geraldine only stared at him. Rather challengingly, actually.

"I am at a loss as to where *Nanny Marie*," and he utterly failed to keep the sardonic inflection from his tone at that name, "would get the impression that she has access to staffing decisions."

"I like her."

"Nanny Marie? I couldn't identify her in a

lineup, I'm afraid. Much less determine whether or not I cared for her one way or another."

"Miss Andrews."

Geraldine sounded testy, but definitive. And that was the trouble. Hugo liked Miss Andrews, too. Definitively.

Even now.

He'd told Eleanor things he'd never told anyone. He'd expected her to understand him when no one else had, ever. And then sure enough, she had. Meanwhile, she'd held on to her innocence far, far longer than most women her age, and she'd gifted it to him. *Him.* As if it had never occurred to her that Hugo the Horrible wasn't a suitable recipient for such a gift.

As if she'd felt completely safe with him, which should have been impossible.

And as if that wasn't enough, Hugo wasn't entirely sure that she was the one who had been rendered fragile by what had happened that night. There were parts of him that no longer fit the way they had before. Parts of him that scraped at all the walls he'd built inside, as if *he* didn't fit anymore.

He had been perfectly content here. Happy enough to live out the consequences of Isobel's decisions far away from prying eyes and telescopic lenses. Perfectly willing to let the country shake in horror at the notion of what he might be doing to their lost saint's precious little girl. No small part of him had thrilled to the idea that he was literally some people's nightmare. Every single night.

He'd taken pleasure in that. They deserved it.

Hugo couldn't understand where all that had gone. How it had disappeared in the course of one very long, very thorough exploration of a prim governess's astonishingly curvy body.

What was it in him that couldn't shrug her off the way he had all the others? Why was it so impossible to draw a line under the latest tabloid scandal and move on? When his past mistakes had aired out his laundry in front of whole nations, Hugo had been unbothered.

He had the sinking, lowering notion that all this time, he'd never known real ruin at all.

"You didn't fire her, did you?" Geraldine demanded, reminding him he was not alone with his brooding.

Hugo eyed her. The little girl had moved further into the room. Now she stood near the fireplace, her hands on her little hips, glaring at her guardian without a seeming care in the world. As if she thought, should there be an altercation, she could take him.

He had tried so hard these past three years, since the accident that had taken Isobel and Torquil. He'd kept his distance from this child. He had tended to Geraldine's needs, but not in a way that could ever hurt her. Or compromise her. He'd been certain—as certain as his critics, if not more so—that left to his own devices, he could only do harm.

That was what he did, he knew. Harm.

He certainly hadn't allowed himself to like Gerladine. Or anyone.

But all he could see was Eleanor, then. Her face, so lovely and so fierce, as she'd stood up for Geraldine. *It's not her fault,* she'd told him.

And Hugo knew that. He'd gone out of his way to make sure he never brought his feelings about

Isobel into any interaction he had with Geraldine. But it hadn't occurred to him until today—until Eleanor—that he hadn't let his feelings enter into anything in a very long time.

Because the fact of the matter was, he rather liked this little girl. He liked how unafraid she was. He liked the fact that she was seven years old and yet had no apparent second thoughts about walking straight into her guardian's library and confronting him. And the more he stared at her, the less she seemed to care. Her little chin tilted up. She even sniffed, as if impatient.

She was a fighter. How could he not adore her for it?

Especially when he'd stopped fighting so long ago.

"If I did fire her, that would be my decision as your guardian and would not require a consultation, Geraldine," Hugo said reprovingly. But when her face looked stormy, he relented. "But I didn't let her go."

He crooked his finger and then pointed to the leather chair across from him. Geraldine made a huffing sound that did not bode well for her teen years, but she obeyed him. With perhaps a little too much stomping, and more attitude than he would have thought possible from a sweet little child, she moved from the fireplace to climb up into the big leather chair. The big piece of furniture seemed to swallow her whole, but that didn't bother Geraldine. She slid back, stuck her feet out straight in front of her, and crossed her arms over her chest.

Mutinously.

"Where is she if you didn't get rid of her?" Geraldine asked as if she'd caught Hugo out in a dirty lie.

"I feel certain Miss Andrews told you that she was taking a few days' break. She does get one, you know. We can't lock her away in a cage and force her to stay here all the time."

Though the idea held some appeal.

The little girl's chin jutted out. "Why not?"

"Excellent question."

"We should go get her back, then," Geraldine said, with a wide gesture of one hand, as if Hugo really was an idiot and she was leading him to the right answer because he was taking too long to get there himself.

And the damnedest thing was, Hugo admired that, too.

Geraldine was not yet ten and yet she was showing more fight than he had in the past fifteen years.

Why had he allowed Isobel to paint him the way she had? Of course there was no fighting a slanted story or a nasty rumor, but he hadn't tried and he hadn't done anything else, either. He hadn't pointedly lived a life completely opposed to the one Isobel claimed he did. He'd never even defended himself. He'd told himself it was because he was too proud to dignify her claims with a response, but was that truly it? Or was it the same sort of martyrdom he'd always abhorred when Isobel faked it?

Had he been waiting all this time for someone to look at him and see him and believe that he wasn't the things that had been said about him?

Maybe there was some virtue in that. Or there could have been—had his father not died believing the very worst of him.

The fact of the matter was, Hugo had never seen the point of fighting battles he'd decided in advance that he couldn't win. He'd never righted a single wrong. He'd simply sat here and taken it. And to what end?

Whether the public loved him or hated him, he was the only parental influence in this child's life. And despite that handicap, Geraldine appeared to be thriving. She was flushed with indignation, and if he wasn't mistaken, love.

Love.

It thudded into him. Then again. Like another fight he was destined to lose. But this time, he didn't intend to go down alone.

Was it virtue to act as if he was a punching bag for all these years or was it an especially noxious version of self-pity?

Hugo didn't know. But he did know this. He was a creature of temper and mood, unable to control himself at any time, the tabloids said.

So he saw no reason to start now.

"Yes," he said slowly, smiling at Geraldine. Until she smiled back, as if they were together in this. Because they were. "We really should get her back. What an excellent idea."

CHAPTER THIRTEEN

RETURNING TO LONDON was like being slapped in the face with the pitiless palm of a little too much reality. But there was nothing to do but grin and bear it.

Eleanor gritted her teeth, figuratively and literally, and set about cleaning up Vivi's mess.

Not the big mess, of course. Not the mess that haunted her, making her feel sick and small and ashamed. Or shaky every time she saw the *Daily Mail* in a newsstand. Not the mess that rolled around inside of her, making her feel as oily and greasy and horrid as what Vivi had done, every time she drew breath—

No, there was no fixing that. Vivi had sold Eleanor's story as her own and asserted, repeatedly and proudly, that she would do it again. She claimed it was for both of their own good, though that prickly, ugly thing inside of Eleanor thought different and left marks every time it did. But it made no difference. It was done.

And Eleanor was just one more scar Hugo would add to his collection. One more lie to add to the rest.

Eleanor concentrated on the things she could fix.

She placated their landlord, pleading their case as sweetly as she could. She did not take Vivi's advice to simply tell the suspicious old woman where she could stuff it, because all that money that Vivi had been promised had yet to come through. She cleaned. Everything. From what passed for baseboards in their tiny tip of a flat to the windows and back. She cleaned every cup and saucer, plate and utensil. She even cleaned out the terrifying old tea mugs, coated in tannins as evidence of their long years of use.

She cleaned as if she was on a mission.

As if it was penance.

And none of that seemed to do a single thing to make her feel better.

Eleanor suspected that there would be no feeling better. That there would be no recovering from this. It didn't matter how she'd come to betray Hugo, surely. It only mattered that she had. Not only had she betrayed him, she hadn't even had the decency to look him in the face and let him know she'd done it.

She hadn't even said goodbye.

Instead, she'd snuck off into the gathering fall evening with her case and her sister, like some kind of thief in reverse.

That was the part she didn't think she could live with. That was the part that scraped to her belly like some ravenous beast with sharp claws. Over and over again.

"You're being a bit dramatic, no?" Vivi asked one evening.

The way she had back in that other life, when Eleanor had never met Hugo Grovesmoor and hadn't had the faintest idea how he would upend her life. The way she did with a little too much frequency, to Eleanor's mind, given her penchant for making an opera out of all and sundry.

Eleanor eyed her sister over the pile of mending that she'd been ruthlessly going through for days now that the flat fairly sparkled. Vivi's trousers.

Vivi's poncey skirts. Vivi's lovely and expensive clothes that Vivi herself didn't bother to treat with anything resembling reverence. Or even the bare minimum of care, it appeared.

"While tending to your sewing?" Eleanor asked mildly, which was getting harder to do all the time. "I didn't realize it was possible to be theatrical while mending."

Vivi lifted herself up from the bit of floor in front of the telly, where she'd been flinging herself this way and that to a DVD of some shiny-toothed and alarmingly narrow American celebrity trainer.

"Everyone's obsessed with this workout," she'd informed Eleanor as she'd contorted about.

Eleanor had responded by finishing off the last packet of chocolate biscuits. *At* her.

Now Vivi plunked herself down on the small sofa next to Eleanor, making the cushion dip alarmingly and a pile of her waiting mending tip over. Eleanor thought she'd switch the telly over to a show and drown her mood out, as she been doing since they'd returned, but instead she twisted her body around so she could look her sister straight in the face.

"I know you think you hate me," Vivi said, her voice serious and an unexpected wallop. "I understand that. I even accept it. You don't have any experience with these things."

Eleanor's teeth ached. She made herself unclench her jaw.

"If you mean making up tawdry stories and selling them to the highest bidder, then no. I certainly don't."

"I mean Hugo." Vivi's voice was soft. Worse, kind. "I mean men."

Eleanor bent her head to the blouse she was attempting to repair. She kept her attention furiously focused on her needle. But she was sure that it was no use, that Vivi could see the flush that crept up the back of her neck and threatened her cheeks as well. She didn't understand how a topic that she'd been so pleased to discuss with Hugo—or not discuss, as the case might be, because he'd known and he'd handled it—she had no desire at all to discuss with her sister.

"I think I'd prefer to skip the 'poor, sad Eleanor' discussion tonight, thanks." Eleanor had to order herself to unclench her jaw. Again. And do something with her shoulders before she lifted them over the top of her head. "I think it's possible that the only thing worse than the story you sold might be your pity."

"I don't pity you, Eleanor," Vivi said, and her voice was different. Almost unrecognizable. It made Eleanor uneasy. "I envy you. I don't think I've ever been soft or dewy-eyed about anything. Not even way back when you cried over me in the hospital and I didn't."

Eleanor paused. She very carefully put down her sewing. And then she turned and held her sister's gaze.

"Vivi. Please tell me you're not about to give me 'the talk.'"

Vivi's eyes gleamed then, and they really did look like shiny gold coins, something that Eleanor wished she could find more annoying than she did.

"You spent all night with Hugo Grovesmoor. I think any attempt at a sex talk at this point would be a waste of breath, don't you?"

Eleanor tried to hide the pain that flashed over her. Or that near-reflexive urge to draw in a sharp breath, as if that would ease it.

"I don't want to talk about Hugo."

It was more that she didn't want to talk about Hugo with Vivi, if she was honest. But either way, thinking about him was painful enough.

"I know you're not going to believe me." Vivi reached over and put her hand on Eleanor's leg, and all Eleanor could seem to do was stare at it. "I know that I'm too selfish and take you for granted and anything else you want to accuse me of. It's all true. I know it's true. But that doesn't mean I don't love you, Eleanor. And I get to protect you, too."

Eleanor frowned at that hand on her leg. Hard. "Is that what you were doing, Vivi? Protecting me? Are you sure?"

Eleanor didn't know how she dared ask that—especially because she wasn't sure she wanted to know the answer. Beside her, Vivi blew out a breath. And when Eleanor looked up, something else glittered in her gaze.

"That's fair enough. I can't deny that I reacted

a bit poorly when I arrived at Groves House. I guess it all took me by surprise."

"You were jealous." Eleanor held her sister's gaze, and dared her to refute it.

But Vivi only shrugged, making the curls she'd piled on the top of her head bob a bit. "I don't know what I was. I've worked hard, for years."

Eleanor wanted to argue that, but something made her hold her tongue. Vivi's gaze darkened.

"I've put up with people you wouldn't tolerate for the length of a simple conversation, thank you. I thought we were on the same page. I thought we had specific roles to play. And then it looked as if maybe everything I was doing was beside the point and I didn't know how to handle that." She shook her head. "I'm sorry I'm not as perfect as you are."

"That's not fair."

"You could have told me how much you liked him." Vivi's voice cracked slightly, startling them both. "You could have told me that, Eleanor."

"I didn't think you would have listened if I had."

Vivi shook her head, as if that had hurt her and

she was reeling. "Of course I would have listened. *You're my sister.* It's you and me against the world, remember?"

"I remember," Eleanor whispered. "Of course I remember."

They sat there for a moment, and something shifted inside of Eleanor as they did. That ugly, clawed weight seemed to dissipate a little.

"But this is what I wanted to talk to you about even if it makes you turn red. You don't know about men like Hugo, Eleanor. I do."

"I was under the impression that there were no men like Hugo."

She knew that was true for her. She thought it might also be true for the world, given the way they talked about him as if he'd rounded them all up, abused them horribly and personally, and then booted them out of a speeding vehicle.

"Men are more alike than not." And there was a weariness in Vivi's voice that pricked at Eleanor. She'd been so concentrated on herself. So focused on all the ways she felt overlooked. Taken advantage of. Why had it never occurred to her to wonder if her sister felt the same way? "Keen to take what they can get. No matter what. But it doesn't necessarily mean more than that."

And Eleanor wanted to argue. She wanted to tell Vivi that she was wrong. That she didn't know Hugo. But the fact was... Neither did Eleanor. She'd lived in his house, true. He'd flirted with her, she'd given him her virginity—but despite what that meant to her, it was likely all in a day's work for the likes of Hugo.

She believed that he wasn't the monster the tabloids had made him out to be. But that didn't make him a monk. It didn't make her any less of a fool. She felt her eyes fill up, and ducked her head to hide it. And blink the tears back before they could fall.

"I feel like such a fool," she whispered.

"I can't think of a woman who wouldn't fall for Hugo Grovesmoor," Vivi said, distinctly. "Not one. He's gorgeous and evil and everyone knows he's wild in bed. You never stood a chance."

She could talk about more of this than she'd thought, it turned out. But she couldn't talk about Hugo's reputation in bed. There was only so much she could be expected to handle, surely.

Without cracking apart into little pieces, all over the floor, that she knew her careless sister would never sweep up.

"And what now?" Eleanor asked instead, lifting up her hands and then letting them drop back to her lap. "What am I supposed to do now?" She moved one hand in a lazy, circular motion that encompassed the whole of her chest. "With all of *this*."

Vivi laughed, then. It was that merry laugh of hers that still warmed up the room. It astonished Eleanor how welcoming she found the sound.

"That I can help with." Vivi got to her feet and reached out her hand, beckoning for Eleanor to join her. "Come on, then. The night is young and filled with trouble for us to throw ourselves into."

"Oh, no," Eleanor said then, with a frown. "I don't get into trouble. I—"

"You don't have a job that you have to go to bed early for. You have nowhere to be in the morning."

"Well—"

"And unless I'm mistaken, you're a bit of a scarlet woman, fresh from a shocking affair with the most hated man in England."

"But it's a Wednesday," Eleanor said. Scandalized.

"Ah, grasshopper," Vivi replied mischievously. "I have so much to teach you."

And that was how Eleanor found herself out at one of those desperately chic clubs that Vivi spent so much of her time in. This one was so new it was considered a coup to get in, Vivi informed Eleanor as she got them waved past the line that snaked off down the block and around the corner. On a blustery Wednesday.

Inside, it was a cavernous place, filled with too many dizzying lights and far too many people dressed sleek and sharp. Not exactly the sort of crowd Eleanor felt at home in. But Vivi had asked Eleanor to trust that she knew what she was doing, and Eleanor had agreed to do it.

That was how she'd ended up in the ridiculous outfit her sister picked out for her, sourced more from Vivi's closet than her own.

"I told you it would fit," Vivi had said with great satisfaction when she'd finished her handiwork back at the flat. "It's quite Cinderella, isn't it?"

"If Cinderella was a bit of a tart."

Eleanor ran her hands over the slinky, stretchy dress that gave her curves absolutely nowhere to hide. For the seventeenth time, and it still accomplished nothing. She was still all breasts and hips. There was only one person alive who had ever made her feel beautiful—

But there was no use thinking about Hugo. The sooner she accepted that, the better. He wouldn't have wanted to deal with an overly sentimental virgin for long anyway. That was what Eleanor kept telling herself. No one liked clingy, especially in an employee. Vivi's tabloid story had only hastened the inevitable.

Strange how that failed to make her feel any better.

"There's nothing wrong with a tart," Vivi had admonished her, then flashed one of her grins. "It's all in the quality of the pastry, I promise you."

Eleanor didn't know what that meant. Or, rather, she opted not to pick up on her sister's innuendo.

What she did know, within seconds of entering the club, was that she was most certainly too old for this scene. Perhaps not chronologically. But she had nothing in common with the blissed-out, gleaming creatures who danced madly and drank deeply and didn't seem remotely aware of the fact that there was a world outside where people were already tucked up in their beds, ready for the next morning.

And yet, as soon as she recognized that she wasn't built to enjoy flinging back spirits and then leaping around the dance floor like Geraldine on too much sugar, she really rather enjoyed herself. It was too loud to worry about Hugo. It was too dark to worry about herself and what on earth she planned to do with her life. It was too noisy and too chaotic to do more than smile and then duck away from the strange men who tried to speak to her now and again.

Maybe tottering around town on a random Wednesday was exactly the medicine she needed, come to think of it. Eleanor decided it was, and let the night wash over her.

It was coming on three in the morning when Vivi was finally ready to leave her pack of posh friends and their innumerable dramas. Eleanor was quite pleased with herself for contriving to keep her eyes open the whole of the night, even if she'd lapsed into a strange state where she couldn't tell if she was actually asleep or not. It hadn't seemed to make much of a difference.

Vivi was chattering, as much to herself as anyone else as far as Eleanor could tell, about summoning a taxi driver with her mobile and about which of her circle she'd rowed with over the course of the evening. And Eleanor let it all wash over her, too. Because yes, she thought she really was half-asleep. But also, none of this felt like life. None of it felt real.

London didn't fit her anymore. The thought slid into her head and stayed there, taking up space. Growing with every breath. She had no idea what she was going do about that, because the only place she'd felt as if she'd fit, she'd lost. Yorkshire was as closed to her as if there was a wall around it and several armies keeping her out.

Stop, she ordered herself. *Stop thinking about Hugo.*

"I cannot imagine what you think you're doing, Miss Andrews."

Eleanor froze. Surely that voice was only in her head, the way it had been all week—but no. It was still going.

"Role models for proper young ladies, the wards of dukes, no less, cannot be carousing in the streets of London at this hour. Whatever would the tabloids say?"

That voice was straight from her dreams. It couldn't be real. Eleanor didn't react—but Vivi did. She froze solid next to her.

And Eleanor let herself believe what was right before her eyes, a car or two down from where she and Vivi had exited the club.

Hugo.

CHAPTER FOURTEEN

OF COURSE IT was Hugo.

He lounged at the curb next to a gleaming sports car that was as sleek and muscular—and expensive—as he was. It was hard to tell the difference between them. Both seemed to light up the dark all around them with the same kind of danger.

She'd dreamed this a thousand times since she'd left Groves House, but now it was happening and Eleanor didn't know what to say. What could she possibly say?

"Hugo…" she whispered.

The Duke straightened, pushing away from his leaning position against the side of the powerful vehicle. He looked elegant and dangerous with the streets of London arrayed there behind him, as if his presence rendered the ancient, ever-settled city as wild and untamed as the moors up north. His dark gaze was almost too hot to bear.

And he focused on Eleanor as if she was the only other person for miles.

For a moment she thought she was.

Then Vivi cleared her throat, and Eleanor felt reality slap her again. Hard.

"I'm sure you must be very angry," Vivi began, looking and sounding as uncertain as Eleanor felt. At a later point, she might reflect on the fact that she'd never actually heard her sister sound remorseful before. But at the moment, she was too busy greedily drinking in the sight of Hugo. Right there in front of her and who cared how.

"I don't get angry," Hugo said in that low way of his that made everything inside Eleanor seemed to run liquid and hot, then shudder before starting all over again. "What is another scandalous story in the tabloids to me? One fiction after the next, without end. One life destroyed by my touch only to appear in a bathing costume in Ibiza the following summer on the arm of a film star. Who can keep track?"

It was the cynicism in his voice that almost killed her, Eleanor thought. The weariness. It felt like a knife straight into her gut.

Because she remembered. She remembered what it had been like in his bedchamber that night. She remembered the look on his beautiful face then. Open. Filled with longing and wonder and almost too much light to bear.

"You should keep track," Eleanor heard herself say, just as she heard the huskiness in her voice that she was sure told him far too much. Gave too much away. Made her far too vulnerable. She didn't care. "Someone should keep track. Someday you will make a note of all the lies and I wouldn't be surprised if apologies followed."

Beside her, she felt Vivi tense, but she couldn't spare a glance for her sister. Not now.

"Don't be so naïve," Hugo murmured, all weary cynicism and a bit of censure besides, as if he was in some snide ballroom making cutting remarks behind a quizzing glass, like the Dukes in Eleanor's favorite novels. And yet his voice seemed to fill the street, then reverberate around inside of her, too. "There are never any apologies. *Especially* when the lies are proven to be falsehoods. No one cares about that. They care about the story, and the more salacious and slanderous it is, the better."

Eleanor stepped in front of Vivi then, because the tension in the air felt like a weapon. "It's not her fault. She was taking care of me."

Hugo smirked, and it made Eleanor flinch.

"Because I am the big bad wolf, after all," he agreed in that same dark way. "Despoiler of maidens when they are so unfortunate as to cross my path. Hunkered down in my Yorkshire cave, picking my teeth with the bones of my enemies."

"It is because you say things like that with such obvious relish," Eleanor pointed out crisply, "that it's difficult to imagine you are anything else."

"I'm not sorry," Vivi said over Eleanor's shoulder. Unwisely, in Eleanor's opinion. "Everyone knows what you're like. If you've come down here to bully us, or make things difficult because of the story, you should know that I'm more than capable of taking care of Eleanor as well as myself."

"Are you now?" Hugo's smirk could have taken chunks out of the old, listed building behind them. Eleanor was surprised it still stood. Or that she did. "Let me guess. You will smile prettily. Eleanor will frown. And before you will fall the whole of London and assorted villains just like me. With a click of your fingers."

Hugo didn't wait for an answer to that. He did that thing with his hand again. He merely lifted it, and just like that a cab came screeching to a halt in front of him. He moved from front of his own sports car to the cab, and opened the passenger door with great flourish.

"Your carriage awaits," he said.

Eleanor blinked. It seemed absurd to her that Hugo would appear before her at three o'clock in the morning only to summon them a taxi, but maybe Vivi was more right than she'd wanted to accept. Maybe men were in fact this mystifying at all times. She set her teeth in that way that was becoming a little too common, straightened her shoulders to match, and she marched toward the cab.

"Not you," Hugo said, a current of something like laughter in his voice. Or maybe Eleanor was so desperate to pretend he didn't hate her that she was imagining it. Either way, he reached out a hand and hooked her arm. "You're coming with me."

Vivi stopped on Eleanor's other side. "Oh, no, she's not. Don't go after the weak link. If you want a fight, fight me."

And Eleanor stood there on a London street in the middle of a Wednesday night that had long since become a Thursday morning, her sister fierce at her back and this maddening, intoxicating, gorgeous man before her.

It seemed as if her whole life had come down to this moment. Did she fall back into what was comfortable and let Vivi do her thing the way she always did—the way she'd done when she'd left Yorkshire without a word to Hugo, in fact? Or did she step forward into all the blistering unknown she could see shining there in Hugo's eyes—whether he hated her as he should...or didn't?

How would she live with herself if she didn't try?

There was a part of her that wanted to wait and see. She wanted to see who Hugo would choose. This wasn't a ballroom, in the middle of the night, empty of everyone save the two of them. This was a London street, and both she and Vivi were dressed for the night they'd just had. That meant skin. Skin and lean, lanky attractiveness on Vivi's part. Skin and abundant curves on Eleanor's.

There was a part of her that wanted to act as if she and her sister were a buffet. Line them both up and watch him as he made his decision, so she could see if she was the one he'd chose because she was convenient, or because he really was the only man she'd ever met who wanted her, not her sister.

And she was tired of everyone around her making decisions for her. Even if they were well-meaning. Even if the decisions were in her best interest.

Maybe it was time for Eleanor to make a choice herself.

"It's okay," she said. She kept her eyes trained on Hugo, but she squeezed her sister's hand. "You can go Vivi. Really."

"But—"

"Go," she said again, with soft certainty. "I'll see you at home."

There must have been something in her tone, then, that brooked no disobedience. Or any back talk. Vivi squeezed her hand back, hard, and then got into the waiting car. She slammed the door behind her, and the cab headed off, chugging down the street and then around the corner.

And Eleanor was left standing on a quiet street in a busy city, with the man she never thought she'd see again. Not face to face. Not anywhere but in her head and on a screen or a glossy tabloid page.

"Eleanor. Little one." Hugo shook his head, and it made heat spiral through her, charging through her where she stood as if he'd lit a match. Making the heels she wore seem that much more precarious. "Whatever are you wearing?"

"In comparison to most of the girls I saw tonight, I might as well be wearing a grandmother's cardi and a suit of armor."

"A suit of armor would be a good start."

"I'm wearing a perfectly lovely dress, thank you," Eleanor said primly, and kept herself from tugging on the hem of it by sheer force of will. "If I was working, I'd be wearing something appropriate for work."

"Your hair."

His voice sounded almost tortured, and Eleanor stopped breathing. He reached out and raked his fingers through the dark mass that Vivi had made wavy and thick.

"I hate your hair up, Eleanor. Have I told you that?"

"It's a good job it isn't up to you, then. Isn't it?"

"Are you certain it isn't up to me?"

Hugo moved closer, but all Eleanor could feel was what hung there between them. That tabloid story. Eleanor's innocence. Geraldine. Or the fact she was in love with him, just like a silly, clingy virgin in a story who didn't know enough to guard her own heart. Too many things to bear.

But Hugo moved closer as if he was as entranced she was. As if he couldn't stay away. And Eleanor stopped thinking about anything but him and the half smile on his face as he looked down at her.

"Maybe you haven't heard. I'm a great and glorious peer of the realm. My every wish is law. Or close enough."

He shifted closer. He moved so he could cup her face in his hands, his hundred-percent-proof eyes intent on hers. And everything inside her shivered. Rocked a little bit, then rolled, deep and low.

And this time, she didn't think it was the shoes.

"The tabloids…" She whispered. "Hugo, I'm so very sorry. I don't know how I can ever make it right."

"I don't care about the tabloids."

Eleanor scowled at him. "Well, you should. It's not a small thing to have all these lies told about you. You should care and you should fight and you should—"

"But that's the thing. In this case, the tabloids are no more than the truth. I did take advantage of you. You worked for me and I shouldn't have touched you. But I did."

"I wanted you to."

"I didn't say I was sorry."

He shifted again, and there was a look on his face that Eleanor thought she'd seen before, though she couldn't quite place it. And then it came to her. It had been that night. Locked away in his bedchamber, just the two of them, with nothing outside his door between them. He'd propped himself over her, he'd sunk himself deep inside of her, and he'd looked at her. Just like this.

Her heart began to beat at her, slow and intense.

"I forgot how to fight," Hugo said. "At first I didn't care. And then I did care, but I thought I was taking the high road. And then the high road somehow became this endless act of self-immolation, acted out in the public eye as if that might make it better. It never occurred to me that the flames would take over. Or that my own father would burn."

"It wasn't your fault," she said fiercely. "This was something that was done *to* you. You shouldn't beat yourself up for the things you did to survive it."

"I'm a selfish man, little one. I want to believe you because it's convenient, not because I think it's true."

"You are not a monster." Eleanor poked her finger in his chest as punctuation, and saw that hint of a smile deepen. It was like the sun coming out. "If anyone's a monster, it's that Isobel."

"I think you're letting me off the hook," Hugo said, his voice serious again. Too serious. "And I like that about you. But the truth is, I was callous. Unfeeling. There were any number of ways I could have handled Isobel at the start to avoid all of this, but I didn't. I suspect I must have hurt her, deeply."

"That's no excuse."

"It's an explanation."

Hugo blew out a breath. Eleanor started to say something else, but he laughed then.

"You need to stop defending me, Eleanor. I'm trying to tell you what I should have realized sooner. I love you."

All the air went out of Eleanor's body. She was too hot. Too cold.

She thought it was a fever.

Or possibly joy.

"Yes," Hugo said, as if he knew every last inch of her insecure little soul. "You." There was a wondering look on his face, and she thought his hands weren't entirely steady as they smoothed over her hair to settle at the nape of her neck. "I was so busy thinking of myself as a dragon in a cave, spouting off fire nonsense whenever anyone dared approach. And then you came. And you didn't see a dragon. You didn't see a duke. You saw a man. An irritating man, if memory serves."

"Surely not, Your Grace." But her voice was barely a whisper. Barely a scratch of sound against the night.

"You treated me like a person, nothing more. Even though you read all the same tabloid stories as anyone else. You took my ward under your wing, and more than that, stood up for her. You actually put her first."

"That's the job."

"You would be shocked how few of Geraldine's governesses considered her at all. You made a lost child feel found, Eleanor." His dark eyes gleamed. "And you made a lost man feel whole. For a few short weeks, and one long night, I completely forgot that I'm meant to be the boogeyman."

Eleanor shook her head at that, her eyes feeling

much too full. "I had no idea Vivi was going to do that, Hugo. You have to believe me."

"I never fought before," he told her, his voice low and intense. "I never stood up for myself. But I'll be damned if those rags will drag you through the dirt. I've already had my attorneys contact them. I am the Duke of Grovesmoor. And I am finished hiding."

"Hugo…"

"And more importantly, I love you." He laughed, and it was a sound so pure, so filled with life and light, that Eleanor forgot it was the middle of the night. "I didn't care enough to fight before, because I never loved Isobel. She was an annoyance, but she never hurt me. I only recognized how much I loved my own father after he died, disappointed in me to the end. I worked so hard to pretend I didn't care about my best friend or the fact he chose Isobel over me. And I decided I'd be damned if I'd soften toward the little girl he and Isobel left in my care. The truth of it was, I was fine."

Eleanor didn't realize that tears had started to slide down her face until Hugo wiped them away. She felt caught in a tight, hot grip. Unable to speak. Unable to do anything but float there, gleaming bright and buoyant.

And Hugo was still talking.

"But then you appeared. You marched up my drive in that ridiculous coat and you ruined everything. In the best possible way."

Eleanor ran her hands up the wall of his chest, indulging herself.

"What's the matter with my coat?" She tipped her head back and frowned at him. "It's very warm, Hugo."

That made him laugh again, and then he was picking her up and spinning her around and around, as if she was weightless. But then, he made her feel that way when her feet were on the ground.

"I don't know how to be anything but everyone's favorite monster," he told her when he stopped spinning them, though he still held her there against him in the cool, close night. "But I want to try. I want to watch you frown at me for the rest of my life. I want your dry tone and your prim little remarks and Eleanor, you need to understand me on this, I want everything."

"I loved you the moment I saw you," she told him, smiling down at him as her tears fell freely, and not a single one of them because she was sad. "On that terrible horse."

"Everything," he said again, as if he thought she might have missed it. "A ring on your finger and my babies in your belly, to start. After that, who knows? We can take over the world. I have no doubt you could topple a regime or two in a few weeks, if you put your mind to it. You did it to me."

"I don't want to do anything unless Geraldine's okay with it," Eleanor said, biting her lip as she considered his ward. "The poor thing doesn't need to feel any more abandoned."

"Geraldine will never be abandoned again." Hugo's words rang out like a vow. "She and I have come to an understanding, you see." He leaned forward and pressed his mouth to hers. "We can't rustle around in that great big house without you, Eleanor. It doesn't work. We need you. *I* need you."

"Your Grace," Eleanor whispered, wrapping her arms around this man who could never be a monster, not to her. "You know your wish has always been my command."

He kissed her on that lonely street, with only the faraway stars as witness, and tossed them straight on into forever.

And then, together, they found their way home.

Hugo married his governess in the spring, when Groves House was bursting with flowers and life, and even the screeching tabloids were as nothing next to the benevolent sunlight of a pretty Yorkshire afternoon.

Geraldine stood in as Hugo's Best Man, which was appropriate on a number of levels. Vivi was Eleanor's Maid of Honor, and it was interesting how she'd changed, Hugo thought. The new Vivi didn't have to worry about making connections or finding a husband or whatever plan it was the sisters had cooked up all those years ago.

"That's a terrible plan," Hugo had said when they'd laid it all out for him after Christmas that first year, probably because everyone was a touch too merry after their sumptuous dinner. "The worst I've ever heard."

The adults had been sitting about like over-stuffed lords and ladies of old in one of Hugo's salons, waiting for their meals to digest a bit so they could stuff in a few more mince pies. Geraldine had been lying in front of the fire, her face in a book.

It was, Hugo had reflected with some surprise, the happiest Christmas he could recall. Ever.

"It's a plan that's worked to change the circumstances of impoverished women since the dawn of time," Eleanor had pointed out.

"It has significant downsides," Hugo had argued. "First and foremost, the rich man in question always knows exactly why he was found so marriageable. Believe me, he'll demand payment for that. Forever."

"There is always some form of payment," Vivi had said quietly. "That's just life."

Eleanor and Hugo had exchanged a look, but neither one of them had said anything—out loud—about that weary cynicism in Vivi's voice.

Later, when they were alone in the rooms that

Hugo had moved her into shortly after he'd taken her home from London and put the Grovesmoor emerald on her finger, Eleanor had settled herself astride him and smiled down into his face.

"Is this part of my payment plan?" she'd asked mischievously.

"Of course." Hugo had run his hands along the crease where her thigh met her hip. "I'll insist on certain sexual favors, to be spelled out in the marriage contract."

"I have only one condition," Eleanor had said, very solemnly, angling herself down so her breasts filled his greedy palms and both of them could feel how slick and ready she was for him, as always.

"Name it."

"Love me," she demanded. "Forever."

On his wedding day, Hugo found that promising her exactly that came easily. So easily he laughed at the tabloids that called him all manner of names. So easily that he found even Vivi amusing, as she seemed to veer between finding the fact her sister had become Hugo's duchess romantic and armoring herself in that world-weariness she seemed infinitely more comfortable with.

"She'll come around," Eleanor said confidently on the dance floor as they'd moved together where everyone could watch them, in that ballroom where everything had changed between them previous autumn. Tonight she was dressed in a white gown and she wore his ring, but he could still see her the way she'd been then, with her hair down and her feet bare. "How can she help herself?"

Time changed everything, Hugo discovered. First Vivi, who took a solid year to relax around him. Then another year to really become comfortable in her new role, as a woman of some means with a very powerful brother-in-law.

"It's amazing how many people I thought I wanted to talk to when I was poor," Hugo overheard her telling Eleanor one lazy weekend in France at Hugo's vineyard. "And how little it turns out I like them now that they're the ones pursuing me."

"Imagine," Eleanor replied with a laugh. "You can spend time with only the people you like now."

And so, Hugo realized, could he.

He stopped paying attention to the papers, the way he should have years ago. He cultivated what friendships he had left, gratified to discover that those who'd truly known him had never believed the stories about him. And he let his beautiful wife guide him, with her quiet resolve and her cheerful determination, away from bitterness. More and more with each day that passed.

She knew the names of every staff member in his employ within a month. She continued Geraldine's schooling herself because she liked it. She quickly became popular in the village, with the no-nonsense demeanor good Yorkshire folk appreciated and that kindness of hers that Hugo thought could set the world alight. She took over some of the managerial aspects of the estate, because her keen mind and attention to detail far outstripped that of some of Hugo's aides.

She even built a bridge with the dour Mrs. Redding.

"She allowed as how she didn't trust me *before*," Eleanor told him, laughing, wrapped around him in their bed as she reported the conversation, "because the women ran all over you like water and none with a single thought about anything but themselves."

"Exactly the image I wish to have implanted in my wife's head."

"And then, of course, she waited to see if I drained the family coffers and attempted to divorce you for half of what wasn't mine."

"As well you should. There was no prenup. You have the Grovesmoor fortune entirely within your control, little one."

Eleanor pressed her mouth against his chest, sending a new heat spiraling through him. And that deeper weight that had nothing to do with sex, but everything to do with her. His miraculous Eleanor. "It's not the fortune I want to control. Just the Duke."

"He's a lost cause."

But he was laughing as he said it, and he grinned at Eleanor when she frowned at him.

"No," she said crisply, "he is not. And more, he never was."

And the more time passed, the more he believed it. Isobel had only ever told stories. Torquil might have believed them, but both of them had paid far too high a price for that.

Hugo didn't need to pay it, too. Not anymore.

And he certainly didn't intend to let Geraldine pay a single penny.

She was nine when she got her hands on the tabloids they'd deliberately kept from her for years.

"Is it true?" she asked, her fierce little face screwed up tight, as if she was keeping herself from sobbing by will alone. "Do you keep me only to get revenge on my mother?"

"How would that work, exactly?" Hugo asked mildly. He and Eleanor were reading in his library, but he noticed Eleanor kept very still. Letting the little girl speak to him directly. "I suppose I could lock you in a cupboard, if that would help. Beneath a stair, perhaps?"

"Do you hate me?" Geraldine had asked. She'd looked at him full on , and there was no mistaking the fact that she was a nine-year-old then, no matter how precocious she seemed at other times.

And this was how Hugo knew that Eleanor had changed him, from the inside out. He remembered sitting in opposite chairs from his ward and deciding that they should get Eleanor back. But that Hugo had been handicapped by his own distrust of everything. This Hugo knew what love was. He lived it every day.

So he reached out and pulled the little girl onto his lap, where she belonged.

"You are my ward by law," he told her gruffly, liking the weight of her solid little body against his. Liking the feeling that rose in him, thick and real, that told him he would protect this child against the world with his own hands if necessary. "But as far as I'm concerned, Geraldine, you have always been my daughter."

And as she snuggled into him he lifted his head, and saw Eleanor wiping tears away across from him, her face wreathed in smiles.

A year or so after that, Geraldine pushed her way into the library one summer evening, already slouching about as she walked, like the teenager she would be entirely too soon for Hugo's peace of mind.

"I'm certain I've asked you to knock," Hugo said mildly, his attention on the drink in his hand and his lovely wife, who was frowning intently over the book in her lap. Eleanor had decided to get the university degree she'd been too busy to get when she'd been younger, and was spending the summer with a reading list.

Hugo wasn't sure it was physically possible to love her more.

Geraldine held his gaze. "Knock, knock," she said, because she was as smart-mouthed as anyone else in this house.

"Charming," Hugo murmured.

"I've thought about it and I've come to a decision," Geraldine told him.

"Have you changed your mind about school?" Eleanor asked, lifting her head.

"I still want to go," Geraldine replied. "It will be fun to board and I'll come home all the time. But you two will be so lonely without me."

Hugo's mouth twitched. "Indeed."

Eleanor's dark eyes danced, but she nodded seriously. "I'm sure that's true."

"Well, I know what you need to do," Geraldine said, and then she smiled. "You need to have a baby. As soon as possible."

And Hugo would never know how both he

and Eleanor kept from laughing at that, but they didn't. They thanked Geraldine and then, when she'd skipped back out again to enjoy the long, blue evening, they'd dissolved into the laughter they'd been holding at bay.

But they obeyed her.

Ten months later, the Duke was delighted to catch his first son and heir as he roared his way into the world. But not, perhaps, as delighted as his ward, who was sure she'd plotted out the whole thing.

And Eleanor had never done one thing when she could do three instead. That was how the future Duke of Grovesmoor found himself with a little brother and a baby sister in short order, all of them loud and rowdy and perfect.

"Look at that," Eleanor said as she shepherded their little brood through the village on a blustery sort of fall afternoon that reminded Hugo of the day they'd met. She was even wearing that hideous puffy coat of hers, that she'd steadfastly refused to throw away no matter how many glorious, sleek, and flattering coats he'd gifted her with over the years. Obstinate woman. "I hardly recognize the man in those headlines."

Hugo glanced over at the newsstand and saw his own face, but didn't bother to read whatever nonsense they'd spouted about him this time. He took his wife's hand in his and raised it to his mouth. His sons were running ahead of him toward the green, chasing Geraldine who was for all intents and purposes their older sister, and he was holding his baby girl against his chest.

"Ah, little one," he said with a deep and quiet contentment that was pressed down into his bones now, a part of him forever. "I don't believe in ghosts."

His family was complete. His heart was whole.

Eleanor looked at him as if he'd always been the man she was so proud of, and Hugo believed, at last, that he was.

And would be for as long as they were together—which would be for the rest of their natural lives and far beyond if he had anything to say about it.

Which he bloody well did. He was the Duke of Grovesmoor, after all.

* * * * *